THE CENTRAL PHILOSOPHY OF BUDDHISM

The vastness of Buddhism is surprisingly immense. An extensive and varied literature, covering period of more than fifteen centuries, is scattered in a score of languages. Its complexity is no less formidable; its school and sub-schools are bewildering in their number and in the twists and turns of their thought. The greatest difficulty facing the student is the lack of an acredited tradition of interpretation.

A revolution in Buddhism was created by the Mādhyamika philosophy from which the countries of Central Asia and the Far East take their philosophy. Professor Murti explores this system with an understanding which comes from a close familiarity with the original texts.

TO MY REVERED TEACHER

PROFESSOR S. RADHAKRISHNAN

THE CENTRAL PHILOSOPHY OF BUDDHISM

A STUDY OF MĀDHYAMIKA SYSTEM

T.R.V. MURTI

Foreword by
KEVIN VOSE

MOTILAL BANARSIDASS PUBLISHERS
PRIVATE LIMITED • DELHI

First MLBD Edition : Delhi, 2016
First Published in Unwin Paper Backs 1980 (1987)
Second Edition : 1960 (Reprinted three times)
First Published in Great Britain by George Allen & Unwin 1955

ISBN: 978-81-208-4007-2

Also available at:
MOTILAL BANARSIDASS
41 U.A., Bungalow Road, Jawahar Nagar, Delhi 110 007
8 Mahalaxmi Chamber, 22 Bhulabhai Desai Road, Mumbai 400 026
203 Royapettah High Road, Mylapore, Chennai 600 004
236, 9th Main III Block, Jayanagar, Bangalore 560 011
8 Camac Street, Kolkata 700 017
Ashok Rajpath, Patna 800 004
Chowk, Varanasi 221 001

MLBD Cataloging-in-Publication Data
The Central Philosophy of Buddhism
by T.R.V. Murti
ISBN : 978-81-208-4007-2
Includes Glossary and index.
I. Buddhism II. Philosophy III. Madhyamika
IV. Murti, T.R.V.

Printed in India
by Thomson Press, India and
Published by JP Jain for Motilal Banarsidass Publishers (P) Ltd,
41 U.A. Bungalow Road, Jawahar Nagar, Delhi-110007

FOREWORD

This reprinting of T.R.V. Murti's classic exposition of Mādhyamika on the sixtieth anniversary of its original publication will undoubtedly spark renewed interest in the work and in the study of Mādhyamika philosophy in South Asia. With this reprinting, Motilal Banarsidass continues its laudatory work of promoting the study of Indian philosophy and Buddhism.

Upon publication, *The Central Philosophy of Buddhism* was widely heralded as the finest synthesis of Mādhyamika then available. Writing in the *Journal of Asian Studies* in 1956, the celebrated American Sanskritist Daniel Ingalls called it "the best exposition of Śūnyavāda philosophy that has been written in English." Murti's work offers a bold and erudite attempt to place Mādhyamika in the history of Indian thought and to present it in a philosophically attuned manner. His efforts to position Nāgārjuna's views in dialogue with European philosophical traditions promoted both learned interest in Mādhyamika and research into its textual foundations. The book helped Mādhyamika receive the serious attention it so deserves.

Following in the line of Stcherbatsky, Murti rightfully rejected the nihilistic interpretation of Mādhyamika that had flourished in European readings of it for many decades prior to his workand that still crops up today. He drew attention to the broader implications of negation in the texts of Nāgārjuna, Āryadeva, and Candrakīrti, showing the "destructive" character of their arguments against rival philosophical positions and common sense views to be in service of the attainment of *prajñā,* which he translated as "intuition." He can further be credited with working out a solution to the seeming contradiction that Mādhyamikas, on the one hand, frequently describe the ultimate (*paramārtha*) as surpassing the realm of the mind (*buddhi,* which he renders as "Reason") but, on the other hand, utilize rational thinking as part and parcel of their presentation of Buddhist teachings and as essential to religious pursuits. Murti's resolution of the conundrum as a dialectic that aims at surpassing "Reason" in aim of an "Absolute" clearly bore the influence of his interests in Kant, Hegel, and Śaṅkara and cannot now be supported. However, he deserves our admiration for his identification of this and a good many other tensions in Mādhyamika thinking and for his intellectual creativity in attempting a coherent resolution of them.

While many have pointed out that Murti offers a view of Mādhyamika at odds with that of the authors on whom he relies, the frequency with which his work has been cited attests to its continued importance. Indeed, a true sign of scholarly contribution lies in the ability to set an agenda for future research, to remain at the center of investigation and refutation. After reading Murti's work a remarkable five times over, Jeffrey Hopkins credits it with inspiring his authorship of *Meditation on*

Emptiness, a work that shows how the Tibetan Gelukpa (*dge lugs pa*) Prāsa´gika-Mādhyamika tradition embraces reason as a tool of insight and as useful in meditation (showing that reasoned analysis is, in fact, a kind of meditation), and so responds to some of Murti's central claims.

In the sixty years since this work was first published, the study of Indian and Buddhist philosophy has provided progressively greater detail on all manner of issues, with greater scrutiny directed at individual authors, texts, doctrines, and social and historical relationships. This makes Murti's grand portrayal of a dialectic driving the history of Indian thought – sweeping up the Upani´ads, the Buddha, Sā´khya, Abhidharma, Mādhyamika, Yogācāra, and Vedānta – all the more striking. These broad strokes Murti works in have been found in many cases to be lacking support from a close study of the texts in question, as has the Hegelian dialectic he proposes as a framework for Indian philosophy. His work, though, forces us to consider the merits of sketching the "big picture": sixty years later, is it time to take up the challenge Murti took for himself? Are we ready for a new grand vision of Indian philosophy? Of Mādhyamika? If so, we would do well to resist the temptation to import a ready-made framework into which we fit these hard-won details. Few now would attempt a Hegelian model for the history of European philosophy; even less would it be appropriate for Indian thought, which Hegel himself falsely believed was not "real" philosophy.

That said, Murti's engagement in comparative philosophy is commendable, as are ongoing efforts to create dialog between disparate traditions. We should keep in mind the long list of western philosophers to whom Nāgārjuna has been declared the Indian forerunner, remembering that comparison is always a matter of "fit" and "unfit," to adopt Jonathan Z. Smith's language. Comparison will illuminate aspects of a given figure's views, bringing to the fore previously unnoticed qualities and, at its best, offersolutions to the difficulties in a given philosophy. However, we will always find an element of "unfit"the alignment between distinct thinkers will never be perfect; unique aspects will remain. Nāgārjuna will never be Kant (or Hegel, or Schopenhauer, or Wittgenstein), nor should we want him to be. In placing Mādhyamika next to Kant, Hegel, and F.H. Bradley, *The Central Philosophy of Buddhism* rightfully situates it as a philosophy every bit as rigorous and sophisticated as its western counterparts, one that, we should note, has a great many current practitioners for whom Mādhyamika constitutes a way of life.

KEVIN VOSE

Associate Professor of Religious Studies
Director of Global Studies, College of William and Mary,
Williamsburg, Virginia, U.S.A.

PREFACE

"ALTHOUGH a hundred years have elapsed since the scientific study of Buddhism has been initiated in Europe, we are nevertheless still in the dark about the fundamental teachings of this religion and its philosophy. Certainly no other religion has proved so refractory to clear formulation." This observation of the late Professor Stcherbatsky made in 1927 (*The Conception of Buddhist Nirvāṇa*, p. 1) remains no less true today. It is also a measure of the difficulties which one encounters in this field. The vastness of Buddhism is surprisingly immense. An extensive and varied literature, canonical, exegetical and systematic, covering a period of more than fifteen centuries, is scattered in a score of languages, Sanskrit, Pāli, Tibetan, Chinese and several Mongolian languages. Its complexity is no less formidable; its schools and subschools are bewildering in their number and in the twists and turns of their thought. The greatest difficulty encountered is the lack of an accredited tradition of interpretation which might set aright many inaccuracies and shortcomings in our understanding. In spite of these admitted difficulties, a determined attempt should be made to understand Buddhism. This is essential for a correct and fruitful understanding of Indian philosophy and religion on which Buddhism has exercised a profound and permanent influence. Moreover, Buddhism forms the staple culture of the south, east and far-east Asian countries. A study of Buddhism should also prove valuable as a contribution to world-culture. And this may not be without significance in the context of the present-day world.

The Mādhyamika philosophy claims our attention as the system which created a revolution in Buddhism and through that in the whole range of Indian philosophy. The entire Buddhist thought turned on the Śūnyatā doctrine of the Mādhyamika. The earlier pluralistic phase of Buddhism, its rejection of substance and the rather uncritical erection of a theory of elements, was clearly a preparation for the fully critical and self-conscious dialectic of Nāgārjuna. The Yogācāra-Vijñānavāda Idealism explicitly accepts the śūnyatā of the Mādhyamika, and gives it an idealistic turn. The critical and absolutist trend in Brāhmanical thought is also traceable to the Mādhyamika.

Considering the rôle and the importance of the Mādhyamika, I have ventured to appraise it as the Central Philosophy of Buddhism.

Modern literature on the subject is neither too plentiful nor free from misunderstanding. Our standard text-books on Indian philosophy content themselves with a perfunctory treatment of the system. There is a tendency on the part of some critics and historians of thought to dismiss it as nihilism; many even identify it with the Vedānta. Such criticism is as uninformed as it is misleading. Stcherbatsky's book, *The Conception of Buddhist Nirvāṇa*, is an exception to this. But it is hardly to be expected that in the course of about 60 pages, most of which are devoted to polemic and the elucidation of the conception of nirvāṇa, anything like an adequate exposition of the Mādhyamika philosophy could be made. The present work is an attempt to fill this gap in our knowledge. It is a full study of the Mādhyamika philosophy in all its important aspects.

The book falls into three well-defined but connected parts of unequal length. The first is mainly historical: it traces the origin and development of the Mādhyamika philosophy, its dialectic, as the attempt to resolve the conflict that was engendered by the two main traditions of Indian philosophy, the ātmavāda (substance view of reality) and the anātmavāda (modal view of reality). The anticipations of the dialectic are to be found in the celebrated 'silence' of Buddha, in his refusal to speculate and to predicate empirical categories of the transcendent reality. The development of the Mādhyamika stages and schools of thought and their literature is dealt with at some considerable length. The possible influence of the Mādhyamika on later philosophy, especially on the Vijñānavāda and the Vedānta, is also indicated. The second and main part is devoted to a full and critical exposition of the Mādhyamika philosophy, the structure of its dialectic, the application of the dialectic to categories of thought, its conception of the Absolute, and its ethics and religion. The chapter on the Application of the Dialectic is chiefly of historical interest and is somewhat technical; it may be omitted on the first reading. The last part of the book compares the Mādhyamika with some of the well-known dialectical systems of the West (Kant, Hegel and Bradley), and undertakes a short study of the different absolutisms (Mādhyamika, Vijñānavāda and the Vedānta) whose different standpoints are not generally appreciated.

There is a measure of risk in comparative studies. No two systems of thought or even aspects of them are quite identical or similar. On the other hand, if they were absolutely unique, we could not differentiate or understand them. My constant endeavour has been to draw distinctions, on every important topic, between the Mādhyamika, the Vijñānavāda and the Vedānta. I have also tried to understand the development of thought here in the light of the known development of similar trends in the West. In particular, I have made pointed references to Kant as elucidating aspects of the Mādhyamika. I have tried to be on my guard with regard to the differences in outlook and background of Indian and Western philosophy. In spite of its shortcomings, the comparative method is perhaps the only way by which Indian thought could be made intelligible to the Western reader in terms of the philosophical ideas with which he is familiar.

It is fortunate that we possess not only the basic Mādhyamika texts but practically all the important ones either in the original Sanskrit or as restorations and translations. Help from Tibetan sources would certainly have added to our information of the system, especially about Buddhapālita and Bhāvaviveka. This is not, however, a serious handicap, as we have Mādhyamika texts in Sanskrit representative of every period right from its inception by Nāgārjuna to Prajñākaramati's *Pañjikā* in the 11th century A.D., when Buddhism practically disappeared from India. Besides, in a system which is all dialectic and no doctrine, such additional information as we may glean from other sources cannot materially affect the main exposition and interpretation of its philosophy.

I have approached my task not as a philologist or an antiquarian, but have tried to reconstruct and recapture the spirit of Mādhyamika philosophy. A history of philosophy is not an out-dated museum piece, but a living exposition of ideas; it is essentially a restatement and a revaluation. It is possible that my critics may not always agree with me in my interpretation of the Mādhyamika and incidentally of many aspects of Indian thought. In philosophy, difference of interpretation is legitimate, and should even be welcome. I shall feel myself amply recompensed if my attempt helps, in some measure, in understanding an important phase of Indian thought.

It is with pleasure that I record my obligations. I must first pay my respects to the revered Professor K. C. Bhattacharyya for the general standpoint of my exposition. I have greatly profited by the published writings of Stcherbatsky, Poussin, Winternitz, McGovern, Radhakrishnan, Vidhushekhar Bhattacharyya and many others. Acknowledgement is made of my indebtedness at the appropriate places. This book was first submitted as the Doctoral Thesis for the D. Litt. Degree of the Benares Hindu University. To my examiners,

Pandit Gopinath Kaviraj, Professor Vidhushekhar Bhattachryya and Dr. Benoyatosh Bhattacharyya, I am grateful for their valued criticism and helpful suggestions. I am greatly indebted to my esteemed friends, Acharya Narendra Deva, Professor G. R. Malkani (Director, Indian Institute of Philosophy, Amalner), Dr. C. Narayana Menon (Professor of English, Benares University), Sri B. K. Mallik of Exeter College, Oxford and to Mr. A. Alston of New College, Oxford, who read the typescript and offered valued suggestions for improving the style and presentation. The book would have been much more faulty without their help. My deepest and most sustained obligations are to my revered teacher, Professor S. Radhakrishnan. The work was undertaken under his inspiring guidance. He very kindly revised the manuscript and sent me full and most helpful suggestions from Oxford. He has also taken a keen interest in the publication of the book, encouraging me to hope that it may prove a useful work on the subject. I am very deeply indebted to him for all his kindness to me. *The Central Philosophy of Buddhism* is respectfully dedicated to him as a token of my gratitude and admiration. Professor Radhakrishnan has done so much to revive interest in Indian philosophy and Buddhistic studies.

I am deeply thankful to Mr. K. J. Spalding, Fellow of Brasenose College, Oxford and to the late Dr. H. N. Spalding for their encouragement and help. Dr. Spalding did me the honour of attending my lectures on the Middle and Last Phases of Buddhism given during the Michaelmas term of 1949 in the University of Oxford where I was Deputy for the Spalding Professor of Eastern Religions and Ethics for a year. Dr. Spalding's death is a great loss to the cause of Indian culture.

I am greatly indebted to my young friends, Dr. Rama Kanta Tripathi, Dr. Ashok Kumar Chatterjee and Sri K. Sivaraman for their active help and co-operation in writing the book; I have been immensely benefited by my discussions with them on many topics dealt with in the book.

My thanks are due to the Editor (Professor P. A. Schilpp) and the Publishers (Messrs. Tudor Publishing Company) of *The Philosophy of Sarvepalli Radhakrishnan*, to Messrs. George Allen and Unwin, Publishers of *The History of Philosophy, Eastern and Western*, and to the Editors of *The University of Ceylon Review* for permission to reproduce some portions of the articles which first appeared in their publications.

T. R. V. Murti.

December, 1954.

CONTENTS

PART ONE

ORIGIN AND DEVELOPMENT OF THE MĀDHYAMIKA PHILOSOPHY

PART TWO

THE DIALECTIC AS SYSTEM OF PHILOSOPHY

PART THREE

THE MĀDHYAMIKA AND ALLIED SYSTEMS

ABBREVIATIONS

AAA	*AbhisamayĀlaṁkārĀloka of Haribhadra*, G.O.S., Baroda.
AK	*AbhidharmaKośaKārikās of Vasubandhu*, text edited by G. V. Gokhale, JRAS, Bombay, Vol. 22 (1946)
AKV	*AbhidharmaKośaVyākhyā of Yaśomitra*. Ed. by Wogihara, Tokio.
ASP	*AṣṭaSāhasrikāPrajñāpāramitā* (Bib. Indica).
BCA	*BodhiCaryĀvatāra* by Śānti Deva (Bib. Ind.).
BCAP	*BodhiCaryĀvatāraPañjikā* by Prajñākaramati (Bib. Ind.).
BUSTON OR BHB	Bu-ston's *History of Buddhism*, 2 Parts. Trans. from the Tibetan by Dr. E. Obermiller (Heidelberg, 1931).
CRITIQUE	*The Critique of Pure Reason* by Kant. Translation by Prof. N. Kemp Smith.
CŚ	*CatuḥŚatakam of Ārya Deva*. Restored into Sanskrit by Prof. V. Bhattacharya, Viśvabhārati, Śāntiniketan, 1931.
CŚV	*CatuḥŚatakaVṛtti* by Candrakīrti (Commentary on CŚ).
HIL	*History of Indian Literature*, Vol. II—by M. Winternitz, University of Calcutta, 1933.
IP	*Indian Philosophy*, 2 Vols., by Prof. S. Radhakrishnan, Library of Philosophy, London.
MA	*MādhyamakĀvatāra of Candrakīrti*, Chapt. VI (incomplete) Reconstructed from the Tibetan version by Pt. N. Aiyāswāmi Śāstri, J.O.R. Madras, 1929 ff.
MK	*Mādhyamika Kārikās of Nāgārjuna*. Ed. by L. de la V. Poussin (Bib. Budd. IV).
MKV	*MādhyamikaKārikāVṛtti* (*Prasannapadā*) by Candrakīrti. (Commentary on MK) (Bib. Budd. IV).
MVBT	*MādhyāntaVibhāga Sūtra Bhāṣya Ṭīkā of Ṣthiramati*, Part I. Ed. by Prof. V. Bhattacharya & G. Tucci (Luzac & Co., 1932).
ŚS	*ŚiṣkāSamuccaya of Śānti Deva*. Ed. by Bendall (Bib. Buddhica, I).
TS	*TattvaSaṅgraha of Śāntarakṣita* (G.O.S., Baroda) 2 Vols.
TSP	*TattvaSaṅgrahaPañjikā* by Kamalaśīla (G.O.S.) (Commentary on TS.)
VV	*VigrahaVyāvarttanī of Nāgārjuna*. Ed. by K. P. Jayaswal and R. Sānkrityāyana, J.B.O.R.S., Patna.

PART ONE

Origin and Development of the Mādhyamika Philosophy

CHAPTER ONE

THE TWO TRADITIONS IN INDIAN PHILOSOPHY

I. THE MĀDHYAMIKA SYSTEM—ITS ROLE AND SIGNIFICANCE

BUDDHISM profoundly influenced the philosophy and religion of India for over a thousand years. It was a challenge to complacency and a call for renouncing dogmatism. It adopted the method of critical analysis (vibhajyavāda) from the very outset.[1] Buddhism occupies the central position in the development of Indian philosophy. Brāhmanical and Jaina systems grew under the direct stimulus of Buddhism. Schools and sub-schools sprang up without number. Doctrines were systematised and details were worked out under this pressure. Great attention came to be paid to logic and epistemology. Precise terminology was evolved, and an immense śāstra-literature came into being. Indian philosophy became critical and richer; it gained in depth and comprehension.

There were sharp twists and turns in Buddhism itself. It had a momentous and varied life. Its schools and sub-schools, judged even by Buddhist standards, are bewildering. The tendency to split and divide itself into sects and sub-sects appeared very early in the history of Buddhism. The several Councils held from time to time to decide the orthodox creed and to stamp out heresy are evidence of this vitality. The *Kathāvatthu* is perhaps the earliest record in Pāli of the doctrinal differences of the schools. Buddhist historians like Buston and Tāranātha speak of the *Three Swingings of the Wheel of Law* (dharmacakra-pravarttana).

At first the earliest Teaching completely excluded the nihilistic point of view (i.e. everything, all the elements, were considered to be real in themselves). Owing to this an (incorrect) realistic imputation could easily grow prominent.

With a view to this (the Buddha) has expounded the Intermediate teaching in which a negativistic standpoint predominates. But this

[1] *Cf.* "I am not a generaliser (dogmatist); I am an analyser (vibhajjavādi)." *Majjh. N.* II, p. 197 (*Subha Sutta*, No. 99).

(scripture of the latest period) introduces (different degrees of Reality), demonstrating the elements in their imputed aspect (parikalpita) as totally non-existing, the elements in their causally dependent aspect (paratantra-svabhāva) as having a real existence from the standpoint of the Empirical Reality (saṁvṛti), and the two forms of the Ultimate Aspect (pariniṣpanna) as representing the Absolute Reality. It is accordingly that which puts an end to the two extreme points of view, contains the direct meaning (nītārtha) and cannot be an object of dispute. On the contrary, the other two (Swingings of the Wheel of the Doctrine) are of conventional meaning (neyārtha) and can be made an object of controversy. This is the opinion of the Vijñānavādins. . . . The Mādhyamikas however say: "The Lord having begun with the teaching that all elements are devoid of a real essence of their own, that they neither become originated (anutpanna) nor disappear (aniruddha) and by their very nature merged in Nirvāṇa and that they are quiescent from the outset (ādi-śānta), has swung the second Wheel of the Doctrine for the sake of those who had entered the Great Vehicle. The teaching, marvellous and wonderful as it is, demonstrates the principle of non-substantiality and Relativity. . . . According to the Mādhyamikas,[1] the earliest and the latest Scriptures are both conventional (ābhiprāyika) and only the Intermediate contains the direct meaning.[2]

Stripped of metaphor and partisan colouring, this means that there were three principal turning-points in the history of Buddhism. And these are:

1. The earlier realistic and pluralistic Phase comprising the Hīnayāna schools—Theravāda and Vaibhāṣika (Sarvāstivāda). This can be called the Ābhidharmika system. The Sautrāntika school is a partial modification of this dogmatic realism;

2. The middle phase or the Mādhyamika system of Nāgārjuna and Ārya Deva advocating Śūnya-vāda (Absolutism);

3. The last idealistic phase—the Yogācāra system of Asanga and Vasubandhu and the later Vijñānavāda of Dignāga and Dharmakīrti.

[1] This is the view of Candrakīrti and others: *tad evam Madhyamaka darśana* evāstitva-nāstitva-dvaya-darśanasyā-prasango na Vijñānavādidarśaneṣ viti vijñeyam . . . tathāvidha-vineya-janabodhānurodhāt tu paramārtha-darśanasyopāyabhūtatvān *neyārthatvena* mahākaruṇāparatantratayā *vijñādivādo* deśitah, Sāmmatīyapudgalavādavat, *na nītārtha* iti vijñeyam. MKV, pp. 275–6.

Cf. also. BCAP, p. 406: yat tu kvacid bhagavatā citta-mātrāstitvam uktam, tat skandhāyatanādivan neyārthatayeti kathayiṣyate. See also p. 484.

[2] BHB (Buston's *History of Buddhism*), Vol. II, pp. 52–4 (quoted with gaps). See also Dr. Obermiller's *The Doctrine of Prajñāpāramitā* (pp. 91–100) for a full exposition of the three phases of Buddhism. Stcherbatsky: *Buddhist Logic*, Vol. I, pp. 3–14; Rosenberg: *Die Probleme der bud. Phil.*, p. 35.

These historians of Buddhism, Buston (1290–1364) and Tāranātha (1574–1608), were neither too near nor too far removed from the movement, and hence they could comprehend it as a whole. The Mādhyamika is the turning-point of Buddhism. It is the central or the pivotal system. Like Kant in modern European philosophy, the Mādhyamika system brought about a veritable revolution in Buddhist thought. "It never has been fully realized," says Stcherbatsky with regard to this system,

> what a radical revolution had transformed the Buddhist church when the new spirit, which however was for a long time lurking in it, arrived at full eclosion in the first centuries A.D. When we see an atheistic, soul-denying philosophic teaching of a path to personal Final Deliverance consisting in an absolute extinction of life, and a simple worship of the memory of its human founder, when we see it superseded by a magnificent High Church with a Supreme God, surrounded by a numerous pantheon, and a host of Saints, a religion highly devotional, highly ceremonial and clerical, with an ideal of Universal Salvation of all living creatures, a Salvation not in annihilation, but in eternal life, we are fully justified in maintaining that the history of religions has scarcely witnessed such a break between new and old within the pale of what nevertheless continued to claim common descent from the same religious founder.[1]

In metaphysics, it was a revolution from a radical pluralism (Theory of Elements, dharma-vāda) to an as radical absolutism (advaya-vāda). The change was from a plurality of discrete ultimate entities (dharmāḥ) to the essential unity underlying them (dharmatā). Epistemologically, the revolution was from empiricism and dogmatism (dṛṣṭi-vāda) to dialectical criticism (śūnyatā or madhyamā pratipad). Ethically, the revolution was from the ideal of a private egoistic salvation to that of a universal unconditional deliverance of all beings. Not mere freedom from rebirth and pain (kleśāvaraṇa-nivṛttiḥ) but the attainment of Perfect Buddhahood by the removal of ignorance covering the real (jñeyāvaraṇa) is now the goal. The change was from the ideal of the Arhat to that of the Bodhisattva:[2]

[1] *Conception Buddhist of Nirvāṇa*. p. 36. See also p. 4 and p. 46 for similar observations.

[2] 'ye'pi te Subhūte, etarhy aprameyeṣv asamkhyeṣu lokadhātuṣu Tathāgatā arhantaḥ samyaksambuddhāḥ daśadiśi loke tiṣṭhanti dhriyante yāpayanti *bahujana-hitāya bahujanasukhāya lokānukampāyai mahato janakāyasyārthāya hitāya sukhāya devānām ca manuṣyānām cānukampāyai anukampām* upādāy-ānuttarām samyak-sambodhim abhisambuddhās te'pi sarve enām eva praj-

Universal love (karuṇā) and Intellectual perfection (prajñā or śūnyatā)[1] are identical. The Theoretic and the Practical Reason coincide.

In Religion, it was a revolution from what was almost a positivism to an absolutistic pantheism. Religion is the consciousness of the Super-mundane Presence immanent in things, the consciousness of what Otto happily calls the 'mysterium tremendum'. Early Buddhism (Theravāda) was not a religion in this sense. It was an order of monks held together by certain rules of discipline (vinaya) and reverence for the *human* Teacher. It enjoined a very austere moral code, primarily for the ordained. But there was no element of worship, no religious fervour, no devotion to a transcendent being. No cosmic function was assigned to Buddha; he was just an exalted person and no more. His existence after parinirvāṇa was a matter of doubt; this was one of the inexpressibles. The rise of the Mādhyamika system is at once the rise of Buddhism as a religion. For the Mahāyāna, Buddha is not an historical person. He is the essence of all Being (dharmakāya); he has a glorious divine form (sambhogakāya) and assumes at will various forms to deliver beings from delusion and to propagate the dharma (nirmāṇakāya). The essential unity of all beings became an integral part of spiritual life. Worship and devotion to Buddhas and Bodhisattvas was introduced, possibly owing to influence from the South.[2]

This laid the foundation for the last development in Buddhism—the Tāntric phase. Tāntricism is a unique combination of mantra,

ñāpāramitām āgamyā 'nuttarāṁ samyaksambodhim abhisambuddhāḥ. ASP. p 255.

Cf. *Itivuttakam* (84), p. 78.

Dr. Har Dayal considers the Bodhisattva ideal as a revival of the genuine teaching of the master. Says he: "They (the monks) became too self-centred and contemplative, and did not evince the old zeal for missionary activity among the people. The Bodhisattva doctrine was promulgated by some Buddhist leaders as a protest against this lack of true spiritual fervour and altruism among the monks of that period. The coldness and aloofness of the arhats led to a movement in favour of the old gospel of 'saving all creatures.' The Bodhisattva-ideal can be understood only against this back-ground of a saintly and serene, but inactive and indolent monastic Order." *The Bodhisattva Doctrine*, pp. 2–3.

[1] śūnyatā-karuṇābhinnam bodhicittam iti smṛtam.

[2] *The Aṣṭasāhasrikā* (probably the oldest *Prajñāpāramitā* text) contains a passage conforming to this reading. It says: ime khalu, Śāriputra, ṣaṭ-pāramitā-samprayuktāḥ sūtrāntās tathāgatasyātyayena *dakṣiṇāpathe* pracariṣyanti, vartanyāḥ punaruttarāpathe pracariṣyanti navamaṇḍaprāpte dharmavinaye saddharmasyāntardhānakālasamaye samanvāhṛtās te, Śāriputra, Tathāgatena." ASP. p. 225.

ritual and worship on an absolutist basis. It is both religion and philosophy. This development occurred in Brāhmanism too, influenced no doubt by the corresponding development in Buddhism.

The *Śālistamba Sūtra* says[1]: "Whosoever sees the Pratītyasamutpāda sees the Buddha, and whosoever sees the Buddha sees the Dharma (Truth or Reality)." Nāgārjuna expresses himself similarly in his *Mādhyamika Kārikās*[2]: "One who perceives truly the Pratītyasamutpāda realises the four sacred truths—pain, (its) cause, cessation and the path." Buddhism has always been a Dharma-theory[3] based on the Pratītyasamutpāda, and every Buddhist system has claimed to be the Middle Path. Pratītyasamutpāda has, however, received different interpretations at different times. The earlier Buddhism of the Ābhidharmika systems took it as denying the permanent Atman (substance) and at once establishing the reality of the separate elements. Pratītyasamutpāda is the causal law regulating the rise and subsidence of the several elements (dharma-sanketa). The middle path is the steering clear of Eternalism (substance or soul) and Nihilism (uccheda-vāda, denial of continuity). The Mādhyamika contends that this is not the correct interpretation of the doctrine. Pratītya-samutpāda is not the principle of temporal sequence, but of the *essential dependence* of things on each other, i.e., the unreality of separate elements (naissvābhāvya, dharma-nairātmya). The entire Mādhyamika system is a re-interpretation of Pratītyasamutpāda.[4] It is now equated with Śūnyatā—the empirical validity of entities and

[1] yo, bhikṣavaḥ, pratītyasamutpādam paśyati, sa buddham paśyati, yo buddham paśyati sa dharmam paśyati. *Śālistamba Sūtra,* quoted in BCAP, p. 386, also partly in MKV. p. 6, 160.
The Pāli text corresponding to this is found in *Majjh. N.* I 191 (28th Sutta): vuttam kho pan'etam Bhagavatā: yo paṭiccasamuppādam passati so dhammam passati; yo dhammam passati so paṭiccasamuppādam passatīti. The other part of the formula may be completed from *Sam. N.* IV 120: yo kho, Vakkāli, dhammam passati so mām passati; yo mām passati so dhammam passati. Cf. also *Itivuttaka,* 92 (p. 91).

[2] MK. XXIV, 40.

[3] Rosenberg makes this characteristic observation in his *Die Probleme der bud. Phil.* Alle Teile der buddhistischen Dogmatik sind in der Terminologie der Theorie von den Trägern den dharma dargelegt . . . *Die Dharma-theorie* ist der Schlüssel zum Verständnis der dogmatischen Literatur des Buddhismus, der alten so wie der spätern (p. 77). Again he says: Der Begriff "dharma" ist in der buddhistischen Philosophie von so überwiegender Bedeutung, dass man das *System des Buddhismus in gewissem Sinne Dharmatheorie nennen kann.* (pp. 78–9).

[4] tad atrānirodhādyaṣṭaviśeṣaṇaviśiṣṭaḥ pratītyasamutpādaḥ śāstrābhidheyārthaḥ. MKV. p. 3.

their ultimate unreality.[1] The middle path is the non-acceptance of the two extremes—the affirmative and the negative (the sat and asat) views, of all views. In the Vijñānavāda, Śūnyatā is accepted, but with a modification. The formula is: That which appears (the substratum, i.e., vijñāna) is real; the form of its appearance (the duality of subject and object) is unreal.[2] The middle path is the avoidance of both the dogmatism of realism (the reality of objects) and the scepticism of Nihilism (the rejection of objects and consciousness both as unreal).[3]

An intelligent reading of the development of Buddhist thought shows the Mādhyamika system as having emerged out of a sustained criticism of the Ābhidharmika schools, which themselves grew as the rejection of the ātmavāda of the Brāhmanical systems. It is thus a criticism of both the ātma and anātma theories. An analogous position in the West is that of Kant in modern philosophy. His *Critique* is primarily a criticism of Empiricism, which itself was a rejection of the standpoint of Rationalism with regard to the origin and scope of knowledge. The Yogācāra Idealism is made possible by the Śūnyatā of the Mādhyamika, just as the Idealism of Hegel is indebted to Kant's *Critique* for its understanding of the function of Reason.

It is possible to perceive the initial stages of the dialectic in the direct teachings of Buddha himself.[4] Buddha pronounced some problems to be insoluble or inexpressible (avyākṛta). This is the so-called agnosticism of Buddha. Criticism is the very essence of Buddha's teaching. He was aware of the antinomical character of Reason. His refusal to answer questions about the beginning and extent of the world or of the unconditioned existence of the soul (jīva) and the Perfect Being (tathāgata) was the direct outcome of the awareness of the conflict in Reason. It is at the same time an attempt to

[1] yaḥ pratītyasamutpādaḥ śūnyatām tām pracakṣmahe; yā prajñaptir upādāya pratipat saiva madhyamā. MK. XXIV, 18.

[2] abhūtaparikalpo 'sti dvayam tatra na vidyate; śūnyatā vidyate tvatra tasyām api sa vidyate. MVBT. p. 9.

Cf. also:

tatra kiṁ khyāty asatkalpaḥ kathaṁ khyāti dvayātmanā;
tasya kā nāstitā tena yā tatrādvaya-dharmatā.
Trisvabhāvanirdeśa, 4.

[3] An entire treatise—The *Madhyānta-Vibhāga* is devoted to an elucidation of the Middle and Extreme views.

See MVBT. pp. 9 ff; *Triṁśikā*, pp. 15–6.

[4] infra, Chapter II.

transcend the duality of Reason. Dialectic was born. To Buddha, then, belongs the honour of having suggested the dialectic first, much before Zeno in the west. Dialectic, as will be shown later, is the consciousness of the total and interminable conflict in Reason and the consequent attempt to resolve the conflict by rising to a higher standpoint. In a conflict there are at least two principal alternative views, totally opposed to each other in their solutions of the problems of existence and value. The two view points were the ātma and anātma systems, like the systems of Rationalism and Empiricism before Kant.

In Buddha, the dialectic is but suggested; as the conflict of view-points which engenders the dialectic had not yet developed. The dialectic in its systematic form is found in the Mādhyamika; for, by that time the divergent views had been cultivated and formulated into well-knit systems—as the Sāṅkhya, Vaiśeṣika and the Vaibhāṣika. There is no doubt, however, that the Mādhyamika dialectic is the systematised form of the suggestions made by Buddha himself. Buddha resolves the conflict by an intuitive perception of the Real as non-dual (advaya); the Mādhyamika does it by turning Reason against itself, through the dialectic.

The development of the Advaita Vedānta offers us a close parallel on the ātma tradition. The Upaniṣads affirm Brahman (Absolute Spirit) as the sole reality of the world. The Upaniṣadic seers reach this absolutism not so much through reasoning as by inspiration. They are more suggestive than systematic. The Advaitism (Non-dualism) of Śaṅkara is established on a dialectical basis by the criticism of the Sāṅkhya, the older Vedānta and other systems. For its dialectical technique the Vedānta is clearly indebted to the Mādhyamika.[1]

A system which engendered this revolution in Indian philosophy and religion deserves to be studied with more sympathy and attention than has been accorded to it. There is a tendency on the part of some critics and historians to dismiss the Mādhyamika system as nihilism or as identical with the Vedānta. Such criticism is as uninformed as it is misleading. An attempt is made in the following pages to study the Mādhyamika system in all its aspects—historically, analytically and comparatively. This may throw light on the development of Indian philosophy, especially of the absolutist (advaita) trends. A study of the Mādhyamika system may prove of value intrinsically as it is a critique of all philosophy.

[1] Infra Chapter IV.

II. THE TWO TRADITIONS[1] IN INDIAN PHILOSOPHY—THEIR GENERAL NATURE

There are two main currents of Indian philosophy—one having its source in the ātma-doctrine of the Upaniṣads and the other in the anātma-doctrine of Buddha. They conceive reality on two distinct and exclusive patterns. The Upaniṣads and the systems following the Brāhmanical tradition conceive reality on the pattern of an inner core or soul (ātman), immutable and identical amidst an outer region of impermanence and change, to which it is unrelated or but loosely related. This may be termed the Substance-view of reality (ātma-vāda). In its radical form, as in the Advaita Vedānta, it denied the reality of the apparent, the impermanent and the many; and equated that with the false. The Sāṁkhya did not go so far; still it inclined more towards the substantial, the permanent and the universal. The Nyāya-Vaiśeṣika, with its empirical and pluralist bias, accords equal status to both substance and modes. Not only did these systems accept the ātman, but what is more, they conceived all other things also on the substance-pattern. The ātman is the very pivot of their metaphysics, epistemology and ethics. In epistemology, substance makes for unity and integration of experience; it explains perception, memory and personal identity better than other theories. Bondage is ignorance of the self or the wrong identification of the non-self with the self (ātmany anātmādhyāsa). Freedom is the discrimination between the two.

The other tradition is represented by the Buddhist denial of substance (ātman)[2] and all that it implies. There is no inner and immutable core in things; everything is in flux. Existence for the Buddhist is momentary (kṣaṇika), unique (svalakṣaṇa) and unitary (dharmamātra). It is discontinuous, discrete and devoid of complexity. The substance (the universal and the identical) was rejected as illusory; it was but a thought-construction made under the influence

[1] The term 'Tradition' is used here not in the sense of dogmatic authoritarianism, but to mean a fountain-source from which stems a continuous stream of thought and culture.

[2] Śāntarakṣita explicitly states that Nairātmyavāda is that which distinguishes the teaching of Buddha from all others:

> etac ca sugataseṣṭam ādau nairātmyakīrtanāt;
> sarvatīrthakṛtām tasmāt sthito mūrdhani tathāgataḥ.
> TS. 3340.

Again: ātmadṛṣṭau hi vinaṣṭāḥ sarvatīrthikāḥ. TS. 3325.

of wrong belief (avidyā). This may be taken as the *Modal view of reality*. The Buddhists brought their epistemology and ethics in full accord with their metaphysics. Their peculiar conception of perception and inference and the complementary doctrine of mental construction (vikalpa) are necessary consequences of their denial of substance. Heroic attempts were made to fit this theory with the doctrine of Karma and rebirth. Avidyā (ignorance), which is the root-cause of suffering, is the wrong belief in the ātman; and prajñā (wisdom) consists in the eradication of this belief and its attendant evils.

The terminology employed here is after the best Jaina epistemological treatises. Philosophical views, they say, are principally two—the dravyārthika naya (substance-view) and paryāyārthika naya (modal view).[1] Each view, carried to the extreme, denies the reality of the other. One emphasises the universal and the continuous to the exclusion of the changing and the different, and *vice versa*. The Vedānta is cited as the exponent of the extreme form of the *Substance-view*,[2] and Buddhism (Tathāgatamatam) represents the exclusive Modal view.[3]

The Jaina ostensibly reconciles these two opposed views by according equal reality to substance and its modes. There is no substance without modes nor modes without substance.[4] Reality is manifold (anekāntātmakam); it is not of one nature; it is unity and difference, universal and particular, permanent yet changing.[5] The Jaina shaped its epistemology on this pattern and formulated the logic of the disjunction of the real (syādvāda). This view may be said to constitute the third stream of Indian philosophy—lying mid-way between the

[1] sāmānyatas tu dvibhedo, dravyārthikaḥ paryāyārthikaś ceti. *Pramāṇā Naya*, VII, 5; *Sanmati Tarka*, Gāthā 3 (pp. 271 ff.). tathāhi paraspara-vivikta-sāmānya-viśeṣa-viṣayatvād dravyārthika-paryāyārthikāv eva nayau, na ca tṛtīyaṁ prakārāntaram asti. (p. 272).

[2] sattādvaitaṁ svīkurvāṇaḥ sakala-viśeṣān nirācakṣāṇas tadābhāsaḥ, yathā *sattaiva tattvaṁ* tataḥ pṛthagbhūtānāṁ viśeṣāṇām adarśanāt, *Pramāṇa Naya*, VII. 17 & VII, 18.

[3] ṛju vartamāna-kṣaṇasthāyi-paryāya-mātraṁ prādhānyataḥ sūtrayan nabhi-prāya ṛjusūtrah.
sarvathā dravyā-palāpī tadābhāsaḥ, yathā tathāgatamatam. *Pramāṇa Naya*, VII, 28, 30–1.

[4] dravyaṁ paryāyaviyutaṁ paryāyā dravyavarjıtāḥ; kva kadā kena kimrūpā dṛṣṭā mānena kena vā. *Sanmatitarka* I.

[5] Cf. Umāsvāti's Sūtra: utpāda-vyaya-dhrauvya-yuktaṁ sat. *Tattvārthādhigama*, V. 30.
also: *dravyaparyāyātmakam vastu prameyam*, quoted in *Syādvādamañjarī* and other works.

two extremes of the ātma—and anātmavādas. Seemingly partaking of both, it was essentially un-Brāhmanical and un-Buddhistic. It was un-Brāhmanical, as it accepted a changing ātman[1] and even ascribed different sizes to it; no Brāhmanical system could ever accept that.[2] It was un-Buddhistic too, as it accepted a permanent entity, ātman, besides change. As such, the Jaina found favour with neither. The synthesis of two views is a third view, and is no substitute for them. The Jaina system exercised comparatively little influence on the course of Indian philosophy, and was little affected by other systems. Jainism has remained practically stationary down the ages.

Indian philosophy must be interpreted as the flow of these two vital streams—one having its source in the ātma doctrine of the Upaniṣads and the other in the anātmavāda of Buddha. Each branched off into several sub-streams with a right and a left wing and several intermediary positions. There were lively sallies and skirmishes, but no commingling or synthesis of the two streams. Throughout the course of their development they remain true to their original inspirations. The Brāhmanical systems took the real as Being, Buddhism as Becoming; the former espoused the universal, existential and static view of Reality, the latter the particular, sequential and dynamic; for one space, for the other time, is the archetype. The Brāhmanical systems are relatively more categorical and positive in their attitude (vidhimukhena), while the Buddhists were more negative (niṣedhamukhena). Again, the former are more dogmatic and speculative, the Buddhists empirical and critical. Subjectively minded, Buddhism is little interested in cosmological speculations and constructive explanations of the universe. The Brāhmanical systems were bound to an original tradition; they all accepted the authoritarian character of the Veda. Buddhism derives its inspiration from a criticism of experience itself. The tempo of development was quicker and intenser in Buddhism than in the Upaniṣadic tradition.

Absolutism (advaitism) came to be established in each tradition by an inner dynamism, by the necessity to self-consistent. Advaitism must be distinguished from monism, which just asserts

[1] A changing ātman is a veritable contradiction for the Brāhmanical systems: the ātman does not change and what changes is not ātman.

[2] Cf. *The Brahmasūtras*: evam cātmākārtsnyam II, ii, 34 ff. Some Brāhmanical systems (Sāṅkhya, Nyāya and the advaita Vedānta) conceived the ātman as all-pervasive (vibhu) in size, while others, especially the Vaiṣṇava schools of Rāmānuja, Madhva etc., conceived it as *atomic* (aṇu) in size. But neither of them could tolerate increase or decrease in the original size.

the existence of a single reality. Advaitism (non-dualism) expressly denies the reality of duality. And this is done, not by positive arguments, but by the negation of appearance. All absolutism is based on the dialectic.

Monism had already been reached in the Upaniṣads, and this was carried on by the older Vedānta with the help of a systematic exegesis (mīmāṁsā). It did not find it necessary to deny the reality of the world nor of the efficacy of works (karma). The monism of the *Brahmasūtras* was compatible with difference and change. All this underwent a change in Gaudapāda and Śaṅkara who consistently deny difference and change. They uphold non-dualism as the truer meaning of the Upaniṣads.

Contemporaneously or slightly earlier, there occurred a revolution in the Philosophy of Language, and an absolutism of the Logos (Śabda-Brahma-vāda) through an analysis of the symbolic consciousness was reached by Bhartṛhari in his *Vākyapadīya*.

This revolution in the Upaniṣadic tradition was not attained without outside help. Absolutism in Buddhism (both the Mādhyamika Śūnyatā and Yogācāra Vijñapti-Mātratā) actually preceded it by several centuries. There is ample evidence not only of precedence but of influence as well. Gauḍapāda appears to us as the Brāhmanical thinker boldly reformulating the Upaniṣadic ideal in the light of the Mādhyamika and Vijñānavāda dialectic. But there was more borrowing of technique than of tenets. The Vedānta philosophers did not and could not accept the Buddhist metaphysics—its denial of the self, momentariness etc.; but they did press into service the Mādhyamika dialectic and the Vijñānavāda analysis of illusion. No absolutism could be established without the dialectic and a theory of illusion.

The Yogācāra, though it severely criticised the Mādhyamika conception of Śūnyatā, was yet directly and immediately influenced by the Mādhyamika. Its difference with the latter was with regard to the nature of the Absolute. While the Mādhyamika refused not only to characterise it—which all absolutism does—but also to identify it with anything in experience, the Vijñānvādins identified it with Consciousness. It only makes for confusion to ignore the different conceptions of the Absolute in the Vedānta, Mādhyamika and Vijñānavāda systems; at least the approaches are different. There is no doubt that it was the Mādhyamika dialectic that paved the way for the other Absolutisms.

The Śūnyatā of the Mādhyamika is the necessary implication of his dialectic, and the dialectic is the maturity of criticism which was born with Buddhism. The rise of sects and schools helped and hastened the birth of the dialectic.

The immediate emergence of the Mādhyamika dialectic must be traced to the rise of the systems of philosophy like the Sāṁkhya, Vaiśeṣika and Nyāya on the one side and the Ābhidharmika philosophy on the other. As they were diametrically opposed to each other, and yet as every one of them claimed to give us the true and only picture of reality, it must have dawned on men, already critically minded like the Buddhists, that speculative systems of thought are mere conceptual construction: they profess to lead us to the real but succeed in landing us in appearance; they claim to be knowledge, but in a sense are only illusion. This awareness of the utter subjectivity of our conceptual devices is the birth of the dialectic.

III UPANIṢADS AND BUDDHISM

Since the opening of the Buddhist scriptures to the Western world, it has become almost a stereotyped opinion among orientalists to regard Buddha as carrying on the work of the Upaniṣadic seers. Indian philosophy is interpreted as having evolved out of one single tradition—the Upaniṣadic. Buddhism and Jainism are treated as deviations rather than as radical departures from the Upaniṣadic tradition (ātmavāda). Such an interpretation is not fully alive to the vital differences and exclusive attitudes inherent in the Brāhmanical and the Buddhist systems. It tends towards *over-simplification.*

Likewise, the differences obtaining in Buddhism itself are overlooked or minimised, and an attempt is made to treat it as one system. This mistake, however, is not made in the case of the systems (Sāṁkhya, Yoga, Mīmāṁsā, Vedānta and Nyāya-Vaiśeṣika) deriving their inspiration from the Vedas. Such attempt engenders partisan spirit in writers; they begin taking sides with one or the other school of Hīnayāna and Mahāyāna, and consider *that* as *the* teaching of Buddha. There is again the *fallacy of over-simplification*. This prevents a correct understanding of the development of Buddhist philosophy. The dialogues of Buddha, as preserved in the Pāli Canons, are suggestive; they are as little systematic as the Upaniṣadic texts. Buddhist systems grew out of them much in the way the Brāhmanical systems grew out of the Upaniṣads. Buddhism is a matrix of systems,[1] and not one unitary system. It does not exclude legitimately different formulations. For a correct and fruitful understanding of the development of Indian philosophy, it is necessary to admit not only the difference between Buddhist and Brāhmanical systems of thought, but also internal differences within Buddhism itself. This would be evident if we consider the nature and development of the Upaniṣadic and Buddhist thought.

The entire Vedic teaching may be construed as knowledge of the deity (devatāy vidyā). The Devatā (deity) is the super-natural personality or essence activating things from within. It is an unseen presence (parokṣa), not overtly perceived, but felt to be the guiding and controlling spirit within. Indra, Varuṇa, Agni and other Vedic gods are not mere natural forces personified, as interpreted by Western scholars. It would be truer to understand them as personalities. Each deity has a characteristic external manifestation, such as thunder and lightning in the case of Indra. Prayers for favour could be addressed to them as they were deities and had power over phenomena; and as personalities they could be gracious. The devatā has both a cosmic (ādhidaivika) and a microcosmic (ādhyātmika) signification. In the Upaniṣads, 'deva' and 'ātman' are often used as interchangeable terms.[2] Impelled by its own dynamism, there was a two-fold movement in the deepening of the devatā-knowledge. As the deity is understood as the soul or inner essence of things,[3] the same logic led to the search for a deeper and innermost deity of deities. This is the movement towards monotheism which is an admitted feature of the Ṛg Vedic hymns. It may be truer to say that the insight into the innermost deity, variously called Virāṭ, Prajāpati or Hiraṇyagarbha,[4] was implicit from the beginning. The characterisa-

[1] Cf. "All the different shades of philosophic theory—realistic and idealistic—are found within Buddhism itself; and we have, so to speak, philosophy repeated twice over in India—once in the several Hindu systems and again in the different schools of Buddhism" (Hiriyanna, *Outlines of Ind. Phil.*, p. 198).

[2] adhyātmayogādhigamena devaṁ matvā dhīro harṣaśokau jahāti (*Kaṭha*, I, ii, 12); seyaṁ devataikṣata (*Chā. Up.* VI, iii, 2); devātmaśaktim (*Śvetāś. Up.* I, 3); cakṣuḥ śrotraṁ ka vu devo unakti (*Kena Up.* I, i); yadaitam anupaśyaty ātmānaṁ devam añjasā (*Bṛ. Up.* IV, iv. 15).

[3] Compare the expressions: gūḍham anupraviṣṭam; guhāhitam gahvareṣṭham; nihitam guhāyām; eṣa gūḍhotmā na prakāśate; ya ātmā sarvāntaraḥ, etc.

[4] tad yad idam āhur amum yajāmuṁ yajety ekaikaṁ devam etasaiva sā visṛṣṭir eṣa u hyeva sarve devāḥ (*Bṛ. Up.* I, iv, 6). yasmād etasyaiva prajāpateḥ

tion of each deity (Indra, Agni, Viṣṇu etc.) as the highest God in turn, the so-called Kathenotheism, is evidence of the awareness of the unity of Godhead. The Vedic religion of devatās is not so much a polytheism as a pantheism.

Side by side with this, there was the movement to identify man and his spiritual functions with the deity. In the Vidyās and Upāsanās, notably in the Vaiśvānara-vidyā and the Onkāra Upāsanā, we can clearly see the process of identification of the aspects of the individual with the macro-cosmic divinities. Here too was the same search for unifying the several psychic functions in a deeper principle underlying them all.[1] That principle is found in Vijñāna (Consciousness) and Ānanda (Bliss). The next step is to identify the essence of the subjective with the reality of the objective. This is expressed in the sentences like, 'I am Brahman', 'That thou art'. Difference between the self and Brahman is looked down upon.[2] This could be done, for both are transcendent (devoid of empirical determinations), and yet are the basis of all. 'Tat tvam asi' (That thou art) sums up the final teaching of the Vedas.

The mode of the development of Vedic thought consists in accepting the ātman as an inner core in things, and then to deepen this insight till a logically stable position was reached. The true self is identical with the Absolute (Brahman).[3] Later systems try to synthesise this original intuition in their own way; but they all take the ātman (Substance) as the basic reality.

In the dialogues of Buddha we breathe a different atmosphere. There is a distinct spirit of opposition, if not one of hostility as well, to the ātmavāda of the Upaniṣads. Buddha and Buddhism can be understood only as a revolt not merely against the cant and hollow-

sā visṛṣṭir devabhedaḥ sarva eṣa u hyaiva prajāpatir eva prāṇaḥ sarve devāḥ. "indraṁ mitraṁ varuṇaṃ agnim āhuḥ" iti śruteḥ. "eṣa brahmaiṣa indra eṣa prajāpatir ete sarve devāh" iti ca śruteḥ.
(Śaṅkara's Bhāṣya on the above, p. 109, Ānandāśrama Edn.)

[1] As in the *Kena* where the Ātman is reached as the foundational principle behind all mental functions; or as in the *Taittirīya* where the bodies (kośas) are shown to be the external trappings of the inner core (ātman); or as in the *Bṛ. Up.* where the self is established as the invariable light (svayaṁjyotiḥ) which illumines the changing states, to mention only a few characteristic modes of approach.

[2] Cf. ātmā hy eṣāṁ sa bhavati, atha yo'nyāṁ devatām upāste' nyo' sāvanyo-'ham asmīti na sa veda. *Bṛ. Up.* I, iv, 10; also, neha nānāsti kimcana.

[3] The movement of thought can be expressed in the equation: Devatā = Ātman = Inner Essence = Sole Reality, Absolute (Brahman).

ness of ritualism—the Upaniṣads themselves voice this unmistakably —but against the ātma-ideology, the metaphysics of the Substance-view. Buddha nowhere acknowledges his indebtedness to the Upaniṣads or to any other teacher for his characteristic philosophical standpoint. Although Brahmā, the deity, is referred to several times, Brahman (the Absolute) is never mentioned. Buddha always considers himself as initiating a new tradition, as opening up a path never trod before.[1] In the *Brahamajāla*, the *Sāmaññaphala Sutta* and elsewhere, current philosophical speculations are reviewed; and all of them are rejected as dogmatic (diṭṭhivāda) and as inconsistent with spiritual life. This is not the way of one who continues an older tradition. It is not correct to hold that the differences are religious and practical, although they are put up as philosophical.[2]

If the ātman had been a cardinal doctrine with Buddhism, why was it so securely hidden under a bushel that even the immediate followers of the Master had no inkling of it? The Upaniṣads, on the other hand, blazen forth the reality of the ātman in every page, in every line almost. Buddha came to deny the soul, a permanent substantial entity, precisely because he took his stand on the reality of moral consciousness and the efficacy of Karma. An unchanging eternal soul, as impervious to change, would render spiritual life lose all meaning; we would, in that case, be neither the better nor the worse for our efforts. This might lead to inaction (akriyāvāda). Nay more; the ātman is the root-cause of all attachment, desire, aversion and pain. When we take anything as a self (substantial and permanent), we become attached to it and dislike other things that are opposed to it. Sakkāyadiṭṭhi (Substance-view) is avidyā (ignorance) *par excellence*, and from it proceed all passions. Denial of Satkāya (ātman or Substance) is the very pivot of the Buddhist metaphysics and doctrine of salvation.[3]

[1] samudayo samudayo ti kho me, bhikkhave, pubbe *ananussutesu* dhammesu cakkhum udapādi, ñaṇam udapādi, paññā udapādi, vijjā udapādi, āloko udapādi. *Sam. N.* II, p. 105. See also *Mahāvagga* (*Vinaya Piṭaka*) I, 5.

na me ācariyo atthi sadiso me na vijjati;
sadevakasmiṁ lokasmiṁ na'tthi me paṭipuggalo.
Majjh. N. I, p. 171 (Sutta, 26).

[2] I.P. Vol. I, pp. 691 ff.

[3] The Upaniṣadic verse: 'ātmānam ced vijānīyād' etc. can, with a slight change, be made to express the Buddhistic formula:

ātmānam ced vijānīyān nāsty ayam iti pūrūṣaḥ;
kim icchan kasya kāmāya tv anusamjvared ātmānam.

The oft-recurring strain in the Pāli Canons is that things are transitory:

> How transient are all component things;
> Growth is their nature and decay.
> They are produced; they are dissolved again;
> To bring them all into subjection that is bliss[1]
> Decay is inherent in all component things;
> Work out your salvation with diligence.[2]

This is the last speech of the Tathāgata, and must therefore be taken as summing up his life-teaching.

In his interesting monograph, *The Basic Conception of Buddhism*, Professor V. Bhattacharya concludes, after a searching analysis, that the denial of the self is the basic tenet of Buddhism. He says: "Thus and in various other ways, too many to be mentioned, the existence of a permanent Self or ātman, as accepted in other systems, was utterly denied by the Buddha, thereby pulling down the very foundation of desire where it can rest."[3] Another distinguished scholar, the late Professor Stcherbatsky, is equally emphatic about this.

> When Buddha calls the doctrine of an eternal self 'a doctrine of fools' it is clear that he is fighting against an established doctrine. Whenever in his Sermons he comes to speak about Soullessness or Wrong Personalism (satkāyadṛṣṭi) a sense of opposition or even animosity is clearly felt in his words. This doctrine along with its positive counterpart—the separate elements that are active in life and whose activity must gradually be suppressed till Eternal Repose is attained—is the central point of the whole bulk of Buddhist teaching, and Mrs. Caroline Rhys Davids remarks, "how carefully and conscientiously this anti-substantialist position had been cherished and upheld." We may add that the whole of the history of Buddhist philosophy can be described as a series of attempts to penetrate more deeply into this original intuition of Buddha, what he himself believed to be his great discovery.[4]

We are now in a position correctly to indicate the relation between the Upaniṣads and Buddha. Both have the same problem, Pain

1 aniccā vata saṅkhārā uppādavayadhammino;
uppajjitvā nirujjhanti, tesam vūpasamo sukho'ti.
Mahāsudassana Sutta, ii, 17; *Mahā Pari Nib.* VI, 10.

2 "vayadhammā saṅkhāra, appamādena sampādethā'ti".
ayam tathāgatassa pacchimā vācā.
Mahā Pari Nibbāṇa, VI, 7.

3 *Basic Conception*, p. 70; see also p. 95.

4 *Soul Theory of the Buddhists*, pp. 824–25.

(duḥkha), and they see it in all its intensity and universality. Phenomenal existence is imperfection and pain. Both again are one in placing before us the ideal of a state beyond all possibility of pain and bondage. The Upaniṣads speak of it more positively as a state of consciousness and bliss (vijñānam ānandaṁ brahma). Buddha emphasises the negative aspect of it: Nirvāṇa is the annihilation of sorrow. Both have to speak of the ultimate as devoid of empirical determinations, as incomparable to anything we know; silence is their most proper language. They also agree that no empirical means, organisational device, sacrifice or penance, can bring us to the goal. Only insight into the nature of the real can avail. For the Upaniṣads, the ātman is real; only its identification with the body (kośas), the states or any empirical object, is accidental. By negating the wrong identification, its unreal limitations, we can know its real nature. Ātman is Brahman; there is no other to it. No fear, aversion or attachment could afflict it.[1] To realise the self (ātmakāma) is to have all desires satisfied (āptakāma), and thus to transcend all desires (akāma).[2]

Buddha reaches this very goal of desirelessness, not by the universalisation of the I (ātman), but by denying it altogether. For, only when we consider anything as permanent and pleasant, as a self, do we get attached to it and are averse to other things that are opposed to it; there is then bondage (saṁsāra). The attā is the root-cause of all passions, and this notion has to be rooted out completely to attain Nirvāṇa. For the Upaniṣads, the self is a reality; for the Buddha it is a primordial wrong notion, not real. The highest experience, brahmānubhava, the Upaniṣads take not as the annihilation of the 'I', but of its particularity and finitude. In fact, we realise the plenitude of our being there as bhūmā (whole). Buddha was impressed by the negative aspect of the highest trance-states as devoid (śūnya) of intellect, consciousness etc. Both reach the same goal of utter desirelessness, but through different means. The spiritual genius of Buddha carved out a new path, the negative path.

There are observations in Professor Radhakrishnan's writings which indicate the difference between Buddha and the Upaniṣads: "If there is a difference between the teaching of the Upaniṣads and

[1] Compare the passages: tatra ko mohaḥ kaḥ śoka ekatvam anupaśyataḥ; yatra sarvam ātmaivābhūt; abhayaṁ vai, Janaka, prāpto'si, etc.

[2] athākāmayamāno yo'kāmo niṣkāma āptakakāma ātmakāmo na tasya prāṇa utkrāmanti brahmaiva san brahmāpyeti (*Bṛ. Up.* IV, iv, 6).

the Buddha. it is not in their views of the world of experience (saṁsāra) but in regard to their conception of reality (nirvāṇa)."[1]

> The fundamental difference between Buddhism and the Upaniṣads seems to be about the metaphysical reality of an immutable substance, which is the true self of man as well. . . . It is true that Buddha finds no centre of reality or principle of permanence in the flux of life and the whirl of the world, but it does not follow that there is nothing real in the world at all except the agitation of forces.[2]

Is not a *fundamental metaphysical difference* the source of all other differences? If Buddhism is "only a restatement of the thought of the Upaniṣads" with a new emphasis,[3] it is desirable to emphasise this 'emphasis,' especially because it is of a fundamentally metaphysical nature. The Upaniṣads and Buddhism belong to the same spiritual genus; they differ as species; and the differentia are the acceptance or rejection of the ātman (permanent substance).

IV WAS THERE A PRIMITIVE BUDDHISM AFFIRMING THE ĀTMAN?

Attempts have been made by not an inconsiderable section of orientalists to discover a primitive Buddhism—the actual teaching of the master as distinguished from later scholasticism and monkish elaboration. Some, like Poussin, Beck and others,[4] aver that Yoga and practice of virtues formed the original teaching of Buddha which scholasticism later on transformed into a soul-denying creed.

Mrs. Rhys Davids[5] holds, on the strength of a number of textual citations, that Buddha advocated the existence of soul and carried on the tradition of the Upaniṣads. She says:

> You may find that genuine Sākya more in what the Piṭakas betray and have suffered to survive than in what they affirm as chief and fundamental.

[1] *Gautama—the Buddha*, p. 33.

[2] I.P. Vol. I, p. 375. [3] *Ibid.*, 676.

[4] See Stcherbatsky—*Buddhist Nirvāṇa*, pp. 6 and 23.

[5] In her later works, *Gotama the Man* (1928), *Sākya or Buddhist Origins* (1931), *A Manual of Buddhism* (1932), *Outlines of Buddhism* (1934) *To Become or not to Become* (1937), *What was the Original Buddhism* (1938), and many of her older works (*Birth of Ind. Psy. and its Development in Buddhism*, 1936 *Buddhism*, 1934; *Milinda Questions* etc. which she has re-edited and revised with the 'ātma-bias' and in reviews and articles in the periodicals (I.H.Q., Viśvabhāratī, Hibbert Journal, N.I.A.; J.R.A.S. etc.) too numerous to mention, Mrs. Rhys Davids elaborates her pet theme with tiresome repetition. She has gone back completely on her previous interpretation.

This happened because the piṭakas are the work of men removed from the Founder by centuries, not far short of five centuries when values were undergoing change."[1]

Buddha, according to Mrs. Rhys Davids, did not deny the soul or self outright, but only that the body, the sense-organs etc., were the self. "The words 'body is not the self', 'mind is not the self', cannot rationally be said to imply that there is no self or soul or real 'man'. As soon might I be held to be denying the existence of the captain, if I said on looking at two sailors, 'you are not the skipper'. Yet this is just the inference that Buddhism has come to draw from this monition! This belongs to the after-history."[2] "But I held that the man *was*, though he was not the things he worked with. I only said he was not these, he was not mind, not body."[3] "Thus the positive word with which I could have helped man was taken from me and the negative word, which by itself makes my teaching worthless, is put forward as the most characteristic note in our philosophy."[4]

"Gotama was both teaching and expanding the Immanent cult of his day."[5] Accepting the Upaniṣadic ideal of the self as the ultimate value, Buddha taught how to realise it, how to become that. He insisted on conduct (sīla), works, concentration (samādhi) and insight (paññā), and dependence on oneself than on ritual or knowledge. The Sākya religion

at its birth, was a new word of a certain 'More' to be recognised in man's nature and life, he was very real, not a 'being' but as one who becomes that, as becoming, he is capable at length of consummation as That (Most) the form which Deity as immanent had assumed in Indian religious teaching of the day.[6]

The utter denial of the self as a reality and its replacement by the Group (skandha) theory is a later but unwarranted accretion.[7]

1 *Sākya or Buddhist Origins* pp. 5; 339.

2 *Outlines of Buddhism*, p. 46.

3 *Gotama the Man*, p. 68.

4 Ibid., p. 121.

5 *Outlines of Buddhism*, p. 20.

6 *Sākya*, p. 419. "Man as safeguarded by the utterance was that who becomes, in a way body and mind do not . . . . But the monk-dressed utterance, as we have it in full, speaks of man not as the *More* but as the *Less*, the worse, and of suffering as held desirable." Ibid, p. 200.

7 "Those facts taken together seem to show, that in the Five Khandha doctrine we have an effort in mental analysis not belonging to the birth of the Sākyan mission." *Buddhist Psychology*, p. 201.

Mrs. Rhys Davids calls it "monkish gibberish." She seeks and finds a primitive Buddhism free from the soulless creed, but with a simple faith in the immanent ātman. Her favourite literary method is to declare Suttas as the *Poṭṭhapāda* and even portions of the same Sūtta (e.g. the *Sāmaññaphala*) which speak of soullessness as later additions.[1] She takes out passages out of their context and reads them arbitrarily as subscribing to her view.

All this raises several issues of considerable importance: exegetical, historical and philosophical; and a correct appraisal of the issues is vital for the understanding of the emergence of the Mādhyamika system.

Yoga and practice of morality are neutral. It is no doubt true that Buddha and Buddhist schools paid the utmost attention to śīla (virtues) and samādhi (concentration of attention); they brought to light deeper and subtler distinctions, and gave us a minute map of the entire terrain of our inner life. However, there is nothing peculiarly Buddhistic about this. We have all the ingredients, if not the detailed prescriptions, of a moral code in the *Śikṣāvallī* of the *Taittirīya Upaniṣad* and similar texts. Yogo practice was much older than Buddhism. Buddha himself was taught Yoga, all our accounts agree, by two Sāṅkhya teachers, Āḷāra Kālāma and Uddaka Rāmaputta. It is an accepted tenet of all Indian philosophical systems that an impure and distracted mind is incapable of perceiving the truth.[2] All systems enjoin, as a preliminary to ultimate insight, the practice of virtues and the training of the mind in concentration. Excepting the materialist and the Mīmāṁsā, every system accepted Yoga as part of its spiritual discipline, although its orientation differs in each system. Buddhism differs in this respect from the other systems only to the extent that it made a systematic and intense study of these spiritual aids. But to reduce Buddhism to a technique of mind-concentration or a code of morals is failure to appreciate the individuality of Buddha's genius and his metaphysical insight. It is failure to discern that even a way of life implies a view of reality.[3] The so-called 'silence' of Buddha and his aversion to speculative theories

[1] *Buddhist Psychology*, pp. 194 ff.

[2] Cf. sa tasmai mṛdita-kaṣāyāya tamasaḥ pāram darśayati bhagavān Sanat Kumāraḥ—*Chā. Up.* VII, 26, 2. tasmai sa vidvān upasannāyā *samyakpraśānta-cittāya* śamānvitāya; yenākṣaram puruṣam veda satyam provāca tām tattvato brahmavidyām. *Muṇḍaka Up.* I, ii, 13.

Brahmacarya is prescribed (e.g. in *Ch. Up.* VIII) as a necessary condition for receiving the highest knowledge.

[3] This point is dealt with later.

cannot be adduced as evidence of his not having a philosophy. The real significance of his silence is discussed in the next chapter.

Mrs. Rhys Davids' contention raises, as already pointed out, three kinds of issues: exegetical, historical and philosophical. What is the proper exegesis to adopt in ascertaining the import of the Buddhist Canons, which admittedly contain different strata of composition and belong to periods of time more or less removed from Gautama the Buddha? They are suggestive rather than systematic, and there are apparent doctrinal differences. It will not, however, do to pick up only those passages that are favourable to our theory and ignore the rest or call them interpolations and later accretions. For, it is possible to adduce against one textual citation which affirms the ātman, ten or even twenty which deny it with vehemence.

Reliance on isolated texts and those too considered out of their context, as is done by Mrs. Rhys Davids, is not calculated to lead to fruitful result. The chronological division of texts into primitive and later accretion is highly conjectural. Two or several parts of the Buddhist scriptures may be at variance with each other; but in the absence of incontestable historical evidence, it is difficult to decide which text is prior to which other. We have to fall back upon the philosophical appraisal of the doctrines for deciding the priority of some texts to that of others. And yet philosophical evaluation of the Canons is itself made to depend on the division into the original teaching of Buddha and later scholasticism, thus involving a circularity in argument. Exception must also be taken to her reading of some passages which amounts almost to a distortion.[1]

[1] Mrs. Rhys Davids quotes (*Buddhism*, p. 73; *Outlines*, p. 55; *Buddhist Psych.* p. 209 and elsewhere) the *Mahāparinibbāṇa* passage "attadīpa attasaraṇa" etc. . . . and translates it: "Live as they who have the self for a lamp, the self for a refuge, as they who have dharma for a lamp, dharma for a refuge, and none other." This interpretation is not borne out by the context. There was no doctrinal discussion of the soul or the self. Buddha was telling Ānanda that he had become old, eighty years of age, and that he had taught all that he knew without reservation (anantaram abāhiram karitvā) and that he did not hold anything up his sleeve like a tight-fisted teacher (ācariya-muṭṭhi). Therefore the Order should do well without him. "Ānanda, be a lamp unto yourself, be a refuge unto yourself; seek not any outside help (anañña-saraṇa) in this matter." To treat this passage as inculcating a metaphysical tenet about the self is not warranted by the context. The *Dhammapada* text: "ātmā hi ātmano nātha, ko nu nāthaḥ paro bhavet" (quoted in Mādhyamika works, MKV. pp. 354–5) and similar ones admit of the interpretation that the empirical reality of the self as a doer and enjoyer of the consequences is accepted. The Mādhyamika teachers have made commendable efforts to reconcile these texts. See *infra*, Chapter VII, the last portion of the section on the 'Examina-

Passages must not be counted, but weighed. We must consider the entire body of texts together and evolve a synthesis, weighing all considerations. We require a synoptic interpretation of the Buddhist scriptures. It is necessary to make a doctrinal analysis of the contents and assess philosophically their value. Such syntheses of doctrines and texts have been made from time to time by the Buddhist schools themselves.[1] We need consider only three such important syntheses—one by the Vaibhāṣika and the Sautrāntika, the second by the Mādhyamika and the last by the Yogācāra. Each is an attempt to reconcile all the texts and doctrines from a definite point of view. In spite of the specific differences they exhibit, they have a generic affinity that is particularly Buddhistic. The Mādhyamika synthesis of the texts and doctrines is on the distinction of existence into paramārtha (absolute) and samvṛti (empirical) and texts into nītārtha (primary) and neyārtha (secondary). According to Nāgārjuna, Buddha has affirmed the existence of the ātman against the materialist, for there is the continuity of karma and its result, act and its responsibility; he has denied it as against the eternalist who takes it as an immutable identical essence; he has also said that there is neither the self nor no-self.[2] Buddha, like a skilful physician, always graduated his teaching according to the need and the capacity of the taught.

This is one way of reconciling the differences of texts and doctrines. It is our contention that traditional explanations must be taken into account, and proper weight must be given to them. To brush them aside by condemning them as scholasticism, as later addition etc., is not evidence of unbiassed criticism. Buddhist or the other Indian schools of thought are not scholasticism in the sense that philosophy is made subservient to theology, as we find in the West during the middle ages. They may be scholastic in the sense that they pay attention to minute details and revel in subtlety. This however is no draw-back.

tion of the Ātma doctrine'. Much cannot be built on the use of such terms as 'brahmacariya', 'brahmavihāra', 'brahmapada', for they connote purity, serenity and 'blessed state'; they have lost all implications of a Brahman—or ātma-metaphysics.

[1] The *Kathāvatthu* is a sustained attempt, on the side of Theravāda, to interpret all texts from its standpoint by rejecting other opposed interpretations. The appeal there is to the texts for deciding an issue.

[2] ātmety api prajñapitam anātmetyapi deśitam; buddhair nātmā na cānātmā kaścid ity api deśitam. MK. XVIII 6. See MKV. pp. 354 ff. for the considered Mādhyamika standpoint on the subject of the ātman.

Every Indian system has passed through three or four well-defined stages of development. A seer or a great man of insight gives utterance to his intimate vision of reality; this is the mūlamantra, the original inspiration, which initiates a new path and is the basis of a new philosophy. The second stage consists in systematising, defining, the suggestions in aphoristic form (sūtra or kārikā); a philosophical system gets formulated. There is further elaboration, drawing of implications, application to details of experience, removing of discrepancies, etc. A further stage is reached when the systems indulge in criticism and refutation of other systems to strengthen their own position. Only the third and fourth stages can be called scholastic, and this too is not undesirable or valueless.[1]

Buddhist systems are the different ways in which the original vision of Buddha has been sought to be formulated in systematic form. Nothing is gained by the theory of a soul-affirming primitive Buddhism followed by a soul-denying scholastic Buddhism. Even if, *per impossible*, it were proved that the historical person—Gautama the Buddha—did teach a soul-doctrine, fundamentally at variance with the doctrines we associate with classical Buddhism, we shall still have to explain Buddhism and to relate it with the Upaniṣadic tradition. Freeing Buddha from the charge of preaching the denial of the ātman may save *him* from any 'guilt'. The question is not a personal one. In attempting to bridge the difference between the Upaniṣads and Buddha, we would have immeasurably increased the distance between Buddha and Buddhism. We cannot find any sufficient and compelling motives for the falsification of the original teaching. Either the monks were too stupid to grasp the master's basic teaching, or they were so clever that they fabricated and foisted on him an opposite doctrine. Neither of the alternatives can be seriously entertained. Why and when precisely the falsification is supposed to have occurred is not specified.

Prima facie, those systems and schools of thought which owe allegiance to the founder of this religion have greater claim to represent and understand Buddhism than the moderns who are removed from him by centuries of time as well as distance of culture and outlook. The Buddhist schools have had an unbroken tradition of development, and most of the leaders of the schools had received their

[1] Doctrinally, the stages are: suggestive, systematic and scholastic; from the literary point of view, these may be put down as the canonical, śāstra or sūtra and ṭīkā stages.

knowledge from some of the celebrated direct disciples of Buddha, like Śāriputra, Maudgalyāyana, Kāśyapa, Ānanda and others. In the course of its progress, a great religion develops and emphazises certain trends and tendencies implicit in the original inspiration of the founder. In the case of Buddhism too we must accept the law of evolution that the later phases are potentially contained in the earlier.

The entire development of Buddhist philosophy and religion is proof of the correctness of our nairātmya interpretation of Buddhism. There is no Buddhist school of thought which did not deny the ātman; and it is equally true that there is no Brāhmanical or Jaina system which did not accept the ātman in some form or other. It may be objected that the ātman the Buddhists deny is the material self identified with the body or with the particular mental states, and that such denial does not touch the position of the Sāṅkhya or the Vedānta etc. But Buddhism never accepted the reality of the ātman, of a permanent substantial entity impervious to change. The Real, for Buddhism, is Becoming. And any species of the ātma-view must take it as a changeless idential substance. The Buddhist schools differed among themselves to a great degree; they have, however, one thing in common—the denial of substance (ātman). It is a mistake to think that the Mahāyāna schools reversed the denial of soul and re-affirmed its reality. If anything, they are more thorough in carrying out the nairātmya doctrine. They deny not only substance (pudgala-nairātmya), but extend the denial to the Elements too (dharma-nairātmya) which the Hīnayāna schools had uncritically accepted as real.

In that great compendium of early Buddhist philosophy—*Abhidharma Kośa*—Vasubandu devotes one whole chapter to the discussion and refutation of the ātma-doctrine (pudgala-viniścaya). It is principally a condemnation of the Pudgalātman-heresy in Buddhism, the special tenet of the Vātsīputrīya school,[1] which admitted a sort of quasi-permanent self, neither identical with nor different from the mental states (skandha). It also refutes the Sāṁkhya and Vaiśeṣika conceptions of the ātman. Vasubandhu observes that of all teachers Buddha is unique in denying the self.[2] Denial of

[1] This forms the first issue to be discussed in the *Kathāvatthu*.

[2] Cf. The stanza of a Stotrakāra referred to by Yaśomitra:

sāhaṁkāre manasi na śamaṁ yāti janmaprabandho,
nāhamkāraś calati hṛdayād ātmadṛṣṭau ca satyām;
anyaḥ śāstā jagati ca yato nāsti nairātmya-vādī
nānyas tasmād upaśama-vidhes tvan-matād asti mārgaḥ.

AKV. p. 697.

substance (ātman) is the foundation of Buddhism down the ages. Śāntarakṣita says that all heretical philosophers have made their position untenable by adhering to the ātman.[1] In later scholastic Buddhism, the denial of the self is fully worked out with all its implications; its metaphysics, epistemology and spiritual discipline were brought in full accord with this basic tenet. There was elaboration and deepening of the original teaching of Buddha and not distortion or falsification.

The Buddhists are not the only ones in taking their philosophy as nairātmyavāda. Jaina and Brāhmanical systems invariably characterise Buddhism as denial of the ātman, substance or soul. Mādhavācārya considers the Buddhist only slightly less objectionable than the materialist (Cārvāka); in the gradation of systems he makes in his *Sarvadarśanasangraha*, Bauddha-darśana immediately follows the Cārvāka. For an ātmavādin nothing could be more pernicious than the denial of the self. Udayanācārya very significantly calls his *Refutation of Buddhistic Doctrines* (*Bauddha-dhikkāra*) Ātmatattvaviveka (Distinction of the Reality of Self). The acceptance of the ātman is what divides the orthodox from the Buddhist systems. The Jainas agree with this characterisation, and sharply distinguish their view from the purely modal view of the Buddhist.

The modern exponent may not feel committed to the estimate of Buddhism by Buddhists and others. But he is required to pause and explain the unanimity with which Buddhism has been taken as anātma-vāda. He is also required to consider the teachings of Buddha in relation to Buddhist schools of thought which, *prima facie*, have the right to be considered as embodying the founder's tenets.

There is another compelling reason for our nairātmya interpretation of Buddhism. If it had subscribed to the ātma-tradition like the Brāhmanical systems, the emergence of the Mādhyamika dialectic should prove an enigma. Dialectic is engendered by the total opposition between *two* points of view diametrically opposed to each other. And the required opposition could have been provided only by the ātma-view of the Brāhmanical systems and the anātmavāda of earlier Buddhism. The *Ratna-Kūṭa-Sūtra* (*Kāśyapa Parivarta*)[2] makes this explicit:

" 'That everything is permanent' is one extreme; 'that everything is transitory' is another. . . . 'that ātman is' (ātmeti) is one end

[1] TS. p. 867 and p. 866.

[2] *Kāśyapaparivarta*, pp. 86–7.

(antaḥ); 'that the ātman is not' is another; but the middle between the ātma and nairātmya views is the Inexpressible. . . . It is the reflective review of things (dharmāṇāṁ bhūta-pratyavekṣā)." This is the Middle Path (madhyamā pratipad) of the Mādhyamika.

V SOME OBJECTIONS AGAINST THE NAIRĀTMYA INTERPRETATION OF BUDDHISM ANSWERED

1. It is sometimes suggested that Buddha could not have propounded the nairātmya doctrine as the India of that period was not ripe for receiving it; the Zeit-geist was against any radical departure from the Upaniṣadic tradition. Further, the success that attended Buddha even during his life-time could not have been achieved, had he preached the denial of the self.

It is wrong to suggest that the times were philosophically premature and unprepared to entertain revolutionary doctrines. If anything, the picture of India that is depicted in the contemporary Jaina and Buddhist scriptures is one which revelled in philosophic speculations of a very daring kind. The objection ignores the originality and genius of Buddha. And if it were accepted, no reform, no change, should be possible as that would mean going against the established order.

The criticism further implies that only a particular type of philosophy or religion deserves to succeed or could succeed. Curiously enough, this is what might be and is actually said by the votaries of other systems. If Buddha succeeded, it was because the monks, following his path, could perceptibly advance towards freedom from all attachment. This is not to say that that could be achieved *only* by this path, but that it is *one* of the paths open to us.

If there is one lesson more than any other which the history of philosophy and religion teaches us, it is this: that differences of outlook are inherent and cannot be ruled out. There will always be advocates and votaries of particular systems. It would be nearer the truth to admit that there are some basic types of philosophy and religion; and some persons evince spiritual affinity to a particular type rather than to others. The refusal to accept this verdict of history is nothing short of intellectual myopia; it savours of intolerance. The issue, in the last analysis, is whether we subscribe to the view that there is only *one way* to reality or that it admits of *alternative paths*. If the former, the criticism of Buddhism is justified; but nothing could justify the criticism itself. One can be positive of one's own way that it leads to the goal and not that others cannot. That would be a species of dogmatism.

If alternative paths are admitted, difference in perspectives has to be admitted, but without a necessary difference in the ultimate goal. Further, the choice of one particular path to the exclusion of others is not a matter of logic, but of spiritual temperament and affiliation. One may succeed better along a particular path than on any other. Logic comes in *after* the choice is made; it is the endeavour consistently to keep to that path and not to stray unwittingly or otherwise into another. Polemic, ostensibly indulged in to refute the opponents out of existence, has value as defining and differentiating one's pattern of reality and mode of spiritual progression from that of others with which it might possibly be confused. It need not, however, be feared that we have no means of discriminating the spurious from the essential spiritual types; for, the spurious dies a natural death through sheer inanity and lack of following. Corruption and vested interests can thrive on spurious as well as on genuine systems; we should be on our guard against this. In the last resort, the criterion of the genuineness of any spiritual discipline lies in one's personal intimate experience of the real. This is accepted as the end by all systems.

2. It is also suggested that Buddha was a practical man; he rigorously eschewed all theoretical considerations as vain; as not conducive to the spiritual life. Support is apparently lent to this by Buddha's rebuke of Mālūnkyaputta and Vaccha Gotta.[1] It is concluded that Buddha inculcated a way of life, but did not care to enunciate a view of reality. He addressed himself exclusively to ethics and left metaphysics severely alone. Votaries of this contention might further say that it was left to the scholastic phase of Buddhism to spin metaphysical theories and distort the teachings of the Master. The Master himself did not preach them, even by implication.

Can we have a way of life which does not imply a view of reality as well? Is it possible to follow an ideal of conduct which claims allegiance of the entire man without raising, by implication at least, questions about the ultimate value, the nature and destiny of the individual undertaking the discipline, and his relation to the ideal? The Mīmāṁsā which is ostensibly concerned with dharma—performance of the sacrifices and rites—finds that the investigation of

[1] See *Majjh. N.* Suttas 63 and 72.

dharma involves metaphysical and epistemological issues about the self, nature of karma etc. It is committed to a form of Realism.[1] Stoicism and Epicureanism which began apparently as ethical schools have always implied a metaphysic.

The modern political modes of life, e.g. Fascism, Communism etc., imply each a distinctive philosophy. They may be materialistic or otherwise, but they imply a philosophy of existence and value. The common man may not be conscious of having a philosophy; he has neither the occasion nor the capacity to formulate a system; nevertheless his conduct *implies* a world-view. The choice then is not between having a metaphysic and not having one; but between one metaphysic and another, between a good one or a bad one. It is possible to have speculative systems of philosophy without at once having an ethics; but the converse is not possible. If it is impossible now to have a way of life without a view of reality, it was impossible for Buddha too not to have had a metaphysic. Western philosophical systems, with a few exceptions, are speculative in character. Being mere playthings of imagination, they do not necessarily lead to a spiritual discipline; they can go with any or no path of life. No Indian philosophical system is merely speculative. Each is a darśana, an insight into the real which is at once a path of perfection and cessation of pain.

Buddha of the Nikāyas appears to be well-acquainted with all the philosophical systems and trends of thought current before and during his time. He rejects them because they are at variance with the path of perfection elaborated by him. Does this not mean that Buddha is alive to the fact that a way of life implies a metaphysic?

The practice of virtues and concentration of mind are not ends in themselves. They are meant for giving us insight into the nature of the real. Buddha inveighs against the mechanical observance of rites and virtues (śīlavrata-parāmarśa). His own discipline would be indistinguishable from mere śīlavrata without the insistence on prajñā (knowledge). And it is this attainment of prajñā that imparts

[1] karmibhyaḥ phalasambandhaḥ pāralaukyaihalaukike;
sarvam ityādy ayuktaṁ syād artha-śūnyāsu buddhiṣu.
tasmād dharmārthibhiḥ pūrvaṁ pramāṇair lokasammataiḥ;
arthasya sadasadbhāve yatnaḥ kāryaḥ kriyām prati.
Śloka Vārt. Nirālambanavāda, 3–4.

The *Kāśikā* thereon says: sarvo hy ayaṁ mīmāṁsā-prapañco bāhyārthāśraya eva.

a unity and singleness of purpose to several isolated acts of morality. Not only this, but it is prajñā that perfects the virtues. One cannot be completely virtuous and freed from pain without insight. Insight makes spiritual life easy and natural. This is so in every system. As Sureśvarācārya says: "To one who has knowledge of the ātman, non-hatred and other virtues come naturally, without any effort."[1]

Indicating the role of prajñā, Śāntideva says: "Practice of virtues and concentration of mind are for the sake of attaining bodhi or prajñā."[2] The *Aṣṭasāhasrikā* speaks of prajñā as the leader of perfections. The other pāramitās cannot even be pāramitās (perfections or excellences) without prajñāpāramitā. He who is not convinced of the hollowness of things (śūnyatā) cannot also practise charity and other virtues to the utmost limit. He would have his reservations and hesitations. It is not possible then to have mere practice of virtue without implying a metaphysic.

3. By far the most serious objection to the view that Buddha taught the nairātmya doctrine (denial of soul or substance) is that it is contradictory to his other doctrines accepted as basic, namely, the efficacy of karma, the adoption of spiritual life and the doctrine of rebirth. Karma without a permanent agent who wills and reaps the fruit of his action is inconceivable. What is the value of spiritual life if there is none at the end of it? Buddha's doctrine would be the acceptance of pain without *any one who* feels the pain, a spiritual discipline without any person who undergoes the discipline and a final result (nirvāṇa) without any individual to enjoy it. Such an absurdity, it might be said, could not have been meant seriously by Buddha.

Buddha himself was aware of these alleged absurdities. In the Canons it is especially stated: "There is action, but the agent does not exist."[3] In the *Sermon of the Bearer of the Burden*, it is again stated that the Five Groups (pañcopādāna skandhāḥ) are the burden, attachment to them is carrying of the burden, detachment from them

[1] utpannātma-prabodhasya tv adveṣṭṛtvādayo guṇāḥ;
ayatnato bhavanty asya na tu sādhanarūpiṇaḥ.
Nāiṣkarmya Siddhi, IV, 69.

[2] BCA IX, 1: imaṁ parikaraṁ prajñārthaṁ munir jagau.

[3] iti hi bhikṣavo'sti karma asti karmaphalam;
kārakas tu nopalabhyate ya imān skandhān vijahāti
anyāṁś ca skandhān upādatte, anyatra dharma-sanketāt.
Quoted in BCAP. p. 474; TSP. p. 11. See also *Sam. N.* I, p. 135.

is laying down of the burden, and the burden-bearer is the empirical individual.[1]

People entertain the fond belief that the rejection of the soul—the permanent substance—vitiates Buddhist metaphysics, and that the difficulties with which it is faced are insuperable. It is further believed that the ātma-metaphysics (substance-view) avoids these pitfalls and affords a more plausible explanation of things. All this, however, is evidence of confused thinking. The anātma doctrine is no more at variance with facts or logic than the ātma doctrine. How does the acceptance of the ātman—the unchanging permanent entity—explain karma, rebirth, memory and personal identity more plausibly? As the permanent is of one uniform immutable nature, it cannot have different volitions when different circumstances call for different actions. It is neither the worse nor the better for the actions performed. It is impervious to any reform or progress. Precisely to avoid this insuperable difficulty did Buddha, taking his stand on the efficacy of Karma (act) as the sole arbiter of an individual's destiny, refuse to accept the permanent soul. A changing ātman (soul) is a contradiction in terms. No ātma-view has accepted or can accept a changing self; for, once we accept change of the ātman, we have no valid argument to confine this change to definite periods, i.e. it remains unchanged for an appreciable stretch of time and then changes. This would mean two different ātmans. Nor can we admit that one *part* of the ātman changes while the other part is permanent. If the changing part does belong to the ātman as integrally as the other part, then we would be having a supposedly unitary entity which has two mutually opposed characteristics. This does violence to our conception of an entity.

Buddha *replaced* the soul by the theory of a mind-continuum, by a series of psychical states rigorously conditioned as to their nature by the causal law governing them (dharma-sanketa). According to him this alone provides for progress (change, efficacy) and continuity (responsibility), as each succeeding state (good or bad) is the result of the previous state. Thus it avoids the futility of karma which is an inescapable predicament of the acceptance of the permanent soul on the one hand and nihilism or materialism which follows from the non-acceptance of continuity on the other. Rebirth does not mean that the soul bodily, as an identical individual essence, transports itself from

[2] Quoted in AKV. p. 106; BCAP. p. 474; TSP. p. 130. See *Sam. N.* XXII 22 for the Pāli text.

one place to another. It only means that a new series of states is generated conditioned by the previous states. Nothing is lost, and the new birth is a result of the previous. The *Śālistamba Sūtra* puts the matter definitely: "There is no element which migrates from this world to the other; but there is recognition (realisation) of the fruition of karma, as there is continuity of causes and conditions. It is not as it were that one, dropping out from this world, is born into another, but there is continuity of causes and conditions."[1] When Buddha says that in a previous birth he was himself Sunetra, a venerable teacher, as he does in the *Saptasūryodaya Sūtra* and in many of the *Jātakas*, this only means that the Buddha-series (buddhasantāna) is one—that both Sunetra and Gautama belong to the same continuum.[2] The identity of the individual is affirmed by ignoring the differences (abhedopacāra) and emphasising only the causal connection.

Memory and recognition might be thought to present insuperable difficulties. "If there is no soul how is it then that detached moments of consciousness can remember or recognise things which have been experienced a long time ago." Remembrance, as Vasubandhu in his *Abhidharma Kośa*[3] says, "is a new state of consciousness directed to the same object, conditioned as it is by the previous states." That the experience of A is not remembered by B is because the series of states conventionally designated as A is different from the series designated as B. This explanation, however ingenious, does not explain memory fully. Memory or recognition is not merely a revival of the object of the previous state, but there is the added consciousness that 'I have experienced it before.' A mental state, being strictly momentary, individual and unitary in content, cannot, on the Buddhist hypothesis, take cognizance of any other state. *Consciousness of change is not change of consciousness*; yet this is exactly how

[1] atra na kaścid dharmo'smāt lokāt paralokaṁ saṁkrāmati asti ca karmaphala-prativijñaptir hetu-pratyayānām avaikalyāt. Quoted in MKV. p. 568; BCAP pp. 481–2.

Cf. also saṁtānasyaikatvam āśritya kartā bhokteti deśitam. BCA, IX, 73 (p. 471).

[2] The AKV. (p. 710) has: Sunetro nāma śāsteti—*Saptasūryodaya Sūtre*'yam eva Bhagavān ṛṣiḥ Sunetro nāma babhūveti—eka-saṁtānatām darśayatīti yasmāt Sunetro Buddha-saṁtāna eva āsīt. See also MKV. p. 574: yat tarhīdam paṭhyate *Sūtre* (probably *Divyāvadāna*, p. 228) "aham eva sa tena kālena tena samayena Māndhātā nāma Rājā cakravartī abhūvam iti." tat kathaṁ veditavyam iti. anyatva-pratiṣedhaparaṁ tad vacanam, naikatva-pratipādakam iti vijñeyam.

[3] *Soul Theory*. pp. 452–3; AKV. pp. 711–2.

the Buddhist explains change. The identity running through the different states is a false ascription, an illusion, according to them.

The opposite hypothesis of a permanent self does not fare much better either. How can an unchanging uniform being like the ātman remember anything at all? Memory is not merely the continuity of consciousness, but the knowing of an object as having been experienced in the *past* and relating it with the present experience. An unchanging uniform ātman might have existed in the past, but as it does *not lapse*, it cannot know anything *as past*. The devices to which the Sāṅkhya and the Vedānta resort for explaining this difficulty are well-known. They differentiate the function of the ātman as mere unchanging awareness (svarūpajñāna) from the function of the changing mind (buddhivṛtti) which alone knows, remembers etc. As ātman and buddhi would then fall asunder and would not make for any coherent experience, both Sāṅkhya and Vedānta further assume a false identification (adhyāsa) between the two, by virtue of which what is true of the one is *mistakenly ascribed* to the other.[1] The Nyāya is oblivious to the difficulty. It posits a non-conscious substance (ātman), and conceives the states as produced *in* it through the co-operation of the inner sense (manas). How the states like knowledge, pain, pleasure etc., which are transitory, can belong to the unchanging ātman is nowhere explained. The difficulty is not solved by simply asserting that the qualities are produced in the ātman from time to time. What prevents two states from being two different things altogether? In the Sāṅkhya and Nyāya, both the changing and the unchanging substances are considered equally real; there is no evaluation whether the changing is real or the unchanging. Vedānta (Advaita) accepts the unchanging alone as real and rejects the other as unreal. The Buddhists do the opposite.

The difficulty is not confined to memory and moral responsibility alone. Even in such rudimentary experiences as sensation or feeling and in higher forms of experience, such as judgment and inference, synthesis and interpretation are involved. The given data have to be classified, compared, related, apperceived and synthesised into a unity; and yet the distinction has to be maintained.

The problem of knowledge is part of the larger problem, namely, the nature of existence. Our interpretation of experience will be of a piece with our interpretation of the real. In every aspect of things we find two opposite standpoints. In causation, we may emphasise the

[1] Cf. *The Sāṁkhya Kārikā*, 20.

emergence of the effect as something new and different, or we may emphasise its necessary connection and continuity. In any presented object, we may attend to the particular and the changing, or to the universal and the abiding feature. The latter may be termed the static or space-view of things, and the former the dynamic or the time-pattern. On the first, change and difference may be taken as appearance; on the second, the permanent and the universal. One emphasises unity, the other difference. What is real for one is appearance for the other, and vice versa. Whatever be the nature of our bias, we have to work out a systematic explanation of things—objects and our knowledge of them—in terms of our view. The Buddhist schools and the Brāhmanical systems in the course of their development did eventually come to formulate a coherent metaphysic and epistemology in consonance with their respective standpoints. It is not contended that Buddha himself formulated this doctrine of anātma in the systematic form with all its implications fully drawn. It is, however, suggested that he gave the inspiration and the impetus to the nairātmya view which came to be formulated in such sharp contrast to the ātma view. That there are difficulties on either conception of reality, on any conceptual pattern, no one realised perhaps more strongly than Buddha. He was thus led to discredit all attempts at *conceiving* reality, and in consequence, to reject all speculative metaphysics. This is the sole meaning of his silence. To this conclusion too he would have been led, because two or more opposed points of view were tried and found unsatisfactory. If the ātma-tradition alone had held the field, Buddha could not have come to his characteristic 'no-metaphysics' position. The systematic form of this 'silence' is the Mādhyamika system. This system could arise only after the two traditions had developed sufficiently to enable their conflict to be appreciated in all its intensity and universality. That alone could engender the dialectical consciousness.

CHAPTER TWO

THE 'SILENCE' OF THE BUDDHA AND THE BEGINNINGS OF THE DIALECTIC

BUDDHA declared certain questions of a distinctly metaphysical character to be unanswerable. For a correct understanding of the Mādhyamika system it is necessary that the 'silence' of Buddha should be properly appraised. It is our contention that the Mādhyamika dialectic is anticipated in essentials by Buddha. The Mādhyamikas have but systematically formulated his suggestions and drawn out their implications fully.[1]

The Inexpressibles (avyākata, Skt. avyākṛtavastūni) occur in very many dialogues.[2] They are invariably enumerated as fourteen and practically in the same order.

I SOME INTERPRETATIONS

Several interpretations of the avyākṛta have been offered by oriental scholars. It has been suggested that Buddha was innocent of metaphysics or was not interested in it, as he was eminently a practical man with a severely practical aim. The *locus classicus* of this view is the *Cūla Mālunkya Sutta*[3] wherein Buddha likens the metaphysician to that foolish man wounded by an arrow who, before being attended to, would like to know what sort of arrow struck him,

[1] This is evident from the whole tenor of the Mādhyamika system, especially from its reasoned opposition to all kinds of dṛṣṭi—speculative theories. See the last Chapter (XXVII entitled *Dṛṣṭi-Parīkṣā*) of the *Mādhyamika-Kārikās* and also pp. 446 ff., 536 ff. MKV; ASP, pp. 269 ff.

[2] Reference to the avyākata: *Majjh. N.* I, pp. 426–32 (Sutta 63); pp. 483 ff. (Sutta 72); *Sam. N.* III, pp. 257 ff. (Vacchagotta Saṁyuttam); *Sam. N.* IV, pp. 374–403 (Avyākata Saṁyuttam). Particular problems: (*Mahānidāna, Brahma Jāla Sutta* (D.N.) *Mahāli Sutta* (D.N.) . . . *Poṭṭhapāda Sutta* (D.N.), *Mahānidāna Sutta* (D.N.) *Maj. N.* II pp. 228–38. *Sam. N.* III, pp. 213–24 (Diṭṭhisaṁyutta). *Milinda Pañho*, pp. 144 ff. *Abhidharma Kośabhāṣya*, Appendix (Pudgala-viniścaya). MK, XXVII, and also XXII and XXV; ASP, pp. 269 ff. *Mahāvyutpatti*, p. 64 (§206); *Dharmasangraha*, p. 67.

[3] *Majjh. N.* I, 426 ff. (*A.N.* IV, 67 ff.)

whence it came, who aimed it etc. The wounded man would have died before he got satisfactory answers to his questions. The moral drawn is that metaphysical enquiries are unnecessary and can even prove harmful to spiritual life. It is contended by some others[1] that Buddha was an agnostic, though his agnosticism was not a cogently reasoned one, and that this alone fits in with his system and moral discipline. Oldenberg suggests that the questions ought not to be answered and even that they could not be answered. A negative answer or the annihilationist interpretation is also given by the same scholar: "Through the shirking of the questions as to the existence or non-existence of the ego is heard the answer to which the premises of the Buddhist teaching tended: the ego is not, or what is equivalent to it—the Nirvāṇa is annihilation."[2]

These three principal interpretations—the practical, the agnostic and the negative—are stated here as specimens of the incorrect reading of Buddhism. These and similar interpretations do not accord with the teaching of Buddha and the doctrines of the Buddhist schools. We cannot have a way of life which does not imply a philosophy,[3] an ultimate appraisal of reality. The human mind cannot for long be in a state of suspense and postponement. As regards the annihilationist interpretation, Dr. E. J. Thomas very pertinently observes:

> It is certain, however, that that is a conclusion which the Buddhists never drew. In this very sutta, annihilation is rejected. It is not really to the point to say that Buddhist premises tended to this conclusion. The only real question is what conclusion did the Buddhists draw and what for them was the logical answer. They could not consider it (Nirvāṇa) as bhāva, for it is not what is cognised by the senses, nor as non-existence.

[1] Cf. "It is quite legitimate to hold that the Buddha was a genuine agnostic, that he had studied the various systems of ideas prevalent in his day without deriving any greater satisfaction from them than any of us to-day do from the study of modern systems, and that he had no reasoned or other conviction on the matter. From the general poverty of philosophical constructive power exhibited by such parts of the systems as appear essentially Buddha's, one is inclined to prefer this explanation." Keith: *Buddhist Philosophy*, p. 63. "This leads clearly to the conclusion that agnosticism in these matters is not based on any reasoned conviction of the limits of knowledge; it rests on the two-fold ground that the Buddha has not himself a clear conclusion on the truth on these issues, but is convinced that disputation on them will not lead to the frame of mind which is essential for the attainment of Nirvāṇa." ibid. p. 45.

[2] As quoted by E. J. Thomas in his *History of Buddhist Thought*, p. 127.

[3] This issue has been discussed in a previous Section.

The Buddhists had reached the conception of a state of which neither existence nor non-existence could be asserted."[1]

A fairly cogent solution of the problem is possible if all the passages, where the questions are discussed in the Buddhist records, are considered together with the characteristic interpretations of the Buddhist schools themselves. We may then critically assess the value of these considerations.

II THE ANTINOMICAL CHARACTER OF THE AVYĀKṚTA

All our authorities agree in enumerating the avyākṛta as fourteen. Actually, there are four sets of questions, three of which have four alternatives each, and the last one concerning the soul (jīva) has only two. One does not however see why the last question too could not be logically formulated in the fourfold way like the others. The questions are:[2]

(1) Whether the world is eternal, or not, or both, or neither;[3]
(2) Whether the world is finite (in space), or infinite, or both, or neither;[3]
(3) Whether the Tathāgata exists after death, or does not, or both, or neither;
(4) Is the soul identical with the body or different from it?

In the composition of the alternatives, there is a positive thesis which is opposed by a negative counter-thesis; these two basic alternatives are conjunctively affirmed to form the third alternative, and disjunctively denied to form the fourth. The similarity of the avyākṛta to the celebrated antinomies of Kant and the catuṣkoṭi of the Mādhyamikas cannot fail to strike us. No insistence need be made on the order or the number of these questions. Importance, however, attaches to their nature and the form of stating them. The first two questions concerning the world—the one with regard to its origination and duration, and the other about its extent—are the two main

[1] *History of Buddhist Thought*, p. 128.

[2] MKV. p. 446.

[3] The first alternative is usually interpreted as referring to the beginning of the world and the second to its end—both with regard to its temporal limitation or otherwise. see MKV, p. 536: antavān loko nāntavān . . . etāś catasro dṛṣṭayo parāntaṁ samāśritya pravṛttāḥ. śāśvato loko' śāśvato lokaḥ . . . ityetāś catasro dṛṣṭayaḥ pūrvāntaṁ samāśritya pravarttante." But it appears more significant to hold that one question refers to the eternity or otherwise of the world and the other to its infinity or limitation in space.

cosmological problems. Human reason seeks to understand the ultimate unconditioned ground of objects. It seeks to find a transcendent substance like the Prakṛti of the Sāṅkhya, the primordial ground of phenomena, an infinite all-pervasive cause capable of producing all things. The aim in the cosmological speculations (Rational Cosmology) is to reach the unconditioned ground of empirical objects by means of a regressive chain of reasoning (i.e. arguing from effect to cause) stretched illegitimately, as Kant points out, beyond the possibility of experience. We will not get the correct orientation to this and other questions, if we understood the alternatives (śāśvato'yam lokaḥ etc.) as referring to the permanence and impermanence of the empirical world. For, the Eternalist does not and cannot deny empirical change. What he does affirm is that there is an eternal transcendent ground of these changing phenomena. The anti-thesis just denies the existence of this transcendent ground. Buddha must have had before him the Sāṅkhya conception of Prakṛti for the thesis and the materialist denial of the non-empirical for the anti-thesis.

The last question is about the self or the soul (jīva). The thesis seeks to reach the ultimate (non-empirical) unity of the subjective states in an independent entity. If the self were distinct from the body and the states (anyo jīvo'nyac charīram) it follows that it enjoys an unrelated, unconditioned existence apart from the body and the mental states. Its separate reality as consciousness (idealism in a broad sense), its simplicity as pure awareness, its immortality as not being composite and its freedom follow as natural consequences. The question is not about the empirical individual who is perceptibly subject to the vicissitudes of birth and death, but about the ultimate essence and separate existence of the soul as a transcendent entity.[1] Such a conception of the soul was advocated in the Sāṅkhya doctrine of puruṣa. Buddha might have had this in view as illustrative of the thesis. The antithesis (sa jīvas tac charīram) denies every one of the above implications of the thesis by identifying the soul with the body

[1] *The Brahma Jāla Sutta* (D.N. I, p. 34) says: "In this case some recluse or Brahman is addicted to logic and reasoning. He gives utterance to the following conclusion of his own, beaten out by his arguments and based on his sophistry. The self which is connected with the eye, ear, nose, tongue and skin is impermanent, not perduring, liable to change. But that self or soul which is called consciousness or mind or intelligence is permanent, stable, perduring, not liable to change or it will remain for ever and ever," (Rhys Davids's Translation).

(upādāna in general). This is the materialist view of Ajita Keśakambalin and others.

The question regarding the Tathāgata is in fact about the ultimate ground of both the soul and objects[1]—about the unconditioned in general. The Tathāgata as the Perfect Man (uttama puriso parama puriso. *Sam. N* IV, p. 380) is the ultimate essence of the universe. His position is analogous to that of God of Rational Theology (*ens realissimum*). The thesis accepts the absolute existence of the Tathāgata free from his empirical adjuncts. The phrase param maraṇāt—really means existence apart from relation to phenomena. The antithesis denies the existence of any such reality. The implication of this would be the confining of the real to be empirical—the sense-experience. This amounts to Positivism and Nihilism.

The questions are threefold, as our interests are mainly concerning the object, the knowing subject and the unity of both. There may, however, be many secondary questions and even questions about the other aspects of these three.

III BUDDHA'S SOLUTION OF THE PROBLEM

The formulation of the problems in the thesis-antithesis form is itself evidence of the awareness of the conflict in Reason. That the conflict is not on the empirical level and so not capable of being settled by appeal to facts is realised by Buddha when he declares them insoluble. Reason involves itself in deep and interminable conflict when it tries to go beyond phenomena to seek their ultimate ground. Speculative metaphysics provokes not only difference but also opposition; if one theorist says 'yes' to a question, the other says 'no' to the same. We know from the dialogues that Buddha was acquainted with the different speculations, especially of the six tithiyas (heretics). The opening dialogue of the *Dīgha Nikāya* (the *Brahmajāla Sutta*) indicates the standpoint of Buddha. He characterises all speculations as diṭṭhi-vāda (dogmatism) and consistently refuses to be drawn into the net (jāla). He is conscious of the interminable nature of the conflict, and resolves it by rising to the higher standpoint of criticism. Dialectic was born. To Buddha, then, belongs the honour of having discovered the dialectic long

1 In the order of statement of the avyākṛta, this stands midway between the cosmic and the psychological speculations. The Tathāgata is not merely man but a cosmic principle as well. Hence, he could be the synthesis or union of both. But too much cannot be built on the order of the avyākṛta.

before anything approximating to it was formulated in the West. We contend that Buddha reached a very high level of philosophic consciousness, and he did give an answer to the problem—the only answer possible for a critic of experience. Had he resiled from this position and given a 'yes' or a 'no' answer, he would have been guilty of that very dogmatism (diṭṭhi) which he so consistently condemned in others. On the opposition of the eternalist and nihilist views (śāśvatavāda and uccheda-vāda), Buddha erected another and more fundamental opposition—that between dogmatism (both śāśvata and ucchedavādas are species of dogmatism) and criticism which is the analytic or reflective awareness of them *as* dogmatic theories. Criticism is deliverance of the human mind from all entanglements and passions. It is freedom itself. This is the true Mādhyamika standpoint. We shall enforce this contention by citations from texts and by arguments. Before we do so, we might profitably consider the Ābhidharmika (Vaibhāṣika-Sautrāntika) interpretation of the avyākṛta.

IV THE ĀBHIDHARMIKA INTERPRETATION OF THE AVYĀKRTA

The Ābhidharmika system is a semi-critical school. It rejected the unchanging identical soul (ātman), declaring it to be a name having conventional meaning in the context of the empirical. It, however, constructed a system of speculative metaphysics—a theory of Elements (dharmas), based on an imperfect understanding of the utterances of Buddha about the skandha, dhātu and āyatana. Vasubandhu discusses the avyākṛta principally with regard to the soul in the concluding portion of his *Abhidharma Kośa*.[1] Coming from an ācārya (teacher), one of the greatest of all times, his interpretation bears the impress of a master-mind. Himself a Sautrāntika, he has summed up the Vaibhāṣika view. It represents the highest level to which the earlier Buddhism could attain.

Questions are of four kinds: those that can be answered directly, multiple questions that require analysis before answer, those that are answered by counter-question and lastly those that cannot be answered at all (sthāpanīya). The *Abhidharma Kośa* enumerates and

[1] The Appendix (Pariśiṣṭa) to the VIII Chapter (Aṣṭama Kośasthāna) entitled an *Examination of the Soul Theory* (Pudgala-Viniścaya). See AKV. pp. 697 ff. This has been translated by Stcherbatsky with his usual thoroughness and understanding in the *Bulletin of the Academy of Sciences, USSR*, 1919, pp. 823 ff. & 932 ff.

explains these.[1] The fourteen avyākṛta belong to the last class—sthāpanīya. The *Milinda Pañha*[2] also holds the same view with regard to the avyākṛta.

The Vātsīputrīya heresy of a quasi-eternal soul (pudgalātman) that cannot be defined as either identical with the states (skandhas) or different from them is the target of Vasubandhu's criticism. His own interpretation emerges through this polemic against the pudgalātmavāda.

The existence of the soul as something identical with or different from the body is denied. The Vātsīputrīya asks:

If the individual represents exactly the elements he is composed of and nothing else, why then did the Lord decline to decide the question, whether the living being is identical with the body or not.[3]

Vasubandhu—Because he took into consideration the intention of the questioner. The latter asked about the existence of the soul as a real living unit, controlling our actions from within. But as such a Soul is absolutely non-existing, how could Buddha have decided whether it did or did not differ from the body. Fancy someone asking: 'are the hair of the tortoise hard or smooth?' This question has already been analysed by quite ancient teachers.[4]

Vātsīputrīya—And why did not the Lord declare that it does not exist at all?[5]

Vasubandhu—Because he took into consideration the questioner's state of mind. The latter could have understood that the living being (jīva) is the same as the continuity of elements of a life (and that this continuity) is also denied. He thus would have fallen into a wrong doctrine, (the Doctrine of Nihilism).

Vātsīputrīya—Why then did not Buddha declare that the 'living being' is a conventional name for a set of constantly changing elements?

Vasubandhu—Because his interlocutor was not capable of grasping the theory of elements. . . . This (method of teaching in conformity with the mental capacity of the taught) can be clearly seen in the express words of Buddha to Ānanda, when he had answered by silence Vatsagotra and the latter had departed. . . . This point has been explained by Kumāralābha thus: 'The Buddha was pleased to construct his doctrine concerning the

[1] AK. V, 22; AKV. pp. 465–7.

[2] *Milinda*. pp. 147–8.

[3] kasmād bhagavatā sa jīvas taccharīram anyo veti na vyākṛtam iti. ayam eṣām abhiprāyaḥ, yadi skandheṣu pudgalopacāraḥ kasmāc charīram eva jīva iti noktam iti. AKV. p. 708. The passages cited here are from Stcherbatsky's translation of the *Soul Theory*. pp. 846 ff.

[4] pūrvakair eveti—Sthavira Nāgasenādibhiḥ. AKV. p. 708.

[5] itara āha—yadi nāvaktavyaḥ kasmān nokto *nāsti eveti* AKV. p. 708.

elements of existence (with the greatest caution) like a tigress who holds her young by her teeth, (her grasp is not too tight in order not to hurt him; nor is it too loose in order not to let him fall). Buddha saw the wounds produced by the sharp teeth of the dogmatic (belief in eternity) on the one hand and by the downfall of (every responsibility for one's) actions on the other. If humanity accepted the idea of an existing soul, it lay down wounded by the sharp weapon of dogmatism. But if it did cease to believe in the existence of a conditioned self, then the tender child of its moral merit would perish![1] The same author goes on and says: 'Since the living being does not exist, the Lord did not declare that it is different from the body. Nor did he declare that it did not exist, fearing that it could be understood as a denial of the empirical self.'

Vātsīputrīya—"And why did Buddha not settle the questions about the Eternity of the world etc.?"

Vasubandhu—"For the same reason! He took into consideration the intention of the questioner. First of all the latter would have meant the (Universal) Soul to be the world. But then as for Buddha no (such) soul did altogether exist, every answer such as: it is eternal, it is not eternal, it is partly eternal and partly non-eternal . . . would have been out of place. If again the questioner would have meant under the Universe the appearing and disappearing of all (its elements), every answer would have been out of place. . . . If eternal, there is no hope of final release; if non-eternal, the world-process would break of its own accord.

For the same reason, Buddha did not solve the four questions regarding the end of the Universe."

Vātsīputrīya—"And why was the question about the existence of a Buddha after death refused an answer?"

Vasubandhu—"A simple answer was not possible, taking into consideration the intention of the questioner. The latter in asking his question was surmising that the term Buddha denoted the (absolute) soul liberated from all bonds of transient existence. Since the existence of such a soul was not admitted, it was impossible to answer whether it did or did not exist after the death of the body."[2]

The realist solution of the avyākṛta amounts to this that Buddha himself advocated a *view* of the soul, of the world of things etc. The view is that the soul is but a name for the states; there is nothing

[1] āha cātreti, bhadanta Kumāralābhaḥ! dṛṣṭi-daṁṣṭrāvabhedaṁ ca bhraṁśaṁ cāvekṣya karmaṇām; deśayanti jinā dharmaṁ vyāghrīpotāpahāravat. AKV. p. 708, also quoted in TSP. p. 129.

yathā vyāghrī nātiniṣṭhureṇa danta-grahaṇena svapotam apaharati, nayati, māsya daṁṣṭrayā śarīraṁ kṣataṁ bhūd iti, nāpy atiśithilena dantagrahaṇena tam apaharati, māsya bhraṁsapāto'smin viṣaye bhūd iti. AKV. p. 708.

[2] Stcherbatsky: *Soul Theory* pp. 846–849.

unitary or identical corresponding to the name. But all our accounts are unanimous in declaring that the Tathāgata characterised all views as things of dogmatic speculation (diṭṭhigatānīmāni) and did not entertain any view himself. Secondly, the Ābhidharmika solution reduces a conflict of reason to a difficulty of verbal formulation—one that would give least offence to the weak-minded. The interpretation is, however, valuable as paving the way for the Mādhyamika standpoint which is the real heart of Buddhism.

V THE REAL IS TRANSCENDENT TO THOUGHT

All the passages should be considered together to have a complete picture. Vacchagotta—the wandering ascetic—is the principal interlocutor who persistently asks the Tathāgata or his distinguished disciples the reason, the justification, why the Lord does not answer the questions definitely while the other philosophers do so. This is evidence of the fact that Vacchagotta has become aware of the difference between Buddha and other philosophers; he is as yet not aware of the ground of distinction.[1] The Lord or his disciples supply the ground of distinction.

The questions are about the Unconditioned. Buddha is alive, unlike other philosophers, to the insuperable difficulties (*ādīnavam sampassamāno*) in conceiving the Transcendent in terms of the empirical. That form by which the Tathāgata is usually known is no longer present; He is free from measure and form (rūpa-saṅkhā-vimutto); he is deep and unfathomable like the ocean. To say with regard to the ocean that it begins here or that it does not, etc., would be a piece of irrelevance. Likewise, the Tathāgata, as the totality of things, is beyond predication.[2] Khemā Therī gives almost an identical reply to King Pasenadi; and this is later on confirmed by the Lord. The Tathāgata cannot be identified with the material and mental forms, nor can he be characterised by the absence of these. The utter inability to relate and characterise the Unconditioned in terms of the phenomenal is the reason why the questions about the Tathāgata

[1] *Sam. N.* IV, pp. 392–3 & 396.

[2] mahāyye samuddo gambhīro appameyyo duppariyogāhoti. evam eva kho, mahārāja, yena rūpena tathāgatam paññapāyamāno paññapeyya, taṁ rūpam tathāgatassa pahīnam ucchinna-mūlam tālāvatthukatam anabhāva-katam āyatim annuppādakatam. rūpasaṅkhāya-vimmutto kho, mahārāja, tathāgato gambhīro appameyyo duppariyogāho . . . etc., same with regard to vedanā, saññā etc. *Sam. N.* IV, pp. 376 ff. *Maj. N.* I, pp. 487–8 (Sutta 72).

and others cannot be answered outright. Dogmatists invariably confound the Transcendent with the empirical. They take the rūpa, vedanā, vijñāna etc. to be the self. The Tathāgata, on the other hand, does not take these to be the self, nor the self to have the rūpa, nor the rūpa in the self, nor the self in the rūpa. Deeply conscious of the empirical nature of these categories, the Tathāgata does not indulge in such unwarranted extensions; he does not spin speculative theories.[1] He has realised that the Real is transcendent to thought.

Buddha tells Ānanda, when Vacchagotta had been answered by 'silence' and had departed, the reason for his attitude.

> If, Ānanda, when asked by the Wanderer: 'Is there a self?' I had replied to him: 'There is a self', then, Ānanda, that would be siding with the recluses and Brahmins who are eternalists. But if, Ānanda, when asked 'Is there not a self?' I had replied that it does not exist, that, Ānanda, would be siding with those recluses and Brahmins who are annihilationists. Again, Ānanda, when asked by the Wanderer: 'Is there a self?' had I replied that there is, would my reply be in accordance with the knowledge that all things are impermanent? "Surely not, Lord." Again, Ānanda, when asked Vacchagotta the Wanderer: 'Is there not a self?' had I replied that there is not, it would have been more bewilderment for the bewildered Vacchagotta. For he would have said: Formerly, indeed I had a self, but now I have not one any more.[2]

If he had answered the questions, yes, or no, i.e. accepted one of the alternatives propounded, he would have been guilty of that very dogmatism (diṭṭhi) which he had so vehemently condemned in others. Consistent with his attitude of a critic of experience, as one rising beyond the relativity which infects every phenomenon, he could not have given any other answer. All the speculations are dogmatic, mere theories. Vacchagotta asks: "But has Gotama any theory of his own?" The Lord answers:

> The Tathāgata, O Vaccha, is *free from all theories*. But this, Vaccha, does the Tathāgata know—the nature of form, and how form arises and how form perishes. . . . Therefore the Tathāgata has attained deliverance and is free from attachment, inasmuch as all imaginings, or agitations, or false notions, concerning an Ego or anything pertaining to an Ego, have perished, have faded away, have ceased, have been given up and relinquished.[3]

[1] *Sam. N.* IV pp. 395–7.

[2] *Sam. N.* pp. 400–1 (*Kindred Sayings.* IV, p. 282. Trans. by Woodward).

[3] *Majj. N.* I, p. 486 (Dis. 72) Trans. by Warren—*Buddhism in Translations*: p. 125.

Instead of the usual opposition between śāśvata-vāda and uccheda-vāda, affirmation and negation, Buddha substituted the more fundamental one between dogmatism and criticism. This is his middle position (madhyamā pratipad), which is not a position in the sense of a third position lying midway between the two extremes, but a no-position that supersedes them both. It is thus on a higher plane.

Why do not the other philosophers rise up to this critical plane, or how could Buddha reach this? Again, the Lord or his disciples, Sāriputta and Moggalāna, provide the answer. The Lord tells Vacchagotta that ignorance of rūpa, vedanā etc., how they arise, how they cease, and of the path leading to their cessation is the cause of dogmatism.[1] To another questioner, Mahākoṭṭhika, Sāriputta gives the same answer.[2] Ignorance of the truth with regard to rūpa etc. is due to attachment to rūpa and being addicted to existence.[3]

Buddha, unlike the dogmatists, knows what rūpa and other skandhas are; he perceives their origin, their nature as pain and the way to suppress them. He does not theorise about them. Others weave theories regarding these, but do not know their inner constitution. And to know this is to be free from the delusion of the 'I' and the 'mine.' The contrast implied is between the dogmatic use of rūpa etc. and the analytic awareness of them, between theory and the critical consciousness of it. To become aware of a theory (diṭṭhi) as such is not to propound another theory, but to be self-conscious of it; and thereby to resolve it. This is freedom.[4]

When do we know rūpa *as* rūpa, a theory *as* theory? Not when we are using it implicitly, putting all our trust in it, enamoured of its externals, but only when we realise its shortcomings. As long as a mechanism is working smoothly, we have no occasion to know its constitution. Interested as we are in its working, we do not take it to pieces. When we use Reason in the dogmatic speculative way to construct theories, we are not aware of its nature, how it works. As Reason becomes involved in antinomies, we grow critical and try to understand the structure of Reason itself. The two may thus be

[1] *Sam. N.* III, pp. 258 ff.

[2] *Sam. N.* IV pp. 386-7.

[3] rūpe kho āvuso avigata-rāgassa avigatachandassa avigatapemassa avigatapipāsassa avigatapariḷāhassa avigatataṇhassa, hoti tathāgato param maraṇā ti pissa hoti *Sam. N.* IV p. 387.

[4] kiñ ca bhikkhave jānato kim passato āsavānaṁ khayo hoti. iti rūpam iti rūpassa samudayo iti rūpassa aṭṭhagamo, iti vedanā . . . evam kho bhikkhave jānato evam passato āsavānaṁ khayo hoti. *Sam. Nik.* III pp. 152-3.

equated; to know what a theory (dṛṣṭi) is, is to know it as false. The very futility of the attempts of Reason to reach the Unconditioned shows it up as a subjective device.

Buddha condemns theories in his characteristic way:

> To hold that the world is eternal or to hold that it is not, or to agree to any other of the propositions you adduce, Vaccha, is the jungle of theorising, the wilderness of theorising, the tangle of theorising, the bondage and the shackles of theorising, attended by ill, distress, perturbation and fever; it conduces not to detachment, passionlessness, tranquility, peace, to knowledge and wisdom of Nirvāṇa. This is the danger I perceive in these views which makes me discard them all.[1]

This contention also necessarily implies that the criticism of views is not itself a view.

VI THE TRUE NATURE OF BUDDHA'S SILENCE

Buddha's silence, then, cannot be construed as agnosticism;[2] for this is an attitude of doubt and despair; but Buddha's answer is decisive. It is not also true that Buddha's attitude was just a suspension of judgment and that he was awaiting a more favourable opportunity to publish the truth. He tells us expressly that he has taught the truth without reservation and without any distinction of the exoteric and the esoteric; he had not kept back anything like a tight-fisted teacher.[3] Nor is it ignorance of metaphysics. He was not only conversant with philosophical speculations of the time, but was himself a metaphysician of no mean order. By his penetrative analysis he had reached a position which transcended and annulled the dogmatic procedure of Reason. His rejection of speculative metaphysics was deliberate and sustained. Criticism itself is philosophy for him.

His position was not Nihilism even in an implicit form. Neither Buddha nor any Buddhistic system ever took this to be so. Buddha avers in the most explicit terms the existence of Nirvāṇa as the implication of his doctrine and the spiritual discipline. Numerous are the passages in which Nirvāṇa is spoken of in positive terms as a reality beyond all suffering and change, as unfading, still, undecaying,

[1] *Majjh. N.* p. 485–6 (Trans. by Chalmers, slightly modified).

[2] Buddha sharply distinguishes his position from the aññāṇavāda of Sañjaya—the Agnostic (vikatthavādin). See *Brahmajālasutta* and *Sāmañña-phala Sutta* etc.

[3] *Mahāparinibbāṇa Sutta*, ii, 25.

taintless, as peace, blissful. It is an island, the shelter, the refuge and the goal.[1] In a celebrated *Udāna* passage[2] Buddha says: "There is a not-born, a not-become, a not-created, a not-formed. If there were not this not-born, this not-become . . . there would not be the escape, the way out of this bondage (samsāra). . . ."

Buddha did not doubt the reality of Nirvāṇa (Absolute); only he would not allow us to characterise and clothe it in empirical terms as being, non-being etc.[3] His silence can only be interpreted as meaning the consciousness of the indescribable nature of the Unconditioned Reality. Professor Radhakrishnan unerringly indicates the nature of Buddha's silence in his works thus:

> If the Buddha declined to define the nature of the Absolute or if he contented himself with negative definitions, it is only to indicate that absolute being is above all determinations.[4] Why, then, did Buddha not admit in express terms the reality of the absolute. Buddha refused to describe the absolute, for that would be to take a step out of the world of relativity, the legitimacy of which he was the first to contest in others. The absolute is not a matter of empirical observation. The world of experience does not reveal the absolute anywhere within its limits.[5]

A close parallel, as is pointed out by many scholars, is the Upaniṣadic way of defining Brahman as 'neti' 'neti', as what cannot be grasped by speech, thought or senses. Brahman is nirdharmaka (asthūlam, anaṇu etc.), devoid of determinations. Far from being unreal on this account, it is the sole reality, the soul of the universe.

While the indescribability of the absolute is common to the Upaniṣads and Buddha, a difference in their approach must be admitted. The Upaniṣadic seers do not concern themselves with the different philosophical standpoints and views of the real. Being pioneers in the field, they had not before them many, right or wrong, views to criticise and to condemn. They appear to start with an intuitive or extra-philosophical knowledge of Brahman and then lead the disciple to that knowledge through arguments and analogies. They are not aware, except in a vague form, of the conflict in Reason. Theirs is not a dialectical approach. Buddha on the other hand is more rational in his procedure. He starts with the total and interminable conflict in Reason as exemplified in the several speculative

[1] *Sam. N.* IV p. 369 ff.

[2] *Udāna* pp. 80–81. cf. *Itivuttaka* p. 37 (§43) and p. 61.

[3] Cf. *Udāna* p. 80 (VIII. 1).

[4] *Gautama the Buddha*, p. 59.

[5] *I.P.* Vol. I pp. 682–3.

systems of his time. The untenability of each view, of all views, condemns them as mere subjective devices. The rejection of theories (diṭṭhi) is itself the *means* by which Buddha is led to the non-conceptual knowledge of the absolute, and not vice versa. It is no accident then that Buddha concerns himself with an analysis of the various theories of reality and rejects them all. Buddha ascends from the conflict of Reason to the inexpressibility of the absolute. The consciousness of the Conflict in Reason and the attempt to resolve it by rising to a plane higher than Reason is dialectic. And the dialectical method is the Mādhyamika way.

Again, the Upaniṣads, with one voice, speak of the knowledge of the self as the knowledge of all and this is the sole means of freedom. Bondage is the ignorance of the self. For Buddha, however, the self is a primary wrong notion. Buddha does not speak of the knowledge of any specific entity as the saving knowledge. For him the awareness of the nature of pain and its cause is itself the knowledge which sets man free. Times out of number we are told that Buddha knows what is pain, how it arises, how it ceases etc. This can only mean that for him knowledge is the self-conscious awareness of the world-process; to realise the inexorability of the Causal Law (pratītya-samutpāda) is to stand aside from it. "Freedom is the knowledge of Necessity." It is an attitude of withdrawal. Avidyā is ignorance of the nature of pain etc; it is the natural but unconscious attachment to things. Buddha's conception of reflective awareness of things as the saving knowledge is the Mādhyamika notion of śūnyatā or prajñā.

It might be asked: if Buddha had no theory of his own, how is it that he appears to have suggested a theory of elements (skandha, dhātu and āyatana) at very many places in his dialogues? To suggest, as is done by some scholars, that the skandha-doctrine is a later scholastic elaboration of the monks is to shelve the question. We must accept that Buddha did formulate such a doctrine; the passages are too numerous and the tradition too weighty to be ignored. On our interpretation, the doctrine of elements was necessary as a preliminary step. If there had been only the substance-view (ātma-vāda) in the field, Buddha could not have been led to the dialectical consciousness. A modal view too was necessary. A thesis had to be opposed by a counter-thesis before there could emerge the dialectical consciousness. Then alone could there be a Conflict in Reason and the attempt to transcend it. As a matter of dialectical necessity then did Buddha formulate, or at least suggest, a theory of elements. The Mahāyāna systems clearly recognise this dialectical necessity when they speak of the pudgala-nairātmya—the denial of substance—as intended to pave the way for Absolutism. Śūnyatā is the unreality of the elements as well (dharma-nairātmya). Modern Buddhist scholars like Kimura[1] who are in touch with a living Buddhist tradition also speak in the same strain.

VII ANTICIPATIONS OF THE MĀDHYAMIKA

That the Buddha did not mean the doctrine of elements to be an ultimate standpoint is evident from certain trends and texts of the Pāli canons, although they have been subjected, as is accepted now, to a careful and partisan revision and editing by the Theravādins.

Buddha declares rūpa, vedanā, etc. to be illusory, mere bubbles[2] etc. In the *Majjhima Nikāya*, it is stated:[3] "Depending on the oil and the wick does the light of the lamp burn; it is neither in the one nor in the other, nor anything in itself; phenomena are, likewise, nothing in themselves. All things are unreal; they are deceptions; Nibbāna is the only truth." Basing himself on this text Nāgārjuna says: "In declaring that it is deceptive and illusory, the Lord means Śūnyatā—dependence of things."[4]

Condemning that incapacity of some of the monks to understand the deeper, inner, meaning of his teaching, Buddha speaks of the Bhikkhus of the future period thus:

[1] "Historically, it must be said that Buddha preached his phenomenological doctrines in an 'Exoteric form' to the people and his Ontological doctrine in the 'Esoteric form' was reserved only for advanced or brilliant men. Teachings on both these lines proceeded simultaneously without implying any periodical or chronological division. However, from the doctrinal point of view, the former is the more expedient (upāya) doctrine, while the latter is the real doctrine. This order equates well with the inherent natural law in the spiritual domain. Here the former or 'exoteric' must come first and the latter or 'esoteric' would come next." *The Terms Hīnayāna and Mahāyāna* etc. p. 60. See also pp. 47 ff.

[2] phena-piṇḍūpamaṁ rūpam; vedanā bubbulūpamā maricikūpamā saññā, sankhārā kadalūpamā, māyūpamañ ca viññānaṃ dīpitādicca-bandhunā. *Sam. N.* III 142. cf. also the *Majjh. N.* (II, p. 261) passage: anicca, bhikkave kāmā tucchā musā moghadhammā māyākatam etam, bhikkave, bālatāpanam. etc. cf. also *Suttanipāta* 757–8. The Sanskrit versions of these texts are quoted at several places in the MKV.

[3] *Majjh. N.* III, p. 245 Dialogue, 140.

[4] tan mṛṣā moṣadharma yad yadi kiṁ tatra muṣyate;
etat tūktam bhagavatā śūnyatā-paridīpakam. MK, XIII 2.

The monks will no longer wish to hear and learn the Suttāntas proclaimed by the Tathāgata, deep, deep in meaning, reaching beyond the world, dealing with the Void (suññatā-paṭisamyuttā) but will only lend their ear to the profane suttāntas proclaimed by disciples, made by poets, poetical, adorned with beautiful words and syllables.[1]

This is a significant admission that the real heart of Buddha's teaching is the doctrine of Śūnyatā, as the Mādhyamikas claim. Nāgārjuna is justified in declaring that the Buddha has nowhere taught the doctrine of Elements as the ultimate tenet.[2]

The Mādhyamika standpoint is clearly stated in some celebrated passages. Buddha tells us that there are two principal viewpoints—the existence and the non-existence views (bhavadiṭṭhi and vibhavadiṭṭhi). No one holding to either of these can hope to be free of this world. Only those who analyse and understand the origin, nature and contradictions of these two views can be freed from the grip of birth and death—saṁsāra.[3] Kaccāyana[4] desires to know the nature of the Right View (sammādiṭṭhi) and the Lord tells him that the world is accustomed to rely on a duality, on the 'It is' (atthitam) and on the 'It is not' (natthitam); but for one who perceives, in accordance with truth and wisdom, how the things of the world arise and perish, for him there is no 'is not' or 'is'. "That everything exists" is, Kaccāyana, one extreme; "that it does not exist" is another. Not accepting the two extremes, the Tathāgata proclaims the truth (dhammam) from the *middle position*. Nāgārjuna makes pointed reference to this passage in his *Kārikās* declaring that the Lord has rejected both the 'is' and 'not-is' views—all views.[5]

The *Ratnakūṭa* (*Kāśyapaparivarta*), which is one of the early formative texts of the Mahāyāna, explicitly mentions the two stand-

[1] *Sam. N.* II p. 267.

[2] sarvopalambhomaśaḥ prapancopaśamaḥ śivaḥ;
na kvacit kasyacit kaścid dharmo Buddhena deśitaḥ. MK. XXV, 24.

[3] *Majjh. N.* I, p. 65. See also *Udāna* p. 33; *Itivuttaka*, pp. 43–4.

[4] dvayanissito khvāyaṁ, kaccāyana, loko yebhuyyena atthitañ ceva natthitañ ca . . . sabbam atthīti kho, kaccāyana, ayam eko anto; sabbaṁ natthīti ayaṁ dutiyo anto. ete te, kaccāyana, ubhe ante anupagamma *majjhena* tathāgato *dhammam deseti*. *Sam. N.* II, p. 17. See also *Sam. N.* II, pp. 61 ff.

[5] kātyāyanāvavāde cāstīti nāstīti cobhayam; pratiṣiddham bhagavatā bhāvābhāvavibhāvinā. MK. XV, 7.

points—ātma and nairātmya-vādas and the middle position as transcending both.[1]

Buddha compares, in the *Alaguddūpama Sutta*, the dharmas to a raft which has to be left off after crossing the stream; they are not meant to be taken as ultimate tenets.[2] The Mādhyamikas take this as the Upāya doctrine, having just a means-value; it is to be abandoned after it had served its purpose.

Indicating that pain is conditioned by imagination and is nothing real in itself, Buddha refers to the parable of the Demon Vepacitta who was bound or freed according to the evil or good nature of his thoughts. That imagination (kalpanā) is bondage[3] and the cessation of Kalpanā is freedom is a fundamental Mādhyamika tenet given expression to at several places in his *Kārikās* by Nāgārjuna.[4] Attention must be drawn, once again, to Buddha's rejection of all speculative philosophies as dogmatism (diṭṭhi or diṭṭhigatānīmāni) and his declaration that the Tathāgata is free from all theories. This is in entire accord with the Mādhyamika standpoint of criticism and rejection of all theory as constituting the highest wisdom.[5] Importance also attaches to the antinomical way of stating metaphysical views; the fourfold formulation of the alternatives which is a regular feature of some of the dialogues[6] anticipates the form also of the Mādhyamika dialectic.

The passages favouring the Mādhyamika interpretation may be few and greatly interspersed with texts of a dogmatic character.

[1] ātmeti, kāśyapa, ayam eko'ntaḥ; nairātmyam ity ayaṁ dvitīyo'ntaḥ; yad ātmanairātmyayor madhyaṁ tad arūpyam anidarśanam . . . iyam ucyate, kāśyapa, madhyamā pratipad dharmāṇāṁ bhūtapratyavekṣā. *Kāśyapaparivarta* p. 87. cf. also the *Samādhirāja Sūtra*: astīti nāstīti ubhe'pi antā ubhe anta vivarjayitvā madhye'pi sthānaṁ na karoti paṇḍitaḥ (IX 27) *Gilgit MSS*. Vol. II, p. 103.

[2] evam eva kho, bhikkhave, kullūpamo mayā dhammo desito nittharaṇatthāya na gahaṇatthāya. kullūpamam vo bhikkhave ājānantehi dhammā pi vo pahātabbā; pāg eva adhammā. *Majj. N.* I, p. 135 (Sutta. 22) cf. the Mādhyamika conception: upāyabhūtam saṁvṛti satyam; upeyabhūtaṁ paramārtha-satyam.

[3] *Sam. N.* IV, p. 202.

[4] MK. XVIII, 5.

[5] *Majj. N.* I, p. 486 (72nd Sutta) cf. also *Mahānidāna Sutta*, 32 (*Dīgh. N.* XV, p. 32) yāvatānanda adhivacanaṁ yāvatā adhivacanapatho, yāvatā nirutti yāvatā niruttipatho, yāvatā paññatti yāvatā paññatti-patho, yāvatā paññā yāvatā paññāvacaraṁ, yāvatā vaṭṭaṁ yāvatā vaṭṭaṁ vaṭṭati, tad abiññā vimutto bhikkhu, tadabiññā vimutto bhikkhu na jānāti na passatīti'ssa diṭṭhīti tad akallam.

[6] *Brahmajāla* and other *Suttas*. This is the catuṣkoṭi of the Mādhyamikas.

Nevertheless, they necessitate a reinterpretation of the entire body of Buddha's teaching. For, it is possible to subordinate the doctrine of elements to the absolutist teaching and not *vice versa*; the skandhas, dhātus and āyatanas may be taken as having phenomenal validity; their formulation would still be significant. But the texts which speak of them as illusory and fit to be rejected as diṭṭhi cannot be understood in any other manner except as the ultimate teaching. An analogous case is the relative value attaching to the 'para' and 'apara' texts of the Upaniṣads. We are told, in what appears to be a canonical text, that we should attach value to the texts of primary and ultimate import (nītārtha) and not to those of secondary import (neyārtha).[1] The Mādhyamika exegesis consistently explains and interprets texts on this distinction.

That the early Buddhist view was like that of the Mādhyamika has not wholly escaped the notice of orientalists like Kern, Otto Franke, Poussin and even of Keith. Kern says that "from the outset Buddhism was an idealistic nihilism;"[2] "that the early Buddhistic view was, like that of the Mahāyāna, negative though the argument establishes, even taken on its own claims, that the view was idealistic with a tendency, not wholly conscious or articulate, to negativism."[3]

"The *Majjhima Nikāya* freely contains the ideas of Voidness," says Keith giving exact references to a number of passages. "Belief in the existence of ideas is merely a raft to enable men to cross the ocean of existence. . . . This accomplished, it should be cast away for the useless thing it is."[4]

Sāriputta confronts Yamaka with the question whether the true self of the Tathāgata is his material form and receives a negative reply. Similar replies are given to the questions whether he is in the material form, or

[1] nītārthaṁ ca sūtram prati-śaraṇam uktam iti: catvārīmāni, bhikṣavaḥ, pratiśaraṇāni. katamāni catvāri? dharmaḥ pratiśaraṇam na pudgalaḥ; arthaḥ pratiśaraṇam, na vyañjanam, nītārtha-sūtra pratiśaraṇam na neyārtham; jñānam pratiśaraṇam na vijñānam iti. Quoted twice in AKV, p. 174; p. 704.

[2] *A Manual of Indian Buddhism*, p. 50.

[3] Franke's view—See his paper: *Negativism in the Old Buddhist Teaching* (*Festschrift Kahn*, pp. 366 ff). Therein Franke tries "to prove that the idea of Voidness has indeed been in the mind of the founder of the creed or that the Singhalese school itself takes up the idea of voidness or that it has been interpreted into the original conception by the authors of the commentaries (aṭṭhakathā) and above all by Buddhagosa." Poussin (E.R.E. VIII, p. 334) says: "There is a great deal of Mādhyamika philosophy in the Pāli Canon."

[4] *Buddhist Phil* p. 49.

it in him, or different from it, and so on with the four other constituents which make up the apparent individual. Yamaka also admits that the five constituents all taken together do not make up the Tathāgata; nor again is he without the five constituents taken together. Sāriputta then confronts Yamaka with the conclusion that even in life he cannot comprehend in truth and essence the Tathāgata and that *a fortiori* it is absurd to make assertions of him after his death. Does this mean that even in life Yamaka cannot show the Tathāgata really to exist and still less of course in death can his nature be stated?[1] The interpretation is possible, and in entire harmony with the Mādhyamika view.[2]

It is not contended that we have a full-fledged dialectic in Buddha; but that there are definite suggestions and indications which led, as a matter of logical development, to the systematic formulation of the dialectic by the Mādhyamika. The reason for this is that the conflict in reason which engenders the dialectical consciousness was itself not in a systematic but suggestive stage then. Only as the rival systems developed and differed radically from each other could their opposition be sharp and sustained. This presupposes a period of several centuries wherein the systems took their definite form. The Mādhyamika represents that systematic stage of the conflict in reason and the solution of the conflict by transcending the alternatives.

[1] This is exactly the conclusion that Nāgārjuna arrives at in his chapter on the *Examination of the Tathāgata* (MK. XXII): prapañcayanti ye buddham prapañcātītam avyayam; te prapañcāhatāḥ sarve na paśyanti tathāgatam.
tathāgato yatsvabhāvas tatsvabhāvam idam jagat;
tathāgato niḥsvabhāvo niḥsvabhāvam idam jagat. MK. XXII, 15–16.

[2] *Buddhist Phil.* p. 67. See also p. 66.

CHAPTER THREE

DEVELOPMENT OF THE TWO TRADITIONS AND THE EMERGENCE OF THE MĀDHYAMIKA SYSTEM

I GENERAL OUTLINE OF THE DEVELOPMENT

SYSTEMS of philosophy are the elaboration, through concepts and symbols, of certain original intuitions. If all of us had those basic intuitions, systems should be superfluous. Every one is not a Buddha or a Yājñavalkya. It happens that the great mass of mankind can but be followers and are not leaders in thought. Systems of thought are intended to lead them to the highest experience through symbols and concepts. The several systems, both of the Upaniṣadic (ātma) and Buddhistic (anātma) tradition, must be considered as so many attempts to embody their original inspiration. In the process of translation the original freshness and flavour are lost to some extent. Besides, all the systems do not equally penetrate to the original inspiration. Some may stay at the periphery, some go a little deeper, while it is only a few that penetrate to the centre. These differences arise because of the spiritual bias and the capacity of the makers of systems. Though all the Brāhmanical systems are derived from the Upaniṣads, there is justification to hold that only the Advaita Vedānta represents the real heart of the Upaniṣads. Similarly, though all the Buddhistic systems (Theravāda, Vaibhāṣika etc.) embody the teachings of Buddha, it is the Mādhyamika system that represents the real heart of Buddhism.

It is a fact exemplified in both the traditions that the Advaita Vedānta and Mādhyamika systems developed as criticism of an earlier realistic formulation, the Sāṁkhya and the Ābhidharmika systems respectively. The historical development is also the logical here. It is admitted on all hands that the Sāṁkhya was the first system to arise in India, and in its earliest formulations it is pre-Buddhistic. The Sāṁkhya grew as the first synthesis, on rationalist basis, of the chief tenets of the Upaniṣads. It tried to remove certain inconsistencies in the Upaniṣadic teaching by bifurcating reality (substance) into the changing object (pariṇāmi nitya) and the unchanging subject (kūṭastha nitya) and by precisely defining change. The inherently unstable standpoint of the Sāṁkhya was tried to be rectified by making reality homogeneous. The Vaiśeṣika realism does this by objectifying all things, the ātman (subject) included, and by converting the dualism into a pluralism. The idealistic Vedānta reasserts monism through a rigorous criticism of the Sāṁkhya dualism. The older Vedānta of the author of the *Brahma Sūtras* and his pre-Śaṅkara commentators, while establishing monism, generally accepted the modification of Brahman, and did not see any contradiction in conceiving Brahman as both unity and difference. It was left to Gauḍapāda and his illustrious successor, Śaṅkara, to revolutionise the Vedānta by introducing the theory of appearance (vivarta); they rejected the earlier conception of a real transformation of the absolute into phenomena (brahma-pariṇāma) and asserted non-dualism (advaita) as the true teaching of the Upaniṣads. This development, which was a turning-point in the history of Indian philosophy, was engendered by two sets of influences: one, the drive towards self-consistency which was at work in the older Vedānta too, and second, the adoption of the technique (dialectical method) already perfected by the Mādhyamika and also used by the Vijñānavāda. We have definite evidence of this influence in Gauḍapāda, though in Śaṅkara the traces are almost obliterated. There was, however, adoption of the technique of the Mādhyamika dialectic and not the borrowing of its tenets. Influence is not necessarily acceptance or borrowing of doctrines. That too is influence which stimulates the systems to modify, revise or even to re-affirm their doctrines. Influence may be expressed as much through opposition as by acceptance. In this sense alone the Brāhmanical systems, Vedānta and Nyāya, have been influenced by Buddhism.

An almost analogous and parallel development obtained within the anātma tradition (Buddhism). Like the Sāṁkhya on the Upaniṣadic side, the first attempt to synthesise the teachings of Buddha was the Ābhidharmika system. We may comprise under this the Theravāda as well as the Sarvāstivāda. Internal evidence of the Mahāyāna systems themselves and historical evidence unmistakably point to the Sarvāstivāda as the matrix from which the Buddhist systems developed as departures and deviations. The Ābhidharmika system is analogous to the Sāṁkhya in a more vital sense. We may consider its dharmas (Skandhavāda) as the Buddhistic version of the Sāṁkhya conception of Prakṛti and Puruṣa.

The inadequacy and inconsistency of the Abhidharma system—the theory of elements—led to the Mādhyamika dialectic. The tempo of development was intenser and quicker in the anātma tradition. Schools and sub-schools multiplied without number, and in the welter of ideas, Mahāyāna was born. It was a revolution in Buddhism, and is in a sense the re-affirming of the oldest and central teaching of Buddha. Here too two influences may be seen at work. One, the passion for consistency: the very dynamism of the nairātmyavāda must have made the realist phase (the Theory of the Elements) seem just a step. Then there was the Sāṁkhya and probably the other systems which conceived reality from a totally different standpoint. The difficulties in each standpoint with regard to philosophical problems were there as ever. This must have led an acute and sensitive mind to reflect that the fault lay not in this or that system; there was something fundamentally wrong about the constitution of Reason itself. Kant was led, in similar circumstances, when faced with the impasse created by Rationalism and Empiricism, to examine the claims of Reason in his *Critique of Pure Reason.* We have reason to think that the opposition in philosophy created by the Sāṁkhya and the Vedānta on the one hand and the Ābhidharmika philosophy on the other was much more total and basic than that between Rationalism and Empiricism. Reflective criticism was inevitable. The Mādhyamika dialectic is the expression of this criticism.

The great contribution that Buddhist thought made to Indian philosophy was the discovery of the subjective—the doctrine of appearance. While the Sāṁkhya took only the relation between puruṣa and prakṛti as appearance, the Buddhists with their nairātmya bias relegated substance, the permanent, the whole and the universal to the realm of the unreal. They maintained them to be purely subjective forms (vikalpa) lacking reality. Not empirical in origin, the vikalpas are *a priori* forms which the uncritical mind (bālapṛthagjana) superimposes on what really are momentary particular elements of existence. Thus is created the illusion of the soul, the permanent, the whole and the universal. Owing to this, there is attachment, aversion, infatuation, etc. (samskāras, kleśas). That these forms are *a priori* is evident from the formula: (avidyā-pratyayāḥ saṁskārāḥ . . .). We might say that the Buddhist metaphysics from the very start partook of the Humean and the Kantian: in admitting the reality of the separate elements the Buddhists were like Hume; and unlike Hume but like Kant they ascribe the origin of the substance-notion to avidyā which is beginningless and non-empirical in origin. This standpoint is present in essentials in the Pāli Canons and is well-developed in the Abhidharma literature and the *Milinda Pañho*.

The Sautrāntika school is a very vigorous form of this critical attitude consistent with pluralism and realism.

To the Mādhyamika it became clear that the subjective was much deeper and wider in scope. Not merely the categories of substance, but causality, change, existence (bhāva), non-existence (abhāva) were equally subjective. To this conclusion he must have been led, as on the ātma tradition there was a parallel movement to deny the reality of change, difference and to take them as subjective *a priori* forms imposed on the real, which is changeless. What was avidyā for the Buddhist was real for the Sāṁkhya or the Vedānta and *vice versa*. The second stage in the development of subjectivity (nairātmya) was reached in the Mādhyamika. There is the denial of all categories and doctrines (ātmā as well as anātmā), of all species of dogmatic philosophy; all dogmatic systems are dṛṣṭi, and Prajñā is the negation of all views—Śūnyatā. Śūnyata (Doctrine of the Void) is the pivotal concept of Buddhism. The entire Buddhist philosophy turned on this. The earlier realistic phase of Buddhism, with its rejection of substance and uncritical erection of a theory of elements, was clearly a preparation for the fully critical and self-conscious dialectic of Nāgārjuna. Not only is the Yogācāra idealism based on the explicit acceptance of Śūnyatā, but the critical and absolutist trend in the ātma tradition is also traceable to this.

The revolution in Buddhist thought exerted a decisive influence on subsequent philosophy. Each system began re-modelling, reforming and readjusting its tenets in the light of this disturbing and devastating discovery of the subjective. Systems with a monistic bias such as the Vedānta and Vijñānavāda accepted the subjective, the *a priori* function of thought and profited in the result; but they restricted the subjective within limits. They seem therefore to condemn the extremism of the Mādhyamika—his so-called nihilism (śūnyatā). They may be taken as a modification of the extremely critical no-metaphysics standpoint of the Mādhyamika.

The Advaita Vedānta with its insistence upon the reality of Pure Being, its identity and universality, defined avidyā as that which makes Being appear as Becoming (vikāra), the universal as particulars, the identical as different (bheda). The Vijñānavāda, with its insistence on the reality of Consciousness as Will or Ideation, defined avidyā to consist in Vijñāna appearing as confronted with an object—with the duality of the apprehender and the apprehended.

Different from monism, both reach advaitism (Absolutism)—the advaita of Pure Being (Brahman) and the advayatā of Pure Consciousness (vijñapti-mātratā) by rejecting appearance through dialectical methods—through negation. Their absolutes partake of the form of the Mādhyamika Śūnyatā in being transcendent to thought and being accessible only to non-empirical Intuition. They also have recourse to the device of two truths and two texts to explain apparent inconsistencies in experience and in the scriptures.

The reaction of the realistic and pluralistic systems was just the reverse. They rejected the subjective and re-affirmed their realism more vehemently.

The Mīmāṁsā and the Nyāya on the one hand and the Jaina on the other take thought-forms to be forms of the objectively real too. Thought *discovers* or *represents* reality, and does not distort it. For the absolutist systems, thought distorts reality and makes it appear as other than what it is. They had thus to make the distinction between what is *in itself* and what *appears* merely, and had, as a logical consequence, to accept two truths etc. The realist systems had no such distinction to make; their reals are just systematised or crystallised forms of empirical thought; they are very close to everyday moulds of experience. This is hardly the place to pursue this topic. The systems of realism—Jaina, Nyāya-Vaiśeṣika, and Mīmāmsā—that emerged out of their age-long duel with the Mādhyamika and other critical systems are no longer the naive formulations they were in the beginning; they are fully conscious of their implications. All this can be amply proved by reference to the works of each system.

II DEVELOPMENT IN THE ĀTMA-TRADITION

A consideration of the Sāṁkhya and the systems that developed out of it is necessary for understanding the emergence of the Mādhyamika dialectic. Dialectic is the Consciousness of the total conflict in Reason and the attempt to resolve the conflict. This cannot be engendered without the systematic and sustained cultivation of the two 'moments' of the dialectic. Nāgārjuna and Āryadeva, the founders of the Mādhyamika, were quite conversant with the classical Sāṁkhya and Vaiśeṣika and possibly with the Vedānta too.[1] They invariably take them to represent the śāśvata or ātma view and were alive to the insuperable difficulties of that view, as they were aware of the difficulties of the opposite view. Hence the dialectic.

The first stages of the Sāṁkhya system are pre-Buddhistic. The teachers of Buddha-Āḷāra Kālāma and Uddaka Rāmaputta were Sāṁkhya philosophers. There might have been a theistic phase of the Sāṁkhya,[2] for aught we know; but as tracing a history of the Sāṁkhya falls outside the scope of the subject, we omit these details. The Sāṁkhya attempted a synthesis of the teachings of the Upaniṣads on a rational or independent basis. There were two prominent tenets—the immutability and purity of the ātman (asango' yam puruṣaḥ), Self as pure consciousness, and the creation of the world from the Self which was taken as the sole reality. To the Sāṁkhya it appeared axiomatic that what changes could not be conscious and the conscious could not change. It tried to remove the apparent contradiction in the Upaniṣads by sacrificing the sole reality of the ātman (brahman); and bifurcating the real into exclusive compartments, it assigned different functions to each. It accepted two kinds of the real (nitya): the unchanging puruṣa (kūṭastha) and the changing Prakṛti (pariṇāmi).

That the Sāṁkhya was a *rational* synthesis of the Upaniṣads is proved beyond doubt by the fact that the *Brahma Sūtras* find it necessary to refute the Sāṁkhya contention that it represents the true import of the Upaniṣad texts. The refutations are so numerous and so sustained that they would be unintelligible if the Sāṁkhya had not been considered a rival in the field of Upaniṣad-

[1] Cf. Nāgārjuna's *Ratnāvalī*:
sasāṁkhyaulūkya-nirgrantha pudgala-skandha-vādiṇam;
pṛccha lokaṁ yadi vadaty asti-nāsti-vyatikramam.
quoted in MKV. p. 275.

Kimura (*Hīnayāna and Mahāyāna* p. 23) gives this interesting information: "If we now look at Nāgārjuna's *Daśa-bhūmi Vibhāṣā Śāstra* we find the names of Sāṁkhya and Yoga mentioned, and in his *Ekaśloka Śāstra* we meet the names of Kapila and Ulūka, and in his *Prajñāpāramitā Śāstra* reference is made to the doctrines of the Sāṁkhya System. And in his *Dvādaśanikāya Śāstra* also we come across the term 'satkārya' which indicates the doctrine of the Sāṁkhya." See Pt. Aiyāswami's note on *Nāgārjuna and Satkāryavāda of the Sāṁkhyas, Sino-Indian Studies*, Vol. IV, Part I (1951).

[2] Dasgupta: *History of Ind. Phil.* Vol. I, pp. 213 ff. Keith; *The Sāmkhya System*. Chapters I and III.

exegesis.[1] The appellations—'aśabdam' (unscriptural) 'anumānam', 'ānumānikam'[2] (conjectured, inferred), by which the Sāṁkhya is referred to in the *Brahma Sūtras*—are significant as revealing that the Sāṁkhya interpretation was considered 'free' and unorthodox, and that the Sāṁkhya did claim to be a correct understanding of the Upaniṣads.

The problem of change occupies the central position in the Sāṁkhya as in other systems. Becoming, change, for the Sāṁkhya is self-becoming, self-manifestation. One and the same thing is at once the stuff that changes and the efficient cause of its change (upādāna and nimitta). Matter is dynamic; it is energy-stuff. Cause is self-efficient and self-contained. Only the universal cause (vaiśva-rūpya) is self-sufficient; particular happenings are organic limitations of the one universal causation. That which changes and that into which it is changed are identical (satkāryavāda). The difference between them is not that of two things but of *two states* of one thing: the effect is the actualised (vyakta) state of the potentital cause (avyakta). Causation is continuous or *legato* movement. The Sāṁkhya does not rule out difference and declare change as appearance (avidyā) as the advaita Vedānta does; but it emphasises the identity-aspect of things rather than that of difference. The Sāṁkhya's is a logic of identity with a tinge of difference. In a rigorous formulation of the real, this has to be rejected. The real cannot be heterogeneous, composite.

The difficulties of the Sāṁkhya are fundamental. There are two reals—one is real as changing, the other is real as unchanging. Nothing is common to both of them and they thoroughly exclude each other. In calling them both existent and real, we are using a common measure. The Sāṁkhya uses two mutually exclusive patterns of the real and does not evaluate them, i.e., prefer one to the other. Apparently, prakṛti is independently real, as real as puruṣa, and in that sense it could be called a 'self', existing by itself. Prakṛti exists and acts by itself; but it is not *for* itself; the value of its existence is for another (sanghāta-parārthatvāt). The Sāṁkhya would not go to the extent of asserting that prakṛti would continue to exist even if

[1] There are about 13 or 14 explicit references to the Sāṁkhya interpretation in the *Brahma Sūtras*. The fifth Adhikaraṇa (īkṣater nāśabdam etc.) makes out that the Sāṁkhya interpretation of the Upaniṣadic texts is unwarranted. Reference may also be made to the other adhikaraṇas (Sections) in the *Brahma Sūtras*.

[2] aśabdam (*Br. Sūtr.* I i 5); ānumānikam (Ibid I, iv, 1) anumānam (Ibid II, ii, 1).

there were no puruṣa. The *raison d'être* of Prakṛti's existence and activity is the satisfaction of the needs of Puruṣa.[1] Not only is the real bifurcated into spirit and matter, but even in Prakṛti's nature, there is the bifurcation of *existence and value*. This necessitates the plurality of puruṣa, to keep the world-process going.[2] Prakṛti exists, but it is not what we attain to in our spiritual effort; in fact it is that from which we dissociate ourselves. Thus what exists and what is valuable are sundered. The same predicament we shall meet with in the Ābhidharmika system too where the impermanent elements are real as ultimate existences; but they are not accepted as the goal of the spiritual discipline (nirvāṇa). This basic defect is unavoidable in any dualistic or pluralistic metaphysics.

The Sāṁkhya position is inherently unstable. In it there are elements which are mutually conflicting. This arises because of the adoption of two patterns of the real (puruṣa and prakṛti). This in turn necessitates the sundering of existence and value, and the admission of identity and difference as equally real. Criticism, as the drive towards rigour and consistency, can take either of the two directions: If change and impermanence is the sole pattern of reality, then puruṣa must be replaced by the states of the mind (buddhi); and change itself must be construed as the momentary flash and flicker of things. For, the acceptance of an *abiding* entity (prakṛti) which *changes* introduces heterogeneity into the structure of the real. It partakes of the substance and the modal views at once. If change is to be accepted as real, the abiding permanent element must be discarded as unreal. This is exactly what the earlier Buddhism did. This was easy for them, for they had no love for the permanent; and so could explain things on one single pattern of impermanence and non-substantiality (anitya, anātman). The other direction in which the Sāṁkhya could be made consistent was to deny change and impermanence; it would be to take puruṣa (Spirit) or the Unchanging as the norm of the real. This would tend towards monism and, in its rigorous form, to the Absolutism of the Vedānta by the denial of difference and change as illusory. A somewhat intermediary standpoint is that of the Vaiśeṣika which accepted the change as well as the permanent. The Sāṁkhya holds that the permanent (prakṛti) itself changes; for the Vaiśeṣika, the permanent (the atoms—the

[1] svārtha iva parārtha ārambhaḥ: *Sāṁkhya Kārikās*, 56.

[2] kṛtārthaṁ prati naṣṭam api anaṣṭam tad anyasādhāraṇatvāt—*Yoga Sūtras*, III, 22.

ultimate parts of things and the other substances like, ātman, kāla, dik, ākāśa) do not change at all; but a new thing is produced *in* them when such parts are brought together. The same mechanical conception underlies its notions of substance and attribute, whole and parts etc.

In the Sāṁkhya, these idealistic and realistic trends are not brought together in harmony. We have already noticed that prakṛti exists for the puruṣa and cannot function without him, though it does not owe its existence and activity to him. That is, the Sāṁkhya accepts the dependence of the object on the subject in the practical sphere of value (tadartha eva dṛśyasyātmā), but not in the sphere of existence. The Sāṁkhya rightly holds that empirical existence (saṁsāra) is owing to the wrong identification of spirit and object; and this is because of ignorance. But it has not much justification in holding that prakṛti will not be affected if the contact ceases on the attainment of viveka (discrimination). Here too there are the two trends—realistic and idealistic. Consistency would demand that one or the other should be made more exclusive. Either spirit is all—idealism in the sense of the supremacy of the spirit and the object is an appearance; or every thing is object, the spirit itself to be conceived as knowable, like an object (jaḍa). The first is the position which the Vedānta came to adopt finally; the second is the Nyāya-Vaiśeṣika realism. There were certainly several stages before these standpoints could be reached.

From the unstable equilibrium of the Sāmkhya there is evolution, on one side, of the Vedānta with its insistence upon one substance (spirit) and its logic of identity and the consequent denial of difference; on the other we have the Nyāya-Vaiśeṣika with its acceptance of many substances conceived equally as objects of thought, and its logic of difference. The Nyāya is a pluralistic, realistic and empirical version of the Sāṁkhya; the Vedānta is the absolutistic version of it.

We know for a fact that the older Vedānta of the Sūtrakāra and the early commentators affirmed the oneness of substance—the sole reality of Brahman by pointing out the untenability of creation from an unconscious substance (prakṛti). It did away with the difference or opposition between spirit and matter, and conceived the world of nature and spirits as the manifestation of the one underlying Brahman. It relied on texts[1] which speak of matter and mind as two aspects of Brahman, and took the accounts of creation from

[1] dve vāva brahmaṇo rūpe, mūrtaṁ caivāmūrtaṁ ca—*Bṛ. Up.* II, iii, 1.

sat or ātman literally. The difference between objects and spirits is that of two forms of one underlying substance. The older Vedānta accepted the logic of the Sāṁkhya, its Satkāryavāda, its notion of identity with some difference, but with the ontology of the Upaniṣads —the reality of Brahman alone. This development does not show any Buddhistic or external influence and can be understood as a very natural reaction of the Aupaniṣada school against the Sāṁkhya dualism. It can be characterised as a Pantheism or Monism.

This type of Vedānta continued to be in vogue for several centuries from the beginning of the Christian era till the time of Gauḍapāda and Śaṁkara. They then substituted the notion of vivarta (appearance) for pariṇāmavāda (modification); monism was turned into advaitism. The main criticism is that just as there cannot be two exclusive or opposed compartments of the real, Brahman too cannot be conceived as having two aspects—one the unchanging and the other changing; it cannot have parts. The real must be of one piece. The jīva (individual self) is completely identical with brahman; their difference is appearance.

The Advaitic stage in the Vedānta was, however, not reached without the influence of the Mādhyamika and Vijñānavada as indicated before. The precise nature of the indebtedness will be dealt with in the next chapter.

From the Sāṁkhya dualism then the stages in the development of the Upaniṣadic tradition are:

(1) Sāṁkhya dualism;

(2) The Pantheism or Monism of the older Vedānta;

(3) Advaitism of Gauḍapāda, Maṇḍana Miśra and Śaṅkara.

In the Nyāya-Vaiseṣika, we may distinguish three similar stages of development. The point of departure must be taken as the Sāṁkhya, because of the considerations already urged. The Sāṁkhya could be made consistent by interpreting everything in terms of the Spirit or in terms of the object; it had to adopt the logic of identity or that of difference exclusively. The former alternative was carried out by the Vedānta; the latter by the Nyāya-Vaiśeṣika.

The initial phase of the Nyāya-Vaiśeṣika does not show any Buddhist influence. We may find the faint beginnings of it in the Seven Ultimates of Pakudha Kaccāyana,[1] who is one of the six important tīrthiyas figuring in the Pāli Canons. From the beginning

[1] Ref.: *Sāmaññaphala* and other Suttas. See Barua's *Hist. of Pre-Buddhistic Ind. Philosophy*, pp. 282 ff.

it had been a realistic pluralism, advocating atomism and mechanical combination and separation of things (ārambhavāda). The influence of Buddhism made it still more realistic; it tended to make the Nyāya-Vaiśeṣika a very consistent and self-conscious realism.

The basic principle of the Nyāya-Vaiśeṣika realism is that everything is object (viṣaya, padārtha, jñeya), ātman and knowledge included. Objectivity (viṣayatā) is threefold—Substantive (viśeṣya), Adjective (viśeṣaṇa) and Relation (sambandha); because, our knowledge is invariably of this form, and there is one-one correspondence between thought and things. Certain entities can exist only as in a thing, as its predicates (qualifying adjectives). To this class belong attributes (guṇas, e.g. colour, taste, pain, pleasure, etc.), motion (karma), generality (sāmānya), particularity (viśeṣa), and even absence (abhāva) which is conceived as a qualifying characteristic of the locus. In contrast to this class, we have the substances (dravya) *in which* the predicates have their being, and which they qualify. Distinct from both is the relation corresponding to the apprehension of "in", "of"; the attribute is *in* or *of* substance. The Real has to be conceived as one of these three distinct and primordial modes. It is not possible to reduce their number or derive one from another.

Relation (samavāya) is not only real, but is one more real, different from the relata (e.g. substance and attribute, whole and parts). This conception alone makes for the co-existence of different entities and their connection. Both the Advaita Vedānta and the Buddhist deny the reality of relation, but from opposite angles. For the Advaita, the substance or the whole alone is real, and the attribute or the part is just an ascription; it is, therefore, nothing apart from the substance (dravyātmkatā guṇasya).[1] The Buddhist denied the reality of substance and the whole, accepting the modes only. Neither of them has any use for relation (samavāya). But it is against the Buddhist that the Nyāya directed its polemic.

The Nyāya-Vaiśeṣika system that emerged at the end of its duel with the Buddhist systems sustained for centuries very rigorously establishes the objectivity of relations (samavāya), of the whole (avayavī), universal (sāmānya) and even of absence (abhāva). It minimised and even denied the work of thought. It objectified and externalised all thought-forms, and put them up as categories of the object. One has to look into the polemic found in the works of

[1] See Śaṅkara's criticism of the Vaiśeṣika doctrines in his commentary on the *Br. Sūtras* II, ii, 17.

Vātsyāyana, Udyotakara, Vācaspati Miśra, Jayanta, Udayana, Śrīdhara and a host of others to realise the truth of this remark. The Nyāya brought its ontology and epistemology in full accord with its basic principle or assumption. The Nyāya resisted the subjectivistic and critical attitude of the Buddhist schools all along the line. Of special note is the *Nyāya Sūtra* criticism[1] of the general position of the Mādhyamika, who condemned thought as subjective and so capable of giving us only appearance. The Nyāya vindicates the objectivity of pramāṇas (valid sources of knowledge) and their inherent capacity to serve as the means of knowing the real as it is.

III THE ĀBHIDHARMIKA SYSTEM

Existence is declared anicca, anatta and dukkha in the Pāli Canons. Classification of things into khandha, dhātu and āyatana is also a well-established feature in them. The Theravāda and the Sarvāstivāda, in spite of some important differences, may be considered as representing one metaphysical standpoint. They were the first to develop the suggestions contained in the teachings of Buddha; they were the first to have an abhidharma, a metaphysical system, much earlier than the other schools. As we have noted, it is the realistic and dogmatic tendency that is expressed first; the absolutist systems arise as a criticism of this.

The philosophical treatises, as distinguished from the *Sūtra* (Discourses) and the *Vinaya Piṭaka* (Rules of Discipline), may be considered as the abhidharma of each system. 'Abhidharma' is defined in the *Abhidharma Kośa* as Pure Intuitive Knowledge of the dharmas with its subsidiary discipline (prajñāmalā sānucarā'bhidharmaḥ).[2] Asanga defines it as the intimate (abhimukhataḥ) and sustained (ābhīkṣṇyāt) perception of the nature of existence; it is the attempt to penetrate to the deeper import of the teachings (sūtrārtha) of Buddha; lastly, it serves to suppress the defilements.[3] Abhidharma is the metaphysic of each system with which its other disciplines are intimately connected.

[1] See *Nyāya Sūtras* II, i, 8–19 and all the commentaries and sub-commentaries thereon. Reference is made to this controversy later down. *Infra*, Chapter VI, Sections iv and v notes.

[2] AKV. p. 8.

[3] abhimukhato'thābhīkṣṇyād abhibhāvagatito'bhidharmaś ca.
abhigamyate sūtrārtha etenety abhidharmaḥ. *Mahāyāna Sūtrālaṅkāra* XI, 3.

The seven Abhidhamma treatises of the Pāli Canon, though put forward as the word of Buddha, are really the Theravāda interpretation and synthesis of the teachings of the Master. Both internal and external evidence clearly proves this. The *Kathāvatthu*, on its own showing even, was composed at the time of the Emperor Asoka. Different and conflicting interpretations were current at that time, and there were eighteen schools of Buddhism. The *Kathāvatthu* is the drawing up of the orthodox creed by the Elders in Council, comparable, as Mrs. Rhys Davids felicitously puts it, to the Nicene creed. The favourite method of the *Kathāvatthu*, in the settling of a disputed tenet, is to cite a passage from the Suttas and ask the opponent to accept it. The style and manner of treatment of subjects in all the seven Abhidhamma treatises is so artificial and cramped that they could hardly be called dialogues. In the *Dhammasanganī* and other treatises, we are treated to interminable lists and classifications of the dhammas, undertaken mostly from the ethical point of view. The underlying general metaphysical principles are hardly stated; they can be elicited only by implication. There is little attempt at argument, and no *a priori* deduction of the categories is made. The statements are mostly headlines or mnemonic aids (mātikās) meant to be supplemented by oral exposition. They are an advance on the suggestions scattered in the Suttas, in so far as they specifically enumerate and classify existences on a realistic and pluralistic basis. It is a dhamma theory, a doctrine of elements.

The Sarvāstivāda can claim to be as old as the Theravāda. The adherents of this school had their canons in Samskrit.[1] Fragments of this have been discovered in Central Asia, and recently considerable portions of its Vinaya were discovered at Gilgit and ably edited by Dr. N. Dutt.[2] Their entire canon is preserved in the Chinese Tripiṭaka. Regarding their Abhidharma literature Takakusu observes thus:

> The evidence we have adduced from Sanskrit, Tibetan and Chinese sources not being conflicting, we are fairly justified in assuming that at

[1] "The learned Buddhist monk Vinīta Deva of 8th Century A.D. makes a statement like this—The Sarvāstivādins used Samskrit, the Māhāsanghikas Prākṛt, the Sāmmitīyas Apabhraṁśa and the Sthaviravādins used Paiśācī"—Kimura, *Hīnayāna and Mahāyāna* p. 7. This is in accord with the permission that Buddha gave his followers to maintain their canons in their own language: "anujānāmi, bhikkhave, *sakāya-niruttiyā* buddhavacanaṁ pariyāpuṇitum" *Cullavagga*, V, 33, 1.

[2] *Gilgit MSS.* 3 Vols. published under the authority of the Kashmir Durbar.

an early period of their separate history, the Sarvāstivādins were in possession of an Abhidharma literature consisting of seven books, one principal and six supplementary, and that these works had been widely studied in Kashmir, the seat of this school, and we can say further that the tradition concerning them is comparatively trustworthy, since it has been preserved in practically the same form in India, Tibet, China and Japan.[1]

Unlike the Theravāda Abhidhamma treatises, the seven works, *Jñānaprasthāna* and its subsidiary Pādas,[2] are attributed to human authors. The works of the Sarvāstivādins do not represent one and the same period of Buddhist philosophy, nor do they agree entirely in content with their Pāli counterparts. A detailed comparison of these treatises with their Abhidhamma counterparts is a task which can be undertaken with satisfactory result only when the whole Sarvāstivāda literature from Chinese, in which alone it is preserved in entirety, is made available in translation. The *Mahā Vibhāṣā* and *Vibhāṣā* are commentaries of epic proportions on the *Jñānaprasthāna*, but incorporating matter from the other *Pādas*. Wholly lost in Sanskrit, they are preserved in Chinese (Nanjio, 1263, 1264; Hobogirin, 1545, 1546). These represent the real Śāstra of the Ābhidharmikas, and give the name to the system (Vaibhāṣika). Vasubandhu's *Abhidharmakośa* is an authoritative treatment of the whole subject by an acknowledged master. Himself a Sautrāntika, like his gifted commentator Yaśomitra, Vasubandhu has, however, faithfully expounded the Vaibhāṣika doctrines.[3] Owing to the labours of savants like Poussin, Stcherbatsky, Rosenberg, Sylvain Levi, Wogihara and others we have before us a fairly complete and coherent picture of the system.

[1] Takakusu—*The Sarvāstivāda Literature* pp. 81–2, J.P.T.S., 1905.

[2] Cf. AKV. (p. 9): anye tu vyācakṣate śāstram iti Jñānaprasthānam. tasya śarīrabhūtasya ṣaṭ pādāḥ. *Prakaraṇapāda* ityādi . . . śrūyante hy Abhidharmaśāstrāṇāṁ kartāraḥ. tad yathā *Jñānaprasthānasya* ārya Katyāyanīputraḥ kartā, *Prakaraṇa-Pādasya* sthavira Vasumitraḥ, *Vijñānakāyasya* sthavira-Devaśarmā, *Dharmaskandhasya* ārya Śāriputraḥ, *Prajñaptiśāstrasya* ārya Maudgalyāyanaḥ, Dhātukāyasya Pūrṇaḥ, *Saṁgītiparyāyasya* Mahākauṣṭhilaḥ iti (Ibid. p. 11). See also *Buston* Vol. I pp. 49–50.

Takakusu's article in J.P.T.S., 1905; McGovern's *Manual of Bud. Phil.* pp. 27 ff.

[3] Cf. AKV. p. 11. "uditaḥ kilaiṣa śāstrā" . . . 'kila' śabdaḥ parābhiprāyaṁ dyotayati. Ābhidharamikāṇām etan mataṁ, na tv asmākaṁ Sautrāntikānām iti bhāvaḥ . . . cf. the kārikā of the *Abhidharmakośa* (VIII 40) "Kāśmīra Vaibhāṣikanīti siddhaḥ, prāyo mayāyaṁ kathito'bhidharmaḥ." At numerous places Yaśomitra refers to Vasubandhu as: "Sautrāntika-pākṣikas tv ayam ācāryaḥ." (AKV. p. 26, etc.)

A correct and adequate understanding of the Vaibhāṣika system is essential for the appreciation of the dialectic of Nāgārjuna; for, it is mainly directed against the Vaibhāṣika system. All mention of the Abhidharma system and its doctrines invariably refers to the Sarvāstivāda. The opinion of competent scholars like McGovern[1] and Stcherbatsky is that the Southern or Ceylonese Sect had little or no direct influence in the development of Buddhist schools in India. For our purpose it may be ignored; at best, it may supply corroborative evidence at places.

The Vaibhāṣika system is a radical pluralism erected on the denial of Substance (soul) and the acceptance of discrete momentary entities. Dharma is the central conception in this, as it is in the other systems of Buddhism.[2] Change, Becoming, is the central problem here, as in the Sāṁkhya, with this difference that for Buddhism this and every problem was approached from the predominantly ethical point of view. There is no doubt that the Ābhidharmikas had before

[1] "One point, however, deserves attention, and that is the complete absence of all North Indian mention of the Abhidharma books of the Pāli Canon. The Pāli School makes very sweeping claims for itself. It claims that Pāli was the original language of the Buddha, that the seven Abhidharma works are part of his gospel, and that they were recited at the first council. It is also stated that Buddhaghosa, the great commentator, came from somewhere in North India and was a scholar of some repute before his arrival in Ceylon. Both of these statements imply a close relationship between the Ceylonese Buddhist school and that of India. It is therefore important to point out the following facts: the only Hīnayāna Abhidharma Piṭaka which we can prove to be known to the Buddhists of North India was that of the Sarvāstivādins. For a long time it was thought that these works were but different versions of the Pāli Abhidharma Canon, or that if different, the Sarvāstivādin works were probably half commentaries or rewritings of the works preserved for us in Ceylon. We now know, however, that there is no connexion between the two sets of works, that the Sarvāstivādin writings were composed by persons whom it is scarcely possible to conceive could have seen the Pāli works, or even to have heard of their categories. Nor do we find any scholar either inside or outside the Sarvāstivādin school who accepted, quoted, or even attacked the Pāli Abhidharma works. They were completely ignored as far as we have any record, and though the Sthaviravādins were cited from time to time, there is no place where we can identify their quoted statements in such a way as to prove the possession of a definite Abhidharma Canon.

In the same way whenever the Mādhyamika philosophers refer to the Hīnayāna Abhidharma works, the Sarvāstivādins are the only ones quoted. In fact, among the Mādhyamikas the term Ābhidharmika is used as a synonym for Sarvāstivādin." *A Manual of Buddhist Philosophy* Vol. I, pp. 16–17.

[2] The Buddhist formula: "ye dharmā hetu-prabhavāḥ etc." fully justifies this remark. See Rosenberg: *Die Probleme der budd. Phil.* p. 17. For the meaning of term dharma see *Buston* Vol. I, pp. 18 ff. and *Central Conception of Buddhism* pp. 2 ff; 73 ff.

them the developed Sāṁkhya and that they moulded their system closely on the Sāṁkhya model.

Viewed as a step in the evolution of Indian philosophical thought, says Stcherbatsky, Buddhism was probably preceded by a fully developed form of the Sāṁkhya system in the elaborate thoroughly consistent shape of an Indian science (sāstra). . . . Both doctrines are sometimes called radical systems (ekāntadarśana), because the one adheres to the doctrine of eternal existence only (sarvam nityam), while the other maintains universal impermanence (sarvam anityam). It is out of place here to go into a more detailed comparison of both systems. Their close affinity has not escaped the attention of scholars. What I should like to insist upon is the fact that a close connection may be expressed not only by points of similarity, but also by opposition, nay by protest.[1]

The characteristic standpoint of the Ābhidharmika system can be expounded as a polemic against substance,[2] the permanent and the universal conceived as real in the systems of the ātma tradition. Though the arguments were formulated in strict logical form later and belong rather to the Sautrāntika school, they are quite relevant here too.

The Real is the efficient (arthakriyākāri). The permanent as the non-efficient is unreal. Efficiency can be either simultaneous or successive. If simultaneous, all the effects being completed at once, it may be asked whether the permanent exists after the first moment or not. If it does, it should produce the same effects in the second and succeeding moments, thus giving rise to an interminable series of the same effect from one cause. This is an absurdity. If it does not produce this series, though continuing to exist in the succeeding moments, then it is evident that there is a manifest difference in its nature between the first and other moments; for, in the first moment it is efficient (samartha), while in other moments it is not so (asamartha) with regard to the same effect. *That cannot be one of which two or more opposed characteristics are predicated.*[3] Nor is the permanent efficient successively, e.g., A first produces X, then Y, then Z. It

[1] *Soul Theory*, p. 824.

[2] This is a classical argumentation expounded and criticised in most Brāhmanical and Jaina works. Reference may be made to the *Kṣaṇabhanga Siddhi* (both versions) in the *Six Buddhist Nyāya Tracts*; TS pp. 131 ff.

Among the modern expositions, Dr. S. K. Mookerjee's *Buddhist Philosophy of Universal Flux* may be consulted, as also Stcherbatsky's *Buddhist Logic*, Vol. I, pp. 79 ff.

[3] This is the Buddhist dictum: yo viruddhadharmādhyāsavān nāsāv ekaḥ.

should be asked whether A is capable of producing Y when it was producing X. If it could do so, A would precipitate all the effects at once, and the second alternative will have been reduced to the first one of simultaneous production. If it is not capable, it will never produce the effect, as a piece of stone cannot produce the sprout given any length of time. If we still think that A is one and the same entity in two or more moments, then it is both efficient and inefficient at once with regard to the same effect.

It may be objected that a cause (e.g. the seed) is the same; only, the efficiency is owing to the presence or absence of auxilliaries. But do the auxilliaries (sahakāri) mean anything to the permanent? The mere inoperative presence of them will not bring about any result. They must therefore first *modify* the seed before it can sprout; it is the seed as *changed* that produces the effect. If the modification were an integral part of the seed, it should have that always. If it were not, then the seed would have two natures—one, what it is in itself and the other, what it becomes in response to its auxilliaries. But accepting two natures of a thing is really to accept two things, according to the Buddhist dictum. Thus things are different every moment; difference of time is difference of thing; at no two moments is a thing identical. Existence is momentary (kṣaṇika).

The same conclusion can be enforced by the consideration of decay and destruction. The vulgar notion is that a thing will continue to exist unless it is destroyed by opposite forces. But if a thing is not capable of destruction by itself, no amount of external influence can affect it, much less reduce it to nothing. The blow from a stick destroys the pitcher, it may be said. But if destruction were not inherent to the pitcher, the blow should mean nothing to it; it should continue to exist untouched as before, like empty space. If the destruction were inherent to the pitcher, the blow of the stick is merely an occasion for its cessation; it does not bring it about. Consider for a moment, what is meant by the ageing or decaying of a thing. It is not the case that a thing continues to exist unaffected for any stretch of time and then suddenly begins to change. It changes every moment, uniformly, unperceivedly, relentlessly. Change or even birth is death every moment; the thing must become different at every moment of its existence. *Permanence of a thing is an illusion*, like the oneness of the flame or of the stream.[1] Existence is flux. A thing is a point-instant,

[1] arciṣāṁ santāne pradīpa iti upcaryate. eka iveti kṛtvā. sa deśāntareṣūtpadyamānaḥ, santānarūpaḥ, taṁ taṁ deśaṁ gacchatītyucyate. evaṁ

having neither a 'before' nor an 'after'; it has no span temporally; there is no duration. Cessation is inherent in things and is entire (ahaituko niranvayo vināśaḥ).

Precisely the same logic is applied to refute the reality of the Whole (avayavī). What constitutes *one* thing? We might hold with commonsense that the table is one entity, the tree is one, though they may consist of parts. But the table is partly seen and partly not, as it is impossible to see all the parts at once. Parts of the tree move and some other parts do not; a part of it is in shade and a part of it is sunlit. How can that be one entity to which two or more opposed characteristics (e.g. seen and unseen, moving and unmoving, dark and sunlit) are ascribed? It is not possible to escape this logic by stating that what is moving is one part and what is not moving is different from it. For, both the parts belong to the *same* thing; the characteristics of the parts belong to the thing—the whole—of which they are parts. Therefore, there are as many things as there are distinguishable 'parts' or aspects. An entity has no extensity or complexity of content. The oneness of many things ('parts' and aspects) is illusory as the oneness of a heap of corn.[1] Horizontally, spatially, a thing has no expanse. It is not only an instant (kṣaṇika) lacking duration, but a spatial point lacking all magnitude and diversity as well.

By the same logic we are led to the denial of the universal (sāmānya) or identical aspect of things. Each entity is discrete and unique (svalakṣaṇa). The existence of the universal, uniform and identical, in all the particulars is beset with insuperable difficulties. How can one entity exist in a number of particulars separated by distance of space and time, in entirety, untouched by what happens to the particulars? Moreover, in cognising a thing, we do not certainly cognise it (the particular) and its duplicate (the universal). The polemic of the Buddhist against the universal is too well-known to need any detailed statement. All existence, for the Buddhist, is particular; the universal is a thought-construct, a vikalpa.

The real is momentary; it is simple, unitary; it is particular, unique. This view militates against the conception of the real as permanent,

cittānāṁ santāne vijñānam ity upacaryate, ekam iveti kṛtvā. AKV. p. 713.

rāśivad dhārāvad iti . . . ekasmin kṣaṇe samavahitānāṁ bahūnāṁ rāśiḥ; bahuṣu kṣaṇeṣu samavahitānāṁ dhārā. rāśidṛṣṭāntena bahuṣu dharmeṣu pudgalaprajñaptiṁ darśayati. dhārādṛṣṭāntena bahutve sati rūpa-vedanādīnāṁ skandhānāṁ pravāhe pudgalaprajñaptiṁ darśayati. Ibid. p. 705.

[1] See footnote No. 1 on previous page.

as substance, as universal and identical. All things, physical and spiritual, exhibit this pattern; there is no exception. It is not, as in the Sāṁkhya, that while the object changes, the self does not change. Nor is change considered as the change *of* a permanent underlying substance that is continuous in the effect. Change is the *replacement* of one entity by another; it is the cessation of one and the emergence of another. Existence is the momentary flash into being and subsidence into non-being of material and mental states—feelings, perception, volition etc. No doubt the states can be grouped, under various combinations, into skandha, dhātu and āyatana etc.; but the combination is not real over and above the constituents. The components are real, *vastusat*; the combination is appearance, *prajñapati sat*. What we usually take as the self or the soul (ātman) can be analysed, without residue, into the several mental states, citta and caitta. There is no abiding and continuous self over-lapping these states and in which they inhere. The pudgala or the Individual is an appearance; it constitutes the primary avidyā—satkāya-dṛṣṭi.[1]

The rejection of substance, soul and all relations is Humean in character. Hume recognises two main principles of his philosophy: "*that all our distinct perceptions are distinct existences*, and *that the mind never perceives any real connexion among distinct existences*. Did our perceptions either inhere in something simple and individual. or did the mind perceive some real connexion among them, there would be no difficulty in the case."[2]

But there is a very important difference which should not be lost sight of. Hume would account for the notion of substance, causality etc. through the operation of the empirical laws of association and habit. The Buddhist was alive, like Kant, to the fact that these notions are *a priori* and are not of empirical origin. Satkāyadṛṣṭi—the inveterate tendency to read permanence, universality and identity into what are really momentary, discrete and particular—is primordial beginningless avidyā. Alongside of their rejection of the substance-view and the acceptance of the real as momentary states (modal

[1] The Ābhidharmika and other treatises usually speak of the 20 peaks of this mountain of satkāya or ātma dṛṣṭi: viṁśati-hoṭikā hi satkāyadṛṣṭiḥ paṭhyate: rūpam ātmeti samanupaśyati, rūpavantam ātmānam, ātmīyaṁ rūpam, rūpe ātmeti; evaṁ yāvad vijñānaṁ vaktavyam, AKV. p. 705. viṁśati-śikharasamunnatatarātipṛthu-satkāya-dṛṣṭimahāśailaḥ MKV. p. 294. viṁśati-śikhara-samudgato'yaṁ satkāyadṛṣṭi-śailaḥ kumatīnām pravarttate yaduta rūpam ātmā etc. TSP. p. 131.

[2] *Treatise of Human Nature*. Appendix pp. 635–6 (Selby-Bigge's Edn.)

view), the Buddhists developed the complementary doctrine of avidyā and vikalpa; with a metaphysic largely Humean, they elaborated their analysis of knowledge more or less on Kantian lines. This is evident from the logical treatises such as the *Pramāṇa Samuccaya* and *Nyāyabindu* where the theory of kalpanā (vikalpa) or the synthesising activity of the mind is worked out. The Buddhists brought their epistemology[1] and ethics into full accord with their anātma-metaphysic.

Though it would be interesting, it is not possible to investigate the fuller implications of the above Buddhistic position. It should, however, be pointed out that it is a very consistent and comprehensive philosophy of the modal or anātma standpoint. If in the consistent ātma metaphysic the problem is how to account for change, plurality, particularity and difference, here it is how to account for the appearance of permanence, universality and identity. Both have recourse to the theory of avidyā or Transcendental construction to account for the appearance of difference or identity respectively.

In this and the previous sections we have investigated the two standpoints of the Sāṁkhya and other systems following the ātma tradition. The trend in one is towards unity, identity and universality; in the other it is towards plurality, difference and particularity. The Sāṁkhya, which is the basic system of the ātma tradition, advocates satkāryavāda or the identity of cause and effect; the Ābhidharmika system conceives them as different. Curiously enough, they lead to the same *impasse*—no production or causation. If the effect were identical with the cause, nothing *new* emerges; there is no causation. If they were different there is no emergence of the effect *from* the cause; the two are unrelated, and there is no causation. A combination

[1] If the momentary and the unique is the ultimately real, (paramārtha sat), that alone is the true object of perception (pratyakṣam kalpanāpoḍham; tasya viṣayaḥ svalakṣaṇam).

The series or the continuum (santāna), although not ultimately real, is still of empirical validity; it is not however perceived, but only 'inferred', known indirectly through the mediation of the categories of thought-construction. There are thus two spheres of objects, svalakṣana (the particular) and sāmānyalakṣaṇa (the general); and to cognise them there are two means of knowledge perception and inference (pratyakṣa and anumāna). In the practical sphere, the (mis) understanding of the separate elements as a self (as a permanent identical substance) gives rise to attachment to it and aversion to its opposite and infatuation generally. These are the kleśas (primary passions) and upakleśa (secondary passions) included under saṁskāras, which are directly derived from avidyā (satkāyadṛṣṭi). The antidote for this is nairātmya bhāvanā, the true view of things as mere dharma without any substance.

of these alternatives fares no better. If the combination were a mere assemblage of the two, it would be open to the objections levelled against each. If on the other hand, it were something unique and indescribable, it might escape these objections; but it would be beyond the purview of thought. The conclusion is inescapable, as the Mādhyamika found, that the fault lies not in this or that thought-pattern, but in this veritable tendency to apply patterns to the Real.

This predicament stares us in the face everywhere. Take what you call a thing, the table. Is it a cluster of qualities or predicates without a unity—(dharmamātram)? Then they cannot form one thing, each being an isolated and self-contained entity. The unity is neither in one nor in all of them collectively. This, however, is the standpoint of the Ābhidharmika system, since it denied substance. Nor is the table a bare unity without the predicates, for such a thing is not experienced at all. A consistent form of the Substance-view advocates the supremacy of Being; it has to deny change, becoming and movement. It is necessarily committed to a block universe. The Buddhist view, promising in its advocacy of the supremacy of Becoming, does not satisfactorily explain change, movement. It reduces change to a series of entities emerging and perishing; each entity however rises and perishes in entirety; it does not become another. Movement for the Buddhist is not the passage of an entity from one point to another; it is the emergence, at appropriate intervals, of a series of entities, like the individual pictures of a 'movie' show; it is a series of full-stops. There is neither flow nor movement in each entity, nor in the series; it is the spectator who projects that into the several static entities. Cutting up of the real into a number of discrete slices cannot make for movement or change.

The realisation of the insuperable difficulties in each of these standpoints led to the emergence of the Mādhyamika dialectic. It is the consciousness of the inherent contradiction present in the attempts of Reason to characterise the unconditioned in terms of the empirical. The dialectic exposes the pretensions of speculative metaphysics which seeks illegitimately to extend thought-categories beyond their proper field. As we have pointed out, there are two principal 'moments' or wings in a Dialectic. The systems of the ātma tradition represent the thesis, and the ābhidharmika system the antithesis of the antinomical conflict. This is the systematic form of the same conflict which was present in suggestive form in Buddha. Buddha's refusal to be drawn into the net of speculative metaphysics is consciousness of the transcendence of the real to thought. In the Mādhyamika, the same attitude is carried out in systematic form. The Mādhyamika system represents the maturity of the critical consciousness within the fold of Buddhism.

There was, however, no sudden jump from the earlier pluralistic Buddhism of the Hīnayāna to the Mādhyamika. A number of transitional and intermediary schools and doctrines paved the way for the advent of the Mādhyamika Absolutism—Śūnyatā.

IV TRANSITION TO THE MĀDHYAMIKA

The rise of Mahāyāna as a religion on a distinctly philosophical basis was the work of several centuries; but its beginnings could be traced shortly after the pari-nirvāṇa of Buddha. Three features sharply distinguish Mahāyāna from the earlier schools:[1]

(i) The conception of the supermundane Personality of Buddha (lokottara) as the essence of phenomena;

(ii) The Bodhisattva ideal of salvation for all beings, as against the private and selfish salvation for oneself of the Śrāvakayāna, and the attainment of full Buddhahood instead of Arhatship;

(iii) The metaphysics of śūnyatā—Absolutism—instead of a radical pluralism of ultimate elements.

The terms Mahāyāna and Hīnayāna came into vogue much later than the tendencies and cults of which they are the labels. In the schism of the Vajjian monks and the secession of the Mahāsanghikas we see clearly the Mahāyāna trends, which must have been germinating much earlier. Kimura, who has made a special historical study of these terms, states that the terms Mahāyāna and Hīnayāna were coined by the Mahāsanghikas as a sort of retaliation against the Theravādins who called them 'Pāpa Bhikkhus' (sinful monks) and heretics. Further, that the Mahāsanghikas have developed the

[1] The ASP (p. 24) takes Mahāyāna to mean the refuge for countless and immeasurable beings, as the path of the Bodhisattvas and as the real that is transcendent to thought, not having origination or decay.

See Asanga (*Sūtrālaṁkāra*, I.) for the distinction of Mahāyāna from Hīnayāna:

āśayasyopadeśasya prayogasya virodhataḥ;
upastambhasya kālasya yat hīnam hīnam eva tat. (I, 10).

. . . śrāvakayāne ātmaparinirvāṇāyaivāśayas tad artham eva prayogaḥ, parīttaś ca puṇyasambhārasamgṛhītaḥ upastambhaḥ, kālena cālpena tadarthaprāptir yāvat tribhir api janmabhiḥ. mahāyāne tu sarvaṁ viparyayeṇa. (p. 4).

esoteric or the ontological teaching of Buddha, while the Theravādins were the conservative literalists who emphasised the phenomenological teaching and could not go beyond the external (exoteric) meaning.[1]

The evolution of the Mahāyāna may be said to have begun from the time of Buddha's parinirvāṇa (544 or 487 B.C.); it was almost complete by the 1st century B.C. The process lasted for more than three or four centuries during which period the deeper and more fruitful ideas of the master gained ground on the religious, ethical and metaphysical fronts. At first, the advocates of these doctrines were branded as heretics and breakers of the Order, although they do not seem to have been insignificant in numbers. Later on, the tables were turned against the Orthodox Elders, and by about the beginning of the Christian era Mahāyāna became ascendent.

No history of the development of Buddhism, as religion and philosophy, can be complete without a proper co-ordination of the undermentioned three aspects:

(i) We have to take into account the external history of the Order, the rise of the Schools, their distribution and migration, together with the various attempts made from time to time in the Councils and Synods to stamp out heresy and to evolve an orthodox creed.[2]

(ii) The literary history of Buddhism will also throw considerable light on our understanding of its philosophy and religion. Under this, we have to consider the language of the schools, the nature and extent of their literary productions (canonical and non-canonical) with the ascertainment of their dates.[3]

[1] *Mahāyāna and Hīnayāna*, pp. 12, 15, 67, 115 ff.

[2] A considerable body of literature has grown round the history of the Buddhist Councils; for References see Hastings's E.R.E. and Winternitz's *History of Indian Literature* (Vol. II, pp. 71, 169 ff.) Regarding the spread of Buddhist Schools and Sects reference may be made to Dr. N. Dutt's *Early Hist. of the Spread of Buddhism*, S. Dutt's *Early Monastic Buddhism* & Kimura's *The Shifting of the Centres of Buddhism in India*. (Journal of Letters, Vol. I, Cal. Uni.) and the *Hist. of the Early Budd: Schools*, Vol. IV (Asutosh Mukerjee. Comm. Volume).

[3] By far the best summary of the Buddhist literature is found in the monumental work of Winternitz, *History of Indian Literature*, Vol. II (abbreviated hereafter as H.I.L.) and Buston's *History of Buddhism* 2 Vols. Trans. by Obermiller. R. L. Mitra's *Nepalese Buddhist Literature* and Nariman's *A Literary History of Sanskrit Buddhism* are out of date and unsystematic.

(iii) But the above considerations are meant for the understanding of its ideological or doctrinal development. And it is with this that we are primarily concerned.

Early Buddhist historians, like Vasumitra and Bhavya, speak of the 18 different schools, all claiming to embody the true teaching of Buddha[1] (aṣṭādaśa-nikāya-bheda-bhinnam bhagavato dharmaśāsanam). The question of historical value apart, this acount supplies us the important links in the evolution of the Mahāyāna. Only four main schools need be considered: the Sthaviravāda, Sarvāstivāda, Mahāsanghika and the Sāmmitīya; others are sub-schools and offshoots of these. The Sthaviravāda, predominant at first, gradually declined in importance and influence from the time of the 3rd Council (Asoka's reign) till it disappeared altogether from the mainland proper; but it continued to thrive in Ceylon, Burma and Siam. The Sarvāstivāda was the most dominant and influential school; it had its ramifications all over the country, including Kāshmir, Gandhāra etc. When the Mādhyamika or the Vijñānavāda writers criticise the Abhidharma philosophy, they invariably mean this school. The Sāmmitīyas (Vātsīputrīyas) must have been a prosperous sect with quite a considerable following. No original works of this sect have come down to us, and there is the disadvantage of having to derive our all too meagre knowledge of this school from its opponents. Its importance is as a transitional stage between the one-sided modal standpoint of the other schools and the no-position of the Mādhyamika. It is however the Mahāsanghikas who can be definitely termed the precursors of Mahāyāna religion and philosophy.

The development of the Mahāyāna literature with its characteristic form and content from out of the Hīnayāna was preceded by a stage of transition. There is extant a considerable body of literary works which constitute a veritable borderland, with one leg in the Hīnayāna and the other in the Mahāyāna.

[1] Vasumitra's *Nikāyālambana Śāstra* (Nanjio, Nos. 1284–6), translated into English by J. Masuda (*Origin and Doctrines of Early Indian Buddhist Schools*), *Asia Major* Vol. II, 1925; Max Welleser's *Die Sekten des alten Buddhismus* (Heidelberg, 1927) gives Vasumitra's (pp. 24 ff) and Bhavya's (Bhāvaviveka's) (pp. 77 ff) account of the schools. See also *Buston* Vol. II, pp. 97 ff., Tāranātha's *Geschichte*—pp. 270 ff. Dr. N. Dutt's *Three Principal Schools of Buddhism* (Calcutta, 1939) is further valuable as making a comparative study of these sources with the *Kathāvatthu*. Rockhill's *Life of the Buddha* (pp. 181–202) gives information about the schools condensed from the Tibetan works: Bhavya's *Nikāyabheda Vibhanga*, Vinīta Deva's *Samayabhedoparacanācakra* and *Bhikṣuvarṣāgrapṛcchā*.

The *Mahāvastu*,[1] *Lalita Vistara*[2] and the *Avadāna*[3] literature constitute, both in literary form and content, a distinct step towards the Mahāyāna. Deification of the Buddha, legendary tales glorifying the Buddhas and Bodhisattvas in the approved Purāṇic style with all manner of exaggeration, a trend towards Buddhabhakti and the glorification of the exalted Bodhisattva ideal are the characteristic features of these. The epics and dramas of Aśvaghoṣa[4] (contemporary of Kaniṣka)[5] served the same purpose. We see in these the steps by

[1] The *Mahāvastu* (Ed. by E. Senart, Paris, 1892–97) claims to be the Vinaya Piṭaka of the Lokottaravādins belonging to the Mahāsanghikas. This is a volume of epic proportions written in easy, fluent Mixed Sanskrit. It belongs to the class of literature called Avadāna, moral stories. It is a veritable storehouse of Jātakas, edifying stories and dogmatic Sūtras. Buddha is treated as God who had descended into the world and who underwent penance etc. as a sort of make-believe. To some extent the *Mahāvastu* also anticipates the Mahāyāna spiritual discipline, especially its conception of the ten bhūmis of the Bodhisattva.

[2] *Lalitavistara* (Ed. by R. Mitra, Bib. Indica, and S. Lefmann, 2 Vols, Halle). Though strictly belonging to the Dharmagupta sect—a branch of the Sarvāstivādins, it is, in style and content, a Vaipulya Sūtra of the Mahāyāna, and has been considered as one of the Nine Dharmas along with such works as *Saddharma Puṇḍarīka*, *Aṣṭasāhasrikā*, *Laṅkāvatāra* etc. The precise date of this work is uncertain (see H.I.L. Vol. II, pp. 253 ff.). For our purpose, it may be stated that it has been one of the secondary formative works that might have possibly influenced the Mādhyamika. We find appreciative references to the *Lalita Vistara* as a canonical authority in Candrakīrti (MKV. pp. 26, 108, 377, 407, 551 etc.), Śānti Deva (ŚS pp. 203 ff and especially 237 ff) and Prajñākaramati (BCAP. p. 532). These Mādhyamika writers appeal especially to the following *Lalita Vistara* passages: that the cause (seed) is not the same as the effect (sprout) nor different etc., bījasya sato yathānkuro na ca yo bīja sa caiva ankuro; na ca anya tato na caiva tat, evam anuccheda aśāśvata dharmatā. (quoted in MKV. pp. 26, 108, 377 and 428 and ŚS p. 238); that a thing that is produced by dependence on others is nothing in itself (MKV. p. 407; ŚS. p. 238. BCAP. p. 532; that things are apparent, māyika, like mirage or reflections is also stated in many places (MKV. p. 532, ŚS. p. 239). These are basic Mādhyamika notions.

[3] Special mention must be made of the *Avadāna Śataka* and *Divyāvadāna*. See H.I.L. pp. 277 ff. The value of this literature is on the religious and ethical side as glorifying the Bodhisattva ideal.

[4] Aśvaghoṣa is the author of *Buddha Carita*, *Saundarānanda* and *Śariputra-Prakaraṇa*, besides many lyrical poems. To Aśvaghoṣa is attributed the *Mahāyāna Śraddhotpāda Śāstra*, wholly lost in Sanskrit but preserved in Chinese only and translated therefrom by Suzuki and T. Richard as "*The Awakening of Faith*." So far, we have come across no reference to this book in any Mahāyāna work. The Bhūta-Tathātā concept elaborated by the author of the *Awakening of Faith* seems to be later to Nāgārjuna. Probably, this is the work of Aśvaghoṣa II, 5th Cent. A.D. See Kimura *Hīnayāna and Mahāyāna* pp. 41, 84 etc.

[5] Kaniṣka's date remains still unsettled. Considered opinion now favours the beginning of the 2nd Cent. A.D. Some scholars continue to adhere to an earlier date (A.D. 78 or even 58 B.C.). See H.I.L. Vol. II, Appendix V.

which Buddhism became a popular religion with attractive legends and a glorious pantheon.

The beginnings of the Mahāyāna can be distinctly traced in the Mahāsanghika schools which seceded from the Sthaviravāda at the Second Council held at Vaiśāli.[1] The doctrinal differences attributed to this influential and progressive section of Buddhism by Vasumitra, Bhavya and others leave little doubt that they were evolving the Buddhakāya conception, the Bodhisattva ideal and Buddhabhakti. By implication, they had some vague notion of an underlying reality as the ground of the changing phenomena. It was natural for them to identify this reality with the Tathāgata whom they considered as lokottara (supermundane, transcendent) and divine.[2] These undeveloped notions mark the incipient stages of the Mahāyāna Buddhology, śūnyatā and Bodhisattva ideal which are fully developed in the *Prajñāpāramitā* and other treatises.

The *Dīpavaṁsa* gives a graphic but biassed description of the method of the Mahāsanghikas and their 'creation' of new canons. "The Monks of the Great Council made a reversed teaching (of the scriptures). They broke up the original collection and made another collection. They put the Suttas collected in one place elsewhere. They broke up the sense and the doctrine in the five Nikāyas. The Parivāra, the summary of the sense (of the Vinaya), the six sections of the Abhidhamma, the *Paṭisambhidā*, the Niddesa and part of the Jātaka, so much they set aside and made others."[3] This account is evidence of the revolutionary nature of the Mahāsanghika doctrines, and of the

[1] A hundred years after the death of the Buddha which is put traditionally at 544 B.C. or by the western scholars at 487 B.C.

[2] Kimura: *Hīnayāna & Mahāyāna* pp. 86–7:
"If we look at the *Nikāyabheda-dharma-mati cakra Śāstra* (or I-pu-tsun-lun-lun) of Vasumitra, we come across the following passages: 'The fundamental and common doctrines of the Mahāsanghika, the Ekavyāvahārika, the Lokottaravāda and the Kaukkuṭika schools: The four schools unanimously maintained that (1) The Blessed Buddhas are all supermundane (lokottara). (2) The Tathāgatas have no worldly attributes (sāsrava dharmas). (3) The words of Tathāgatas are all about the Turning of the Wheel of Law (dharmacakrapravartana). (4) Buddha preaches all doctrines (dharmas) with one utterance. (5) In the teachings of Bhagavān (Buddha) there is nothing that is not in accordance with the Truth. (6) The physical body (rūpa-kāya) of Tathāgata is limitless. (7) The majestic powers of Tathāgata also are limitless. (8) Lives of Buddhas too are limitless. (9) Buddha is never tired of enlightening living beings and awakening pure faith in them etc.' "
See also: Masuda's *Origin & Doctrines of Early Ind. Buddhist Schools*, pp. 18 ff.

[3] Quoted from E. J. Thomas's *Hist. of Buddhist Thought*, p. 32.

negative reaction it raised in the Orthodox fold. On the Mahāsanghika side, the complaint was that the Sthaviras were literalists and did not understand the deeper and truer meaning of the Scriptures.

External (Brāhmanical) influence on the rise of Mahāyāna has been surmised by some scholars, e.g. Kern, Max Müller, Keith, Stcherbatsky[1] and others. Possibly, the influence exerted was with regard to the conception of Godhead and Bhakti and the absolute as the transcendent ground of phenomena, an idea which is well-defined in the Upaniṣadic conception of Brahman. The question is difficult to decide as there is little direct evidence. If there was any borrowing, it was indirect and circumstantial. More probable it is that by its own inner dynamism Buddhist thought too was heading towards Absolutism in metaphysics and Pantheism in religion.

The part played by some philosophical schools, notably the Vātsīputrīyas and the Sautrāntika, in proving as a sort of transitional link, must be mentioned. Universally condemned by all the other Buddhistic schools as heretical,[2] the Vātsīputrīyas held tenaciously to the doctrine of the pudgalātman (the Individual) as a quasi-permanent entity, neither completely identical with the mental states, nor different from them. However halting this conception may be, it is evidence of the awareness of the inadequacy of a stream of elements to account for the basic facts of experience, memory, moral responsibility, spiritual life etc. The Vātsīputrīyas showed the hollowness, at least the inadequacy, of the doctrine of elements; the states (skandhas) cannot completely substitute the ātman; a permanent synthetic unity must be accepted. Of course, they could not attain to the critical (middle) position of the Mādhyamika, viz. that there are no states without the self, nor is there the self without the states, and therefore both are unreal, being relative.

The Sautrāntika,[3] as a critical realist, developed the doctrine of

[1] Kern sees distinct parallels between the *Bhagavad Gītā* and the *Saddharma Puṇḍarīka*. Keith even hints at Greek and Christian influence (*Buddhist Phil.* pp. 216–7). Stcherbatsky says: "That the Mahāyāna is indebted to some Aupaniṣada influence is probable" (*Buddhist Nirvāṇa* p. 51; see also p. 61).

[2] The Pudgalātmavāda has come in for vehement criticism at the hands of the other schools. Vasubandhu devotes an entire section (the Appendix to his *Abhidharma Kośa*) for a refutation of this doctrine. The *Kathāvatthu* opens with a condemnation of this. Even the Mādhyamika does not spare him. (MK. Chaps. IX & X). See *Infra* Chap. VII, the section on *ātmaparīkṣā* for a detailed criticism of the Pudgala theory.

[3] Saṅkrāntivāda and Dārṣṭāntikavāda were other names or stages of the Sautrāntika. See Masuda, op. cit. pp. 66–7.

conceptual construction (vikalpa) as complementary to the doctrine of elements. They were aware of the subjectivity of phenomena to a much greater extent than the Vaibhāṣika. They cut down the inflated lists of categories accepted by the Vaibhāṣika, and roundly declared many of their reals as merely ideal (prajñāpti-sat).[1] The application of Occam's razor could have but one logical limit; all phenomena, without exception, are dependent on construction, and are without any real nature of their own. This certainly paved the way for the more logically developed position of the Mādhyamika. The Sautrāntika by his insistence on the creative work of thought and the doctrine of Representative Perception (bāhyānumeya-vāda or jñānākāra as viṣaya-sārūpya) directly led to the Idealism of the Yogācāra. If we knew only our ideas and the external object was always inferred, the conclusion is irresistible that only ideas are real; the external world of objects is an ideal projection. The Vijñānavāda arises by a trenchant criticism of the Sautrāntika doctrine of sārūpya (resemblance) between Viṣaya (object) and Vijñāna (knowledge)—the doctrine of representative perception. In the West too, the Idealism of Berkeley arises as a criticism of the Representative perception advocated by Descartes and Locke. This known parallelism of development should help us to understand a similar line of thought here.

The Satya Siddhi school of Harivarman is sometimes claimed as an intermediary school between Hīnayāna and Mahāyāna. Yama-Kami Sogen says:[2] "Harivarman's doctrine (the Satya Siddhi School) is to be regarded as the highest point of philosophical perception attained by Hīnayānism, and in a sense it constitutes the stage of transition between Hīnayānism and Mahāyānism." But as the date of Harivarman is the 3rd Century A.D., long after the advent of Nāgārjuna and Ārya Deva, the Satyasiddhi school may be considered as an attempt at a synthesis between Hīnayāna and Mahāyāna rather than as a precursor of Mahāyāna.[3]

[1] The Sautrāntikas based themselves on the scriptural text: pañcemāni bhikṣavaḥ saṁjñāmātraṁ pratijñāmātraṁ vyavahāramātraṁ saṁvṛti-mātraṁ yad utātīto'dhvānāgato'dhvākāśaṁ nirvāṇaṁ pudgalaś ceti. Quoted in MKV. p. 393; CŚV. pp. 59–60. They also refused to accept the citta-viprayukta-saṁskāras. MKV. p. 444. The Sautrāntikas reduced the number of Dharmas (75 in the Vaibhāṣika) to 43. See Appendix D of Pt. Aiyāswāmi's edn. of *Ālambana Parīkṣā*. (Adyar, Madras).

[2] *Systems of Buddhistic Thought*, p. 173, as quoted in Dr. Dutt's *Aspects of Mahāyāna*.

[3] This remark is from Dr. Dutt's *Aspects*, p. 65.

V PRAJÑĀPĀRAMITĀS AND THE FORMULATION OF THE MĀDHYAMIKA SYSTEM

The Mādhyamika system is the systematised form[1] of the Śūnyatā doctrine of the *Prajñāpāramitā* treatises; its metaphysics, spiritual path (ṣaṭ-pāramitā-naya) and religious ideal are all present there, though in a loose, prolific garb. With the *Prajñāpāramitās* an entirely new phase of Buddhism begins. A severe type of Absolutism established by the dialectic, by the negation (śūnyatā) of all empirical notions and speculative theories, replaces the pluralism and dogmatism of the earlier Buddhism. The *Prajñāpāramitās* revolutionised Buddhism, in all aspects of its philosophy and religion, by the basic concept of Śūnyatā. In them is reached the fruition of criticism that was born with Buddhism. Earlier Buddhism was semi-critical: it denied the reality of the substance—soul—(pudgala-nairātmya), but dogmatically affirmed the reality of the dharmas, separate elements. The new phase denies the reality of the elements too (dharma-nairātmya). The *Prajñāpāramitās* are not innovations; they can and do claim to expound the deeper, profounder teachings of Buddha, The fourteen avyākṛta (Inexpressibles) of Buddha receive their significant interpretation here. The dialectic that is suggested in Buddha is the principal theme here.

There is evidence to believe that the *Aṣṭasāhasrikā* is the oldest and basic Prajñāpāramitā text from which there has been expansion and abridgement, expansion into the *Śatasāhasrikā* and *Pañcaviṁśatisāhasrikā*[2] and abridgement into the *Saptaśatikā, Adhyardhaśatikā* etc.

[1] Candrakīrti says of Nāgārjuna that he had unerringly and deeply understood the Prajñāpāramitā way: Ācārya-Nāgārjunasya viditāviparītaprajñāpāramitā-nītеḥ (MKV. p. 3) and saddharmakośasya gabhīrabhāvaṁ yathānubuddhaṁ kṛpayā jagāda (ibid p. 1). From the Chinese sources we learn that Nāgārjuna is the author of a voluminous *Mahāprajñāpāramitā Śāstra* (*Nanjio* No. 1169; Hobogirin, 1509; translated into Chinese by Kumārajīva, A.D. 402–5). This circumstance might have led some to consider Nāgārjuna as the author of the *Prajñāpāramitā Sūtras*; but it is definitely established now that they had existed a considerable time before him and that he is only their systematiser. See H.I.L. Vol. II, pp. 341–2. Kimura: *Hīnayāna & Mahāyāna*, pp. 10 ff.

[2] This is in spite of the orthodox opinion that the *Śatasāhasrikā* has been abridged into the *Pañcaviṁśati, Aṣṭa*, etc. See AAA. p. 14.

The Prajñāpāramitā Sūtras range from the *Śatasāhasrikā* (100,000 verses in length) to the *Prajñāpāramitā Hṛdaya Sūtra* consisting of a few lines only: this is more or less a Dhāraṇī. The printed texts of these are:

1. The *Śatasāhasrikā*, Bib. Indica, (1902–13), Chapts. 1–13 or a little over a fourth has been published so far;

down to the shortest *Prajñāpāramitāhṛdaya Sūtra* consisting of a few lines. The *Aṣṭasāhasrikā*[1] was translated into Chinese as early as A.D. 172 by Lokarakṣa, and this affords us the lower limit. Allowing for the fact that the work must have established its reputation in India itself and for the difficulties of travel to a distant country etc., we may not be far wrong if we hold that the *Aṣṭasāhasrikā* might have been in existence in the 1st century B.C., if not earlier. The

2. The *Pañcaviṁśati*, redacted to conform to the *Abhisamayālaṁkāra*, edited by Dr. N. Dutt in the Calcutta Oriental Series, 1934. The first Abhisamaya or about a third of the entire work is all that is published. The original *Pañcaviṁśati* seems to be lost in Sanskrit, but is available in Tibetan.

3. The *Aṣṭādaśa* (fragments only) edited by Bidyabinod (1927) and Sten Konow (1942) in the *Memoirs of the Arch. Survey of India*, Nos. 32 & 69 respy.

4. The *Daśasāhasrikā* is lost in the original; the I & II chapters have been restored from Tibetan into Sanskrit by Sten Konow, Oslo, 1941.

5. The *Aṣṭasāhasrikā*, complete text edited by R. Mitra in the Bib. Indica (1888) and by Wogihara, Tokyo, 1932–35.

6. A summary or nucleus of the *Aṣṭa* is the *Ratnaguṇasaṁcaya Gāthā* consisting of about 300 verses in Gāthā Sanskrit ed. by Obermiller, *Bib. Buddhica*, 1937.

7. The *Suvikrāntivikramiparipṛcchā* or the *Sārdhadvisāhasrikā*, the first two chapters of which have been edited by Matsumoto; ch. 1 (Bonn, 1932); ch. 2 (*Kahle Studien*, 1935.).

8. The *Mañjuśrī parivarta* or *Saptaśatikā* edited by Tucci in *Mem. d. R. Acc. N. dei Lincei*, Vol. XVII, Rome, 1923; First Part only (corrected and ed.) by J. Masuda in the *Taisho Uni. Journal*, 1930, Tokyo.

9. The *Vajracchedikā* (the well-known *Diamond Sūtra*) ed. by Max Müller, Oxford, 1881.

10. The *Adhyardha Śatikā* has been edited by E. Leumann (*Zur nordarischen Sprache und Literatur*, Strassburg, 1912; and by Izumi, Toganoo and Wogihara, Kyoto, 1917.

11. The *Prajñāpāramitā Hṛdaya Sūtra*, easily the most popular of the Prajñāparamitā sūtras, has been edited and translated several times over by different scholars: by Max Müller, Oxford, 1884; by Shaku Hannya in the *Eastern Buddhist*, 1922–23; by D. T. Suzuki in his *Essays in Zen Buddhism*, 1934; and by Dr. E. Conze in the JRAS, 1948.

Fairly complete and detailed information about these and other Pāramitā texts which exist in MS only with the Chinese and Tibetan versions is given in Matsumoto's *Die Prajñāpāramitā Literatur*, Bonner Orien. Studien, Heft. I, 1932.

Many and varied are the problems connected with the *Prajñāpāramitās*. To mention some of them only: the inter-relation of the various recensions, the settling of the different stratifications to which each of them has been subjected, the fixing up of the dates for each, and the doctrinal analysis of their contents etc. A vast exegetical literature too has grown on these. Many of the commentaries are in Chinese and Tibetan, especially in the latter. The *Abhisamayālankārāloka* of Haribhadra (G.O.S. No. LXII, Baroda) is also a free commentary on the *Abhisamayālaṅkāra* and the *Aṣṭasāhasrikā* at once.

[1] *Die Prajñāpāramitā Literatur* pp. 4, 22 (Nanjio No. 5, *Daśasāhasrikā* is the same as our *Aṣṭa*).

formulation of the Mādhyamika as a system belongs, therefore, to the beginning of the Christian era.

It is difficult to say with any definiteness regarding the other canonical works that might have preceded and influenced Nāgārjuna and Ārya Deva. The Nine Dharmas[1]—*Āṣṭasāhasrikā, Saddharma Puṇḍarīka, Lalita Vistara, Laṅkāvatāra, Gaṇḍavyūha, Tathāgata-guhyaka, Samādhirāja, Suvarṇa Prabhāsa and Daśabhūmikā Sūtras* are held in great veneration by both the Mādhyamika and Yogācāra. There is evidence that Nāgārjuna was acquainted with the *Saddharma Puṇḍarīka*, for he quotes[2] from it. Probably, the Gāthā portions of the *Samādhi-rāja*[3] (*Candra-Pradīpa*) *Sūtra* were also utilised by Nāgārjuna. Candrakirti however quotes very freely from this in almost every chapter of his commentary *Prasannapadā*. The *Tathāgata Guhyaka*[1] and *Laṅkāvatāra* and other works are probably later than Nāgārjuna. Nothing definite can be said about them in the present state of our knowledge.

"The *Kāśyapa*[2] *Parivarta* (*Ratnakūṭa*) belongs to the comparatively small group of Mahāyāna works whose existence before the year A.D. 200 can be confidently assumed." The Mādhyamika standpoint of steering clear of the two extremes of nitya, and anitya, of ātman and nairātmya, is brought out with emphasis and clarity in this important text. The Madhyamā Pratipad is very suggestively characterised as the self-conscious or critical awareness of things as they are (dharmāṇām bhūtapratyavekṣā); it is not a position at all,

[1] All these nine are available in print; some (*Saddharma, Laṅkāvatāra, Suvarṇaprabhāsa* and *Samādhirāja*) have been edited twice over.

[2] See *Hist. of Ind. Lit.* Vol. II, p. 304.

[3] Candrakīrti refers to this as *Samādhirāja Sūtra*, while Śāntideva calls it *Candrapradīpa Sūtra* after the principal interlocutor there. This (chapters I–XVI) has been recently critically edited with introduction and notes by Dr. N. Dutt as part of *Gilgit MSS*. The earlier edition of this work, printed by the Buddhist Text Society, Calcutta, is faulty and incomplete. K. Regamey has published 3 chapters, VIII, XIX & XXII of this Sūtra, Warsaw, 1938. The characteristic Mādhyamika standpoint is stated thus:

astīti nāstīti ubhe'pi antā
tasmād ubhe anta vivarjayitvā
madhye'pi sthānaṁ na karoti paṇḍitaḥ. IX 27.

The distinction between nītārtha and neyārtha is also clearly drawn (VII 5, *Gilgit MSS.* Vol. II, p. 78).

[4] In his learned introduction to his edition of this work, Dr. B. Bhattacharya discusses the date and authorship of *Tathāgataguhya* or *Guhya Samāja*. After a thorough analysis, this scholar concludes that "it is very likely, therefore, that Asanga who belonged to the 3rd Century A.D. is the author of the *Guhya Samāja Tantra*" (p. XXIV).

[5] *Kāśyapa Parivarta* Ed. by Baron A. von Staël-Holstein, Shanghai, 1926.

and is indescribable.[1] In all probability, this was one of the shorter formative texts of the Mādhyamika system—one that is quoted with respect by Candrakīrti and Śānti Deva.

About 48 other Sūtras are included in the *Ratnakūṭa* class in the Chinese and Tibetan collections;[2] most of them are *Paripṛcchās*, short tracts dealing with a particular problem, and still others like the *Pitāputra Samāgama* etc. are considerable treatises going over the entire ground of Mādhyamika philosophy. Śānti Deva's *Śikṣāsamuccaya* remains our main, and in most cases the only, source for excerpts and specimens from these Sūtras. Candrakīrti quotes, among others, from *Akṣayamati*, *Upāliparipṛcchā*, *Pitāputra Samāgama*, *Ratnamegha*, *Ratnacūḍa Paripṛcchā*, *Satyadvayāvatāra* etc. From this it is not possible to conclude that these were necessarily prior to Nāgārjuna and Ārya Deva.

In the *Prajñāpāramitā* and the subsidiary Canonical (Sūtra) literature of the Mādhyamika, the one basic idea that is reiterated *ad nauseum* is that there is no change, no origination, no cessation, no coming in or going out; the real is neither one, nor many; neither ātman, nor anātman; it is as it is always. Origination, decay etc. are imagined by the uninformed; they are speculations indulged in by the ignorant. The real is utterly devoid (Śūnya) of these and other conceptual constructions; it is transcendent to thought and can be realised only in non-dual knowledge—Prajñā or Intuition, which is the Absolute itself. We are also expressly warned not to consider Śūnyatā as another theory, the Dharmatā as other than the phenomenal world. The Absolute in one sense transcends phenomena as it is devoid of empiricality, and in a vital sense is immanent or identical with it as their reality. The distinction between two truths, Paramārtha and Saṁvṛti, is emphasised. The butt of their criticism is the dogmatic speculations (the reality of skandha, dhātu, āyatana etc.) of earlier Buddhism; rūpa, vedanā etc. are *not anitya* (impermanent); but they are *Śūnya*, lacking a nature of their own. Pratītya-Samutpāda is *not the temporal sequence* of entities but their *essential dependence*. Nairātmya receives a deeper interpretation as appearance (niḥsvabhāvatva); and by a relentless dialectic it is shown that nothing escapes this predicament. All this finds the fullest expression in the works of Nāgārjuna and his followers.

[1] Ibid. pp. 82–90. This is quoted at many places in this work.

[2] The Kanjur lists 49 works as belonging to this class. The Tôhoku University *Cat. of the Tibetan Buddhist Canons* (Nos. 45–93).

VI THE MĀDHYAMIKA SCHOOLS AND LITERATURE (c. A.D. 150–800)

The Mādhyamika[1] system seems to have been perfected at one stroke by the genius of its founder—Nāgārjuna. There have not been many important changes in its philosophy since that time. In a system that is all dialectic, criticism, progress cannot be measured in terms of doctrinal accretion or modification. The Mādhyamika system performs the high office of philosophy in taking stock of itself from time to time. A close study of the system reveals to us the stresses and strains to which philosophy was subject in India down the ages.

The Mādhyamika system has had a continuous history of development from the time of its formulation by Nāgārjuna (A.D. 150) to the total disappearance of Buddhism from India (11th Cent.). We have a succession of brilliant teachers practically in every period. It is possible to distinguish three or four main schools or rather stages in the course of its development. The first is the stage of systematic formulation by Nāgārjuna and his immediate disciple—Ārya Deva. In the next stage there is the splitting up of the Mādhyamika into two schools—the Prāsangika and the Svātantrika, represented by Buddhapālita and Bhāvaviveka respectively. In the third period Candrakīrti (early 7th cent.) re-affirms the Prāsangika (*reductio ad absurdum*) as the norm of the Mādhyamika; the rigour and vitality of the system is in no small measure due to him. Śānti Dva (691–743), though coming a generation or two later, may also be taken as falling within this period. These two account for the high level attained by the Mādhyamika system. The fourth and last stage is a syncretism of the Yogācāra and the Mādhyamika—the chief representatives of which are Śāntarakṣita and Kamalaśīla. It is they who culturally conquered Tibet and made it a land of Buddhism. The Mādhyamika remains to this day the official philosophy of the Tibetan Church.

1. *First Period—Nāgārjuna* (c. A.D. 150) *and Ārya Deva* (c. 180–200).

Though the traditions of his life are greatly overlaid with legendary

[1] 'Madhyamaka' or 'Madhyamaka Darśana' is an alternative, and perhaps an earlier term used for the Middle Way of Nāgārjuna; it is derived from 'Madhya' (Middle) by the addition of 'taddhita' suffixes. 'Mādhyamika' is used both for the system and its advocates. Non-Buddhist writers invariably refer to the system as well as the adherents of it as Mādhyamika. Nāgārjuna or even Ārya Deva do not seem to have used either of these terms.

details, there is no reason to doubt that Nāgārjuna was a real person.[1] The circumstances of his life[2] are briefly told. He was, in all probability, a Brāhman from the South who came to Nālandā and propagated the new Prajñāpāramitā teaching. The legend which credits him with having brought the *Śatasāhasrikā* from the abode of the Nāgas means that he was the founder of a new and important phase in Buddhism. All our accounts also agree in connecting his abode with Dhānyakaṭaka or Śrīparvata[3] in the South, and of his personal friendship with the King Śātavāhana (Āndhra) for whom he wrote the *Suhṛllekha*. Tradition places him four hundred years after the parinirvāṇa of the Lord, whereas the consensus of opinion among European scholars is that he lived about the middle of the 2nd century, A.D.[4]

According to Buston (Vol. I, pp. 50–1) six are the main treatises of Nāgārjuna. *Prajñā-mūla* (*Mūla-Madhyamaka Kārikās*[5]) which is

[1] Max Walleser (*Life of Nāgārjuna, Asia Major* Hirth Ann. Vol.) writes in a sceptical vein about the historicity of Nāgārjuna: "The systematic development of the thought of voidness laid down in the *Prajñāpāramitā Sūtras* is brought into junction with the name of a man of whom we cannot positively say that he has really existed, still less that he is the author of the works ascribed to him. This name is Nāgārjuna." (p. 1). Possibly, the Chinese and Tibetan accounts used by this scholar confound the philosopher with the Alchemist and the Tantrika Nāgārjuna.

[2] See Buston—Vol. II, pp. 122 ff.

[3] Reliable historical evidence is available for associating Nāgārjuna with the remains of the great Buddhist monastery and temple, Nāgārjonikoṇḍa, in the Andhra province. See *Buddhist Remains of Āndhra*, pp. 53–63.

[4] "It has to be agreed that even to-day, an exact fixing of Nāgārjuna's life-time must remain entirely doubtful, having regard to the contradictory source of the tradition, always supposing that a writer of this name existed at all." (Walleser, ibid, p. 6).

"It is a good working hypothesis, though nothing more, that he lived in the latter half of the 2nd century A.D." (H.I.L. Vol. II, p. 342).

[5] This is the basic text of the Mādhyamika; it is comparable in influence and importance to the *Brahma Sūtras* or the *Nyāya Sūtras*. The text with the *Prasannapadā* of Candrakīrti has been edited by the Buddhist Text Society, Calcutta and by L. da Vallee Poussin in the Bibliothica Buddhica No. IV, 1913. The latter edition is a very valuable piece of scholarship. The text consists of 27 chapters beginning with *Pratyayaparīkṣā* and ending with *Dṛṣṭi Parīkṣa*; it consists of 448 verses. Each chapter is an examination of a particular category or doctrine. The Ābhidharmika doctrines are the ones chiefly criticised. Eight commentaries have been written on this by celebrated men, by Nāgārjuna (*Akutobhaya*), Buddhapālita, Bhāvaviveka (*Prajñāpradīpa*), Guṇamati, Sthiramati, Candrakīrti (*Prasannapadā*), Deva Śarman (*Sitābhyudaya*) and Guṇaśrī. All commentaries, except that of Candrakīrti, are lost in the original, but are preserved in Tibetan. According to Wassilief (quoted by Stcherbatsky, *Nirvāṇa* p. 66), "the authenticity of the work (*Akutobhaya*)

the Mādhyamika Śāstra *par excellence*; *Śūnyatā Saptati*[1] expounding the theory of the unreality of things in 66 anuṣṭub stanzas; *Yukti Ṣaṣṭikā*[2] is a work of 60 stanzas in anuṣṭup metre; the original of this and the above work is lost; but they are preserved in Tibetan. *Vigraha-Vyāvartanī* is the refutation of possible objections that may be raised against the negative method of Śūnyatā (Dialectic); it is very valuable for the light it throws on the nature of the Mādhyamika dialectic. The text is available[3] with the commentary of Nāgārjuna. We have the evidence of Candrakīrti to say that the Ācārya[4] wrote his own commentary on the work. At places, the *Vigraha Vyāvarttanī* almost repeats verses[5] from the *Mādhyamika Kārikās*. "*Vaidalya Sūtra* and *Prakaraṇa*, the self-defence of Nāgārjuna against the charge of perverting logic" is to be had in Tibetan. The sixth[6] work, according to Buston, is *Vyavahāra Siddhi*, "showing that from the point of view of the Absolute Truth—Non-substantiality, and from the empirical standpoint—wordly practice, go along together."

was doubted even by the credulous Tibetans." Some chapters have been translated: I & XXV in English by Stcherbatsky, and V, XII–XVI by Schayer in German.

[1] There are three commentaries on the *Śūnyatā Saptati*, one by Nāgārjuna, the second by Candrakīrti and the third by Parahita—lost in the original but preserved in Tibetan (Mdo. XVII 4). A stanza from *Śūnyatā Saptati* (paṭaḥ kāraṇataḥ siddhaḥ etc.) is quoted in MKV. p. 89.

[2] Preserved in Tibetan and Chinese. Translated from the Chinese Version by Phil. Schaeffer in German; Heidelberg, 1923. Candrakīrti quotes from this half a verse:

tat tat prāpya yad utpannaṁ notpannaṁ tat svabhāvataḥ (MKV. pp. 9 & 10.) to decide the exact meaning of pratītya-samutpāda as dependence. Another verse from the *Yukti-Ṣaṣṭikā* (hetutaḥ sambhavo yeṣām) is cited in MKV. (p. 413) and in BCAP. (p. 583) and a slightly different verse in BCAP. (p. 500). A replica of this idea is found in BCA. IX, 145.

[3] *Vigraha-vyāvarttanī* Ed. by K. P. Jayaswal and R. Sankrityayana, Appendix to J.B.O. R.S. Vol. XXII; Translation into English from the Chinese and Tibetan versions by G. Tucci, in the *Pre-Diṅnāga Buddhist Texts*, G.O.S. No. XLIX. Probably, this book was written after the *Mādhyamika Kārikās*, as the Vṛtti of VV. quotes the MK. Kārikā: vyavahāram anāśritya paramārtho na deśyate, etc.

[4] MKV. p. 25: *vigrahavyāvartanyā* vṛttiṁ kurvatāpy ācāryeṇa prayoga-vākyānabhidhānāt.

[5] VV 37 = MK VII 12; VV 38, 39, 40 = MK VII 9, 10, 11 respectively.

[6] According to Tāranātha only the first five are by Nāgārjuna. Some take the sixth work to be *Akutobhaya*, but this is wrong. This commentary is not by Nāgārjuna. See Obermiller—*Doc. of Prajñā-pāramitā* pp. 4–5.

There is good evidence to hold that *Ratnāvalī*,[1] which is profusely quoted by Candrakīrti and Prajñākaramati, is the work of Nāgārjuna. There is no reasonable doubt with regard to *Catuḥ Stava*[2] (Nirupama, Lokātīta, Cittavajra and Paramārtha-stava in anuṣṭup metre) being the work of Nāgārjuna. These are feeling verses of the highest devotion; they show that Nāgārjuna, like Śankara, had the religious strain also well-developed in him. Both these great Ācāryas have the same felicity of language and the capacity to express their thoughts even in shorter pieces. A number of spurious works have been fathered upon them, and in many cases it is difficult to reject them as not genuine.

Pratītya Samutpāda Hṛdaya[3] (Tanjur Mdo XVII) is a small tract in seven āryās by Nāgārjuna; one verse (svādhyāya-dīpa etc.) from this has been cited by Candrakīrti (MKV. p. 428, p. 551.). The *Bodhicaryāvatārapañjikā* (p. 351) quotes, apparently from this, a couplet and a half to the effect that in the phenomenal sphere, pratītya samutpāda, or the twelve-link causal chain with its three sub-divisions, continues without intermission in this and other lives conditioned as it is by kleśa and karma.[4] There is a commentary on this by Candrakīrti.

On the strength of a verse from Śānti Deva,[5] it may be hazarded that Nāgārjuna was the author of a collection of Mahāyāna Sūtras—

[1] This work is utilised in our exposition of the Mādhyamika doctrines. G. Tucci has edited the text with a translation of some parts in the J.R.A.S. 1934, 1936. (Incomplete; Parts 1, 2 and 4 only).

[2] The *Catuḥstava* is quoted at many places in MKV. pp. 55, 64, 215 and in BCAP (numerous places). These citations are utilised in this work. *Nairaupamya* and *Paramārtha Stavas* have been edited by Tucci in the JRAS (1932), pp. 312 ff. Prabhubhai Patel has restored the entire *Catuḥstava* from Tibetan into Sanskrit in the IHQ. Vol. VIII (1932), pp. 316–331; 689–705). According to Patel the titles of the four Hymns are: *Nirupama, Lokātīta, Acintya* and *Stutyatīta.*

[3] Tibetan Text and Translation ed. by Poussin as Appendix IV to his *Theorie des douze Causes*, Gand, 1913. Pt. N. Aiyaswami has translated this into English from the Chinese version (Taisho, Vol. XXXII, 1654) in the *K. V. Rangaswami Aiyangar Com.* Vol. pp. 485–91. A commentary on this by Ullangha named *Pratītyasamutpādaśāstra* has been translated from the Chinese by V. Gokhale, Bonn, 1930.

[4] BCAP. p. 389.

[5] BCA, V. 106:
saṁkṣepeṇāthavā paśyet Sūtrasamuccayam;
ārya-Nāgārjunābaddhaṁ dvitīyaṁ ca prayatnataḥ.

Sūtra Samuccaya.[1] Buston too includes it in the list of the works of Nāgārjuna "dedicated to the practical side of the Doctrine."[2]

There exist a great number of small tracts such as *Upāyahṛdaya, Mahāyāna Viṁśaka,*[3] *Akṣara śataka* (rightly a work of Ārya Deva), *Abuddha Bodhaka, Bhavasaṁkrānti Sūtra Vṛtti,*[4] *Prajñā Daṇḍa,*[5] *Dharma Saṅgraha,*[6] etc. which are attributed to Nāgārjuna. It is difficult to decide about the real authorship of these works. In the *Chinese Tripiṭaka* (Nanjio, p.368) 24 works are ascribed to Nāgārjuna, some of which have been noted already. Of the rest, the important ones[7] are: *Mahāprajñā-pāramitā Śāstra* (No. 1169), *Daśabhūmivibhāṣā Śāstra* (No. 1180), *Dvādaśa nikāya* (*Mukha*) *Śāstra* (No. 1186) and *Ekaśloka Śāstra* (No. 1212); the first three were translated into Chinese by Kumārajīva about A.D. 405 and the last by Prajñāruci (A.D. 538–43). Besides these, a large number of Tantric and Medical works are attributed to Nāgārjuna in the Tibetan Collection (Tanjur).

[1] Mr. Anukulchandra Banerjee, in a note on this topic in the I.H.Q. Vol. XVII, pp. 121 ff., gives interesting information about this work. He concludes: "From these evidences, it is clear that there were two texts of the *Sūtra Samuccaya*, one by Śānti Deva and the other by Nāgārjuna, and that Śānti Deva regarded the work of Nāgārjuna as of great importance and recommended its more careful study than that of his own." (p. 126).

[2] Buston, Vol. II, p. 125.

[3] Reconstructed Sanskrit Text, edited with the Tibetan and Chinese versions and an English translation by Prof. Vidhushekhar Bhattacharya, Sāntiniketan. Concensus of opinion among scholars is that this work is by another Nāgārjuna who lived about the first half of the 7th century. This work however is quoted in *Jñānasiddhi*.

[4] *Bhavasaṁkrānti Śāstra* by Nāgārjuna. Restored into Samskrit by Pt. Aiyāswāmi Śāstri, Adyar, 1938. As some of the verses are quoted from this work, *e.g.* 'na cakṣuḥ prekṣate rūpam etc.) this is most probably a genuine work of Nāgārjuna.

[5] A book of 260 sayings, edited and translated by Major W. L. Campbell, Calcutta, 1919. There is nothing particularly Buddhistic about them.

[6] Ed. by Kasawara and Max Müller—Oxford, 1885. This is just a glossary of Buddhist technical terms.

[7] "There are no grounds for denying Nāgārjuna the authorship of the commentaries, *Prajñāpāramitā Sūtra Śāstra* and *Daśabhūmi vibhāṣā Śāstra*. A translation of the *Mahāprajñāpāramitā* into French by Professor Lamotte is in progress. 2 Volumes (pp. 1–1118) have already been published. (Louvain, 1944, 1949). The short treatise, *Ekaśloka Śāstra,* which has come down only in Chinese, and which sets out to prove that true existence (*svabhāva*) is non-existence (abhāva), is perhaps rightly ascribed to Nāgārjuna." H.I.L. Vol. II, p. 348. This has been translated into English by Edkins (*Chinese Buddhism*, pp. 302–317) and restored into Sanskrit by H. R. R. Iyengar, *Mysore Univ. Journal*, I, 2; 1927.

Ārya Deva (Kāṇa Deva, Piṅgalākṣa, Nīla-Netra, Deva) was the chief pupil and worthy successor of Nāgārjuna. The Mādhyamika system owes much of its popularity and stability to him. Nāgārjuna directs the dialectic mainly against the Ābhidharmikas and establishes Śūnyatā as the true import of the scriptures. His references to the ātma tradition are slight and indirect. He was however fully acquainted with the classical Sāṁkhya and even the Vaiśeṣika.[1] The Mādhyamika system is primarily a revolution in Buddhist thought, and so the concentration of Nāgārjuna on earlier Buddhism is understandable. In Ārya Deva, we find not only criticism of the Ābhidharmika but greater attention is paid to the Sāṁkhya and Vaiśeṣika conceptions. This is done in his chief work *Catuḥ Śataka*. There was need to consolidate the Mādhyamika position against the non-Buddhist systems and to show that the dialectic is equally valid against them. Coupled with the accounts we have of him that Ārya Deva was a great debater and that in many discussions he vanquished his adversaries, there is no doubt that he shares the honour of founding the Mādhyamika system with his master, Nāgārjuna.

The most trustworthy account of the main incidents of his life is given by Candrakīrti in the introductory part of his commentary on the *Catuḥ Śataka*:[2] "Ārya Deva was born in the island of Sinhala and was a son of the King of the land. After having become the crown prince he renounced the world, came to the South, and becoming a disciple of Nāgārjuna, followed his doctrine. Therefore the truth of his *Catuḥ Śataka Śāstra* is not different from that of the *Mādhyamika Śāstra* (of Nāgārjuna). The assertion that there is difference between their doctrines simply shows one's rashness; for, it is a false imagination."

Deva "most probably lived at about the turning point of the second and third centuries, A.D."[3]

Catuḥśataka (*Catuḥ-Śatikā* or simply *Śataka*) is the most celebrated work of Ārya Deva. Except for some fragments,[4] the work is lost in

[1] See *Supra*–pp. 55–6 n.

[2] Prof. V. Bhattacharya's Restoration of *Catuḥśataka*, Intr. XIX. Dr. N. Dutt questions the authenticity of these incidents, and Prof. Bhattacharya answers the criticism. See I.H.Q. ix (1933) pp. 18 ff. and 193 ff.

[3] H.I.L. Vol. II, p. 350.

[4] Fragments mixed up with vṛtti discovered and published by MM. Pt. H.P. Śāstri, *Memoirs of the A.S.B.* Vol. III, No. 8, pp. 449–514. This contains only 129 verses or about a third of the whole work.

the original, but is preserved in entirety in Tibetan, from which it has been reconstructed[1] into Samskrit. Dharmapāla and Candrakīrti have written commentaries on the work, the first probably on the first half and the latter on the whole work. It consists of 400 verses[2] arranged symmetrically under 16 chapters, each consisting of 25 verses. The first half is devoted to the Mādhyamika spiritual discipline and the second to a refutation of dogmatic speculations of Buddhists and non-Buddhists, e.g. Sāṁkhya and Vaiśeṣika.[3] In style and content it is equal to the *Mādhyamika Kārikās*; and its importance in the system is only second to the *Kārikās*. Candrakīrti quotes the *Śataka* frequently in his MKV as authority for his statements. The correct Mādhyamika standpoint is upheld by Ārya Deva, and the work ends with a verse[4] characteristic of the dialectic.

The *Śata Śāstra*[5] (translated by Kumārajīva A.D. 404, into Chinese) and the *Śata Śāstra Vaipulya* (trans. by Hieun Tsang A.D. 650) are probably the last 8 chapters of the *Catuḥ Śataka*, the contents being reshuffled.

The *Akṣara Śatakam*[6] is in all probability the work of Ārya Deva. It is lost in the original, but is preserved in Chinese (*Śatākṣara Śāstram*, Nanjio, No. 1254; Hobogirin, 1572) and also in Tibetan where it is wrongly ascribed to Nāgārjuna. With regard to the genuineness of the work, Mr. Gokhale remarks: "As regards the short basic text—the *Akṣara Śataka* proper—it is by no means improbable

[1] Part II, Chapter VIII–XVI, reconstructed and edited with copious extracts from the commentary of Candrakīrti by Prof. Vidhusekhar Bhattacharya, Visvabharati, 1931. This work grew as a criticism of the restoration made by Dr. P. L. Vaidya in his *Études sur Ārya Deva et son Catuḥ Śataka*, Paris, 1923. Prof. Bhattacharya had also previously restored the VII chapter in the *Proc. of IV Oriental Conference*, (Allahabad, 1926) pp. 831 ff. I have unhesitatingly used the restorations of this eminent scholar in my exposition of the Mādhyamika system.

[2] Regarding the number of verses and arrangement of the chapters, see the Preface to the Fragments from *Catuḥ Satikā* cited above and Dr. Vaidya's Intr. to his restoration (*Études*).

[3] See Chaps. IX, X, XI of CŚ.

[4] sad asat sadasac ceti yasya pakṣo na vidyate;
upālambhaś cireṇāpi tasya vaktuṁ na śakyate. CŚ XVI 25.

[5] Translated by Prof. G. Tucci in the *Pre-Diṅnāga Buddhist Texts on Logic*, G.O.S. XLIX, Baroda.

[6] *Akṣara Śatakam*—The Hundred Letters—A Mādhyamika Text by Ārya Deva, after Chinese and Tibetan materials. Trans. by V. Gokhale; Heidelberg, 1930.

that Ārya Deva was the author of it; the title in itself is so typical of an Ārya Devic production that one might easily be tempted to suggest a chronological sequence among the works: *Catuḥ Śataka, Śataka* (*Śata Śāstra*) and *Akṣara Śataka*, where beginning from the *Catuḥśataka* the logical arguments become more and more systematic and pointed till in the present text they develop into a short and neat refutation solely directed against the Sāṁkhyas and Vaiśeṣikas, who probably formed in Ārya Deva's time the most powerful opponents of Buddhism."[1] It must be admitted, however, that the *Akṣara Śatakam* does not seem to be very intelligible even with the commentary. The general drift of the treatise is to refute both identity and difference (bhāvā naikatvaṁ bhinnatvam api), sat and asatkāryavāda and to establish that things are apparent (svapnasamam). The twenty odd propositions which form the entire subject-matter of the treatise are introduced so abruptly and with so little argument that it singularly fails to add to our knowledge of the Mādhyamika system.

The *Hasta-vāla-Prakaraṇa*[2] (The Hand Treatise), (Chinese, *Muṣṭiprakaraṇa* . . . Nanjio Nos. 1255–6; Hobogirin, 1620, 1621, wrongly attributed to Dignāga) may be taken as another attempt by Ārya Deva at summarising the doctrines in six verses. Just as the appearance of the 'rope-snake' is unreal, likewise things of the world too, when closely scrutinised, are nothing apart from their parts; but indivisible parts are equally unreal. The wise one should abandon attachment, just as one shakes off fear of the unreal 'rope-snake.' The distinction between the empirical (laukika) and Absolute Truth (paramārtha) is drawn in the last verse.

Cittaviśuddhi Prakaraṇa[3] and *Jñānasāra Samuccaya*[4] are also attributed to Ārya Deva, perhaps with less justification. In the *Chinese Tripiṭaka*, the *Refutation of Four Heretical Hīnayāna Schools*

[1] *Akṣara Śatakam*, p. 14.

[2] Prof. F. W. Thomas has edited the Tibetan and Chinese texts with a restoration in Samskrit of the text and Commentary and an English translation in the J.R.A.S. 1918, pp. 267–310. In his prefatory note to this, Dr. Thomas discusses the authenticity of the work and the peculiar nature of the title.

[3] Fragments discovered and edited by MM. Pt. H. P. Shastri, JASB, 1898, pp. 178–184; Ed. by Prabhubhai Patel, Visvabharati Series, 1933, 1949. The work belongs to the Vajrayāna school. See I.H.Q. ix (1933) pp. 705 and the introduction to his edition for a discussion of the contents and authorship of this work by Patel.

[4] Prof. V. Bhattacharya quotes a couplet (*Basic Conception*, p. 11) from this. This is also quoted in TSP. pp. 72, 878.

and of the *Conception of Nirvāṇa according to 20 heretical schools* mentioned in the *Lankāvatāra Sūtra* are also attributed to Ārya Deva. If these are genuine, it affords information about a number of sects and religions, such as Māheśvara, Vaiṣṇava,[1] etc.

2. Buddha-Pālita and Bhāvaviveka[2] initiate a new phase in the development of the Mādhyamika system. Buddhapālita takes the essence of the Mādhyamika method to consist in the use of *reductio ad absurdum* arguments alone (prasanga-vākya). The true Mādhyamika cannot uphold a position of his own; he has therefore no need to construct syllogisms and adduce arguments and examples. His sole endeavour is to reduce to absurdity the arguments of the opponent on principles acceptable to him. We have the evidence of Candrakīrti to say that Buddhapālita held prasanga (*reductio ad absurdum*) to be the real method of Nāgārjuna and Ārya Deva. He therefore initiates the Prāsangika School of the Mādhyamika.

Bhāvaviveka (Bhavya), a younger contemporary of Buddhapālita, criticises the latter for merely indulging in refutation without advancing a counter-position.[3] He seems to have held that the Mādhyamika could consistently advance an opposite view. When the satkāryavāda is criticised, the opposite view of cause and effect being different should be set forth. It is not quite clear what exactly Bhāvaviveka, who was himself a Mādhyamika, meant by this. Probably, he would have liked to take a particular stand with regard to empirical reality, or his aim was to vindicate the empirical validity of both the alternatives in turn. It is unfortunate that we have no extant work of his in Sanskrit which could have thrown light on the distinction between the two schools. Bhāvaviveka is the founder of the Svatantra (Svātantrika) Mādhyamika School which had some following and which later on gave rise to combination with the Sautrāntika and Yogācāra. Candrakīrti criticises him severely for being inconsistent, although a Mādhyamika,[4] in advancing independent arguments and

[1] See Kimura: *Hīnayāna and Mahāyāna* pp. 28–9 and 350.

[2] Regarding the date, N. Peri says: A propos de la date de Vasubandhu j'ai place Buddhapālita dans la premiere moitie du cinquieme siècle (1st half of the 5th Century A.D.) BEFEO, 1911, as quoted in Dr. Vaidya's *Études sur Āryadeva* etc. p. 17. Winternitz agrees with this date. H.I.L. Vol. II, p. 362.

[3] ācārya-Bhāvaviveko dūṣaṇam āha: tad atra prasangavākyatvāt etc. MKV. p. 36. See also pp. 38, 14–15.

[4] angīkṛta-madhyamaka-darśanasyāpi yat svatantraprayoga-vākyābhidhānam . . . asya tārkikasyopalakṣyate. MKV. p. 25.

for his fondness for exhibiting his skill as a logician.[1] He is even castigated for his inaccuracy[2] in stating the opponent's position. From another reference to Bhāvaviveka, it appears that he held that the realisation of Śūnyatā was not absolutely necessary for Nirvāṇa and that he conceded that the Śrāvakas[3] and Pratyekabuddhas could also attain final release. This is certainly opposed to the ekanayavāda[4] of Nāgārjuna according to which eventually the votaries of the other paths have to be initiated into the Śūnyatā discipline for attaining final release.

In his *Karatalaratna*,[5] Bhāvaviveka attempts to establish the basic Mādhyamika standpoint by syllogistic arguments. He formulates the syllogisms thus:[6] The conditioned things (saṁskṛta) are unreal (śūnya) from the standpoint of ultimate truth (tattvataḥ), because they are produced through causes and conditions (pratyayodbhavāt), like things created by magic (māyāvat). The unconditioned (asaṁskṛta), such as Space, Nirvāṇa etc., are non-existent from the standpoint of ultimate truth, because they are non-originating (anutpādāḥ), like the sky-lotus (khapuṣpavat). The syllogisms are mainly intended to convince the Hīnayānist of the truth of the Void (Śūnyatā). Bhāvaviveka defends his argument against possible formal and material objections. He points out that he does not mean to deny the empirical validity of things (saṁvṛtisat), but only their ultimate reality.[7] The argument therefore is not vitiated by the evidence of sense-perception etc., as these acquaint us only with appearance.[8] Nor is it opposed to the testimony of the scriptures or

[1] ātmanas tarkaśāstrātikauśalamātram āviścikīrṣayā MKV. p. 25, tasmāt priyānumānatām evātmana ācāryaḥ prakaṭayati, MKV. p. 16.

[2] . . . iti paravyākhyānam anūdya dūṣaṇam abhidhatte, tasya parapakṣānuvādākauśalam eva tāvat sambhāvyate. MKV. p. 8 also pp. 9–10.

[3] See MKV. pp. 351–3. Candrakīrti concludes on this with regard to Bhāvaviveka: tad ayam ācāryo yathaivamvidhe viṣaye nācārya-matānuvartī tathā pratipāditaṁ *Madhyamakāvatāre* 'dūraṅgamāyāṁ tu dhiyādhika ity atreti na punas tad dūṣaṇe yatna āsthīyate.

[4] See AAA. p. 120: ārya Nāgājunapādās tan-matānusārinaś caikayānanayavādina āhuḥ. 'labdhvā bodhidvayam' . . . etc. See *infra* Chapter X.

[5] Poussin has translated this work *Mahāyānatālaratna Śāstra* of Bhāvaviveka into French (*Le Joyau dans la Main*) in MCB ii (1932–33) pp. 68–138. Pandit N. Aiyāswāmi Śāstri has restored this from the Chinese translation of Hieun Tsang (Nanjio, 1237, Taisho, 1578) into Sanskrit under the title, *Karatalaratna* (The Jewel in Hand) Visva-Bharati, Santiniketan, 1949.

[6] *Karatalaratna*, p. 34.

[7] Ibid—p. 35.

[8] Ibid—pp. 40 ff.

even of commonsense. It may be objected[1] that for the Śūnyavādin there is no subject of negation, as he does not accept any entity. The objection is not valid; for it is not necessary that a thing must be accepted as real before we could negate it; it is enough that it is taken to be real in common parlance. Realists may advance the counter-argument[2] that what is efficient e.g. the sense-organ, is real (not unreal like the barren woman's son). This is clearly wrong, for efficiency is also possible in the case of apparitional things.

Another possible objection is that the argument that proves the voidness of *all* things is itself void, as it is itself subject to the same predicament (i.e. is conditioned by causes).[3] Far from being a defect, this only serves to bring out the universal applicability of the law; the proof that all things are śūnya is itself śūnya, within appearance. Bhāvaviveka further clarifies his position by stating that śūnyatā does not mean the assertion of the non-existence of things, but only the denial of the dogmatic assertion of existence.[4] He also distinguishes his standpoint from that of the Vijñānavādin.[5] He rightly points out that Śūnyatā does not nullify things or make them disappear, but shows up their real nature as devoid of essence (niḥsvabhāva).[6]

Does Bhāvaviveka succeed in 'proving' sūnyatā by positive arguments? There can be no doubt about his ingenuity and scholarship; nor does he fare worse than other speculative philōsophers. Can we, however, establish the concomitance (vyāpti) between 'dependent origination' (the middle term) which is claimed to be a universal factor of all things and their unreality, śūnyatā (the major term)? As all things are brought within the compass of the rule, there can be no negative example (vipakṣa-dṛṣṭānta): we are not in a position to say: what is not unreal is also not dependent in origination. The argument is inconclusive, as the method of Agreement alone is used and not the method of Difference or Exclusion. To say, as Bhāvaviveka does, that the Sāṁkhya or the Vaiśeṣika or even the Buddhist realists make use of the same method merely means that they are equally inconclusive, or that the Mādhyamika is equally dogmatic. The characteristic Mādhyamika stand as a review or criticism of all positions and theories does not emerge from Bhāvaviveka's procedure. And to review a position, we should not have a position of our own but be alive to the contradictions of other

[1] Ibid, p. 42.
[2] *Karatalaratna*, p. 43.
[3] Ibid—pp. 44 ff.
[4] Ibid—pp. 49–51.
[5] Ibid—pp. 56 ff.
[6] Ibid—pp. 62 ff.

positions. The Mādhyamika is a philosophy of higher order; it is a philosophy of philosophies.

Both Buddhapālita and Bhāvaviveka developed their respective standpoints by writing commentaries[1] on the *Mādhyamika Śāstra*; these are lost in the original but are available in Tibetan. Bhāvaviveka was evidently a man of great scholarship; for his *Tarkajvālā*[2] gives full exposition of the views of Sāṁkhya, Vaiśeṣika and Vedānta, often quoting from the original texts. In his *Madhyamakārtha Saṅgraha*,[3] he accords to the Absolutes of Hīnayāna and heretical systems the status of paryāya paramārtha.[4] This makes him out as a liberal-minded Mādhyamika unlike Candrakīrti. Besides these works and *Prajñāpradīpa* the commentary on the *Mādhyamika Kārikās*, Bhāvaviveka has written an independent work—*Madhyamakāvatāra-Pradīpa*, (mdo XVII I) and another prakaraṇa: *Madhyamaka Pratītya Samutpāda*.

3. It is Candrakīrti and Śānti Deva that give to the Mādhyamika system its rigorous, orthodox form. Candrakīrti is a commentator and author of unequalled merit; his dialectical skill is of the highest order. Stcherbatsky rightly describes him as "a mighty champion of the purely negative method of establishing monism." "He succeeds in driving Bhāvaviveka's school into the shade and finally settles that form of the Mādhyamika system which is now studied in all monastic schools of Tibet and Mongolia, where it is considered to represent the true philosophic basis of Mahāyāna Buddhism."[5]

[1] According to Stcherbatsky (*Nirvāṇa* p. 66) these two celebrated champions of the Mādhyamika system appeared in the South. Buddhapālita is the author of the *Madhyamakavṛtti* (Tibetan version partly pd. in the Bib. Buddhica); no other work of his has come down to us. *Prajñāpradīpa* (Tibetan version partly pd. in the Bib. Indica) is the name of Bhavya's commentary.

[2] This is an auto-commentary on the *Mādhyamika-Hṛdayakārikā*. Probably, *Madhyamakahṛdayavṛtti Tattvāmṛtāvatāra* is another name of this work (See pp. 58 & 76 of Bhāvaviveka's *Karatalaratna*). A Sanskrit palm-leaf MS of *Tarkajvālā* was discovered by R. Sanskrityayana in the Shalu Monastery (Tibet) in the year 1936. A copy of this was made by him there itself; and it is now awaiting publication. Interesting details of this MS are given in the JBORS Vol. XXIII, Part I. (p. 48). The opening Ślokas are given. Some of the names of the chapters are: (1) Bodhicintāparityāga, (2) Munivrata-samāśraya, (3) Tattvajñānāvatāra, (4) Śrāvaka-Tattva-niścaya, (5) Yogācāra-tattva-niścaya, (6) Sāṁkhya-Tattva-niścaya, (7) Vaiśeṣika-tattva-niścaya, (8) Vedānta-tattva-niścaya etc.

[3] Text restored into Sanskrit by Pt. Aiyāswāmi Śāstri; JOR (Madras) Vol. V, pp. 41 ff.

[4] See *infra* Chap. IX (Section, *Two Truths*).

[5] *Budd. Con. of Nirvāṇa*, p. 67.

Candrakīrti, according to Buston[1] and Tāranātha, was born in the south in Samanta; he entered the Order, and studied the holy texts from Kamalabuddhi—the disciple of Buddhapālita and Bhavya. Candrakīrti has written lucid and authoritative commentaries on the works of Nāgārjuna and Ārya Deva. His *Prasannapadā* (The Clear-worded)—a commentary on the *Mādhyamika Kārikās*—is probably his mature and latest work. It was certainly written later than the *Madhyamākavatāra*, which is very freely quoted and referred to. From Tibetan sources, we also know that he wrote commentaries on Nāgārjuna's *Śūnyatā Saptati* and *Yukti Saṣṭikā*. His commentary on Ārya Deva's *Catuḥ Śataka*[2] is next only to *Prasannapadā* in merit and importance. Candrakīrti has written an independent work of great value, the *Madhyamakāvatāra*[3], with his own commentary on it. This is unfortunately lost in the original, but is preserved in Tibetan and part of it has been restored into Sanskrit.[4] Two other small manuals (prakaraṇas) *Madhyamaka-Prajñāvatāra* and *Pañcaskandha* are also attributed to him in the Tanjur collection. (Mdo. XXIII 5, and XXIV 3).

Candrakīrti re-affirms the prāsangika standpoint of Buddhapālita against Bhāvaviveka, whom he severely criticises for his un-Mādhyamika position and several other inaccuracies. Candrakīrti is the chief exponent of the Prāsangika School which has, mainly through his efforts, become the norm of the Mādhyamika. He has also refuted the Vijñānavāda at several[5] places, and has shown the unsoundness of its doctrines of Self-Consciousness (svasaṁvitti) and the existence of Knowledge (vijñāna) without the object. In a sustained dialectic, Candrakīrti shows, in his *Madhyamakāvatāra* (Chapter VI), that without object, Vijñāna too is nothing; we cannot even apprehend it, much less remember it. He even suggests that 'Vijñāna' is the Ātman[6] of the heretics (Tīrthakaras) in disguise. He

[1] See Buston, Vol. II, pp. 134 ff, for an account of his life and works. Tāranātha's *Geschichte* pp. 147 ff.

[2] Chaps. VII–XVI restored into Samskrit with copious extracts from Candrakīrti's commentary by Professor V. Bhattacharya.

[3] Partly translated into French by Poussin in *Le Muséon*, 1907, 1910, 1911. Tibetan Text published in the Bib. Buddhica. There is a commentary on this by Jayānanda.

[4] Chapter VI (Incomplete) restored into Sanskrit with the commentary by Pandit N. Aiyāswāmi Śāstri, J. O. R. (Madras) 1929 ff.

[5] See MKV. pp. 61 ff—274 ff; MA. pp. 40 ff. The Mādhyamika criticism of Vijñānavāda is dealt with in a subsequent chapter (Chap. XIII) of this work.

[6] MA. p. 59.

has no hesitation in concluding that Vijñānavāda is inconsistent with the truth of empirical[1] reality. Vijñānavāda is not, according to Candrakīrti, the middle position, which is the non-acceptance of both 'is' and 'is not' ('astitva' and 'nāstitva') whereas Vijñānavāda *accepts both*, the non-existence of the Parikalpita and the existence of the Paratantra.[2] For him, Vijñānavāda is not the final teaching (nītārtha), but is just a step to it (neyārtha).[3]

Candrakīrti also vindicates, from the standpoint of empirical truth, the soundness of commonsense notions with regard to the objects of sense-perception against the Sautrāntika-Vijñānavāda[4] doctrines of the Unique Particular (svalakṣaṇa) and Perception as devoid of determination (kalpanāpoḍha). According to him, these refinements have not much use either as a statement of the empirical or of the ultimate reality.

His criticisms directed against the Vijñānavāda and the Sautrāntika and his intimate knowledge of their technicalities afford evidence of the ascendence of these schools at that time and the Mādhyamika reaction to them. Candrakīrti's time[5] is certainly subsequent to Diṅnāga and probably contemporaneous with Dharmakīrti.

Śānti Deva[6] follows the prāsangika method, and his works are equally important and popular. According to Tāranātha and Buston,[7] Śānti Deva was the son of King Kalyāṇavarman of Saurāṣṭra, and was himself to be crowned king in succession to his father, but he renounced this on the advice of Mañjuśrī who appeared to him in a dream. "He fled and took orders in Nālandā with Jayadeva: henceforth he was known by the name of Śānti Deva."

[1] MA. p. 64 bhraṣṭā hi te saṁvṛtitattva-satyāt.

[2] tasya parikalpitasyāvidyamānatvāt paratantrasya ca vidyamanatvād astitva-nāstitva-darśanadvayasyāpy upanipātāt kuto'ntadvayaparihāraḥ MKV. p. 275.

[3] MKV. p. 276.

[4] MKV. pp. 596.

[5] There is some difference of opinion with regard to the exact time of Candrakīrti. Winternitz (H.I.L. Vol. II, p. 363) says: "One of Dharmapāla's pupils is Candrakīrti, who must accordingly have lived in the 6th century and not, as is usually taken for granted, in the 7th." Peri and others place him between A.D. 575–625.

[6] "The evidence of *Tattvasiddhi* where Śāntarakṣita quotes a full śloka from the *Bodhicaryāvatāra* once for all settles the question (of Śānti Deva's date). It proves that Śānti Deva flourished in a period between the departure of I-Tsing from India in 695 and before Śāntarakṣita's first visit to Tibet in A.D. 743." Dr. B. Bhattacharya's Foreword to the *Tattvasaṁgraha* p. xxiii.

[7] Buston, Vol. II, pp. 161 ff. Tāranātha, pp. 163 ff.

Śānti Deva's *Śikṣā Samuccaya*[1] and *Bodhicaryāvatāra*[2] are the two[3] most popular works in the entire Mahāyāna literature, and they well deserve their popularity. The *Śikṣā* is a compendium of the doctrines of the Mahāyāna, especially of the Mādhyamika. The entire work is a string of excerpts from important Sūtras, most of which are now lost in the original. Śānti Deva supplies 27 verses that serve as the Chapter headlines under which the citations from the Sūtras are arranged. Śānti Deva's pre-occupation, in this and the *Bodhicaryāvatāra*, is with spiritual discipline, the cultivation of the Bodhicitta. These two works are our chief sources for the Mādhyamika path of spiritual realisation. The ninth chapter of the *Bodhicaryāvatāra* called *Prajñāpāramitā* is extremely valuable for a knowledge of the metaphysics of the Mādhyamika. Like Candrakīrti, Śānti Deva is consistent in following the Prasanga method, and he is as thorough in his criticism[4] of Vijñānavāda.

A very high order of spiritual serenity and detachment pervades his works. One is invariably reminded of the *Imitation of Christ* in reading the *Bodhicaryāvatāra,* which is the stronger in appeal, as it is born of deep philosophical insight. Devotion (bhakti) to the Buddhas and Bodhisattvas, and confession of one's transgressions (papadeśanā) before them are enjoined as part of spiritual purification. This is by no means an innovation; Nāgārjuna's *Catuḥstava* is in the same strain.

4. In Śāntarakṣita and Kamalaśīla we find a new phase in the development of the Mādhyamika system. They accept the Sautrāntika-Vijñānavāda position with regard to the empirical, and the

[1] Ed. by C. Bendall and published in the Bib. Budd. No. 1. An English translation of this by Bendall & Rouse is available; London, 1922.

[2] Text with Prajñākaramati's *Pañjikā* edited by Poussin in the Bib. Indica. The popularity of this work is evinced by the fact that as many as 11 commentaries have been written on this. The *Pañjikā* of Prajñākaramati (*c.* A.D. 1078) is the one extant in Sanskrit, and is one of the very best.

[3] Tāranātha p. 165 and Buston, Vol. II, pp. 163, 166, speak of 3 works of Śānti Deva, *Śikṣāsamuccaya, Sūtra-samuccayya* and *Bodhicaryāvatāra*. Dr. Vaidya (in his *Études sur Ārya Deva* etc.) suggests that *Śikṣāsamuccaya* refers to the 27 Kārikās of Śānti Deva forming the skeleton of the work and the *Sūtra Samuccaya* are the extracts from the Mahāyāna Sūtras which form the bulk of the present *Śikṣā*. This enumeration might have had its origin in Śānti Deva's own reference to Nāgārjuna's *Sūtra Samuccaya* and a second one of his own. See Winternitz op. cit. p. 366 n.

[4] BCA pp. 389 ff.

Mādhyamika with regard to the ultimate reality. They represent a syncretism of the Mādhyamika with the Yogācāra.

The evidence for our contention is two-fold: the nature of their works and the testimony of Tibetan historians. The entire structure of the *Tattvasaṅgraha* is Mādhyamika in character; every chapter of it is devoted to the examination (parīkṣā) of a particular category or system; refutation is the predominant note. The prefatory verses in the beginning are an echo of Nāgārjuna's opening verse in the *Mādhyamika Kārikās*. Śāntarakṣita makes his obeisance to Buddha—the foremost among teachers—who has taught the Pratītya Samutpāda[1] that is characterised by negative predicates. It has been pointed out that at places the author shows his manifest inclination to Vijñānavāda.[2] But he likewise expounds the doctrine of momentariness, svalakṣaṇa etc. All this can be explained on the hypothesis that Śāntarakṣita accepts the Vijñānavāda contention about the non-existence of objects from the empirical (vyāvahārika) point of view.

Besides the *Tattvasaṅgraha*, Śāntarakṣita has also written *Mādhyamikālaṅkāra Kārikā*[3] and its Vṛtti, on which there is the commentary (*Pañjikā*) by his disciple, Kamalaśīla. His other works are on Tantra and on Prajñāpāramitā. There is no independent work on Vijñānavāda as such.

The evidence of Buston and other Tibetan historians almost settles the issue. We read: "Buddhapālita and Candrakīrti are the chief representatives of the Mādhyamika-prāsangika school. The teacher Bhavya and the rest are the Mādhyamika-Sautrāntikas. Jñānagarbha, Śrīgupta, Śāntarakṣita, Kamalaśīla, Haribhadra and others belong to the school of the Yogācāra-Mādhyamikas."[4]

[1] Cf. the opening stanzas of the *Tattvasaṁgraha* which serve as the key to the whole book with that of the *Mādhyamika Kārikās*:
cf. prakṛtīśobhayātmādi-vyāpāra-*rahitaṁ* calam; . . .
yaḥ pratītya-samutpādaṁ jagāda gadatāṁ varaḥ
taṁ sarvajñaṁ praṇamyāyaṁ kriyate *Tattvasaṁgrahaḥ*
with
anirodham anutpādam— . . .
yaḥ pratītyasamutpādaṁ prapañcopaśamaṁ śivam;
deśayāmāsa sambuddhas tam vande vadatām varam. MK (Opening Verse).

[2] See both the English and Samskrit Intr. to the *Tattvasaṁgraha* pp. xxi ff and 14 ff.

[3] See Buston, Vol. II, p. 136; Bhattacharya, *Āgama Śāstra* p. lxxvi.

[4] Buston, Vol. II, p. 135. Poussin, writing about Bhāvaviveka (MCB, ii, p. 67), says: that the Tibetans divided the Svātantrikas into two branches;

Dr. Obermiller in a note quotes from the work of Tson-kha-pa's pupil Khai-dub the following: ". . . Thereafter, the teacher Śāntarakṣita composed the *Mādhyamikālaṅkāra* and laid the foundation of another school of the Mādhyamikas which denies the Empirical Reality of the External world, acknowledges the introspective perception, but on the other hand does not consider consciousness to have an Ultimate Reality (differing in this from the Yogācāra-Vijñānavādins). The *Mādhyamikāloka* and the 3 *Bhāvanākramas* of Kamalaśīla, as well as the texts of Vimuktasena, Haribhandra, Buddhajñānapāda, Abhayakara Gupta etc., agree with Śāntirakṣita with the main standpoint (which is that of the Yogācāra-Mādhyamika-Svātantrika, whereas Bhāvaviveka and Jñānagarbha express the point of view of the Sautrāntika-Mādhyamika-Svātantrikas."[1]

Śāntarakṣita and Kamalaśīla[2] introduced and spread Buddhism in Tibet. Owing to their efforts and those of other teachers such as Dīpaṁkara Śrījñāna (Atīśa), the Mādhyamika has continued to be the dominant philosophy in Tibet and Mongolia to this day. We are also told that even in distant Japan it consituted the faith of the Sanron[3] sect.

Svātantrika-Sautrāntika (Bhāvaviveka etc.) and Svātantrika-Yogācāra (Śāntarakṣita and others). The distinction is based on their conception of empirical reality only.

[1] Buston, Vol. II, p. 136 n; see also Obermiller's *The Doctrine of the Prajñāpāramitā*, p. 90 n.

[2] Śāntarakṣita lived between 705–762 and Kamalaśīla, 713–763. For a discussion of the dates and the personal life of these great teachers see Dr. Bhattacharya's Foreword to the *Tattvasaṁgraha*, G.O.S. XXX–XXXI, Baroda.

[3] See H.I.L. Vol. II, p. 351.

CHAPTER FOUR

THE INFLUENCE OF THE MĀDHYAMIKA DIALECTIC

I INFLUENCE OF THE MĀDHYAMIKA ON VIJÑĀNAVĀDA

PHILOSOPHY never returns to its former placid state after the shock of a great philosopher. It is again a saying of Hegel that the opposition that a philosophy evokes is evidence of its vitality and fruitfulness. The Śūnyatā—advayavāda—of the Mādhyamika had come to stay. It was generally accepted that the Real is Absolute—at once transcendent of empirical determinations and immanent in phenomena as their innermost essence. A necessary distinction had also to be made between what is in itself and what appears to untutored perception. Absolutism entails the distinction between the paramārtha and the vyāvahārika; it formulates the doctrine of two 'truths'; it also implies a theory of illusion.

These basic ideas of the Mādhyamika were accepted; but there was a reaction against what appeared to some as its extremism and unqualified negation of phenomena. The Idealism of the Yogācāra (Vijñānavāda) school has to be understood as a significant modification of the Mādhyamika Śūnyatā on a constructive basis. The formula now is: That which appears is real but not the manner of its appearance;[1] *that which* is devoid is real, while that *of* which it is devoid is unreal. . . .[2] 'All is real' or 'All is nothing' are both incorrect forms of śūnyatā. The rope is inherently devoid of the 'snake'-appearance, which is foreign to it; but it is not devoid of its own

[1] yat khyāti paratantro'sau yathā khyāti sa kalpitaḥ;
pratyayādhīnavṛttitvāt kalpanāmātra-bhāvataḥ.
tasya khyātur yathākhyānaṁ yā sadā vidyamānatā;
jñeyaḥ sa pariniṣpanna-svabhāvo'nanyathātvataḥ:
Trisvabhāva Nirdeśa, 2, 3.

[2] aviparītaṁ śūnyatālakṣaṇam udbhāvitaṁ: yac chūnyaṁ tasya sadbhāvād, *yena* śūnyaṁ tasya tatrābhāvāt. sarvabhāvaḥ sarvābhavo vā viparītaṁ śūnyatālakṣaṇaṁ śūnyatāyā evābhāvaprasangāt. MVBT. p. 13.

intrinsic nature as rope.[1] With this logic, the Vijñānavādins contend that the reality of vijñāna (consciousness) must be accepted as it cannot be denied at all, while the duality of subject and object with which it is apparently infected must be considered non-existent; śūnyatā[2] applies to this unreal aspect. The real is identified with vijñāna.

The Vijñānavādin maintains two contentions; Vijñāna is *real*, not apparent; vijñāna *alone* is real, not the object. The first is against the Mādhyamika, for whom both the knowing consciousness and the object known are relative to each other, and are therefore nothing in themselves, i.e. unreal. The second is against the realist (like the Ābhidharmika) who uncritically accepts the object as real on a par with vijñāna. Both are extreme positions, and the Vijñānavāda steers a middle course between them.[3]

It is convinced of the unreality of the object on certain plausible grounds: (1) There is want of conformity between the usual form of knowledge (viz. chair, table etc.) and the object which is the atom, singly or in combination. The cognition is of the gross object (sthūla-pratibhāsa); but the atom cannot serve as the object-condition (ālambana pratyaya) for the cognition.[4] What appears in knowledge has no counterpart outside, and what is supposedly outside does not appear in knowledge. The whole or a real combination consisting of parts is not accepted, as the Nyāya-Vaiśeṣika does; the Vaibhāṣika-Sautrāntika theory had already condemned the reality of the avayavī (whole). (2) The manifest difficulties inherent in accounting for cognition on a dualistic basis, viz., knowledge here and object there with a sārūpya relation (representation) between them and the

[1] yathā rajjuḥ śūnyā sarpatvabhāvena tatsvabhāvatvabhāvāt sarvakālaṁ śūnyā, na tu rajjusvabhāvena. tathehāpi. MVBT. p. 12.

[2] Cf. the first Kārikā of the *Madhyāntavibhāga*:
abhūtaparikalpo'sti dvayaṁ tatra na vidyate;
śūnyatā vidyate tv atra tasyām api sa vidyate. MVBT. p. 9.

[3] vijñānavad vijñeyam api dravyata eveti kecin manyante;
vijñeyavad vijñānam api saṁvṛtita eva na paramārthata
ity asya dviprakārasyāpy ekāntavādasya pratiṣedhārthaḥ prakaraṇārambhaḥ. *Triṁśikā Bhāṣya*, p. 15.

[4] na tadekaṁ na cānekaṁ viṣayaḥ paramāṇusaḥ;
na ca te saṁhatā yasmāt paramāṇur na siddhyati. *Viṁśatikā*, 11
Cf. also yady apīndriya-vijñapter grāhyāṁśaḥ (aṇavaḥ) kāraṇam bhavet;
atadābhatayā tasya nākṣavad viṣayaḥ sa tu (aṇavaḥ).
yadābhāsā na tasmāt sā dravyābhāvād dvicandravat, evaṁ bāhya-dvayaṁ caiva na yuktaṁ matigocaraḥ. *Ālambana Parīkṣā*. 1, 2. See also TS. pp. 551 ff.

CHAPTER FOUR

THE INFLUENCE OF THE MĀDHYAMIKA DIALECTIC

I INFLUENCE OF THE MĀDHYAMIKA ON VIJÑĀNAVĀDA

PHILOSOPHY never returns to its former placid state after the shock of a great philosopher. It is again a saying of Hegel that the opposition that a philosophy evokes is evidence of its vitality and fruitfulness. The Śūnyatā—advayavāda—of the Mādhyamika had come to stay. It was generally accepted that the Real is Absolute—at once transcendent of empirical determinations and immanent in phenomena as their innermost essence. A necessary distinction had also to be made between what is in itself and what appears to untutored perception. Absolutism entails the distinction between the paramārtha and the vyāvahārika; it formulates the doctrine of two 'truths'; it also implies a theory of illusion.

These basic ideas of the Mādhyamika were accepted; but there was a reaction against what appeared to some as its extremism and unqualified negation of phenomena. The Idealism of the Yogācāra (Vijñānavāda) school has to be understood as a significant modification of the Mādhyamika Śūnyatā on a constructive basis. The formula now is: That which appears is real but not the manner of its appearance;[1] *that which* is devoid is real, while that *of* which it is devoid is unreal. . . .[2] 'All is real' or 'All is nothing' are both incorrect forms of śūnyatā. The rope is inherently devoid of the 'snake'-appearance, which is foreign to it; but it is not devoid of its own

[1] yat khyāti paratantro'sau yathā khyāti sa kalpitaḥ;
pratyayādhīnavṛttitvāt kalpanāmātra-bhāvataḥ.
tasya khyātur yathākhyānaṁ yā sadā vidyamānatā;
jñeyaḥ sa pariniṣpanna-svabhāvo'nanyathātvataḥ:
Trisvabhāva Nirdeśa, 2, 3.

[2] aviparītaṁ śūnyatālakṣaṇam udbhāvitaṁ: yac chūnyaṁ tasya sadbhāvād, *yena* śūnyaṁ tasya tatrābhāvāt. sarvabhāvaḥ sarvābhavo vā viparītaṁ śūnyatālakṣaṇaṁ śūnyatāyā evābhāvaprasangāt. MVBT. p. 13.

With his bias in favour of vijñāna as the sole reality, the Yogācāra criticises the Mādhyamika for denying the reality of vijñāna. His most effective argument against the Mādhyamika is that everything may be dialectically analysed away as illusory; but the illusion itself implies the ground on which the illusory construction can take place.[1] Accepting the Śūnyatā[2] of the *Prajñāpāramitās* and even protesting that they interpret it correctly, they modify the Śūnyatā of the Mādhyamika; they give substance to the śūnya by identifying it with Pure Consciousness (vijñapti-matratā) that is devoid of duality (dvaya-śūnyatā). They consider themselves the true Mādhyamika—adopting the middle course between the extremes of Nihilism and Realism.[3] A whole treatise—*The Madhyānta Vibhāga*—is devoted to an elucidation of the Vijñānavāda position in contradistinction to that of others.[4] The Yogācāra-Vijñānavāda school is the third and last comprehensive synthesis of Buddhistic doctrines. It could certainly incorporate the Vaibhāṣika 'dharmas' taking them as citta and caitta (mental states); the Yogācāra even increased the number to a hundred.[5]

The founder of the Yogācāra school is Maitreya(nātha) (A.D. 270–350) whose historicity[6] is now generally accepted. But he is represented solely by his illustrious disciple Asanga (*c.* 350) and his brother Vasubandhu.[7] Their position here corresponds to that of

[1] upacārasya ca nirādhārasya cāsambhavad avaśyaṁ vijñānapariṇāmo vastuto'stīty upagantavyo yatrātmadharmopacāraḥ pravarttate. *Triṁśikā Bhāṣya*, p. 16.

[2] nanv evaṁ sūtra-virodhaḥ, sarvadharmāḥ śūnyā, iti sūtre vacanāt. nāsti virodhaḥ, yasmād dvayaṁ tatra na vidyate etc. MVBT. p. 9.

[3] na śūnyaṁ nāpi cāśūnyaṁ sarvaṁ vidhīyate Prajñāpāramitādiṣu sattvād iti, asattvād iti . . . madhyamā pratipac ca seti . . . sarvāstitve sarvanāstitve vānta eva syān na madhyamā pratipat. MVBT. pp. 13–14. See also p. 18.

[4] A comparison between the Vijñānavāda and the Mādhyamika Absolutes and the logical merits of their respective standpoints is undertaken in a subsequent chapter entitled "The Mādhyamika, Vijñānavāda and Vedānta Absolutism." (Chapter XIII).

[5] See McGovern: *Manual of Buddhism* pp. 109 ff. Pt. Aiyāswāmi: *Ālambana Parīkṣā* Appendix C. pp. 111 ff. This gives a restoration from Chinese of Vasubandhu's *Mahāyāna Śatadharma Vidyāmukham*.

[6] See Tucci—*Some Aspects of the Doctrines of Maitreyanātha and Asanga*. pp. 2 ff. H. Ui and, previous to him, M. M. H. P. Sastri have established the historicity of Maitreyanātha.

[7] There is difference of opinion with regard to the date of Vasubandhu. "The two most important are those that place him between A.D. 280–360 and between A.D. 420–500." (Foreword to TS. p. LXVI). The former is the one now generally accepted.

Nāgārjuna and Āryadeva in the Mādhyamika system; they founded and systematised the Yogācāra philosophy. The Yogācāra was continued by the Vijñānavāda of Dignāga and Dharmakīrti who both had strong Sautrāntika leanings; this is reflected in their logical works.

Asanga is a very interesting and dominating figure in the development of Mahāyāna philosophy. His three works *Mahāyāna Sūtrālaṁkāra*, *Dharma Dharmatāvibhanga* and *Madhyānta Vibhāga* are from the Yogācāra point of view and interpret Śūnyatā on an idealistic basis.

In the *Abhisamayālaṁkāra*, not a single word is said about the store-consciousness (ālaya vijñāna), about the three aspects of existence, etc. The main teaching is that of non-substantiality and Relativity of all elements of existence, without any limitations whatever. This is the strict Mādhyamika point of view. . . .

The *Uttaratantra* also is a treatise devoted to an exposition of the strictest Absolutism of the Mādhyamika type. Obermiller makes this interesting observation with regard to this: We have thus two categories of texts to consider: On one side there are the *Saṁdhinirmocana*, the *Laṅkāvatāra*, etc., containing the Yogācāra teachings and a compromising interpretation of the Prajñāpāramitā; the three Yogācāra treatises of Maitreya, and the whole literature founded upon them. On the other we have the pure uncompromising Monism of the Prajñāpāramitā, summarised in the *Abhisamayālaṁkāra*, brought to a further development in the *Jñāna-āloka-alaṁkāra*, the *Śrī-mālā-devīsiṅhanāda* and similar Sūtras and fully expounded in the *Uttaratantra*. As the central figure here we have the Saint Asanga, as the expounder and the interpreter of two different systems. How is this strange position of one of the most celebrated Buddhist ācāryas to be explained? What was Asanga's real standpoint?

In our introduction to the *Uttaratantra* we have indicated two possibilities, viz. that there may have been an evolution in the conceptions of Asanga, from Idealism to pure Monism, or that he could have simply written his works from different points of view. Before we are put in possession of new materials that will help us in the solution of the question, we shall have to state merely that Asanga 'has evidently fluctuated between the two divisions into which the Mahāyāna was split.'[1]

Asanga is an important figure in one other respect. He seems to be one of the leaders of the Tantric Buddhism (Vajrayāna), if his connection with the *Guhya Samāja Tantra* (*Tathāgata Guhyaka*) is

[1] *The Doctrine of Prajñāpāramitā*. pp. 99–100.

accepted.[1] Tantra is certainly much earlier than Asanga, and the basic ideas and practices have been present in all ages. Tantra is the unique combination of mantra, ritual, worship and yoga on an absolutistic basis. It is both philosophy and religion, and aims at the transmutation of human personality, by tantric practices suited to the spiritual temperament and needs of the individual, into the Absolute. What the student of philosophy, especially of the Mādhyamika system, is interested in is to point out that it is Śūnyatā that provided the metaphysical basis for the rise of Tantra. With its phenomenalising aspect, karuṇā (corresponding to the Hindu conception of śakti), the formless Absolute (Śūnya) manifests itself as the concrete world. But the forms neither exhaust nor do they bring down the absolute. It is through these forms again that man ascends and finds his consummation with the universal principle. The various deities, each with a physical form, a bīja mantra (a secret symbol), a mode of worship etc., constitute the pantheon from which Buddhist, Hindu and even Jaina Tantras have drawn, sometimes through mutual borrowing. It is not relevant to our work to enter into these details. It is however the Śūnya of the Mādhyamika that made Tantricism possible. It may thus be said to have initiated a new phase in Buddhist philosophy and religion; this had its due influence on the corresponding phase on the Brāhmanical side.[2]

II RELATION BETWEEN THE MĀDHYAMIKA AND VEDĀNTA

With regard to the influence of the Mādhyamika on Vedānta we are on less sure ground. It is a matter of conjecture and presumption whether and to what extent there had been borrowing on either side. The question is vast and complicated; scant justice can be done to it in the compass of a few pages. For the sake of completeness however, we have to indicate the possible influence of the Mādhyamika on the development of Vedānta. Only the barest outline can be attempted here.

[1] See Dr. B. Bhattacharya's Intr. to the *Guhya Samāja* pp. XXIV ff.

[2] "There is hardly a Tantra in Hindu literature," says Dr. Bhattacharya in his *Buddhist Esoterism* (p. 163), "which is not tinged with Buddhistic ideas of Vajrayāna and its leading tenets, including the Mahāsukhavāda; it is no exaggeration to say that some of Tantras of the Hindus, such as the *Mahācīna-krama-tantra* are entirely Buddhist in origin. . . . It is thus amply proved that the Buddhist Tantras greatly influenced the Hindu Tantric literature."

To appreciate the possible influence, we may begin by considering the nature of the revolution in Aupaniṣada thought ushered in by Śaṅkara and Gauḍapāda. It is unfortunate that we have no extant Vedānta exegetical literature prior to them. The main features of the older Vedānta have to be pieced together from references to and citations from the commentaries of those writers found in the works of Śaṅkara and the non-advaita Vedāntins, especially Rāmānuja. We have evidence of the existence of these Vedānta teachers beginning shortly after the author of the *Brahma Sūtras*: Bodhāyana, Upavarṣa, Guha Deva, Kapardī, Bhāruci, Bhartṛmitra, Brahmanandī, Tanka, Dramiḍa, Brahmadatta, Bhartṛprapañca, and Sundara Pāṇḍya. Competent scholars[1] have gleaned the views of these and have tried to present a picture of pre-Śaṅkara Vedānta. The views of Brahma Datta and Bhartṛprapañca deserve special notice; Śaṅkara criticises, at numerous places[2] in his bhāṣya on the *Bṛhadāraṇyaka*, the views of Bhartṛprapañca. Ignoring minor differences and details, we may characterise pre-Śaṅkara (Gauḍapāda) Vedānta as follows:

(1) Upholding the sole reality of Brahman against the Sāṁkhya dualism, it however accepted modification of Brahman (pariṇāma), and even ascribed parts to Brahman. The Upaniṣad texts regarding creation are taken literally; jīva (the individual) and the world of nature are conceived as real parts (aṁśa) of Brahman.

(2) Brahman was conceived to have qualities and aspects. It has concrete form (rūpa), and is also formless (arūpa). It is one as the whole and many with regard to its aspects; unity and diversity are not mutually incompatible.[3] While difference in kind was denied, internal diversity

[1] MM. Pt. Gopinath Kaviraj makes a comprehensive survey of Pre-Śaṅkara Vedānta in his Introduction, in Hindi, (pp. 8 ff) to the translation of *Br. Sūtra Śāṅkara Bhāṣya with the Ratna Prabhā* (*Acyut*, Vol. III, 4). This article, which is almost a fair-sized book, deserves to be more widely known for the wealth of information and fruitful suggestions.

See also Hiriyanna: *Brahma Datta—an Old Vedāntin.* Proc. IV. Oriental Conf. (pp. 787 ff); *Bhartṛprapañca—Ind. Ant.* 1924, pp. 76–86 and Proc. III *Orient. Conf.* pp. 439 ff.

[2] *Bṛ. Up. Bhāṣya* (Ānandāśrama Edn.): pp. 150 ff., 190, 207, 236, 293 ff, 323 ff, 331, 560, 622–3 etc.

[3] atra kecid vyācakṣate: ātmavastunaḥ svata evaikatvaṁ nānātvam ca, yathā gor godravyatayaikatvaṁ sāsnādīnām dharmāṇām parasparato bhedaḥ. yathā sthūleṣvekatvaṁ nānātvaṁ ca taṭhā niravauaveṣv amūrtavastuṣv ekatvaṁ nānātvaṁ cānumeyam. *Bṛ. Up. Bhāṣya* p. 622. See also *Br. Sūtr. Bhāṣya* on II, i, 14. ekatvaṁ nānātvaṁ cobhayam api satyam eva, vṛkṣa ityekatvam śākhā iti nānātvam, etc.

and even individual distinctions were admitted. The resultant philosophy could be called the theory of Identity with difference (Viśiṣṭābheda) or both Identity and difference (bhedābheda).

(3) Freedom is not through knowledge alone. On various grounds all the pre-Śaṅkara Vedāntins have accorded an important and even equal status to upāsanā (devotional contemplation) and karma (works). They advocated the combination of knowledge and works (jñāna-karma samuccaya-vāda) which Śaṅkara and his disciple, Sureśvarācārya, have repeatedly refuted. Probably also, they did not advocate complete identity between jīva and brahman in the state of mukti, but only similarity (sārūpya).

(4) As a consequence of the above position, they had the closest affinity with the Pūrva Mīmāṁsā; the enquiry into Brahman was considered an integral part of, or at least a necessary sequel to, the karma jijñāsā (Pūrva Mīmāṁsā). It is Śaṅkara who makes a total break from this tradition, and comes in for criticism at the hands of non-advaita Vedāntins.[1]

(5) The nature of avidyā[2] is hardly clear. It was taken as a function of brahman to become many; there was real transformation and re-transformation of the world into Brahman again (prapañca-pravilaya-vāda).[3] The notion of appearance (adhyāsa) does not seem to have been understood or appreciated.

No doubt, there are many other differences; but these are enough to indicate the distinction we want to draw between pre-Śaṅkara Vedānta and Śaṅkara's standpoint. The former did not formulate a theory of appearance (vivartavāda); no need was felt to draw the distinction between the paramārtha and the vyāvahārika or of the texts into para and apara; Pre-Śaṅkara Vedānta is best described as ekatvavāda, monism; it is not advaita—Absolutism. Advaitism is the conscious rejection of duality and difference as illusory. Brahman is established, not positively, but by the denial of duality.

This is the nature of the revolution in the Aupaniṣada tradition ushered in by Śaṅkara. All these are present in essentials in Gauḍapāda's *Māṇḍūkya Kārikās*. He very explicitly declares that

[1] Cf. *Śrī Bhāṣya* I, i, 1.

[2] Cf. *Bṛ. Up. Bhāṣya* (p. 330) avidyāyāś ca svata utthānam ūṣarādivad ity ādikalpanānupapannaiva.

[3] See Śaṅkara's Bhāṣya on *Br. Sūt.* III, ii, 21 for a criticism of this doctrine and its implications.

duality (dvaita) is unreal (mithyā) and advaita (non-duality) is ultimate (paramārtha);[1] there is complete unqualified identity between jīva and Brahman; their difference is only apparent and is circumstanced[2] by delimiting adjuncts (upādhi). There is no creation or parcelling out of Brahman, and all accounts of creation in the scriptures are to be taken as but devices to teach the identity of brahman and the world.[3] Gauḍapāda makes, in the first three books of his *Kārikās*, a sustained and successful attempt to show the deeper meaning of the Upaniṣadic texts.[4] By appeal to arguments too, he shows plausibly how a thing could appear and be mistaken as real; he adduces as examples dream-objects, 'rope-snake' etc; ajāti-vāda,[5] vivartavāda and māyāvāda are all established as the true import of the Vedānta.

Śaṅkara's greatness consists in his seizing upon these suggestions and coherently working them into a system. Even if his identity with Śaṅkara, the commentator on the *Kārikās*, is questioned, as it can well be, there can be no doubt that our Śaṅkara was fully acquainted with the *Kārikās*; he quotes two verses[6] from them, and reverentially refers to Gauḍapāda as the master conversant with the Vedānta-tradition.[7] Tradition also makes out that Gauḍapāda was the teacher of his teacher.

The question can now be put; pre-Gauḍapāda-Śaṅkara Vedānta is monistic, not advaitic; how could it suddenly take an absolutistic turn? Two hypotheses are possible: one that of borrowing, or at least of copying, from the absolutism and dialectic already well-established in the Mādhyamika and Vijñānavāda systems; and second, that owing to its own inner dynamism the Upaniṣadic tradition too was heading towards absolutism. There is nothing incongruent in either of the hypotheses, nor are they mutually exclusive. But it is to be noted that after its criticism of the Sāṁkhya dualism and establishment of the reality of Brahman, there was not much development

[1] māyāmātram idaṁ dvaitam advaitaṁ paramārthataḥ. (I, 17) advaite yojayet smṛtim (II, 36); advaitaṁ paramārtho hi (III, 18) etc.

[2] See *Māṇḍ. Kā.* II 3–7, 13–14.

[3] Ibid. III 15.

[4] *Māṇḍ. Kāri.* II 3, 11–15; III 23–26.

[5] Ibid. II 32, III 2 ff. III 20 ff.

[6] "anādi māyayā" is quoted in *Br. Sūt. Bhāṣya* II, 1, 9 and "mṛlloha visphulinga" etc. in II, iv, 14 (ibid).

[7] atroktaṁ vedantārtha-sampradāyavidbhir ācāryaiḥ.

in the Aupaniṣada school; it produced a considerable amount of exegetical literature and evolved a mīmāṁsā, but as regards originality and striking a new path, it remained stagnant and sluggish. There is, however, nothing inherently impossible for the older Vedānta-thought in developing into advaitism; for, if the radical pluralism of earlier Buddhism could lead to the absolutism of the Mādhyamika, a similar development could happen here too, perhaps with greater ease. The Upaniṣads themselves unmistakably suggest the sole reality of Brahman; difference is decried as apparent; Śaṅkara's reference to Gauḍapāda, as one knowing the tradition (sampradāyavid),[1] may mean that there was an advaitic school of Vedānta too, although it might not have been a dominant one. It is possible, even probable, that such a school existed and exerted its influence on the Mādhyamika and that it became the dominant Vedāntic school owing to the efforts of Gauḍapāda and Śaṅkara.

Though this hypothesis of evolving absolutism without external help cannot be ruled out completely, it is however a fact that absolutism (advayavāda) had already been evolved in the anātma tradition. There were lively interchanges between the Buddhist and the Brāhmanical logicians for centuries. The Mādhyamika and Aupaniṣada schools were not enclosed in water-tight compārtments. We have undeniable evidence of Mādhyamika and Yogācāra influence in the *Māṇḍūkya Kārikās*: The whole problem has been ably and thoroughly treated by Professor Bhattacharya in his *Āgama Śāstra of Gauḍapāda*.[2] The question has been brought as near a solution as our present knowledge of Mahāyāna Buddhism and Vedānta warrants.

The questions about the priority of the *Māṇḍūkya Upaniṣad* to the *Kārikās*, how much of it is Upaniṣad and even the question about the identity of the commentator of the *Kārikās*—Śaṅkara with the Bhagavatpāda, may be waived aside as not germane to our enquiry. One cannot fail to be struck by points of close similarity between the *Kārikās*, especially the IV Chapter of it and Mahāyāna works. These

[1] Gauḍapāda himself uses expressions which indicate that he is following a Vedāntic tradition, e.g. "vedānteṣu vicakṣaṇaiḥ;" "vedapāragaiḥ . . . dṛṣṭaḥ;" "āhur manīṣiṇaḥ" etc.

[2] *The Āgama Śāstra of Gauḍapāda*, ed., translated and annotated by Prof. Vidhushekhara Bhattacharya, Calcutta, 1943; Sanskrit version by the same author, 1950.

fall under three heads: use of technical words[1] which have significant meaning only in Buddhist philosophical literature; verses[2] which are almost verbatim quotations or adaptations from well-known Mādhyamika and Yogācāra works; and third the doctrines like non-origination, the non-predicability of the four kinds of alternatives (sad asad, etc., svataḥ parataḥ etc.) to things, all things being pure and quiescent, the object as creation of citta-spandana (mind-vibration), etc. These are too numerous and persistent to be laid away as accidents and insignificant coincidences. The conclusion is irresistible that in the *Māṇḍūkya Kārikās*, Gauḍapāda, a Vedānta philosopher, is attempting an advaitic interpretation of Vedānta in the light of Mādhyamika and Yogācāra doctrines. He even freely quotes and appeals to them.

This conclusion is however subject to two important considerations—one textual and the other doctrinal. To take the first. We have so far proceeded on the *assumption* that all the four chapters (Āgama, Vaitathya, Advaita and Alātaśānti) organically belong to the *Māṇḍūkya Kārikās*, and are of one authorship. It is to be noted however that in the first three chapters of the *Kārikās*, nothing is said to which any orthodox Vedāntin could take exception as regards language and logical content. In fact, the author of these three chapters impresses us as a keen Vedāntin giving the deeper interpretation of Upaniṣadic texts. His arguments are all Vedāntic, and there is little Buddhistic flavour about them.[3] The examples adduced by him, viz., rope-snake (II, 17–8), ghaṭākāśa (III, 3–7) have become integral to subsequent Vedānta. No Vedānta writer has quoted from the fourth chapter, while verses are quoted from the first three.

[1] sāṁvṛta (II, i, 4, IV 33, IV 57): kalpita saṁvṛti and paramārtha IV 73, 74. dharmāḥ in the sense of elements (IV, 10, 33, 58, 81, 91, 92, 93, 96, 98, 99); ajāti (IV 19, 42 etc.) . . . buddha IV 19, 42, 80, 88, nāyaka IV 98, 99—sambuddha, dvipadāṁ vara IV, 1. prajñapti, saṁkleśa, paratantra (IV 24), abhūtūbhiniveśa IV 79; lokottaram IV 88. Vaiśāradyam IV 94. tāyin—IV 99, advayatā, prapañcopaśama, asparśayoga II 39. II 2.

[2] Quotations from Mādhyamika works: svato vā paroto vā, IV 22, hetor ādiḥ phalam IV 15, asti nāstyasti . . . IV 83, koṭyaś catasraḥ IV 84, ādiśāntāḥ . . . sarvadharmāḥ IV 93.

Quotations from Yogācāra works:
abhūtābhiniveśo'sti dvayaṁ tatra na vidyate—IV 75.
cittaspanditam evedam, IV 72; cittaṁ na saṁspṛśatyartham IV 26.

All references are traced to their original sources with relentless thoroughness in the *Āgama Śāstra*, especially in the annotations to Book IV.

[3] Such expressions as sāṁvṛta, advaya, prapañcopaśama, ajāti, vikalpa etc., do occur; but on such slender foundations nothing can be built.

Bhāvaviveka and Śāntarakṣita[1] have also quoted, in their exposition of the Aupaniṣada school, from this part alone.

We breathe a different atmosphere in chapter IV (*Alāta Śānti*). Professor Bhattacharya himself observes that "in Book IV Gauḍapāda has discussed nothing directly of the Vedānta, as nothing Vedāntic will be found therein; even such words as brahman and ātman are not to be found there."[2] This part begins with a salutation (mangalācaraṇa) in praise of Buddha (dvipadāṁ varam) and ends with another. This shows that it is an independent work. With regard to their content, the Professor remarks that the relationship between this and the previous books is not "such as between a work and its different chapters."[3] Ajātivāda is established again, but this time as the true import of the Buddha's teachings. Almost every line of this Book IV has reference to the Mādhyamika and Vijñānavāda treatises. Everywhere we are told that such is the teaching of the Buddhas, and such is not. It can be considered as an attempt to synthesise the two schools of Mahāyāna. On internal evidence alone, we may treat the *Alātā Śānti Prakaraṇa* of the *Māṇḍūkya Kārikās* as an independent work, written most probably by a Buddhist. Therefore establishing a concordance between this part (Book IV) and Mahāyāna works proves little; for it is concordance between two Buddhistic works, and not between a Vedānta treatise and Buddhism. Professor Bhattacharya comes almost to the same conclusion when he says: "This leads one to think that Book IV is an independent work" and even more drastically: "Thus we arrive at the conclusion that these four Books are four independent treatises and are put together in a volume under the title of *Āgama Śāstra*."[4]

If the independence of the Books, especially of Book IV, were accepted,[5] it alters our contention with regard to the alleged borrowing. We have no *direct-textual* evidence for that. We can only presume and conjecture from the acknowledged priority of the Mādhyamika and Yogācāra advayavāda to the advaita of Gaudapāda and

[1] See *Āgama Śāstra* pp. lxxv–vi.

[2] Ibid—p. cxliv.

[3] *Āgama Śāstra* p. iv.

[4] *Āgama Śāstra*, p. lvii.

[5] By what chance these independent works were brought together and were foisted upon one author is a matter of conjecture. The similarity of form (ajātivāda and advayavāda) might have been responsible for this accidental alliance.

Śaṅkara and from the absence of such a trend in their predecessors.

This brings us to the doctrinal consideration. We have been talking of borrowing, influence and relationship in rather general terms. It is necessary to define the possible nature of the borrowing, granting that it did take place. It is our contention that there could not be acceptance of any doctrinal content by either side from the other, as each had a totally different background of tradition and conception of reality. The Vedāntins stake everything on the ātman (Brahman) and accept the authority of the Upaniṣads. We have pointed out at length the nairātmya standpoint of Buddhism and its total opposition to the ātman (soul, substance, the permanent and universal) in any form. This barrier was always there. Besides, it is readily assumed that there is no difference between the Absolute of Vedānta and that of the Mādhyamika or Vijñānavāda.[1] If we carefully analyse their respective standpoints, we would find that all these agree with regard to the logical *form* of the absolute, as free of empirical determinations and as the essence of phenomena and also as realised in an intuitive experience. But they differ with regard to the *nature* of the absolute (that with which they identify it) and the mode of their approach. It can only make for confusion to ignore the differences.[2]

Consistent with the above contention, we can only expect the Vedāntin to have profited by the technique or method of the Mādhyamika. He had before him the Mādhyamika distinction of paramārtha and saṁvṛti, of texts into nītārtha and neyārtha, his reaching the real by the method of negating the unreal appearance etc. The Mādhyamika and Yogācāra also had a theory of illusion to account for the emergence of appearance. Knowledge of this turn in Buddhism

[1] This is the usual opinion about these absolutes. MM. Pt. Kaviraj, however, makes the pregnant suggestion (op. cit. p. 73) that these are not identical, and that though they are all absolutism, yet the Śūnyavāda of the Mādhyamika, Vijñānādvayavāda of the Yogācāras, Śaktyadvayavāda of the Śāktas, the Śabdādvayavāda of the Grammarians and the older Vedāntins like Maṇḍana Misra differ in themselves to a greater or lesser extent. The Advaita taught by Gauḍapāda has its own special feature. In the circumstances, it is difficult to estimate whether and to what extent Śaṅkara has been influenced by other systems.

[2] What is real for one is appearance for another. Throughout this work, the characterisitic standpoint of the Mādhyamika has been kept in view, and distinctions between the Mādhyamika, Vedānta and Vijñānavāda have been drawn with regard to important doctrines. The problem is discussed in a separate chapter (Chap. XIII) entitled *The Mādhyamika, Vijñānavāda and Vedānta Absolutism.*

must have sent the Vedāntin back to his own texts and enabled him to perceive the truer meaning of the Upaniṣads in advaitism. Presumably, there has been borrowing of technique[1] and not of tenets.

[1] Śrī Harṣa, as is well known, employs the Mādhyamika method in his *Khaṇḍana Khaṇḍa Khādya* and even says so in so many words. Our explanation of similarity of method and technique accounts for the accusation by Bhāskara and other non-advaita Vedāntins against Śaṅkara and his followers as introducing Mahāyānika-naya (praveśa) and as being Buddhists in disguise (pracchanna-bauddhas); it at once preserves the doctrinal originality of the Vedānta.

PART II

The Dialectic as System of Philosophy

CHAPTER FIVE

THE STRUCTURE OF THE MĀDHYAMIKA DIALECTIC

I ORIGIN AND PLACE OF THE DIALECTIC

It is difficult to conceive of two view-points more diametrically opposed to each other in their metaphysics than the ātmavāda and the nairātmyavāda. The Sāṁkhya and the older Vedānta representing the ātma tradition advocated and formulated the substance-view—the supremacy of being. They emphasised the permanent and universal aspect of experience; they understood the effect as identical with the cause (satkāryavāda). Gauḍapāda and Saṁkara merely bring out the implications of this standpoint when they declare change, difference and plurality as illusory; they formulate the complementary doctrine of avidyā to explain the appearance of difference.

For the earlier Buddhism, the real as the efficient (arthakriyākāri) could not be permanent; only the momentary (kṣaṇika) is real. Things are different at different times; there is no duration; permanence is a subjective construction put upon discrete momentary entities. There are as many entities as there are distinguishable aspects. Each entity is unique; the universal is an appearance. With a Humean metaphysics, the Buddhists worked out the complementary doctrine of conceptual construction largely on Kantian lines. Rejecting the permanent, they elaborated the doctrine of Elements. Causation was taken as the co-ordination of these separate elements (dharma-saṁketa).

It is significant that both the Buddhist and the Brāhmanical systems establish their real by a critique of causality; this is the central problem in Indian philosophy. Curiously enough, both views lead, when consistently pressed, to the same predicament.[1] If the effect were identical with the cause, there is no production, as nothing new emerges; if they were different, there is no continuity between cause and effect. The Mādhyamika shows by his dialectic that not only causality but every category or doctrine leads to contradiction.

[1] Many Mādhyamika treatises begin the dialectic by an analysis of causation. cf. MK. I (*Pratyaya-Prakaraṇa*), BCA. (IX). TS (Opening Chapters).

These views appear to give the truth as long as we are not reflective, critical. Criticism dissolves their plausibility, and establishes the real as Absolute, as devoid of thought-determinations (śūnya).

Further, the Mādhyamika urges that the earlier Buddhism was critical by halves. It was right in denying the reality of substance (pudgalanairātmya); but it was dogmatic when it converted this nairātmya into a *doctrine* of the reality of discrete momentary entities (dharma). Cutting up the real into a series of rigid self-sufficient entities does not make for the production of one thing from another. Each entity being absolutely self-contained, there is no dependance, movement or change; the effect becomes a fortuitous emergence. As Nāgārjuna says:[1] "If you take entities to exist by themselves (svabhāvāt), you take them as unconditioned, uncaused." If things depend on each other, as the doctrine of pratītyasamutpāda should mean, they are relative to each other *in nature*, and not merely in point of time. There are no rigid elements of existence. If things cannot be conceived as permanent, they are not momentary either. Buddha has taught the doctrine of momentariness not as an ultimate proposition, but as a step leading to relativity (śūnyatā).[2]

Like the Advaitism of Śaṅkara, the Mādhyamika is a revolutionary interpretation of Buddhism. It deepened Buddhism by analysing fully its implications. It is a sustained attempt to synthesise the teaching of the Buddhist scriptures by the adoption of the transcendental (paramārtha) and the phenomenal (saṁvṛti)[3] standpoints. Texts are divided into neyārtha and nītārtha, corresponding to Śaṅkara's distinction of parā and aparā śrutis.

Pratītyasamutpāda, the cardinal doctrine of Buddhism, means, according to the Mādhyamika, the dependance of things on each other, their having no nature or reality of their own (nissvabhāvatva or śūnya).[4] The Mādhyamika dialectic was born immediately of the

[1] MK. XXIV, 16, 17.

[2] BCA. IX, 7: lokāvatāraṇārthaṁ ca bhāvā nāthena deśitāḥ; tattvataḥ kṣaṇikā naite:

The Vijñānavādin also says that the earlier doctrine of elements is a step towards the final denial of the elements too:

tathā pudgala-nairātmya-praveśo hy anyathā punaḥ;
deśanā dharma-nairātmyapraveśaḥ kalpitātmanā.
Viṁśatikā, 10

[3] MK. XXIV, 8, 9. See also BCA. IX, 2.

[4] Cf. the oft-quoted text from the *Laṅkāvatāra Sūtra*:

svabhāvānutpattiṁ saṁdhāya, mahāmate, sarvadharmāḥ.
śūnyā iti mayā deśitaḥ. MKV. p. 504.

criticism of the two radical points of view—the substance-view and the modal view, especially of the latter.[1] But like the Kantian dialectic, the Mādhyamika is a critique of all philosophy.[2]

II THE 'COPERNICAN REVOLUTION' IN INDIAN PHILOSOPHY

The position occupied by the Mādhyamika in Indian philosophy is similar to that of Kant in modern European philosophy. The emergence of criticism in Kant was the direct outcome of the *impasse* created by the two trends of thought, Rationalism and Empiricism. Each had been cultivated for three or four generations with great intensity; they advocated diametrically opposed views about the real and our knowledge of it. A similar, perhaps an intenser, conflict emerged in Indian philosophy by the clash of ātma and anātma views. Dialectic is the consciousness of this conflict in Reason. In Kant are gathered the two trends, Rationalism and Empiricism. Both are species of dogmatism, and the critique is their solution as revealing this dogmatism. Likewise, the Mādhyamika characterizes both the ātma and anātma views as dogmatic (dṛṣṭi). Critically analysed, each dṛṣṭi reveals its inner contradiction. Prajñā (intuitional insight) is the abandonment of all dṛṣṭi. Both the Mādhyamika and Kant can justly be credited with having initiated the critical phase in philosophy in their respective spheres. The Copernican revolution in Indian philosophy was brought about by the Mādhyamika.

For both the Mādhyamika and Kant criticism itself is philosophy. They arrive at the devastating conclusion that speculative metaphysics is untenable. Speculation does not give us knowledge, but only illusion. Neither the Mādhyamika nor Kant has any doctrine or theory of their own. The Mādhyamika is more decided and consistent.[3]

The critical philosophy of Kant led to the rise of the great Idealist

[1] Reference must be made to Part I of the work, especially to Chapters 1–3, for a discussion of the nature and development of the two Traditions (ātma and anātma views) and the consequent origin of the Mādhyamika Dialectic.

[2] *śūnyatā sarvadṛṣṭīnāṁ* proktā nissaraṇaṁ jinaiḥ. MK. XIII, 8. The MK ends with the same note: sarvadṛṣṭiprahāṇāya etc. MK. XXVII, 30.

[3] See *infra* the Chapter on the *Mādhyamika Conception of Philosophy as Prajñāpāramitā.*

Kant is hesitant, and at places states his intention of giving us a system of philosophy. "Such a system of pure (speculative) reason I hope myself to produce under the title of Metaphysics of Nature." *Critique*, p. 14.

and Absolutist systems of Fichte, Hegel and Schopenhauer. Likewise, the two great absolutist systems of India, Vijñānavāda and Vedānta, although they did not accept the Śūnyatā of the Mādhyamika, are still the direct outcome of the Mādhyamika dialectic.[1]

III DIALECTIC—THE CONFLICT OF REASON

'Dialectic' is generally, but incorrectly, applied to any closely reasoned argument or refutation of doctrines. Zeno is considered to be the first discoverer[2] of the dialectic, because he invented irrefutable arguments against motion, change and the void. This only means that he was fully aware of the implications and absurdities of 'Becoming'; it is a critique of Becoming. It is not a critique of Being as well. Zeno refutes others, but is not alive to the shortcomings of his own position. In the *Parmenides* of Plato we find for the first time the beginnings of the dialectic. Therein Plato exhibits, with wearisome detail, the contradictions involved in the notions of 'One' and 'Many,' 'Being' and 'Becoming'; there is also an attempt to get beyond these opposites. If our interpretation of Buddha's 'silence' is accepted, then to Buddha belongs the honour of being the first discoverer of the Dialectic.[3]

Dialectic is a self-conscious spiritual movement; it is necessarily a critique of Reason.[4] This is not possible without the consciousness of the opposition of the thesis and the antithesis. There must be at least two view-points or patterns of interpretation diametrically opposed to each other. A dilemma is not a dialectic, for that is a temporary predicament having reference to a particular situation. The Dialectic is a universal conflict affecting every sphere of things.

[1] See *supra* . . . (Chap. IV) for an assesment of the nature and extent of the influence of the Mādhyamika Dialectic on the Vijñānavāda and the Vedānta.

[2] "Because of this method, which he employed with masterly skill, Zeno was called by Aristotle the inventor of Dialectic and Plato says that he could make one and the same appear to his hearers, as like and unlike, as one and many, as in motion and at rest." Zeller, *History of Greek Phil.*, Vol. I, p. 613.

[3] See Chapter II, *Silence of the Buddha and Beginnings of the Dialectic.*

[4] We are not accepting the disreputable meaning of the term dialectic as semblance-knowledge, as sophistry consciously employed to create illusion. See *Critique*, p. 99. Dialectic is rightly understood as a "Critique of the understanding and reason in respect of their hyper-physical employment." ibid., pp. 100–101.

In common-sense and science such an opposition does not arise, although two or more opposed concepts are used in interpreting things. Some things are taken as fleeting and momentary like the flash of lightning; some as permanent, even unchanging. The organic pattern of development is applied in the biological and humanistic sciences; the mechanical in the purely physical sciences. Both these, however, are not offered as explanations of one and the same set of facts; nor is any one pattern universalised. This, however, is inevitable in philosophy. Philosophy selects a particular pattern from among several exemplified in things, exaggerates it out of all proportion and universalises it to infinity. The pattern or concept so selected and universalised becomes an Idea of Reason, as Kant calls it. What impels us to select one particular point of view and not any other is a matter of our spiritual affiliation. The Mahāyānists would call this our spiritual gens (gotra).[1] But having chosen one, consciously or rather unconsciously, we universalise it and take it as the norm of evaluation. Though innocently stated as a description of facts, every philosophical system is an evaluation of things or a prescription to view them in a particular way. There is nothing scientific or philosophic about ideas and concepts. The concept used with restraint, within experience, is scientific; the same used without those limiting and validating conditions becomes an Idea of Reason. With the Mādhyamika, we can call that a dṛṣṭi or anta. Division of spheres among sciences is natural; but within each science itself there cannot be alternative and conflicting systems of explaining the same set of facts. Restriction of spheres among philosophical systems is unthinkable; each philosophy is, or claims to be, a complete and the only picture of all things. In science, a dispute regarding rival hypotheses can, at least in principle, be settled by an appeal to sense-experience in the last resort; in philosophy hypotheses cannot be proved or disproved by any such appeal. Disputes become interminable conflicts. Science is experimentation with things presented to us by sense; philosophy is speculation with regard to the supersensible. "No actual experience has ever been completely adequate to an Idea of Reason, yet to it every actual experience belongs."[2] There is thus no hope of alighting upon an empirical fact

[1] Cf. *Mahāyānasūtrālaṁkāra* III, 2 (p. 10):
dhātūnām adhimukteś ca pratipatteś ca bhedataḥ;
phalabhedopalabdheś ca gotrāstitvaṁ nirūpyate.

[2] *Critique*, p. 308.

which will upset any philosophy. Philosophy, when cultivated seriously and systematically, leads to interminable and total conflict. Dialectic is implicit in philosophy. Dialectic is at once the consciousness of this interminable and total conflict in reason and the attempt to resolve it.

IV DIALECTIC AS RESOLUTION OF THE CONFLICT

Two or three ways have been suggested to get over this conflict. We may recognise that each philosophical system embodies and emphasises a valuable view of reality; its fallacy however lies in its extremism, abstraction from other aspects. The opposition can be got over by incorporating all the views in a comprehensive system. This is the way of the Jaina system and Hegel. Or, despairing of any settlement in this anarchical state of affairs, one may easily be led to scepticism and positivism. Positivism, as denial of metaphysics, is chronic in philosophy. Its resurgence is almost periodic; it invariably appears after a period of great philosophic activity.[1]

Scepticism usually takes a positivist turn by restricting the realm of significant discourse to the empirical.[2] Though confused with positivism, the Mādhyamika position, like Kant's, is totally different; it is spiritual to the core. The Mādhyamika denies metaphysics not because there is no real for him; but because it is inaccessible to Reason. He is convinced of a higher faculty, Intuition (prajñā) with which the Real (tattva) is identical.[3]

It is instructive to consider the solution of the conflict in Reason

[1] To illustrate this from the history of European philosophy:

The scepticism of the Sophists—Protagoras and Gorgias—followed on the heels of the Eleatic (Being) school and Heracleitus (Becoming); the great systems of Plato and Aristotle were followed by the Scepticism of Pyrrho; it invaded the Academy itself, and distinguished masters of the academy—Arcelaus and Carneades—were its great exponents. Hume's scepticism was the natural result of the conflict of the great systems of Rationalism and Empiricism in the modern age. The Positivism of Comte came in the wake of the great systems of Fichte, Hegel and Schopenhauer. In our own times, Logical Positivism may be considered as the negative reaction to Idealism and Realism.

[2] Positivism is anti-metaphysical. It considers metaphysics or philosophy proper as a body of pseudo-propositions, as nonsense. Only science is significant. The function left for philosophy is to analyse linguistic forms employed in science. See the works of Wittgenstein, Carnap, Max Scheler, Ayer and others.

[3] For a fuller discussion of the nature of this intuition see the subsequent Chapter on *The Mādhyamika Conception of Philosophy as Prajñāpāramitā.*

attempted by the Jaina and Hegel, if only because it throws light on the structure of the dialectic and shows in what manner the Mādhyamika dialectic differs from theirs.

By a criticism of several systems representative of different points of view like the Sāṁkhya, Nyāya and Buddhism, the Jaina shows that each view is true in so far as it draws attention to an actual and indispensable aspect of the real. It becomes an exaggerated travesty of facts (nayābhāsa) when it excludes other views. A truer view is to comprehend these views in our conception of the real. Both the substance-view and the modal view (dravyārthika and paryāyārthika naya, or asti and nāsti) are equally true of the real. The basic alternatives (mūlabhangas) are two—affirmation and negation. These can be asserted successively (kramārpitobhayam) or simultaneously (sahārpitobhayam)—engendering a composite view (asti *and* nāsti), and an indeterminate standpoint (avaktavyam) respectively. The indeterminate, as the indifference of emphasis, allows of combination with the previous three, thus giving rise to three more derivative alternatives.[1] The formulation of the real cannot be complete with less than these seven disjunctives. It must be noted that a subsequent alternative does *not* supersede the previous, but is an addition to it. Thus there can be no higher or lower view as in Hegel; each is equally a true view of things. The real is not a unity, but a *manifold of differences* (anekāntātmakaṁ vastu). The Jaina logic is a disjunctive synthesis.

Hegel too inveighs against abstraction which is but partial truth; the whole alone is real. Hegel derives the opposite not by an appeal to experience, but by a logical analysis of the concept. How one concept, by being insisted upon, passes into its opposite has always seemed a puzzle to students of Hegel. The dialectic is a passage, a movement, from concept to concept; it is at once creative of newer, more comprehensive and higher concepts. It is a negative and a

[1] *Syādvādaratnākara*, IV, Sūtras 17–18 (pp. 62 ff). *Sanmatitarka* pp. 441 ff. *Syādvādamañjarī* pp. 189 ff (Poona Edn.). *Prameya-Kamala-Mārtaṇḍa* pp. 681 ff.

tatra praśna-vaśāt kaścid vidhau śabdaḥ pravartate;
syādasty evākhilaṁ yad vastusvarūpādi catuṣṭayāt.
syān nāsty eva viparyāsād iti kaścin niṣedhane;
syād dvaitam eva tad dvaitād ityastitva-niṣedhayoḥ.
krameṇa; yaugapadyād vā syād avaktavyam eva tat;
syādastyavācyam eveti yathocita-nayārpaṇāt.
syān nāsty avācyam eveti tata eva nigadyate;
syād dvayāvācyam eveti saptabhangyavirodhataḥ.

Tattvārtha-Śloka-Vārt. (p. 128.)

positive function of Reason. It presses each concept (e.g. Being), squeezes out all its implications, as it were; and at this stage it becomes indistinguishable from its very opposite (Non-Being). But through this negation there arises a new concept. And as this concept has been engendered by its opposite, it is richer in content, and includes the previous one. Negation is not total annulment but comprehension without abstraction. This new idea itself is the starting point for another process, the thesis of a newer triad. The dialectical movement is a spiral. Rather, it may be conceived as an inverted pyramid. Its beginning is determined by the idea with the least content (Pure Being), and the end by the most comprehensive concept (Absolute Idea). The objection that the entire dialectical movement is merely ideal—formal—is attempted to be solved by Hegel by asserting the identity of Thought and Reality. The investigation of thought-structure is at once the investigation of the Real.

The Hegelian dialectic is a *conjunctive* or integrating synthesis: at every stage the alternatives are unified and transcended; and this leads to a higher and a lower view. The Jaina dialectic is a disjunctive synthesis of alternatives, as we have seen; it is more a syncretism than a synthesis. They further differ in the function they assign to thought: for Hegel thought is *creative*, while for the Jaina it is *representative* of the real. The Jaina's is a logic of realism and pluralism; Hegel's is a logic of idealism and absolutism. However, both may subscribe to this common formula: *distinctions in thought are not merely in thought*, not subjective; *they are truly indicative of the real.* This the Mādhyamika denies. For him thought-distinctions are purely subjective, and when taken as the texture of the real they are nothing less than a falsification of it.

The Mādhyamika dialectic tries to remove the conflict inherent in Reason by rejecting both the opposites taken singly or in combination. The Mādhyamika is convinced that the conjunctive or disjunctive synthesis of the opposites is but another view; it labours under the same difficulties. Rejection of all views is the rejection of the competence of Reason to comprehend reality. The real is transcendent to thought. Rejection of views is not based on any positive grounds or the acceptance of another view; it is solely based on the inner contradiction implicit in each view. The function of the Mādhyamika dialectic, on the logical level, is purely negative, analytic.

V THE FOUR ALTERNATIVES IN EVERY PROBLEM

Four alternative views are possible on any subject.[1] The basic alternatives are two: Being and Non-Being, Affirmation and Negation. From these, two others are derived by affirming or denying both at once: both Being and Non-Being (ubhayasaṁkīrṇātma),[2] and neither Being nor Non-Being (ubhayapratiṣedhasvabhāvatā).[2] It may be thought that in avoiding the two extremes, the Mādhyamika takes a middle position in between the two. No; he does not hold any middle position.[3] Or, the middle is no position; it is beyond concept or speech; it is the transcendental, being a review of all things.[4]

Four and only four views are possible: two are primary and the other two secondary. It is not possible to reduce affirmation or negation to each other. It may be held that "all affirmation is negation"; because, to affirm that 'this is a triangle' is to deny that it is a square, etc. Likewise, negation may be taken as affirmation; for, to deny the existence of a thing is to affirm its presence elsewhere or in some other form. These attempts however are more fanciful than plausible. For, whatever may be the real nature of any *concrete thing* (whether it is all Being or Non-being or both at once), the *two*

[1] In the examination of each category, causality etc., four types of views are invariably formulated in the Mādhyamika texts. In the chapter on the *Examination of Views* (*Dṛṣṭiparīkṣā*, MK. XXVII) the schema of four views is given. "dṛṣṭayo na bhaviṣyāmi . . . etc." MK. XXVII, 2. The *Vṛtti* thereon says: ihāpi dṛṣṭidvayopādānam upalakṣaṇārthaṁ *catasras tvetā dṛṣṭayaḥ* (MKV. pp. 572, 573). Āryadeva gives the number and order of the alternatives:

sad asad sadasac ceti nobhayaṁ ceti ca kramaḥ; eṣa
proyojyo vidvadbhir ekatvādiṣu nityaśaḥ (CŚ. XIV, 21).

Haribhadra puts the thing logically as:

vidhānaṁ pratiṣedhañca tāveva sahitau punaḥ;
pratiṣedhaṁ tayor eva sarvathā nāvagacchati—AAA. p. 61.

[2] In BCAP (p. 358) these characteristic expressions are used.

[3] astīti nāstīti ubhe'pi antā
suddhī asuddhīti imepi antā
tasmād ubhe anta vivarjayitvā
madhye' pi sthānam na karoti paṇḍitaḥ—*Samādhirāja Sūtra* IX, 28 (p. 103, Vol. II, *Gilgit MSS*); also quoted in MKV. pp. 135, 270.

The tattva for the Mādhyamika, according to the well-known verse, "na san nāsat", is *catuṣkoṭivinirmuktam*.

[4] ātmeti, Kāśyapa, ayam eko'ntaḥ, nairātmyam ity ayaṁ dvitīyo'ntaḥ. yad etad anayor antayor *madhyaṁ*, tad *arūpyam* anidarśanam apratiṣṭham anābhāsam avijñaptikam aniketam iyam ucyate, Kāśyapa, *madhyamā pratipad* dharmāṇāṁ bhūta-pratyavekṣā. (*Ratnakūṭa*—quoted in MKV, p. 358. *Kāśyapa Parivarta*. p. 87).

attitudes (affirmation and negation) are entirely different, and one cannot be derived from the other. Affirmation posits, identifies, includes or relates a predicate of a subject; while negation denies, differentiates, excludes or rejects the predicate of the subject. They may be like the two sides of a shield, still they are *two* sides and must be considered as distinct.

It might be thought that affirmation and negation being both exclusive and exhaustive, there is no scope for other alternatives, and that the affirmation and denial of *both of them at once* do not mean new attitudes. This may be the dictum in formal logic which works within a restricted sphere. The acceptance of both 'is' and 'is not' may be affirmation; but it is on a different footing, as here we have the consciousness of the one-sidedness of mere 'is' or mere 'is not'. Likewise, the rejection of both 'is' and 'is not' may be denial; but it is done with the full consciousness that no corresponding affirmation[1] is available. This is an extreme form of non-committal. It is not an attitude of decision, but of doubt and despair. As the competence of thought is not questioned and Reason is not transcended, it is still a view (dṛṣṭi) and not the giving up of views. It may correspond to the agnostic position, but it is not the Mādhyamika standpoint.

The four sets of views serve as schema for classifying all systems of philosophy. The consideration of the real as Being, uniform, universal and identical everywhere is the affirmative view (sat-pakṣa). This is in the main represented by the systems of the ātma-tradition, especially by the Vedānta which takes sat (ātman) alone as real. The Buddhist or Humean view is a good example of the negative attitude; it is a denial of substance, of the universal and the identical, and the acceptance of the asat. The synthetic view like

[1] The third alternative is clearly an affirmation of both 'is' and 'not-is' at once (ubhayavidhānam). With regard to the fourth there may be this doubt whether it is to be construed as denial of both the alternatives 'is' and 'not-is' together (conjunctive denial, ubhayābhāva or viśiṣṭābhāva) of the form—not both 'is' and 'not-is'; or as the denial of each alternative (disjunctive negation or pratyekābhāva) of the form—neither 'is' nor 'not-is'. If it is construed as not both (ubhayābhāva), then it is incompatible with the assertion of both 'is' and 'not-is' *together*, but is perfectly compatible with the acceptance of 'is' and 'not-is' singly; cf. the Nyāya dictum: eka-sattve'pi ubhayaṁ (dvayaṁ) nāstīti pratīteh. But this is clearly opposed to the construction put upon this by Nāgārjuna and other Mādhyamika ācāryas. For instance, in examining the conception of Nirvāṇa, the fourth alternative is stated as a disjunctive negation of the form: neither 'is' nor 'not-is': naivābhāvo naiva bhāvo nirvānam iti yāñjanā. MK. XXV, 15.

that of Jaina or Hegel is an example of the third alternative. The Agnostic or the Sceptic like Pyrrho or Sañjaya[1] can be cited as examples of the fourth.

VI DIALECTIC IS REJECTION OF VIEWS BY *REDUCTIO AD ABSURDUM*

How does the Mādhyamika reject any and all views? He uses only one weapon. By drawing out the implications of any view he shows its self-contradictory character. The dialectic is a series of *reductio ad absurdum* arguments (prasangāpādanam).[2] Every thesis is turned against itself. The Mādhyamika is a prāsangika or vaitaṇḍika, a dialectician or free-lance debater. The Mādhyamika *disproves* the opponent's thesis, and does *not* prove any thesis of his own.

Prasanga is not to be understood as an apagogic proof in which we *prove* an assertion *indirectly* by disproving the opposite. *Prasanga* is disproof simply, without the least intention to prove any thesis. All the arguments which Kant adduces to prove the thesis and the antithesis in his *Antinomies of Reason* are well-known examples of the apagogic proof. The Sāṁkhya proof of the satkāryavāda by disproving the opposite theory of asatkārya-vāda (asadakaraṇāt etc.) as also the Buddhist proof of momentariness (momentary as the efficient) by the disproof of the permanent are typical examples in Indian Philosophy. Such proofs, however plausible they may appear, fail to carry conviction. For, the disproof of the opponent, even if it is cogent, does not necessarily mean the establishment of one's position as true. For both the opponent's view as well as one's own may be false. The apagogic proof can have cogency and compulsion in spheres where by tne nature of the subject matter, such as in mathematics, we so completely possess the field *in concreto* that the alternatives are narrowed down to two, and by rejecting one we indirectly prove the other. It must fail with regard to empirical facts and especially with regard to the supersensuous.[3] For, we not

[1] The Aññāṇavāda of Sañjaya: amarā-vikkhepam—evam pi me no;
tathā ti pi me no; aññathā ti pi me no; no ti pi me no;
no no ti pi me no ti. *Dīgh, N.* I, ii, 24 (Vol. I, p. 25).

[2] ācāryo bhūyasā prasangāpatti-mukhenaiva parapakṣaṁ nirākaroti sma MKV. p. 24). cf. also: prasangasādhanaṁ ca na svapakṣasthāpanāyopādīyate kiṁ tu parasyāniṣṭāpādanārtham; parāniṣṭaṁ ca tadabhyupagamasiddhair eva dharmādibhiḥ śakyam āpādayitum. *Nyāyakandalī*, p. 197. cf. *Nyāyasūtra* I, i, 3 and the *Bhāṣya* thereon.

[3] See Kant's *Critique* (pp. 626 ff) for a discussion of the nature and scope of the apagogic proof.

only lack any sensuous intuition of the latter, but we do not also have an adequate representation of it. It would be circular reasoning to arrive at this very knowledge through the apogogic proof, which, to be cogent, does itself presuppose this intuition. The *reductio ad absurdum* of the Mādhyamika does not establish any thesis. It accepts a particular thesis *hypothetically*, and by eliciting its implication shows up the inner contradiction which has escaped the notice of the opponent.

Nor does the rejection of a thesis entail, as a necessary consequence of this rejection itself, the acceptance of a counter-thesis. For example, the rejection of self-becoming does not mean that the other view of production from the other (cause and effect as different) is accepted. It is pure negation (prasajyapratiṣedha).[1] The *reductio ad absurdum* is for the sole benefit of the holder of the thesis; and it is done with his own logic, on principles and procedure fully acceptable to him.[2] The Mādhyamika dialectic is a spiritual *ju-jutsu*. The Mādhyamika does not have a thesis of his own. He does not construct syllogisms and adduce arguments and examples of his own.[3]

There was indeed a sub-school of the Mādhyamika which believed in advancing counter-theses. This was the Svatantra Mādhyamika school, the chief exponent of which is Bhāvaviveka.[4] This school does not seem to have had much vogue. All the chief Mādhyamika teachers —Nāgārjuna, Āryadeva, Buddhapālita, Candrakīrti and Śāntideva— invariably adduce prasanga (*reductio ad absurdum*) arguments.

VII CAUSALITY DIALECTICALLY ANALYSED

To illustrate the dialectical procedure of the Mādhyamika we may consider the problem of causation. The relation between cause and

[1] nanu ca naiva svata utpannā' ity avadhāryamāṇe, 'parata utpannā,' ity aniṣṭaṁ prāpanoti. na prapnoti; prasajyapratiṣedhasya vivakṣitatvāt. parato'pyutpādasya pratiṣetsyamānatvāt. MKV. p. 13.

[2] paraḥ 'cakṣuḥ paśyatīti pratipannaḥ', sa *tatprasiddhenaivānumānena* nirākriyate. MKV. p. 34.

[3] yadi kācana pratijñā syān me tata eva me me bhaved doṣaḥ; nāsti ca mama pratijñā tasmān naivāsti me doṣaḥ. VV. 29.
mādhyamikānāṁ pakṣahetudṛṣṭāntānām asiddheḥ, svatantrānumānānabhidhāyitvāt—MKV. p. 18; 16 and 34.

[4] Bhāvaviveka, the author of *Tarkajvālā* and other treatises, is severely criticised by Candrakīrti at several places in the MKV (pp. 14, 25, 36, 196, 351–52). He comes in for special censure for adducing, though a Mādhyamika, syllogisms of his own and advocating a thesis. This is against the correct standpoint of the Mādhyamika.

effect has been conceived in four different ways. The Sāṁkhya advocates identity between the two (satkāryavāda), and thus holds the theory of self-becoming; things are produced out of themselves (svata utpannā bhāvāḥ). The Buddhist and even the Nyāya to a certain extent oppose this by maintaining difference between cause and effect. The Jaina view combines the above two views by insisting on the continuous as well as the emergent aspect of the effect (utpādavyayadhrauvyayuktam sat). The materialists and the sceptics, rejecting all the alternatives, take things as produced by chance (ahetutaḥ).

The Sāṁkhya thesis that things are produced out of themselves is wrong; for there is no point in self-production, reduplication. The Sāṁkhya too does not admit that the thing which is already present (fully manifest like the pitcher) produces itself. Besides, there will be no conceivable limit to this process of self-duplication.[1] The Sāṁkhya might parry the argument by saying that it does not deny all difference; the manifestation (abhivyakti) is certainly new; but this does not amount to a difference in substance, but only in form or the states of the same substance. Does not this difference militate against the identity of the underlying substratum? The Mādhyamika further urges that the manifestation itself[2] might be taken as the essential meaning of causation, for it is that which makes any entity efficient. Are the cause and the effect identical with regard to this emergent form? Obviously not. Identity militates against causation. Propositions true of the effect (of the pitcher as holding water etc.) are not true of the cause (clay). Either the cause is not identical with the effect, or if identity is insisted upon, causation must be given up. The Sāṁkhya thesis is not consistent with itself. It sets out to explain causal relation as identity, and yet it cannot do so without admitting differences. Absolute identity is not even assertible. Even to affirm A is A, we have to take the help of difference of time, place and circumstances of A's occurrences etc. Absolute identity is inexpressible by thought. A critique of the Sāṁkhya reveals the inner fissure present in its thesis, and in removing this inconsistency we reach an inexpressible absolute identity. We have not the right to call it identity even. It is beyond thought, outside the range of predication.

To take the other alternative. If the cause and the effect were different, the effect is an *other* to the cause. And being totally different,

[1] na svata utpadyante bhāvāḥ. tad utpādavaiyarthyāt; atiprasangadoṣāc ca. MKV. p. 14, also p. 22.

[2] MKV. p. 22.

nothing should be able to produce things or anything should emerge from anywhere.[1]

This however is not the case. The insistence upon difference thus leads to non-relation, to the abandonment of causation. Absolute difference is not even expressible as a proposition. No attribute can be predicated of a subject; for, being different, they are not relevant to each other. No two entities can be compared; they cannot even be known as different, each being unique and incommensurable. We cannot find a common concept or term even to call them 'things'; for, this is still to identify them as belonging to a class. Pure difference is beyond thought.

The Buddhist is faced with a dilemma: Either insist on difference and thereby give up causation and relation, or accept causation and other relations and give up absolute difference. The Buddhist must give up either difference or causation. But he hopes to retain both; hence he implicitly contradicts himself. The dialectic exposes the implications and the flaws inherent in his position.

It may be thought that both the Sāṁkhya and the Buddhist might considerably better their respective position and remove the contradiction by incorporating some elements from the other. The Buddhist might accept identity along with difference in his view of causation. The Sāṁkhya might admit difference along with identity. Would they be escaping the dialectic then? If identity and difference were simply plumped together, this will add to the difficulties instead of decreasing them.[2]

There was at least the merit of simplicity in each thesis that is admittedly gone now. The real must be conceived as having two different aspects. It is then subject to the Buddhistic dictum: 'that

[1] na parata utpadyante bhāvāḥ, sarvataḥ sarva-sambhava-prasangāt. MKV. p. 36.

[2] The third alternative (ubhayataḥ) is hardly criticised at any great length in the Mādhyamika treatises. It is taken as subject to the difficulties of both the previous ones (sat and asat); sat and asat are mutually opposed to each other. Nāgārjuna says at one place:

> parasparaviruddhaṁ hi sac cāsac caikataḥ kutaḥ. MK. VIII, 7.
> bhaved abhāvo bhāvaś ca nirvāṇam ubhayaṁ katham;
> na tayor ekatrāstitvam ālokatamasor yathā. MK. XXV, 14.

Śāntarakṣita criticises the Jaina view of the Real which is the best example of this view in his TS. pp. 486 ff.

He says:

> vidhānapratiṣedhau hi paraspara-virodhinau;
> śakyāv ekatra no kartuṁ kenacit svasthacetasā. TS. 1730.

is not one which is invested with two or more opposed characteristics.'[1] To say roundly that reality is so is to be dogmatic: philosophy then becomes a mere description of what appears to untutored perception. We may accord prominence to one ingredient and subordinate the other to it. There is, however, no ground for this preferential treatment. We may take identity as the prius, and subordinate difference to it, or *vice versa*. But the notion of subordination is unintelligible in the case of entities which are mutually dependent and indispensable to each other. In the last resort, the subordinate can only mean the dispensable; that is, the real nature of a thing is not affected when the subordinate is absent. This alternative then will be reduced to either of the first two. If the synthesis is under a third something, a *tertium quid*, we have a new pattern. What is the relation between this synthetic unity and each one of the constituents: is it identity, difference or both?[2] The theory is not so simple as it appears. If, to escape this, we say it is beyond the range of identity and difference, it is tantamount to accepting that it is unrelated to the opposites and is inexpressible in itself. This is exactly what the Mādhyamika desires to point out. The real is beyond Reason.

The fourth alternative that things are produced neither from themselves nor from others etc., that is, they emerge at random can be disposed of easily. If no reason is assigned for the thesis, it is a mere dogmatic assertion; it falls to the ground through sheer inanity. If a reason is assigned, there is a manifest self-contradiction between what we assert and how we assert it: for we have a conclusion (that things are produced at random without cause) sought to be cogently, causally, derived from premises.[3]

[1] yo viruddhadharmādhyāsavān nāsāvekaḥ.

[2] If the elements of the synthesis retain their nature and individuality to any extent, then this alternative is certainly subject to the objections against the two previous alternatives. If they do not, and the synthesis is taken to be a unique position devoid of distinction and difference, then it would be indistinguishable from the Mādhyamika standpoint. If it is averred, as is done by Hegel, that the synthesis unifies and yet retains the differences, we have a new problem on our hands: what is the relation between this synthesis and each one of the differents; is it identity or difference or both? If a new synthesis is resorted to, this will lead to a *regress ad infinitum*.

[3] This view has always been taken as that of the Svabhāva-vādin (Naturalist, Materialist). see BCAP. 540 ff.

Cf. na heturastīti vadan sahetukam;
nanu pratijñāṁ svayam eva śātayet.
athāpi hetupraṇayālaso bhavet;
pratijñayā kevalayāsya kiṁ bhavet.

Quoted in BCAP. p. 544; and TSP. p .66 (as tathā coktam ācarya Sūripādaiḥ).

VIII EVERY THESIS IS SELF-CONVICTED, NOT COUNTERBALANCED

In rejecting one thesis the Mādhyamika does not accept its counter-thesis. He does not set one opponent against another. Not only would this be sharp practice but it would be illogical in the extreme. This may be adopted by a sophist trickster out to confute the opponent by any handy means; but a self-conscious dialectic with a spiritual end cannot and does not stoop to this. In refuting the Śāṁkhya view of causation we do not enlist the support of his opponent. The Śāṁkhya stands self-convicted by the implications of his own thesis: production and self-identity cannot go together. Likewise with the other theses. The consideration of several views does not mean that one is false *because* of the other. The knowledge of the opposite thesis merely makes us critical, helps us in discovering the flaw within it. It is false because of its inherent weakness. Every thesis is self-convicted and not counter-balanced by an anti-thesis.

A view is plausible because we prize it; we are enamoured of its externals. We hold fast to it as the truth (grāha, abhiniveśa). No doubt the process is unconscious and goes beyond empirical experience; it may even be beginningless. Nevertheless, it acts as a cover (āvaraṇa) in hiding the real from us. In that state we do not even know that it is a view. So long as we are in illusion, we do not know it as illusion. We become aware of its contradictions, as we analyse it and know it inside out. Self-conscious reflection is not possible if anything were taken as true and unitary, as simple. When we entertain a view, we are possessed by it; we look at things in this coloured way and are not even conscious of it. Only as a contrast is felt between what appeared and what it really turns out to be, there is self-consciousness. We must stand aside and perceive the inner flaw or fissure in our position. This is analysis or Śūnyatā which splits up entities and exhibits their inner nature.

IX PRINCIPLE OF THE DIALECTIC

NOTHING IN ITSELF: ALL IS RELATIVE (PRATĪTYA-SAMUTPANNA):

Why are all views rejected? What is the principle on which it is done? Any fact of experience, when analysed, reveals the inner rift present in its constitution. It is not a thing in itself; it is what it is in relation to other entities, and these in turn depend on others. This process thus proceeds indefinitely and leads to a regress.

Practically minded, commonsense does not care to go deep. Philosophical systems, in their anxiety to uphold their own views, slur and gloss over the inherent flaw and instability of their contentions. For instance, in causation we must differentiate between the cause and the effect and at the same time identify them. The relation between the two cannot be conceived as identity, difference or both; nor can we give it up. Nāgārjuna says: "Neither of those things is established (as real) which cannot be conceived either as identical or different from each other."[1]

The principle is enunciated in almost every chapter of the *Mādhyamika Kārikās*. The substance-view thinks that it could have substance without attributes or modes; the modal view believes that it can dispense with substance altogether. There is, however, no attribute without substance nor is substance without attribute. They are not intelligible even together; for how can we then distinguish them? Nāgārjuna in discussing the relation between a person and his emotions (rāga and rakta) says: that they are not anything either together or separately; likewise, no entity is proved (to exist) as together or separately.[2] There is no self apart from the states (upādāna), nor is the latter without the self that gives unity to them; nor are they anything together.[3] The relation between fire and fuel (agnīndhana) is examined at length by Nāgārjuna to illustrate this predicament. Fire is not fuel, lest the consumer (agent or kartā) and the consumed (object-karma) should be identical; nor is fire different from fuel, for it cannot be had without the latter.[4] All entities, like the Self and its modes (ātmopādānayoḥ kramaḥ) as well as particular empirical things such as table and chair, are completely covered by this analysis.[5]

[1] **ekībhāvena vā siddhir nānābhāvena vā yayoḥ;**
na vidyate'tayoḥ siddhiḥ kathaṁ nu khalu vidyate. MK. II, 21.
sahānyonyena vā siddhir vinānyonyena vā yayoḥ;
na vidyate tayoḥ siddhiḥ kathaṁ nu khalu vidyate. MK. XIX, 6.

[2] **evaṁ raktena rāgasya siddhir *na saha nāsaha*;**
rāgavat sarvadharmāṇāṁ siddhir na saha nāsaha.
MK. VI, 10.

[3] **ātmanaś ca satattvaṁ ye bhāvānāṁ ca pṛthak pṛthak;**
nirdiśanti na tān manye śāsanasyārthakovidān.
MK. X, 16.

[4] **yad indhanaṁ saced agnir ekatvaṁ kartṛkarmaṇoḥ;**
anyaś ced indhanād agnir indhanād apy ṛte bhavet.
MK. X, 1.

[5] **agnīndhanābhyāṁ vyākhyāta ātmopādānayoḥ;**
sarvo niravaśeṣeṇa sārdhaṁ ghaṭapaṭādibhiḥ.
MK. X, 15.

Again, it is pointed out that the agent is dependent on the act; and this in turn depends on the agent. All things are to be understood as on a par with the Agent and the Act.[1] If the definition (lakṣaṇa) were different from the definitum (lakṣya), the latter would be bereft of any distinguishing mark; and if both were identical, then there would be the absence of both as such.[2] There is no whole apart from the parts and *vice versa*.[3] Things that derive their being and nature by mutual dependence are nothing in themselves; they are not real.[4]

Relation has to perform two mutually opposed functions: as *connecting* the two terms, in making them relevant to each other, it has to *identify* them; but as connecting the *two*, it has to *differentiate* them. Otherwise expressed, relation cannot obtain between entities that are identical with or different from each other.[5]

These insuperable difficulties impel us to the conclusion that cause and effect, substance and attribute, whole and parts, subject and object etc., are mutually dependent, relative; hence they are not things-in-themselves.[6]

[1] MK. VIII, 12, 13.

[2] lakṣyāl lakṣaṇam anyac cet syāl lakṣyam alakṣaṇam;
tayor abhāvo' nanyatve vispaṣṭaṁ kathitaṁ tvayā.
MKV. p. 64.

[3] rūpakāraṇanirmuktaṁ na rūpam upalabhyate;
rūpeṇāpi na nirmuktaṁ dṛśyate rūpakāraṇam.
MK. IV, 1.

rūpādivyatirekeṇa yathā kumhbo na vidyate
vāyvādivyatirekeṇa tathā rūpaṁ na vidyate.
CŚ. XIV, 14.

[4] parasparāpeksā siddhir na svābhāvikī.
MKV. p. 200.

[5] na tena tasya saṁsargo, nānyenānyasya yujyate.
MK. XIV, 8.

Cf. Bradley: "Relation pre-supposes quality, and quality relation. Each can be something neither together with, nor apart from, the other; and the vicious circle in which they turn is not the truth about Reality."
Appearance and Reality. p. 21.

[6] pratītya yad yad bhavati na hi tāvat tad eva tat.
MK. XVIII, 10.

pratītya yad yad bhavati tat tac chāntaṁ svabhāvataḥ.
MK. VII, 16.

pratītya-samutpannaṁ vasturūpaṁ saṁvṛtir ucyate.
BCAP. p. 352.

Thus Pratītyasamutpāda is equated with Śūnyatā.
See MK. XXIV, 18.

What is relative is subjective, unreal. The categories are so many conceptual devices (vikalpa, prapañca) by which Reason tries to apprehend the Real that cannot be categorised and made relative (buddher agocaras tattvam). Reason (buddhi) is therefore condemned as falsifying the real (saṁvṛti). No phenomenon, no object of knowledge (bhāva or abhāva), escapes this universal relativity.[1]

Relativity or mutual dependence is a mark of the unreal. A Hegel would have welcomed this inherent dependence of things as the dialectical necessity of Reason working through the opposites, differentiating and at once unifying them. For him that is the mark of the Real. And this, because he does not go beyond Reason; in fact, for Hegel Reason and Real are identical. For the Mādhyamika reciprocity, dependence, is the lack of inner essence. Tattva or the Real is something in itself, self-evident and self-existent.[2] Reason which understands things through distinction and relation is a principle of falsity; as it distorts and thereby hides the real.[3] Only the Absolute as the unconditioned is real, and for that very reason it cannot be *conceived* as existence (bhāva) or non-existence (abhāva) or both etc.

The detailed application of the dialectic to some of the important categories is undertaken in a subsequent chapter. But this would merely *examplify* the dialectical principle. The analysis of even one relational mode must be enough to convince us of the inherent hollowness of things. In induction even one instance, carefully analysed, is enough to enable us to arrive at the principle in question. Important generalisations have been made from single instances. Number of instances is of subjective value only, as facilitating the isolation of the principle sought. Ārya Deva gives expression to this truth when he says:[4]

[1] apratītya samutpanno dharmaḥ kaścin na vidyate;
yasmāt tasmād aśūnyo hi dharmaḥ kaścin na vidyate.
MK. XXIV, 19; cf. also CŚ. IX, 2.

[2] aparapratyayaṁ śāntaṁ prapañcair aprapañcitam;
nirvikalpam anānārthaṁ etat tattvasya lakṣaṇam.
MK. XVIII, 9.

[3] Bradley comes to the same conclusion: "The conclusion to which I am brought is that a relational way of thought—any one that moves by the machinery of terms and relations—must give appearance, and not truth.
Appearance and Reality p. 28.

[4] bhāvasyaikasya yo draṣṭā draṣṭā sarvasya sa smṛtaḥ;
ekasya śūnyatā yaiva saiva sarvasya śūnyatā.
CŚ. VIII, 16.

He, that perceives the nature of a single ens,
perceives the nature of all;
The Śūnyatā of one is indeed the Śūnyatā of all.

X MOMENTS OF THE DIALECTIC

The 'moments' or the stages of the dialectic may be schematised thus. These moments are also the stages in the development or maturation of the philosophical consciousness.

There is first the moment of dogmatism—the indulgence in speculative philosophy (dṛṣṭi-vāda). This natural metaphysical disposition gives rise, sooner rather than later, to two or more philosophical systems. They are not merely different, but are opposed to each other as contraries; they explain all things from mutually conflicting points of view. And as this conflict is not empirical in origin and scope, we become not only aware of the gravity of the conflict but also suspicious of the claim of thought to acquaint us with reality. Criticism is born.

The second moment arises with the awareness of the transcendental illusion, the subjectivity of thought. Dialectic, as a critique of reason, thoroughly exposes the pretensions of speculative reason. This is done by revealing the inner contradiction present in each one of the views, i.e. by *reductio ad absurdum* arguments. As in exposing a thesis the counter-thesis is not accepted, the opposition is resolved without residue. The dialectical movement does not precipitate another triad, nor does it lead to the spiral. The Mādhyamika dialectic, unlike the Hegelian, is purely analytic in character. Criticism is Śūnyatā, the utter negation of thought as revelatory of the real. All judgments, all philosophical systems, are vikalpa, prapañca, false-ascriptions or thought-constructions.

The awareness of the transcendental illusion is possible because of an ideal or norm to which thought tries, fruitlessly, to conform. Thought is subjective, false, in relation to the objectively real. If there were no unconditioned (nirvikalpa, tattva or dharmatā) to which we are denied access in thought, there could not be the consciousness of the subjectivity of thought. The unconditioned (paramārtha) is transcendent to thought; it is certainly accessible to us in intuition. The death of thought (dṛṣṭijñānā) is the birth of Prajñā, knowledge devoid of distinction (jñānam advayam). Kant is convinced of the subjectivity of Reason because it gives us only a semblance of knowledge. He thoroughly exposes the transcendental illusion in his *Dialectic*. Inconsistently enough, he denies that we can have knowledge of the Noumenon by Pure Reason (Dialectic). He should have, as complementary to his doctrine of transcendental illusion, accepted a knowledge of the real; though necessarily, it could not be in the thinking way. He even denies that the illusion can ever disappear[1] or that we can have intellectual intuition.[2] For the Mādhyamika, the effective and complete disappearance of thought is intuition of the real; it is not a new emergence from somewhere; it has been there always[3] (tathatā sarva-kālaṁ tathābhāvāt). Only, it had been obscured by thought (sāṁvṛta). Nāgārjuna declares that they do not understand the heart of Buddha's teaching who do not distinguish between the unconditioned truth and the conventional one.[4]

The Absolute is not one reality set against another, the empirical. The Absolute looked at through thought-forms (vikalpa) is phenomenon (saṁsāra or sāṁvṛta, literally covered). The latter, freed of the superimposed thought-forms (nirvikalpa, niṣprapañca), is the Absolute. The difference is epistemic (subjective), and not ontological.[5] Nāgārjuna therefore declares that there is not the least difference between the world and the absolutely real.[6] Transcendent to thought, the absolute, however, is thoroughly immanent in experience. A critique of experience, like the Mādhyamika dialectic, is conscious of this immanence, the phenomenalisation of the absolute. The phenomenalising activity is of two kinds: one through ignorance, through avidyā and its satellites, the kleśas; and the other is the free conscious assumption of phenomenal forms activated by prajñā and karuṇā. The former is the unconscious activity of the ignorant (pṛthagjana), and the latter is that of the Enlightened Buddhas and Bodhisattvas.

Philosophical consciousness attains its fruition through the working of its inner dynamism, through the three moments of the

[1] Cf. "Transcendental illusion, on the other hand, does not cease even after it has been detected and its invalidity clearly revealed by transcendental criticism". *Critique*, p. 299.

[2] *Critique*, p. 268.

[3] aprahīṇam asaṁprāptam anucchinnam aśāśvatam;
aniruddham anutpannam etan nirvāṇam ucyate.
MK. XXV, 3.

[4] MK. XXIV, 9.

[5] MK. XXV, 9.

[6] MK. XXV, 20.

dialectic: dogmatism (dṛṣṭi), criticism (śūnyatā or prasanga) and intuition (prajñā). In its natural speculative employment, philosophy is dogmatic (dṛṣṭi); this finds expression in the various systems of thought. As this inevitably leads to a conflict, philosophy becomes critical, self-consciously aware of the assumptions and inadequacies of Reason. This is the consciousness of the relativity of phenomena, their unreality. Phenomena are Śūnya as they are dependent, and are thus void of the essence of reality (niḥsvabhāva).

The completion of criticism effectively does away with the speculative or conceptual functions of Reason. Philosophy then culminates in intellectual intuition, Prajñā. Here knowledge (Reason) and its object (the Real) coincide; there is non-duality (jñānam advayam). This too is Śūnyatā, as Prajñā or the Absolute is *devoid of duality* (śūnya of dṛṣṭis or views).[1]

The Mādhyamika dialectic as culminating in intuition is not only the fruition of the theoretic consciousness; it is the fruition of the practical and the religious consciousness as well. The root-cause of pain and imperfection is avidyā or the tendency to conceptulise the real. Mistaking as this or that do we get attached to things or evince aversion towards them. Nāgārjuna says: "Freedom is the cessation of acts (karma) and the roots of evil (kleśa); these are born of vikalpa and this of prapañca (the conceptual function of Reason); prapañca ceases with the knowledge of Śūnyatā."[2] The dialectic as non-conceptual intuitional knowledge takes us beyond the possibility of pain. It is the *summum bonum* of all our endeavour. It is Freedom itself (Nirvāṇa).

The dialectic as Prajñāpāramitā is identified with the tathāgata (dharmakāya)—the *Ens perfectissimum,* which all beings are in essence and which they attain by spiritual discipline. Religion is this mystic pull of the Transcendent (the Ideal) on the actual. The dialectic consummates the union of all beings with the perfect Being (buddha-kāya).[3]

[1] The terms 'Śūnya' and 'Śūnyatā' are applied both to phenomena and the absolute. Phenomena are Śūnya as they are devoid of thinghood (niḥsvabhāva); for they are dependent on each other (pratītya-samutpanna). The Absolute is Śūnya as it is utterly devoid of the conceptual distinctions of 'is' and 'not-is', free from all subjectivity (nirvikalpa, niṣprapañca). See I.P. Vol. I, p. 702.

[2] MK. XVIII, 5; see also MK. XXIII, 1.

[3] Nāgārjuna says in his *Catuḥstava* (quoted in BCAP. p. 590):

buddhānāṁ sattvadhātoś ca yenābhinnatvam arthataḥ;
ātmanaś ca pareṣāṁ ca samatā tena te matā.

In Kant, the *Critique* silences theoretic (Pure) Reason; its function is thus merely negative. It is the Practical Reason that alone guarantees to Kant his ideals, God, freedom and immortality. There is thus the severance of the intellectual form the ethical and the religious. The Mādhyamika Dialectic as negation of thought is intuition of the Absolute; as the rooting out of passions it is Freedom (Nirvāṇa); and it is perfection as union with the Perfect Being.[1]

[1] See the Chapter on the *Mādhyamika Conception of Philosophy as Prajñāpāramitā* and subsequent Chapters for elucidation of these aspects of the Dialectic.

CHAPTER SIX

SOME OBJECTIONS AGAINST THE DIALECTIC CONSIDERED

CERTAIN objections, logical and metaphysical, might be urged against the soundness of the dialectic. A consideration of these should be of help in appreciating the implications of the dialectic. That the Mādhyamika system, even if logically sound, is nihilistic and is a species of positivism and that it has been sterile in the past and does not hold out any hope for the future are broader philosophical issues. They are dealt with in a subsequent chapter. Objections of a formal or epistemological character against the value of the dialectic as a method of knowledge are considered here.

I IS CRITICISM POSSIBLE WITHOUT HOLDING A POSITION?

The foremost objection that cannot fail to strike us is the question —Is criticism of any thesis possible without the acceptance of a counter-thesis? It is commonly held that to criticise a theory we should have a rival theory or stand-point of our own, or that some tenets should be held in common by the disputants. But the acceptance of a common tenet, a common platform, cannot serve to favour any one of the rival hypotheses. Nor does a special tenet or thesis peculiar to one party fare better; for, to claim peculiar strength on the basis of a special tenet would cut both ways. The holding of a position cannot by itself decide the issue in favour of either of the disputants. How then is any hypothesis to be demolished at all? It is done by pointing out that the consequences of a hypothesis either contradict the hypothesis itself or are mutually contradictory. The holding of a rival hypothesis is not only unnecessary, but is clearly irrelevant. Nor is it necessary that the consequences of a hypothesis should be believed in by one who urges the objections, but merely that the consequences should be shown to be implied in the hypothesis to the satisfaction of the party concerned.[1] This is

[1] kiṁ punar anyataraprasiddhenāpy anumānenāsty anumānabādhā?

the only way to confute an opponent. The absurdity of his position must be brought home to him on principles and arguments accepted by him. The Mādhyamika claims to do nothing else. He is a prāsangika —having no tenet of his own and not caring to frame a syllogism of his own. "An opponent in putting forward a thesis is expected, as he is a believer in pramāṇas (valid sources of knowledge) to validate it. He must prove to his opponent the validity of that very argument by which he himself has arrived at the right conclusions."[1] But the case of the Mādhyamika is different; he does not vindicate any assertion in order to convince an opponent. He has no reasons and examples which he believes to be true. Every endeavour of the Mādhyamika is, therefore, exhausted in reducing the opponent's position to absurdity on principles and consequences which the opponent himself would accept.[2] Self-contradiction is the only weapon that can convict an opponent. If he does not desist from his position even after his assertion has been proved to be self-contradictory, we must give up arguing with him. He is not disinterested enough to arrive at the truth.[3] To criticise a position, then, it is not only unnecessary but irrelevant to advance another position.

II CRITICISM IS SELF-CRITICISM

It might be thought that though the Mādhyamika dialectic may be correct as a logical method, it nevertheless savours of ill-will symptomatic of a disposition which sees no good in others. How does it escape being a species of philosophical sadism? The Mādhyamika dialectic is not refutation; it is pre-eminently a *critique* of Reason.[4]

asti sā ca svaprasiddhenaiva hetunā, na paraprasiddhena; lokata eva dṛṣṭatvāt. MKV. pp. 34–5. Cf. also: niścitam idaṁ vākyaṁ lokasya svaprasiddhayaivopapattyā, nāryāṇām. MKV, p. 57.

[1] MKV. p. 19.

[2] na vyaṁ svatantram anumānaṁ prayuñjmahe; parapratijñā-niṣedhaphalatvād asmad-anumānānām. MKV. p. 34.

[3] atha svābhyupagama-virodha-codanayāpi paro na nivarttate, tadāpi nirlajjatayā hatudṛṣṭāntābhyam api naiva nivartteta. na conmattakena sahāsmākaṁ vivāda iti. MKV. p. 15.

[4] A Critique of Reason is the criticism *of* Reason undertaken *by* Reason itself. The genitive 'of' is both accusative and nominative in import. Reason is both the object of the inquiry and the subject (agent) conducting the inquiry. Dogmatic Reason is the subject-matter of enquiry by critical Reason. The Dialectic, as the Critique of philosophical consciousness, is self-consciousness of the higher order. Regarding the correct interpretation of the title of Kant's *Critique of Pure Reason*, see Kemp-Smith's *Commentary*, pp. 2–3.

Refutation is the rejection of an opponent's view by an interested party having a view of his own to establish. A critique is the disinterested analysis of Reason by itself. Reason occupies at once the position of the judge and the accused brought before the tribunal. All sound criticism is self-criticism. Only then can it serve the spiritual purpose of self-culture. For, how can the refutation of most or all views profit anybody, unless it is helpful in saving him from the same mistakes which others have inadvertently committed? It is an antidote and a safeguard against future mistakes. The Mādhyamika is exorcising the devil of dogmatism from his own soul. The outward form of refutation is employed by him so that he can the better dissociate himself from the inherent dogmatic tendency of the human mind. The Mādhyamika dialectic is actuated by the spiritual motive of purifying the mind and freeing it of the cobwebs and clogs of dogmatism (sarvasaṁkalpaprahāṇāya śūnyatā 'mṛtadeśanā).[1]

III DIALECTIC AND THE LAW OF EXCLUDED MIDDLE

Another line objection may be adopted to confute the Mādhyamika. When one alternative is rejected or accepted the other is *eo ipso* accepted or rejected, else the Law of the Excluded Middle would be violated. The Mādhyamika flagrantly violates this law at every step; we find him cutting down all the alternatives that are, by the canons of formal logic, both exclusive and exhaustive. For instance, four alternatives are framed by him with regard to causation, but none is accepted: "Neither out of themselves nor out of others, nor from both, nor at random have entities come into being anywhere."[2] Is not the rejection of satkāryavāda (Identity of cause and effect) tantamount to accepting asatkāryavāda (difference between cause and effect), this being its contradictory? Does not the rejection of motion entail the acceptance of rest—this being its material contradictory? The Mādhyamika rejects both.

[1] The sole aim of Mādhyamika system is to free the human mind of the net of concepts 'vikalpa-jāla' and verbal elaboration (prapañca). The dialectic, as Prajñāpāramitā, is venerated as nirvikalpam, prapañcopaśamam, śivam etc., in the Mādhyamika treatises. (ASP. Opening verses, MK. Opening Kārikā etc). Nāgārjuna ends his great work with the same note:

sarvadṛṣṭiprahāṇāya yaḥ saddharmam adeśayad;
anukampām upādāya taṁ namasyāmi Gautamam.
MK. XXVII, 30.

[2] MK I, 1.

The Mādhyamika is not the only sinner in rejecting the Excluded Middle. Kant does not accept it when he formulates his antimonies and rejects both of them, e.g., "the world has a beginning in space and time" and "the world has no such beginning etc." Hegel himself does not recognise the Law; had he done so, he should have chosen either Being or Non-Being instead of seeking a third.

No logical flaw is involved in not observing the Excluded Middle. If any one wants to vindicate this law, he must not only resolve the antimonies which a dialectic presents, but show that in rejecting one alternative, we do so by covertly accepting its contradictory, or *vice versa*.

The law of Excluded Middle assumes a sort of omniscience and makes capital out of our ignorance. That any two alternatives together exhaust the universe of discourse and that no third is possible cannot be known from the alternatives themselves.[1] Such is not the case with the law of contradiction; it derives all its force from the material in hand, from what is actually presented to us. We can, even on the strength of immediate experience, say that both the contradictories cannot be true. The Excluded Middle too, it may be urged, does not presume anything more than the particular kind of disjunctives called the Contradictories—as Being and Non-Being, Affirmation and Negation. Such contradictory alternatives can easily be recognised by any one, it may be said. To this our reply is that the doctrine of Contradictories as conceived by Formal Logic is defective; for it is always possible to suggest one other alternative in all cases; besides being and non-being, we can admit the indefinite; affirmation and negation do not exhaust all attitudes towards an assertum; we may not assert anything at all, but simply entertain a datum without committing ourselves to any one of these modes. The contention is not academic. Consider for instance the two propositions—"An integer between 3 and 4 is prime"; "An integer between 3 and 4 is composite, not prime." Neither of these propositions is true, though they are contradictories in the formal sense. Can the Excluded Middle help us here? This is a case where *no* adjective, no alternative, can be predicated without absurdity. The illusory snake is another example; it cannot accept the predicates sat and asat, for it is not an existent.

[1] This is possible in the case of mathematics and other purely deductive sciences, where we possess a knowledge of the entire field so completely and unerringly, that we can formulate the alternatives exhaustively, and by the negation of the one we can affirm the other, and *vice versa*.

If we want to formulate the contradictory of any proposition—'S is P'—it is not only 'S is not-P' but also 'S is not'; i.e. the proposition is contradicted if the subject does not exist. It is clear that because there are two contradictories to any position, we can never pass from the denial of the position to any one of the contradictories, or *vice versa*. This is tantamount to giving up Excluded Middle.

A formal objection, pointed out by Johnson,[1] can also be raised against the law. If it were true, the existential import of a proposition and that of its obverse, which is based on the Excluded Middle, must be neither more nor less. 'S is not P' says nothing about the existence of S or P; the proposition would be valid even if they had not existed. What is required is that the combination SP should not be found, and this is available with or without the existence of these terms. Following formal logic, 'S is not P' can be positively rendered into 'S is non-P'. But this is more than a mere verbal change. The new proposition *affirms* a negative predicate of a subject S. If S were not an existent, the proposition would be meaningless, as it would be even if there were no P and non-P. But as we have seen, the original proposition gives no guarantee of the existence of S or P. The obverse imports, tacitly under the cover of an indubitable law, existential matter not to be found in the original proposition. The obverse will be valid, only if one implied premise is supplied. Therefore it is clear that the principle on which obversion is based, namely the Excluded Middle, is not valid. 'S is not P' does not commit us to any position, while 'S is non-P' commits us to the existence of S and possibly of P and non-P. It is apparent that Excluded Middle is not a purely formal principle, but a device to serve a metaphysical doctrine, in which to negate a judgment is taken as affirming a negative predicate. It seems to be a very easy device for asserting the existence of any subject; its only trouble seems to be confined to the assignment of a positive or a negative predicate; the fundamental question about the existence of the subject of a judgment is left to take care of itself.

The Law of Excluded Middle is for the regulation of thought. But here the question is whether thought itself is competent to grasp reality, and not the internal ordering of thoughts. The Law, even if formally valid, is applicable within thought, and has no relevance with regard to the metaphysical problem about the relation of Thought to Reality.

[1] *Logic*, Part I, pp. 71 ff.

IV IS CRITICISM POSSIBLE WITHOUT THE ACCEPTANCE OF PRAMĀṆAS?

The Mādhyamika need not have a thesis of his own nor need he admit any of the alternatives suggested. He has, however, to accept the valid sources of knowledge, the pramāṇas. Otherwise, he would be putting himself out of court at the very outset; he cannot participate in a discussion as a disputant.[1]

He has to urge and bring home to the opponent the consequences of a view. This can be done only by accepting principles of logic and canons of evidence. If without argument and evidence any statement, even this that 'Everything is relative', could be proved, then the most extravagant statement about the reality of all things would be valid.[2] If, to escape this predicament, the proofs and sources of knowledge are accepted, universal scepticism or śūnyatā must be abandoned. The Mādhyamika will then be compelled to formulate, like others, his theory about the number, nature and the object of the pramāṇas. And he will further be compelled to discuss the question of their validity.[3]

The acceptance of the pramāṇas may thus be forced on the Mādhyamika on one of the following grounds: (i) that they are indispensable for any philosophical investigation, criticism included; (ii) that they are indubitably certain, axiomatic, and to doubt them will be self-stultification; (iii) or that they are universally accepted by all, philosophers and others.

This objection is based on a misconception of the nature of the

[1] Śrī Harṣa, influenced as he is by the Mādhyamika dialectic, raises this objection in the very beginning in his *KhaṇḍanaKhaṇḍakhādya* (p. 5). Is any discussion possible without a previous acceptance of the pramāṇas by both the participants in the dispute?: atha kathāyāṁ vādino niyamam etādṛśaṁ manyante, pramāṇādayaḥ sarvatantrasiddhāntatayā siddhāḥ padārthāḥ santīti kathakābhyām abhyupagamyam. tad apare na kṣamante. tat kasya hetoḥ etc.

[2] Nāgārjuna himself raises these objections in his *Vigrahavyāvarttanī*: hetos tato na siddhir naiḥsvābhāvyāt kuto hi te hetuḥ; nirhetukasya siddhir na copapannāsya te'rthasya. yadi cāhetoḥ siddhiḥ svabhāvavinivarttanasya te bhavati; svābhāvyāstitvam mamāpi nirhetukaṁ siddham. atha hetor astitvaṁ bhāvaṇaiḥsvābhāvyam ity anupapannam; loke naiḥsvābhāvyāt na hi kaścana vidyate bhāvaḥ. VV. 17–19 (p. 9).

[3] atra kecit paricodayanti; anutapannā iti kim ayam pramāṇajo niścaya utāpramāṇajaḥ. tatra yadi pramānaja iṣyate, tadedaṁ vaktavyam: kati pramāṇāni, kim lakṣaṇāni kiṁ viṣayāni, kiṁ svata utpannāni, kiṁ parata ubhayato' hetuto veti. athāpramāṇajaḥ sa na uktaḥ. pramāṇādhīnatvāt premeyādhigamasya. MKV. p. 55.

dialectic. It may be the correct and fruitful procedure in commonsense and the sciences where we have to deal with the objective world to accept the logical canons. Here it would be suicidal. If these principles are accepted on the strength of other principles, this would lead to a *regress ad infinitum.*[1] If they are accepted without proof, an element of arbitrariness is introduced: of certain propositions we demand proof and of certain others we waive that.[2] These principles, it might be urged, should be taken as axiomatic, self-valid, and hence require no proof. They make proof possible, but themselves require no proof like the lamp which illumines objects illumining itself, or the balance (tulā) which serves as a standard for itself and other things.[3]

There is, however, a vital difference between the example of the lamp (pradīpa) or the balance (tulā) and the Pramāṇas. Light itself does not stand in need of illumination. It is unlike the object which is shrouded in darkness first and is later revealed by the lamp by dispelling darkness.[4] Logical canons and pramāṇas are not indubitably certain like light. They are themselves object of knowledge, and divergent views are held with regard to them.

It might be held that there is some immediate experience which gives us direct access to these principles. There is, however, no such

[1] yadi pramāṇādhīnaḥ prameyādhigamas tāni pramāṇāni kena paricchidyanta iti *Vigrahavyāvartanyāṁ* vihito doṣaḥ; tadaparihārāt. MKV. p. 59. anyair yadi pramāṇaih pramāṇasiddhir bhavaty anavasthā; nādeḥ siddhis tatrāsti naiva madhyasya nāntasya. VV. 32 (p. 16).

[2] teṣām atha pramāṇair vinā prasiddhiḥ vihīyate vādaḥ; vaiṣamikatvaṁ tasmin viśeṣahetuś ca vaktavyaḥ. VV, 33 (p. 16).

[3] This example of the lamp (pradīpa) or fire is subjected to a detailed analysis by Nāgārjuna in his *Vigrahavyāvartanī* (34–40) and the *Mādhyamika Kārikās* (VII, 8–12) and by Śānti Deva in his *Bodhicaryāvatāra* (IX, 18–19). These examples are also cited in the *Nyāya Sūtras* (II, 1, 8–11) in answer to the objection of the Mādhyamika about the untenability of the relation between Pramāṇa and Prameya. The two cannot be conceived as one prior to or dependent on the other, pramāṇa as prior to the prameya and vice versa; nor are the two simultaneous (mutually dependent) . . . The *Tātparyaṭīkā* explicitly states that the objections are by the Mādhyamika: ayam atra pūrvapakṣiṇo Mādhyamikāḥ (*Tāt. Ṭīkā* pp. 360, 362, Chowkhambha Edn.).

[4] An object that is illumined by the lamp passes through two phases: it is first shrouded in darkness and then the darkness is destroyed. This destruction of darkness is the illuminating function of the lamp, prakāśo hi tamovadhaḥ. The lamp does not pass through these two stages. If it did, if it were in darkness first, it would itself stand in need of being lighted up. When the lamp reveals objects, it is not an object itself, and if it is itself made an object, then it does not function as revealing objects.

empirical experience that is without the mediation of the categories or the interpretative function of the intellect.[1] It is possible to show, as Kant has done, that all experience is subject to conditioning by the *a priori* categories of the understanding. Though this knowledge may be considered true for practical purposes, yet when we strive for the ultimate and immediate truth, the categorising function has to be eliminated. A direct intuitive experience of the canons of knowledge free from the possibility of doubt, distortion, and interpretation is thus not possible. Intellectual intuition is not denied by the Mādhyamika; only it is transcendent to thought as well as to phenomena.

Nor is there unanimity among philosophers about the nature, number and function of the logical canons and sources of knowledge.[2] If there were to arise a dispute concerning the number and nature of these, it would hardly be consistent to suggest their initial acceptance in settling the issue in dispute. It would be circular reasoning to accept the pramāṇas in order to determine these very pramāṇas. And if a discussion could be begun without having to accept the pramāṇas, the rule that no discussion is possible without the previous acceptance of the pramāṇas, is nullified. If one discussion can be begun and conducted unconditionally, other discussions can fare equally well.[3] In any case we have to make a distinction between any ordinary enquiry about objects and one which is concerned with the fundamental presuppositions of knowledge.

[1] athāpi syād anubhava eṣo'smākam iti. etad apy ayuktaṁ, yasmād anubhava eṣa mṛṣā, anubhavatvāt, taimirikadvicandrādyanubhavavad .iti. tataś ca anubhavasyāpi sādhyamānatvāt tena pratyavasthānam ayuktam iti. MKV. p. 58.

[2] It is a commonplace that different systems give different answers to the four sets of questions that may be raised with regard to the pramāṇas: their number, the specific nature of each, their object, and the result they lead to. cf. *Nyāya-bindu-ṭīkā* (B. Ind.) p. 7: caturdhā cātra vipratipattiḥ, saṁkhyā-lakṣaṇa-gocara-phala-viṣayā;" *Prakaraṇapañcikā*; p. 38: "svarūpa-saṁkhyā-rtha-phaleṣu vādibhir yato vivādā bahudhā vitenire; tato vayaṁ tat-pratibodhasiddhaye pramāṇapārāyaṇam ārabhāmahe." *ParīkṣāmukhaSūtra Ṭīkā*, I: "svarūpa-saṁkhya-viṣaya-phala-lakṣaṇāṣu catasṛṣu vipratipattiṣu madhye", etc.

[3] The *Khaṇḍana* gives this answer (p. 10–11): yad idaṁ bhavatā dūṣaṇam uktam, tad api na vaktuṁ śakyam; kīdṛśīṁ maryādām ālambya pravṛttāyāṁ kathāyām idam dūṣaṇam uktam . . . tathaiva kathāntarasyāpi prasakteḥ . . . tasmāt pramāṇādi-sattvāsattvābhyupagamaudāsīnyena vyavahāra-niyamena samayaṁ baddhvā pravarttitāyāṁ kathāyāṁ bhavatedaṁ dūṣaṇam uktam ity ucitam eva tathā sati syāt.

Moreover, there is no such thing as a neutral logic which every philosopher accepts or has to accept. The Realist has his own logic and the Idealist's is different from this. The various interpretations given of the Law of Identity or any other fundamental dictum illustrate the point. They are not agreed even about the nature of judgment. The logic of a philosophical system is the way in which its fundamental position is elaborated through concepts and verbal symbols. Different logics are the inevitable expression of different metaphysical standpoints. If you accept consciously or otherwise a particular metaphysic, you also accept a particular technique of elaboration, which is the logic of that system. Logic is metaphysical to the core. Nothing is more common in philosophical discussions than to find the disputants emerging at the end of the discussion with their differences more accentuated. It is not an accident then that different philosophical systems have continued to the present day without any indication of their going out of existence. If a neutral logic acceptable to all had been available to us, the differences could have been composed long ago. It need not be pointed out that philosophers differ because they tenaciously stick to their initial prejudice. For, this initial and unconscious bias is what we have called a metaphysical standpoint or dṛṣṭi (abhiniveśa). Entering a discussion to settle differences merely proves that the disputants are not as yet aware of their fundamental differences, and they entertain the fond hope of composing them through the discussion.

The most serious objection is that no criticism of knowledge is possible if this contention, that some canons of knowledge are to be accepted as true and sacrosanct, were conceded unquestioningly. By this simple device of raising a sort of point of order or veto, criticism would be stifled. That the pramāṇas or other principles condition our knowledge of thinking is true. They function as the *a priori* factors, more or less in an unconscious way. But a critique which tries to lay bare the *a priori* cannot itself be conditioned by the *a priori*: for this would be to make the *a priori* perform a two-fold function at once: as the conditioning factors of knowledge and the object known (conditioned). If the *a priori* were known by another set of *a priori*, this would lead not only to a regress, but we should never become aware of the working of the *a priori*, the constitution of knowledge. This is really to deny the possibility of a critique of knowledge. The insistence on the unquestionable acceptance of the pramāṇas or other canons of knowledge is really the device of dogmatism to stifle criticism, dialectic. It is the denial of the self-sufficiency of Reason to sit on judgment over itself. The dialectic tells us how Reason works and fashions theories, how experience itself is constituted. This enquiry then cannot, from the nature of the case, presuppose or postulate anything as valid and inviolable.

Possibly, the objection might be the result of faulty terminology. Terms such as 'Knowledge', 'Reason', 'Proof' etc., are used in a two-fold sense. 'Knowledge' is used for the knowledge of objects as also for knowledge of this knowledge itself; 'Reason' is used not only to mean particular arguments, but also for the awareness of what reason is and how it works. Knowledge *of* the *a priori* categories is not knowledge *through* the *a priori*. The proof that the *a priori* function in knowledge (the entire *Critique* of Kant is a brilliant example of this) is not scientific proof of the empirical kind, which is mediated *through* the *a priori*. Knowledge *of* the *a priori* is not an empirical activity at all; it is no knowledge comparable to the knowledge of objects. The procedure and value of the two are entirely different. Empirical knowledge works *through* and because of the pre-suppositions; it is saṁvṛti, and is directed towards understanding and handling objects. Critical knowledge is just the awareness of these presuppositions; it is thus the disabusing of the mind of its pre-suppositions. Its value is clarity and freedom, and not any secular utility. It is Śūnyatā or paramārtha-satya. The Mādhyamika distinguishes between dṛṣṭijñāna which is conditioned through concepts and words (savikalpa, prapañca) and prajñā or śūnyatā which is totally free of these (nirvikalpa, niṣprapañca).

The unhappy terminology used even in philosophical treatises is a predicament of language. Language is pre-eminently an instrument to express the empirical. This is not only natural, but pragmatically the more important. Very often philosophy, especially absolutism, has to convey through the usual symbols what admittedly cannot be symbolised. This it does by superimposing an induced or artificial signification on conventional words. Many of the ambiguities and apparent inconsistencies in the Mādhyamika or other absolutist systems are traceable to this necessary predicament. They are ever trying to convey through language and concepts things for which language was not intended as an instrument of expression.

V DIALECTIC AND SIGNIFICANT NEGATION

Is unqualified, universal, negation—a thorough-going śūnyatā like the Mādhyamika Dialectic—consistent?[1] And even if consistent, is it significant?

1. If A is negated here, it is possibly existent elsewhere. When a person's mistaken identity is negated, it necessarily leads to his correct identification. We cannot stop with mere denial. Negation is significant only as *affirming* a real existing in some form or in some place other than what and where it was mistaken for.[2] Moreover, 'A is not B' may and does usually mean that A is Y. The coin is not elliptical, because it is circular. The latter statement is not only the ground for the negative judgment, but is also the completion of it: 'A is not B, *because* it is Y.'

Every judgment without exception challenges the question: 'Why it is so?' or at least 'How do you know it to be so?'; the former question demanding the cause or real ground, the latter demanding the cause of knowledge or logical ground. . . . In denial then there must be *this* element also of positive import, the attribute which justifies the denial for us.[3] Denial, as a form of judgment, must be capable of contributing something positive to knowledge. . . . We must assume with Plato that knowledge is knowledge of something; and if the nature of 'nothing', as e.g. the abstraction of empty thinking, can be known, the nothing is so far and in that

[1] Universal negation is self-stultifying, it may be contended, as is done by the *Nyāya Sūtras* (II, i, 13–14). If a reason were assigned for the negation, that reason has to be excluded from the scope of negation, (tat-prāmāṇye vā na sarva-pramāṇa-pratiṣedhaḥ). Negation ceases to be universal. If no reason were assigned, the negation is not valid, as it is unsupported by any reason. (sarva-pramāṇa-pratiṣedhāc ca pratiṣedhāsiddhiḥ). The objection misses the essence of the dialectic. Śūnyatā (Universal relativity or the non-existence of any thing-in-itself) is not established by some reason or condition outside the things criticised. It is shown to be the very nature of things, and the showing is not another thing. Just as when it is held that 'Things are momentary' or 'Things are eternal' momentariness or eternity characterises all things, and is therefore not another thing. This objection is taken up for consideration at the end of the chapter.

[2] The *Vigrahavyāvartanī* (11–12) states the realist's contention almost in the same words: sata eva pratiṣedho nāsti ghaṭo geha ity ayaṁ yasmāt; dṛṣṭaḥ pratiṣedho' yaṁ sataḥ svabhāvasya te tasmāt. (VV–11). iha ca sato' rthasya pratiṣedhaḥ kriyate, nāsataḥ, tad yathā nāsti ghaṭo gehe iti sato ghaṭasya pratiṣedhaḥ kriyate, nāsataḥ. evam eva nāsti bhāvo dharmāṇām iti sataḥ svabhāvasya pratiṣedhaḥ prāpnoti, nāsataḥ (VV. p. 7).
atha nāsti sa svabhāvaḥ kin nu pratiṣiddhyate tvayā-nena vacanenarte vacanāt pratiṣedhaḥ siddhyate hyasataḥ. (VV. 12.)

[3] Bosanquet—*Logic*, Vol. I, p. 287.

sense something. All significance then is in this sense ***positive*** significance, and significant negation must, therefore, convey something positive.[1]

For significant denial bare exclusion (the contradictory negation of formal logic) is but a necessary step, a movement towards a determinate position. This means that all possible alternatives proposed for understanding the real or some aspect of it can be rejected only at the peril of giving up thought altogether. And even if negation is thorough-going without any positive counterpart, we have to take into account the negating act, the person who pronounces the negation and possibly the thing negated etc.[2] In the absence of these, negation itself will not be possible.

Against this interpretation of negation the following considerations must be urged. Negation has to be understood only in the context of the correction of an error or the cancellation of an illusion. It is admittedly more subjective than affirmation. As Sigwart says: "The judgment 'A is not B' means, it is false, it must not be believed, that A is B; hence immediately and directly the negation is a judgment concerning a positive judgment that has been essayed or passed; only indirectly is it a judgment concerning the subject of this judgment."[3]

Affirmation and negation do not stand on the same footing, and the demand to have something positive in negation is not to understand it correctly. Negative judgment is the *negation of judgment*, and not one more judgment. It is on a higher level of self-consciousness. In affirming we need not be conscious of the affirmation; in negating we are necessarily conscious of the negating function. The two, affirmation and negation, cannot be taken as co-ordinate and equal. They function in different ways.

The truth of the statement to be negated is not presupposed as a necessary condition of negation;[4] every negation then would be a self-contradiction. If negation implied the truth of the corresponding

[1] Ibid, p. 283.

[2] Cf. nanv evaṁ saty asti grāho grāhyaṁ ca tad grahītā ca; pratiṣedhaḥ pratiṣeddhyaṁ pratiṣeddhā ceti ṣaṭkaṁ tat. atha naivāsti grāho na ca grāhyaṁ na ca grahītāraḥ; pratiṣedhaḥ pratiṣeddhyaṁ pratiṣeddhāro' sya tu na santi. pratiṣedhaḥ pratiṣedhyaṁ pratiṣeddhāraś ca yadyuta na santi; siddhā hi sarvabhāvā yeṣām evaṁ svabhāvaś ca. VV. 14–16.

[3] Sigwart, *Logic*, Vol. I, p. 122 (Eng. Trans.).

[4] "We have not always judged a matter to be true before we deny it. And if an affirmation of the same content is to subsist as a condition of the negation, it seems doubtful whether a negation would not always have to be self-contradictory"—(Bosanquet, *Logic*, Vol. I, pp. 277–278) cf. also Sigwart—*Logic* Vol. I, pp. 119 and 149—(Eng. Trans.)

affirmation, no negative judgment can be made, no statement can be contradicted, no error can be corrected. To say that negation annuls the previous statement but partially is really no answer. For, of the rejected part again it cannot be maintained that that too is partly real, as this would be to reject nothing at all, not even a part.[1] In the last resort it has to be admitted that the negated, to some extent or other, is not real in any sense. It is purely subjective, an appearance.

A dialectical answer given by Nāgārjuna to this question may be mentioned. If negation of itself implied the truth of the corresponding affirmation (the thing negated) (yadi sata eva pratiṣedhaḥ), then the denial or negation of Śūnyatā itself would, according to this dictum, imply the truth of Śūnyatā.[2] What is negated need not be real, is not real. In fact, negation is relevant only as excluding arbitrary interpretations and conjectures of the real. It is significant as doing this pruning work.

Even in the limited sense in which negation is accepted by different systems of philosophy, it is possible to show that there is an element of subjectivity—constructive interpretation or distortion—for which there is no counterpart in reality. The flower-vase is not on the mantelpiece; it may be present elsewhere, but its relation with the object here as its mode is non-existent. The mistaken *identification* of a man with the lamp-post has no objective counterpart. It may even be cogently urged that not only the mistaken *relation*, but the appearance itself, is no object, having merely an epistemic existence. For, the illusory cannot be had apart from the context of that experience. It has no existence apart from knowledge;[3] but the real must have substantive existence of its own.

[1] 'Partially real' may be taken to mean approximately or imperfectly true. Partial truth is an abstraction, as a mere part is put for the whole and is misleading when taken as giving a *complete* picture. Though a complete view may incorporate elements from an incomplete view, the former must be taken as a *substitution* and not as an addition of partial views. For, the respective places accorded to things in a complete picture are bound to differ from those in the incomplete one. And the *claim* of each incomplete view to give us the whole picture and the only picture can never be incorporated. There is thus a great deal of subjectivity (unreality) in the view that is negated.

[2] VV. 62–63.

[3] Cf. the Vedānta notion of the prātibhāsika as the pratibhāsa-mātra-śarīratva; the appearance has no existence apart from our apprehension of it. But this is no existence at all; the sat (real) is in itself and not in and through our knowing of it. Being real, it *may* be known; but the knowing does not make it: being a vastu, it is not puruṣatantra. The prātibhāsika is mithyā (unreal), as it is annulled by knowledge. (jñānanivartyattvaṁ mithyātvam). See *Advaita Siddhi* pp. 160 ff.

2. As for the question: 'how do we negate'—the ground of negation, it might be thought that we already know what the thing in question really is, and are, therefore, in a position to reject wrong views about it. But if we are already in possession of the truth, negation becomes a gratuitous procedure. Negation is not a necessary instrument, a movement, in our reaching the real. On the Mādhyamika view, negation is just that instrument by which we know the real.

It is not always the case that we have first known what a thing is before we negated its imputed character. The 'snake' that I misperceive may be realised to be no snake from my shouts and cautious proddings, made from a safe distance, not evoking any response in the 'snake'. In fact, my conviction that the presentation before me is not a snake at all—the negation itself—may lead me, by dissipating fear and ignorance, to the knowledge that it is a rope and not *vice versa*. The extravagant claims and inconsistencies of a philosophical position may be sufficient ground to condemn it as false without our being in a position to supply the real solution. No thesis can be accepted as true simply on the ground that a better one is not produced.

The question may be more specifically stated in the context of the Mādhyamika philosophy; which comes first: knowledge of the Real and then condemnation of phenomena as Śūnya, because they fail to measure up to the criterion of the Real? or is it the other way round, that we are led to discover the nature of the real through our realisation of the inconsistencies in phenomena? If the first, it is unintelligible how we could have had a knowledge of the real at the very outset. And having had access to the heart of reality, why did we turn away from it to indulge in a thoroughly gratuitous condemnation of the world. This negative act has no discovery-value; it does not light our pathway to reality. It may be said that though we do not have a full and direct knowledge of the real to start with, we still have a formal criterion of it, and this enables us to pass judgment on phenomena. This contention too is not sound. If the criterion were purely formal, it is inexplicable why we have started with that particular criterion of reality and not with any other, any criterion being formal. The entire procedure would then be highly hypothetical: *if* you accept A as the standard, then c, d, e are the consequences; and if instead B were accepted x, y, z, will be the consequences. In such a case, the starting-point cannot be justified; and besides, we shall have nothing to decide between the rival hypotheses. This might be the method of speculative dogmatic metaphysics; it is not the spirit of the Mādhyamika dialectic.

All this arises because we invert the real order of our discovery. The progression is from the appearance to the real, from the false to the true[1] and not *vice versa*. There is no passage from the real to the unreal. Nor is it needed. Our natural attitude is to take anything that appears as real. For instance, we mistake the body for the self. This is an unconscious process of identification; for none can consciously fall into illusion. Then occurs the shock of disillusionment. Consequent on this, we become reflective. Disillusionment or the cancelling consciousness reveals the soul of the appearance by tearing off its superficial vestures as it were. Only this experience provides us with the criterion of the real as *abādhya*, nirvikalpa, or aparapratyaya (the uncontradicted, the non-conceptual thing-in-itself) and the illusory as bādhya (the cancelled); and not any *a priori* formal conception.

The criterion itself must be elicited through criticism. A seeker after truth cannot start with any *a priori* criterion; that would be dogmatically to prejudge the issue. What is implied in the philosophical consciousness as embodied in the different systems is the *urge* to know the Unconditioned, the ultimately real. Through gropings and trials, through systems of dogmatic speculative metaphysics and their necessary clash, the light of criticism breaks out. That takes us to the Real.

The above may be taken as the Mādhyamika conception of the function of negation. It is instructive to compare this with the Vedānta and Vijñānavāda conceptions. In all the three systems, Reason (discursive thought) is transcended, and the Absolute is reached through negation. The differences of these absolutist systems may, however, be treated as different ways of formulating negation.

In the Vedānta, negation applies to becoming and difference, which are falsely ascribed to Pure Being. It is prompted by an extra-philosophical or theological revelation.[2] The Upaniṣads (Vedānta)

[1] Cf. the Upaniṣadic text: asato mā sad gamaya, tamaso mā jyotir gamaya, mṛtyor ma'mṛtaṁ gamayeti (*Bṛ. Up*. I, iii, 28). From the unreal lead me to the real, from darkness to light, from the mortal to the immortal.

[2] Brahman is aupaniṣada—known only through the Upaniṣad; it is therefore, declared as śāstra-yoni (*Br. Sūt.* I, 1–3). The oft-recurring texts, ācāryavān puruṣo vedo, tadvijñānārthaṁ gurum evābhigacchet etc., make out the system as based on revelation to start with.

reveal and declare to us verbally that the non-dual ātman (Pure Being, Self) alone is real. We start our spiritual journey already in possession of the map of the real. The initial verbal knowledge is helped by the dialectic of difference which makes for the removal of doubt and conflict.[1] The process begun in revelation is perfected in the intuitive knowledge of Brahman (nididhyāsana, anubhavāvasānatvād brahma-vijñānaṣya).

In the Mādhyamika system no *ab extra* revelation is relied on. The dialectical consciousness, implicit in speculative systems of philosophy, matures through their necessary mutual conflict. Negation applies *directly to the warring views* of reality, to all vikalpa, and only *indirectly* to the false appearance. Negation is purely logical as it takes its cue from the contradictions of the philosophical systems.

In the Yogācāra system negation is cancellation of objectivity—the independent existence of the object. This is not prompted by theological revelation as in the Vedānta nor by purely logical criticism as in the Mādhyamika. The Yogācāra bases himself on the psychical experience of trance-states, where the object progressively dwindles and vanishes altogether in the highest reaches (in the asamjñi or nirodha samāpattis). The highest state of trance is taken as the Norm of the Real, and this supplies him the metaphysical dictum: Citta (Vijñāna), Consciousness, is all;[2] the object is nothing but a false imputation. The dialectic against realism (the reality of object) gets started, and the sole reality of Consciousness (Vijñaptimātratā) is reaffirmed and reassured. The cue for the negation is psychological in origin.

3. It has been urged, as an implication of significant denial, that we cannot stop with mere negation; it demands completion. The Mādhyamika dialectic is apparently a sinner in this respect, and critics have not hesitated to dub the system as nihilistic. Against such uninformed opinion, it may be stated at once that the system is not nihilism as it rejects the negative attitude too. It is not that the judgment must be replaced by another judgment. The completion may belong to a different order of knowledge; it may be by intuition. Negation is the pointer to the breakdown of the judgment-attitude.

[1] manana or śrutyanukūla tarka (criticism in conformity with revelation) is valuable as removing want of understanding (apratipatti) and misunderstanding (vipratipatti) with regard to the real.

[2] cittamātraṁ, bho, jinaputrā, yaduta traidhātukam iti vacanāt.

It shows that Reality does not accept our ideal construction.[1] Negation reveals to us the purely subjective character of thought. Thought is not an organon of the real, but a distortion of it. It is even wrong to speak of the negative judgment. To judge is to interpret and ideally to reconstruct reality in thought. Judgment *qua* judgment must always be affirmative, ascriptive. Negative judgment is as little meaningful as the negative copula of traditional logic. Negative judgment is the *negation of judgment.*

Negation is thus the despair of thought; but it is at once the opening up of a new avenue—the path of intuition. Negation is the threshold of intellectual intuition. Śūnyatā is not only the negation of dṛṣṭi (view, judgment), but is Prajñā. As spiritual life is born of the abandonment of the secular, intuition is made possible by universal negation. Śūnyatā is negative only for thought; but in itself it is the non-relational knowledge of the absolute. It may even be taken as more universal and positive than affirmation. For to affirm 'A is B', that a figure is a triangle, is inplicitly to deny that it is a square or circle. Every affirmation implies an element of negation. Both affirmation and negation are determinations, limitations or negations. The dialectic as Śūnyatā is the removal of the constrictions which our concepts, with their practical or sentimental bias, have put on reality. It is the *freeing* of reality of the artificial and accidental restrictions, and *not the denial* of reality. Śūnyatā is negation of negations; it is thus a re-affirmation of the infinite and inexpressibly positive character of the Real.

VI IS ŚŪNYATĀ A THEORY?

Very often the objection is advanced that Śūnyatā which criticises all theories is but another theory. The Mādhyamika dialectic which negates all positions is but one more position. And as a new position has been advanced, this would require to be negated by another dialectic and that by another, thus leading to a regress.

The first criticism considered in the beginning of this chapter is: how criticism is possible without a position; the present objection is

[1] Any and every kind of thought-construction has to be denied of the Real. The *Prajñāpāramitā* and other texts speak of 18 or 20 kinds of Śūnyatā: Śūnyatā of external objects (bahirdhā-śūnyatā), of internal states (adhyātma) etc. See AAA. pp. 89 ff; *Śatasāhasrikā Prajñā Pār.* pp. 77, 886, 1407; *Mahāvyutpatti* Sect. 37. *Dharma Saṇgraha*, section 41. BCAP. p. 416.
Pañcaviṁśati pp. 195–8. See Appendix I. *The Twenty Modes of Śūnyatā.*

that criticism itself is a position. As such one can be treated as the converse of the other. Both these objections spring from a common misunderstanding of the nature of dialectic.

The objection that Śūnyatā is itself a theory is on a par with the one urged against the Vedānta. It is said that when the world is declared and cancelled as illusory, the illusoriness (mithyātva) itself would stand out as a fact, may be a negative fact, against Brahman. This is thought to militate against Absolutism—as the Absolute is confronted by an other.[1]

Criticism of theories is no theory. Criticism is but the awareness of what a theory is, how it is made up; it is not the proposing of a new theory. Negation of positions is not one more position. Dialectic, as analysis, does not impose any new thing; it reveals rather than add or distort. Its function is like that of light which merely shows up things in their true character. Suppose the analysis of theories, instead of merely revealing, were to distort or to add to what it analyses, how is this awareness that 'analysis adds or distorts' possible? For, *ex hypothesi*, this awareness of the analytic function may itself be of the nature of distortion; hence no statement about it can be valid.

[1] The Vedānta is considerably exercised over the status of the cessation of avidyā (avidyā-nivṛtti) or the illusoriness of the world (prapañca-mithyātva). Is the cessation of avidyā another fact, different from Brahman as well as from the world—a sort of fifth category different from sat, asat, both, and anirvacanīya; (pañcama-prakārā avidyā-nivṛttiḥ) or is it identical with Brahman? The first view is advocated by some Vedāntins—(see *Siddhānta-leśa*.), and perhaps Maṇḍana Miśra took the cessation of the world to be a negative fact and not a positive one and not therefore militating against the positive non-dualism of Brahman (bhāvādvaita). See Hiriyanna (*J.R.A.S.*, April 1923 and Jan. 1924), M. M. Kuppuswami Śāstrī Intr. to ***Brahma Siddhi*** pp. XI ff.

The accepted view of knowledgeable Vedāntins is that cessation of ignorance as absence (abhavā) is not distinct from, but identical with, Brahman, the substratum (adhikaraṇa-svarūpa). tasmād ajñāna-hānir ātmasvarūpaṁ tadākārā vṛttir veti siddham. ye tu pañcama-prakārādipakṣās, te tu manda-buddhi-vyutpādanārthā iti na tatsamarthanam arthayāmaḥ. *Advaitasiddhi* p. 885. The allied question whether a fresh effort is called for to prove the illusoriness of 'the illusoriness of the world' is put dilemmatically by the realists (e.g. *Nyāyāmṛta-Taraṅgiṇī*) thus: Is the illusoriness of the world illusory or real (prapañca-mithyātvam mithyā or satya); if the former, it means, as a case of double negation, the emphatic assertion of the reality of the world; (the world is not not-real); if the latter, the world too should be real likewise. In either case, absolutism will not be tenable. The objection is based on a misconception of the nature of mithyātva; for dṛśyatva (being object), the reason by which we pronounce anything illusory, is equally present in the pronouncement itself. prakṛte tu niṣedhyatāvacchedakam ekam eva dṛśyatvādi . . . etc. *Advaita-Siddhi* pp. 212–13.

In the last resort then, we have to accept pure analysis or mere awareness without any trace of distortion at some ultimate stage. The knowledge of what theories are cannot itself be a theory; knowledge of what a hypothesis is is not hypothetical. Analysis or criticism does not add to the stock of our existing knowledge. We gain in depth and not in extension. As no new fact is added, there is no necessity for launching on a regressive series of Śūnyatā.

Dialectic is reflective or self-conscious awareness of the previous state of dogmatic speculation, Reason (dṛṣṭi). A state which is merely subsequent in time is not necessarily reflective of the previous state. The content of the two states must be identical; otherwise one would be irrelevant to the other. And yet the reflective state is not a duplication of the other. The same content is more closely, clearly, *re*viewed. Reflective awareness of Reason, and this is Śūnyatā, belongs to a higher level of consciousness. Then alone can it be a review of views. Criticism is nothing but the theories turned inside out.[1]

In keeping with this contention that Śūnyatā (the dialectic) does not add anything to that to which it applies nor is it a different thing, it is stated at very many places in the *Aṣṭasāhasrikā* and other *Prajñā-pāramitā* texts, that rūpa is śūnya and śūnyatā is rūpa (rūpaṁ śūnyaṁ, śūnyataiva rūpam), and similarly with regard to vedanā, saṁjñā, saṁskāra, and vijñāna. If Śūnyatā were different from them, things will not be Śūnya (devoid of essential reality).[2] Therefore it is that saṁsāra and nirvāṇa are identical, there being not a trace of difference between them as Nāgārjuna declares.[3] Nirvāṇa is the reality of saṁsāra or conversely, saṁsāra is the falsity (saṁvṛti) of Nirvāna. Nirvāṇa is saṁsāra without birth and

[1] The argument of this contention is that Śūnyatā is Reflective awareness of theories; reflection cannot be understood except as analysis of the content of a previous state (theories); i.e. it does not have another content nor does it add anything to it but merely *re*veals, *re*views or *clarifies* the presented content. This revelation is not possible if the content analysed were absolutely unitary. Analysis (viveka or parīkṣā) is possible, only if the analysed contains incongruous elements. Thus reflective awareness or analysis has a content identical with the previous state, but it reveals its inner incongruity and is thus on a higher level of consciousness.

[2] na ca śūnyatā bhāvād vyatiriktā, bhāvasyaiva tat-svabhāvatvād; anyathā śūnyatāyā bhāvād vyatireke dharmāṇāṁ niḥsvabhāvatā na syāt. niḥsvbhāvatā tat-svabhāva iti sādhitaṁ prāk. BCAP pp. 416–7.

[3] MK. XXV 19–20; MKV. p. 535.

decay.[1] The difference between them is in *our way of looking at them*; it is epistemic, not metaphysical.

A further vital consideration with regard to Śūnyatā is that it is truly universal, the whole reality. If it were a theory or view, however exalted and useful it might be, it would still be a determination and limitation, a constriction of the real into this or that conceptual mould. To analyse a proposition is not to make another proposition. If that were the case, we cannot make any universal statement. For, the statement about the nature of *all* propositions will, on this contention, be itself a proposition; and it cannot be included in the "all" from the nature of the case (as being that which *states* and not falling within the *stated*). Nor can it be left out; for being a proposition (*ex hypothesi*) it ought to be included within the 'all' for the sake of completeness.[2] The predicament is insoluble, because the premise from which we have started, that statement about all propositions is itself a proposition, is wrong. The right way is to take the truly universal as not falling within the realm of judgment. Likewise, the self-conscious awareness of *all* points of view, or Reason as such, cannot itself be a view. Hence the true universal cannot be a view-point (a dṛṣṭi); and conversely all points of view and positions are particular, not universal.

The Mādhyamika very happily brings out the truth of the considerations urged above by stating that "Śūnyatā (the awareness of the hollowness) of *all* views is prescribed by the Jinas (Buddhas) as the way of deliverance; incurable indeed are they who take Śūnyatā itself as a view——"[3] "It is as if one were to ask,[4] when told that there was nothing to give, to be given that nothing."

Elsewhere it is stated that Śūnyatā should be handled with skill; it does great harm if wrongly understood, like a snake caught at

[1] MK. XXV. 9; MKV. p. 524.

[2] The dilemma is: as *making* a statement about propositions, it is the apprehension of them and not the apprehended; thus it *cannot be included* within the propositions, for that would mean the confusion of the knowing and the known (karma-kartṛ-virodha); nor *can it be excluded* from the 'all', for that would make our statement less universal; as the statement, being a proposition *ex hypothesi*, is not included within the 'all'. The predicament cannot be avoided even if the stating act were sought to becovered by a subsequent act of apprehension; for this would be repeating the difficulty without removing it.

[3] MK. XIII, 8.

[4] yo na kiṁcid api paṇyaṁ dāsyāmīty uktaḥ, sa ced 'dehi bhos tad eva mahyaṁ na kiṁcin nāma-paṇyam' iti brūyāt, sa kenopāyena śakyaḥ paṇyābhāvam grāhayitum. MKV. pp. 247–48.

the wrong end.[1] We are also expressly warned not to consider Śūnyatā as a theory, as one more theory. To quote the *Kāśyapa Parivarta*:

> Those, Kāśyapa, that (mis)apprehend Śūnyatā as a negative fact, I consider them the forlorn, the irrevocably lost. . . . Better it is to entertain the substance-view (pudgala-dṛṣṭi) of the magnitude of the Mount Sumeru than the Śūnyatā-view of the nihilist (abhāvābhiniviśinaḥ). Why is it so? Of all theories, Kāśyapa, Śūnyatā is the antidote. Him I call the incurable who mistakes Śūnyatā itself as a theory (dṛṣṭi). It is as if a drug, administered to cure a patient, were to remove all his disorders, but were itself to foul the stomach by remaining therein. Would you, Kāśyapa, consider the patient cured? . . . Likewise, Kāśyapa, Śūnyatā is the antidote for all dogmatic views; but him I declare incurable who misapprehends Śūnyatā itself as a theory.[2]

[1] MK. XXIV, 11.

[2] *Kāśyapa-Parivarta*, p. 97; sec. 65. also quoted in MKV. pp. 248–9.

CHAPTER SEVEN

APPLICATION OF THE DIALECTIC

THE application of the dialectic to some of the important categories of thought such as causality, motion, substance and quality, and self may be considered. This will show the concrete procedure of the dialectic, and help us in understanding its value as an organon of criticism. In fact this might have well preceded the general considerations of the dialectic; but in the interests of exposition the order has been reversed. It is not possible to exhaust the concrete applications of the dialectic or even to enumerate the general spheres with any measure of adequacy. The applications will be many and varied according to the opponent criticised and the occasion calling for criticism. In a system which is all dialectic, progress or development could be measured not in terms of doctrinal accretion, but in the criticism that it levels against particular systems and doctrines from time to time. Not having a content itself, the Mādhyamika dialectic receives its orientation from its criticism of human thought at every stage of its history. The dialectic performs the high office of philosophy in analysing the "absolute pre-suppositions" of thought. As analysis, the application will not add to the presuppositions, but only make us aware of them.

Nāgārjuna himself applied the dialectic against the Ābhidharmika system—the doctrine of Elements. The *Mādhyamika Kārikās* are a sustained attempt to evolve the Śūnyatā doctrine out of a criticism of the realistic and dogmatic interpretations of early Buddhism. His criticism of the Sāṁkhya and other systems of the ātma tradition is rare and implicit. His disciple and successor, Ārya Deva, pays considerable attention to the criticism of the Sāṁkhya and Vaiśeṣika systems. Buddhapālita and Bhāvaviveka carry on in a similar way. In Candrakīrti not only is the opposition to the Brāhmanical systems more evident, but a new line of criticism is met with. At several places, both in his *Prasannapadā* and the *Madhyamakāvatāra*, Vijñānavāda is criticised; the Mādhyamika standpoint is maintained as the true teaching on rational and textual grounds (yuktyāgamābhyām).[1] Dialectical criticism is turned against an inconsistent turn in the Mādhyamika fold itself, against the Svatantra (speculative) tendency of Bhāvaviveka.[2] In Śānti Deva, we find explicit criticism of the Brāhmanical systems and also of Vijñānavāda.[3] This shows that during the period between Candrakīrti and Śānti Deva Vijñānavāda was on the ascendent. Śāntarakṣita and his disciple Kamalaśīla pay particular attention to the Nyāya arguments and also to the Jaina. Vijñānavāda is accepted, and the doctrine of self-awareness (sva-saṁvedana) is even established. The force of their criticism, however, falls against the Mīmāṁsaka, especially against the arguments of the *Ślokavārttika* of Kumārila. The *Tattvasaṅgraha* also contains refutation of the Aupaniṣada and the Śabda-Brahma systems.

The successive application of the dialectic to systems of thought reveals the strains and stresses to which philosophy was subject in India down the ages.

II CRITIQUE OF CAUSALITY

The *Mādhyamika Kārikās* and other Mādhyamika treatises open with a critique of causality.[4] This is the central problem in Indian philosophy. The concept of causality a system advocates exhibits the logic of the entire system. There is a special reason why the Mādhyamika should pay particular attention to causality. The entire Buddhist thought revolves on the pivot of Pratītya Samutpāda; the Mādhyamika system is the interpretation of Pratītya Samutpāda as Śūnyatā.[5]

[1] MKV. pp. 61 ff. pp. 275–6. MA. pp. 40 ff. See Chap. XIII for the Mādhyamika criticism of the Vijñānavāda.

[2] MKV. pp. 14 ff., 36 ff., 196 ff., 351 ff.

[3] BCA. pp. 389 ff. and 523 ff.

[4] The importance of the problem may be gauged from the consideration that in the *Mādhyamika Kārikās* several chapters—I. (*Pratyaya Parīkṣā*), XV (*Svabhāva Parīkṣā*), XX (*Sāmagrī Parīkṣā*) and XXI (*Sambhava Vibhava Parīkṣā*)—directly deal with this at length, while several others deal with its practical application to pain, (duḥkha) Bondage and Freedom (*Bandha Mokṣa*), saṁskāra (motive Forces), karma-kartā (doer and the deed).

[5] yaḥ pratītya-samutpādaṁ paśyatīdaṁ sa paśyati; duḥkham samudayaṁ caiva nirodhaṁ mārgam eva ca MK. XXIV, 40, also 18 already quoted.
"yaḥ pratītya samutpādaḥ śūnyatā saiva te matā,"
Quoted in BCAP. p. 417.

A critique of causality has necessarily to be a criticism of the views held by different systems. It does not directly concern itself with the causal phenomenon; that is the work of science and common sense. Philosophy can only take into account our *understanding* of things; the datum of philosophy is not the raw fact, but the facts which have already been subjected to a measure of unification and synthesis by the understanding at work in science. The sciences formulate laws; they reduce sense-data to order through the application of relevant forms or categories. Philosophy strives to achieve a greater, a higher kind of, unity that is possible for Reason.

Except the materialists (the svabhāvavādins) who advocated the chance-origin of things, no serious philosophical system in India denied causality or took it as subjective; i.e., as formed through habit and association of ideas, and therefore as merely probable. The Buddhist, the Jaina and the Brāhmanical systems all subscribe to the principle of causality as governing all phenomena. Each interpreted it in its own way, and all of them, before the advent of the Mādhyamika, took it as ultimately real, as a feature of the unconditioned noumenon. The problem for the Mādhyamika is thus confined to proving that causality and other categories are of empirical validity only; they constitute the texture of phenomena. But with regard to the noumenon (tattva) they are mere ascriptions—vikalpa. To adopt Kantian phraseology, we might say that the categories are *empirically real but transcendentally ideal* (subjective, false). This conclusion the Mādhyamika establishes by showing that all the possible ways in which the categories can be understood under the forms of identity, difference, or both, or neither are riddled with contradiction. This shows their relativity and their limitation to the phenomenal realm.

For Kant the problem was first to vindicate the empirical reality, the *a priority* of causality, substance etc., against the contention of Hume, who reduced them to association of ideas and habit. For Hume causality etc. were invalid (subjective) even empirically; they are not true of phenomena even. As such his position militated against science and commonsense. It has been already pointed out that though Buddhism is usually thought to be Humean in its outlook, this should be confined to the dictum that existents are discrete atomic entities. Unlike Hume, the Buddhists accepted causality as a universal and objective principle, ultimately valid of the unconditioned too. Even with regard to the notion of substance (soul), they held that this was not of empirical origin, being beginningless as avidyā (satkāyadṛṣṭi). For Kant then there was a double task: to prove the categories of the understanding to be *a priori* (this he does in the *Analytic*), and then to show that they are valid within phenomenon alone and are not constitutive of the noumenon. This he does in the *Transcendental Dialectic*. The Mādhyamika procedure is simple and direct. He had not to vindicate the empirical reality of the causal principle, but only to urge its restriction to the sphere of phenomena.

III SATKĀRYA VĀDA (SVATA-UTPATTI) DIALECTICALLY ANALYSED

Four alternative views are usually considered with regard to causality and other categories. We may consider the effect as the self-expression of the cause, or as caused by factors other than itself, or both, or neither.[1] The last alternative amounts to giving up the notion of causation, as it means that things are produced at random through sheer chance. The third alternative is really an amalgam of the first two. In fact the first two are the principal alternatives to be considered. Self-production, or the identity of cause and effect, is the Sāṅkhya view of causation (satkārya vāda); the Buddhist takes them to be totally different. One emphasises the continuity between cause and effect, the other the emergent aspect of the effect. Dialectical criticism discloses the inherent flaw in each conception.

Some of the arguments have already been set forth in a previous chapter. Additional arguments and objections may be considered here. It has already been shown that there is no point in mere self-duplication (utpāda-vaiyarthyāt); production must mean change, the emergence of a more useful factor not already present. There is also no end to the process of self-duplication (anavasthā-prasanga-doṣāc ca). In self-becoming, what prevents the seed from duplicating itself *ad nauseum* without producing the sprout, the leaves, the flowers, fruits etc., one after the other?

One may attempt to improve the position by stating that an entity is potential in the beginning, and then it becomes actual, and that there is a difference of states, not of substances, between the cause and the effect. If the cause is fully actual (niṣpanna), there is no purpose in its reproducing itself.[2] Besides, the entity that is

[1] MK. I, 1; MA. VI, 8 (p. 7); BCAP. 355 ff.

[2] BCAP. pp. 355–56; TSP. pp. 23 ff; MKV. pp. 14 and 22.

produced, being an other, cannot be identical with the cause. If the cause were partly actual and partly potential, the thing would *not be one*; it would then be containing two opposed natures. If the cause were wholly potential (aniṣpanna), then it cannot manifest itself, become actual of its own accord; the factor (the efficient cause) by which formless matter becomes actual must be different from it. And if it contained the efficient cause of its change within itself, there would not be any state in which it remains purely potential. For, having all the necessary and sufficient conditions for its production within itself (i.e. if the cause were self-contained and self-sufficient as the doctrine of satkāryavāda should mean logically), it still continues to be in the potential state for an appreciable period, then it would either not produce at all; or be dependent on an external factor. This would be to give up self-causation. This criticism is very pertinent with regard to the Prakṛti of the Sāṁkhya. What causes it to pass from the state of pure potentiality (sāmyāvasthā) to the manifest form. Although the Sāṁkhya tries to slur over this fact, it is the presence of the Puruṣa who, in the ultimate analysis, supplies just that element of disturbance which sets Prakṛti on its course of evolution, very much like the piercing of the dam releasing the impounded waters.[1]

If the cause and effect were identical, how is one to function *as cause* and the other *as effect*.[2] Their natures are different. Propositions true of the one are not true of the other. The distinction between the two cannot be made except on the ground of different notions; otherwise there would be a distinction without a difference.[3] As Nāgārjuna puts it, "The identity of cause and the effect (act and the result) is utterly untenable; if so, there would be no difference between the doer and the thing done.[4] In fact, acceptance of satkārya-vāda would logically lead to the abolition of all difference. The entire universe must collapse into a colourless, differenceless mass.[5]

[1] A similar example is given in the *Yoga Sūtras*, IV 3.

[2] na hi yad yasmād avyatiriktaṁ tat tasya kāryaṁ kāraṇaṁ vā yuktaṁ, bhinna-lakṣaṇatvāt kāryakāraṇayoḥ. anyathā hīdaṁ kāryam idaṁ kāraṇaṁ vety asamkīrṇa-vyavasthā kathaṁ bhavet. TSP. p. 22.

[3] MA. VI, 13.

[4] MK. XX 19, 20.

[5] anyathā bhedavyavahārocheda eva syāt. tataś ca sattvarajastamasāṁ caitanyānāṁ ca parasparaṁ bhedābhyupagamo nirnibandhana eva syāt. sarvam eva ca viśvam ekarūpaṁ syāt. tataś ca sahotpattivināśa-prasangaḥ, eka-yogakṣema-lakṣaṇatvād abheda-vyavasthānasya . . . etc. TSP. p. 23.

IV CRITICISM OF ASAT KĀRYA VĀDA (PARATA UTPATTIḤ)

If the doctrine of self-becoming logically leads to the abolition of differences and the concentration of all causes in one, the doctrine of production from another as logically leads to ultimate differences and the dispersal of causes. A single entity can never be the cause (na hy ekam ekasmāt). Four kinds of causes, rather conditions (pratyayas), are usually enumerated in the Abhidharma treatises, and these are detailed for criticism in the *Mādhyamika Kārikās.*[1] The four are hetu, ālambana, samanantara and adhipati. The principle of division is not clear. They are not like the Nyāya-Vaiśeṣika notion of causes (samavāyi, asamavāyi and nimitta) which are necessary and invariable in the production of every effect. Nor do they bear any resemblance to the Aristotelian four-fold division of causes. The hetu[2] is the direct cause corresponding in some respects to the material or samavāyi kāraṇa. It is defined as nirvarttako hetuḥ—that which (directly) brings about the result; the seed as producing the sprout is adduced as example. Usually six kinds of hetu are listed.[3] Ālambana is the object-condition which is taken as the cause in the production of knowledge and mentạls (citta and caitta). All saṁskṛta and asaṁskṛta dharmas are ālambanapratyaya.[4] The Samanatara too

[1] AKV. p. 231 ff., AK. II, 61. catvāraḥ pratyayā uktāḥ. MK. I, 2.

[2] Really there is not much difference between hetu and pratyaya except one of emphasis. See AKV (p. 188).

[3] AK. II, 49. kāraṇaṁ sahabhūś caiva sabhāgaḥ samprayuktakaḥ; sarvatrago vipākākhyaḥ ṣaḍvidho hetur iṣyate. AKV. pp. 188–9. For a fuller description of the six hetus and their inter-distinction consult McGovern: *A Manual of Buddhist Philosophy*, Vol. I, pp. 182 ff. and *Central Conception* p. 106. The six hetus are not considered here, as no Mādhyamika treatise enters into any detailed criticism of these.

[4] ālambana pratyayo'pi sarvadharmā iti mano-vijñānāpekṣayā. AKV. p. 236. This corresponds to the viṣayatā-sambandha of the Nyāya. "Ālambana pratyaya or percepient condition. This corresponds to what the Cartesians would call the occasional cause. Conditioned by various external objects different types of consciousness arise. The Sarvāstivādins believed that the nature of the newly arising consciousness is conditioned by the external objects, but that the cause of the origination remains karma and the passions. Hence the action of the external objects is called ālambana pratyaya. All objects or all the dharmas of the universe can act as ālambana-pratyaya inasmuch as all dharmas can act as objects of perception, rūpa being the ālambana pratyaya of the five sensuous aspects of consciousness, while all dharmas whatsoever can act as the ālambana pratyaya of the sixth or manovijñāna. In this way even the asaṁskṛta dharmas and the saṁskṛta dharmas of the past and future can function as ālambana-pratyaya." McGovern. op. cit., pp. 190–1. The Yogācāras

plays a part in the production of mentals only. It is the immediately preceding moment of cessation which engenders a succeeding mental state.

According to the *Abhidharma Kośa* and its *Vyākhyā* (the *Sphuṭārthā*) the samanantara is applicable only in the case of mind and mental states.[1] But from the criticism of this cause by Nāgārjuna and Candrakīrti, it is more logical to hold that the samanantra was understood as the immediately precedent cessation of the cause (kāraṇanirodha), like that of the seed, facilitating the emergence of the sprout. The examples given and the point of criticism make this interpretation clear.[2]

The adhipati pratyaya is the indirect influence[3] which one dharma has over another. It is not merely the dominant condition, as the Theravādins too literally interpreted this term to be, but the comprehensive and universal cause. Any entity (sarvaḥ dharmaḥ) exerts influence over all entities except itself. It is thus identical with the kāraṇa hetu,[4] which is defined as all except itself.[5] The adhipati-

introduced a great modification of this notion by refusing to accept the external object as cause of vijñāna. Vijñāna contains within itself the ingredients of the subject-object relation.

[1] The AK. (II, 62) defines the samanantara thus: "citta-caittā acaramā utpannāḥ samanatarah."

samaś cāyam anantaraś ca pratyaya iti samanantara-pratyaya iti. samānārthe *saṁ* śabdaḥ, (AKV. p. 232).

An immediately preceding mental state gives rise to a succeeding homogeneous state (samānārtha—vedanā of vedanā, saṁjñā of saṁjñā etc.); cittaṁ cittāntarasya samanantarapratyayaḥ, na vedanāyāḥ, vedanā vedanāntarasya na cittasyeti. saṁtānasabhāgaḥ sabhāgahetur ity arthaḥ. (AKV. p. 233).

"When one set of dharmas is uniformly and without interval succeeded by another, the preceding group is called the samanantara-pratyaya of the succeeding group. This has special reference to the relation of two different moments of consciousness within the same personality. Any group of mental dharmas (i.e. cetasikas) has the duration of only a singlę kṣaṇa, but at the moment when this group disintegrates a new one arises to take its place and inherit its potential energies." McGovern—*A Manual of Buddhist Philosophy*, p. 189.

[2] MK. I, 9. anutpanneṣu dharmeṣu nirodho nopapadyate; nānantaram ato yuktaṁ niruddhe pratyayaś ca kaḥ. Candrakīrti says: "tatra kāraṇasyānantaro ṇirodho kāryasyotpāda-pratyayaḥ samanantara-pratyayalakṣaṇam," and gives the example of the seed (bījanirodhaḥ). MKV. p. 86. anantaraḥ kāraṇanirodhaḥ kāryotpatti-pratyayaḥ, tadyathā anantaro bījanirodhaḥ ankurasya samanantara-pratyayaḥ. MA. p. 12.

[3] sarvaḥ saṁskṛtā-samskṛtaḥ sarvasya saṁskṛtasya svabhāva-varjyasya sālambanasyānālambanasya ca pratyayo'dhipati-pratyayaḥ. AKV. p. 236.

[4] patiḥ kāraṇam ucyate AK. II, 62.

[5] svato'nye kāraṇa-hetuḥ AK. II 50, 51.

pratyaya is thus wider in scope than all the pratyayas, including the ālambana which conditions only mental phenomena. It is a co-present cause, and is on this very ground criticised by the Mādhyamika.

All the four types of conditions engender the mind and mentals except in the case of the two nirvikalpa trances; with regard to these there is no object-condition (ālambana pratyaya). Two pratyayas only, hetu and adhipati, condition matter and material phenomena, including the forces called citta-viprayukta dharmas. Ālambana and samanantara pratyayas, for reasons already urged, cannot apply to non-mental events.[1] God, primeval matter (prakṛti), time (kāla), chance and others are non-causes, as they cannot account for the order, succession, variety and uniformity of the world-process. This is common ground with the Mādhyamika.[2]

The points of note in the Sarvāstivāda theory of causation is that not a single entity is the cause of an effect,[3] and that the cause is different from the effect. These are the two main points in the Mādhyamika criticism of this theory.

If the effect were an other to the cause, there is lack of relation between the two. In principle anything should be capable of being produced from anything and anywhere; a piece of stone may as well sprout into a plant as the seed does, otherness to the plant being equally present in both.[4] Otherness may be of time, the cause and effect taken as successive, not simultaneous; or it may be of nature, the cause and effect being different in nature. The two kinds of otherness may imply each other. Production is inexplicable on this theory.

The effect is not found in the causes taken singly or collectively. How is it then produced from them?[5] The effect has no standing, no

[1] caturbhiś citta-caittā hi samāpatti-dvayaṁ tribhiḥ; dvābhyām anye tu jāyante AK. II, 64, AKV. p. 20.

[2] neśvarādeḥ kramādibhiḥ. AK. II, 64; īśvarādayas tu pratyayā eva na sambhavantīti. MKV. p. 77, BCA. pp. 544–60.

[3] na hy ekapratyaya-janitam iti svalpapratyayatve'pi avaśyaṁ dvau pratyayau staḥ, AKV. p. 20.
Cf. "na kiṁcid ekam ekasmāt sāmagryāḥ sarvasambhavaḥ." quoted in TSP. p. 155.

[4] MA. VI, 14 (p. 12–3) also quoted in MKV. p. 36. pṛthaktve phalahetvoḥ syāt tulyo hetur ahetunā. MK. XX, 20.

[5] na hi svabhāvo bhāvānāṁ pratyayādiṣu vidyate;
avidyamāne svabhāve parabhāvo na vidyate.
na ca vyasta-samasteṣu pratyayeṣv asti tatphalam;
pratyayebhyaḥ kathaṁ tac ca bhaven na pratyayeṣu yat.
MK. I, 3, 11. See MK. XX, 2–4.

bond of unity, with the causes. There should be as many effects as there are causes, or at least the effect must come into being piecemeal (ekasya kāryasya khaṇḍaśa utpatti-prasangāt).

It might be thought that though the cause may be an other to the effect, it does not necessarily mean that any two entities sustaining the relation of otherness to each other are cause and effect. For, this would depend upon other factors. It is a matter of observation that B is invariably preceded by A and does not otherwise come into being. But how is this necessary relationship between A and B established? To say that we so observe it is no logical answer; it is to beg the question,[1] for we want the *reason* why A is the cause of B while C, D or E are not, when these are equally other to it. The question remains unanswered, and an empirical fact of observation is not the rule but an instance which has itself to be brought under the rule. It cannot establish a rule.

Moreover, the Vaibhāṣika holds that if the causes (like the seed etc.) were to continue to be present in unmodified form, the effect (sprout) cannot be produced. The seed has to cease to be before the sprout could emerge.[2] If that were so, the cause does not exist when the effect is produced? They belong to two different moments of time. It is inexplicable how they can be related to each other as cause and effect. The two relata must be present together for the relation to obtain between them.[3] Relation presupposes, as an essential condition, the togetherness of the relata.

It might be argued that there is no interval between the destruction of the seed and the emergence of the sprout; the occurrence of the one means the occurrence of the other. Cause and effect might well be conceived as the two pans of a balance which go up and down in invariable succession. When the cause goes down (goes out of exis-

[1] idam eva tāvad asmai kāryakāraṇavādine praṣṭavyam. śālyaṅkurasya hetuḥ śālibīja eva nānyaḥ, śālibījasya ca kāryam śālyaṇkura eva ityākāro yo niyamaḥ sa eva kasmād iti. āha, niyamasya darśanād iti. kasmād evaṁ niyamo dṛśyata iti paryanuyoge, yasmān niyamo dṛśyate tasmān niyamo dṛśyata iti tanmātraṁ vadatānena niyamahetum anabhidhāya uktadoṣaḥ kathaṁ cid api nāpākartuṁ śakyate. MA. p. 14.

[2] MK. I, 3. and MKV. p. 78.
Cf. *Br. Sūtras.* II, ii, 26.

[3] asty aṅkuraś ca na hi bījasamānakālaḥ; bījaṁ kutaḥ paratayāstu vinā paratvam; janmāṅkurasya na hi siddhyati tena bījāt. santyajyatām parata udbhavatīti pakṣaḥ. MA. VI, 17. (pp. 14–15.)
tat kim apekṣaṁ paratvam pratyayādīnāṁ, vidyamānayor eva hi maitropagrāhakayoḥ parasparāpekṣam paratvaṁ; na caivaṁ bījāṅkurayor yaugapadyam. MKV. p. 78.

tence) the effect goes up, emerges.[1] This analogy does not, however, hold good here. The two pans are available together and are also connected through a rod, and owing to this one raises the other. The seed and the sprout, on the Vaibhāṣika hypothesis, are never to be had together; one is destroyed, but the other is yet to come into existence.[2]

The gap may be attempted to be bridged by supposing that the cause puts forth an activity (kriyā), and through that the effect is brought about.[3] This intermediary step, far from helping, only serves to complicate matters. When does this activity come into being? Not after the effect has emerged, for this would be perfectly useless. Nor before the effect; for, as an activity, it must be embodied, i.e., belong to an entity. It cannot belong to the seed, for the seed, *ex hypothesi*, is already non-existent; nor to the sprout either, for it has not come into being yet. Nor is the activity existent when the effect is *being born*; for there is no moment of time apart from the preceding and succeeding moments.[4] It is possible to understand the activity not as an effort put forth by an enduring agent or body that is present at the time, but as one or more steps, modifications, between the cause and the final emergence of the effect. And this would be in keeping with the Buddhistic conception of momentariness.[5] How is this intermediary step or series of steps which paves the way for the final effect produced? The same pattern is repeated here in principle. Before the seed produces the sprout, we may interpolate one or several steps; it first swells, then splits, and finally there is the extrusion of a tiny stock, first within the ground and lastly above it; and in between any two of these steps we may suppose any number of other intermediary steps. However, this device will not yield the desired result—the causing. Any two members of the series that are

[1] This analogical argument is given in the *Madhyamakāvatāra* (VI 18): and also in MKV. p. 544–5. daṇḍadvyasya namanonnamanau tulāyāḥ; dṛṣṭau yathā na bhavato hy asamānakālau; janyasya janma janakasya tathā nirodhaḥ. It is suggested in the *Śālistamba Sūtra*.

[2] yady ekadāsty asad idaṁ tviha naikakālyam. janmonmukhaṁ na sad idaṁ yadi jāyamānam, nāśonmukhaṁ sad api nāma nirudhyamānam; dṛṣṭam tadā katham idam tulayā samānam. MA. VI 18–19.

[3] MKV. p. 79. MK. I, 4. Also MA. pp. 16 ff.

[4] MKV. pp. 79–80. For a sustained argument regarding the untenability of the divisions in time see the subsequent section—*Motion and Rest* (MK. II).

[5] Cf. kṣaṇikāḥ sarvasaṁskārā asthirāṇāṁ kutaḥ kriyā; bhūtir yaiṣām kriyā saiva kārakaṁ saiva cocyate. Quoted at various places. BCAP. p. 376; TSP. p. 11. This probably represents the well-defined Sautrāntika position, but the Vaibhāṣika too would accept this.

contiguous might be considered as the cause and the effect, but there would still be a gap between them. Recourse may be had to the device of supposing some more intermediary steps, of a subtle kind, to account for the relation. We may repeat the process *ad infinitum* without our alighting on the relation; the gap will still yawn between any two steps.[1] There is really no simplification, much less a solution, of this causal relation. The effect will remain an *other* to the cause; there is lack of relation between them.

As causation, on the Vaibhāṣika view, is not self-becoming but the co-operation[2] of several factors (pratyayās) in generating an effect, the question arises: what makes factors A, B, C, D etc., which by themselves are disconnected entities and no causes and conditions, into causes? What co-ordinates them for a united effort, for a common end? If some other factor were assumed as bringing about this co-operation, a further question arises: what makes this co-ordinating cause too a cause? This clearly leads to a *regress ad infinitum.*[3] This difficulty is peculiar to all theories of external causation which take the causes to be several, each one of the co-operating causes being a separate entity and coming into contact with the others only accidentally. The difficulty is almost insurmountable, as Buddhism, unlike the Nyāya, does not accept God or other conscious and universal co-ordinating agency.

Logically, this theory of difference between cause and effect leads to occasionalism. As the cause does not give rise to the effect out of itself, the two entities are total strangers, and are utterly unconnected. The cause, even repeated occurrences of it, does not produce the effect but only *indicates* that the effect would occur.[4] The interpolation of

[1] Cf. Hume's analysis of the notion of cause: *Treatise of Human Nature.* pp. 88 ff. (Selby-Bigge's Edn.)

[2] sahakāritva is not sambhūyakāritvam but ekakāryakāritvam. Cf. *Six Bud. Nyāya Tracts.* (*Kṣaṇabhaṅga-Siddhi*).

[3] See MK. I, 5. atha mataṁ, pūrvam apratyayāh santaḥ kiṁcid anyaṁ pratyayam apekṣya pratyayatvaṁ pratipadyanta iti.
etad apy ayuktam. yat tat pratyayāntaram apratyayasya tasya pratyayatvena kalpyate, tad api pratyayatve saty asya pratyayo bhavati: tatrāpy eṣaiva cinteti na yuktam etat. MKV. p. 82.

[4] See Śaṁkara's criticism of this doctrine in the *Brahma Sūtras* II, ii, 19. bhaved upapannaḥ saṁghāto yadi kiṁcin nimittam avagamyeta, na tv avagamyate. The *Bhāmatī* (p. 530) makes out clearly that the sequence of succession (avidyā etc.)can only be an *indication* (jñāpanam) and not production: tathā ca jñāpitasyānyad utpādakam vaktavyam, tac ca sthirapakṣe'pi saty api ca bhoktary adhiṣṭhātāraṁ cetanam antareṇa na sambhavati, kim anga punaḥ kṣaṇikesu bhāveṣu.

other entities in the middle does not alter the situation, but only repeats the same predicament within a shorter segment. Causation is reduced to a universal occasionalism—a dharma saṁketa.

The Mādhyamika criticism with regard to the different types of causes conceived by the Ābhidharmika systems need not be dealt with in great detail. The four pratyayas[1] are subject to the general criticism adduced above.

The other two alternatives of the theories of causation—effect as at once identical and different from the cause, and chance-occurrence—have already been considered before.[2] They are equally inconsistent and contradictory.

The conclusion to which the Mādhyamika is led, as the result of his examination, is that causation cannot rationally be explained. All theories of causation are conceptual devices and make-shifts. Practice does not entail the acceptance of any theory. It is not that the peasant, if he subscribed to the satkāryavāda, would reap a richer harvest, or that he would be spared the trouble of having to manure and water the seeds; for although the theory advocates self-becoming, these efforts would be necessary for the self-manifestation. On the opposite view they are needed to bring a new thing into existence. These theories have no bearing on practical every-day happenings. Every theory can cogently explain all phenomena from its own standpoint. Empirical facts cannot settle the issue between the rival philosophical theories.

The contradictions stare us in the face when they are pressed and brought home to us in metaphysics, when we go beyond the empirical

[1] The hetu-pratyaya is defined as the producer (nirvarttakaḥ) of the effect. This is untenable, for the produced cannot be understood as already present (sat), or as non-existent (asat), or both etc. If already present, there is no need for it to be produced; if non-existent, how could it be produced at all. The third alternative is subject to the criticism of the above views (MK. I, 7; MKV. p. 83). The ālambana is the object-condition governing the rise of mental states. If the state is already present, the object is superfluous; if it is absent, then there can be no relation between the two (MK. I, 8; MKV. p. 84). The samanantra, as the cessation of the cause immediately precedent to the effect, cannot be taken as a cause; for if the seed were to cease before the sprout came into being, how will it exert any influence on the effect? and if the sprout were still to be produced, it would be through chance. MK. I, 9; MKV. p. 86.

The adhipati, as the general influence of all entities, is defined as "that being, this comes into existence." This implies that entities are rigid and well-defined, and have a nature of their own (sasvabhāva). This, however, militates against their dependent origination. In the absence of a rigid nature how could the distinction of the cause and the effect be upheld. MK. I, 10; MKV. p. 87.

[2] Supra Chap. V.

to the noumenon. The essence of the contradiction is that if the cause and the effect were conceived as identical or continuous, there is no distinction between the two; we have a colourless static mass; nothing new emerges, and there is no production. If, however, they are conceived as distinct and discontinuous, then they become external to each other and the cause is on a par with the non-cause, and the effect has emerged from nowhere as it were; it is uncaused.[1] Differently expressed, causation cannot obtain between entities which are identical with or different from each other.

All these views, which are mutually exclusive and collectively exhaustive, try to explain the causal relation through one or other of the thought-patterns—identity, difference, existence, non-existence etc., or a combination of them or a denial of them. The insuperable difficulties which confront all these attempts condemn the relation as mere appearance. Like origination, destruction is neither self-caused nor brought about by others.[2] The conclusion that is forced on us is that causation is inexpressible, like the illusory appearance. "Origination, existence and destruction" says Nāgārjuna, "are of the nature of māyā, dreams or fairy castle."[3] Repeated observation of the seed being followed by the sprout does not prove that it is produced out of itself; nor does it prove the opposite theory. The mystery of production remains. Repeated observation serves but to deaden our sensitivity and to hide the mystery from us. In principle there is no difference between a magical apparition and one produced in the ordinary way of causes and conditions. In either case we are unable to explain wherefrom and how has the effect been produced.[4]

[1] MK. XX, 19–21. Cf. Bradley *App. and Reality*, p. 46. The dilemma is: "causation must be continuous;" "causation cannot be continuous." *ibid.*, pp. 51–2.

[2] na svātmanā nirodho'sti nirodho na parātmanā;
utpādasya yathotpādo nātmanā na parātmanā. MK. VII, 32.

[3] yathā māyā yathā svapno gandharva-nagaraṁ yathā;
tathotpādas tathā sthānaṁ tathā bhaṅga udāhṛtaḥ,
MK. VII, 34.

See *Catuḥśataka* XIII, 25. alāta-cakra-nirmāṇa-svapna-māyāmbucandrakaiḥ; dhūmikāntaḥ-pratiśrutka marīcyabhraiḥ samo bhavaḥ.

[4] māyātaḥ ko viśeṣo'sya yan mūḍhaiḥ satyataḥ kṛtam.
māyayā nirmitaṁ yac ca hetubhir yac ca nirmitaṁ;
āyāti tat kutaḥ kutra yāti ceti nirūpyatām. BCA. IX, 143–4.

Cf. also a verse of Nāgārjuna from the *Yukti Ṣaṣṭikā* (quoted in MKV. p. 413; BCAP. p. 583).
"hetutaḥ sambhavo yeṣāṁ tadabhāvān na santi ye;
kathaṁ nāma na te spaṣṭaṁ pratibimbasamā matāḥ."

Does this amount to the denial of causation altogether and accepting that things are produced at random through chance? It would be a misapprehension of the Mādhyamika stand-point to take it thus. Answering such an objection, Candrakīrti says in a revealing passage:

> That which originates dependent (on others) is Nothing by itself; there is thus no self-hood, independent existence. What is in itself, by its own nature, is not produced by causes and conditions. All phenomena are conditioned. The conditioned is not a thing-in-itself. The relativity or non-absolute nature of things is their Śūnyatā.[1]

II MOTION AND REST

1. Change as transformation of things (causation) cannot be explained rationally. Change, as change of place or locomotion, is equally inexplicable. An examination of motion by the Mādhyamika is specially helpful as revealing to us the nature of space, time, and the substance-attribute relation.

Zeno also denied motion, but he did not disturb rest. Had he been aware of the equally insuperable difficulties that beset rest, Zeno's argument would have been a dialectic instead of being a refutation which it now really is. A consistent dialectician, Nāgārjuna denies both motion and rest. Each is nothing by itself or together.

Three factors are essential for the occurrence of motion—the space traversed (moved in), the moving body and the movement itself. Without motion the divisions of space into the traversed, yet to be traversed, etc., cannot be made; and motion itself cannot be understood without these distinctions.[2] The mover is not intelligible without motion; nor is the latter anything without the mover.[3] To take each of these factors in turn.

What is traversed, moved in? Not that which has already been 'traversed' (gatam), nor even that to be done so (agatam); and there is no third division of space as the "being traversed" (gamyamānam):[4] When a foot-step is put forward it divides the space, *without residue*, into the one already traversed, and the other yet to be done so. It

[1] tasmād iha pratītyasamutpannasya svatantra-svarūpavirahāt, svatantra-svarūparahito'rthaḥ śūnyatārthaḥ. CSV. pp. 226–28.

[2] MK. II, 14.

[3] MK. II, 18.

[4] MK. II, 1. gataṁ na gamyate tāvad agataṁ naiva gamyate; gatāgata-vinirmuktaṁ gamyamānaṁ na gamyate.

may be urged that the place on which the foot is set can be taken as the 'being traversed' (gamyamāna). As the foot itself consists of distinguishable parts, the front portion (the toes) will fall within the traversed, and the back portion (the heel) into that to be traversed. Even in the toes and in the parts of them such distinctions can be made *ad infinitum*, without our alighting upon any part that is 'being traversed.'[1] It would be pointed out that there is some such space as the 'being traversed'; for that is the place where the activity is present; and this activity does not pertain to the traversed or that portion yet to come.[2] But as the activity belongs to the moving body and not to the space, this consideration also will not help us to distinguish that space. It is not possible to ascribe motion to both, to the space covered and the moving body.[3] If there were only one motion—and this naturally belongs to the moving body—how could the space, though unrelated to motion, still be said to be 'being traversed'. There is nothing to differentiate it from other spaces. If two motions were accepted, two moving bodies have perforce to be accepted.[4] For it is inconceivable how motion can exist without a support, without the body that moves. We are here faced with an *impasse*. There is no space that is being traversed. The divisions in space are relative and unreal. Space considered in itself does not have these distinctions—gata (traversed), agata (not traversed) and gamyamāna (being traversed); there is no intrinsic property by which any space could be singled out and distinguished from others.

2. Motion, it might be said, is possible because there is the mover in whom it inheres. Can we say that the *mover* moves or the non-mover? The latter alternative is a manifest contradiction. But is the other alternative—a mover moving—more intelligible? Is the mover anything with or without the motion, and vice versa? We must at

[1] atha syād, gantur gacchato yaś caraṇākrānto deśaḥ sa gamyamānaḥ syād iti. naivam; caraṇayor api paramāṇusaṁghātatvāt, angulyagrāvasthitasya paramāṇor yaḥ pūrvo deśaḥ, sa tasya gate'ntargataḥ; pārśnyavasthitasya caraṇaparamāṇor ya uttaro deśaḥ sa tasyāgate'ntargataḥ. na ca paramāṇuvyatirekeṇa caraṇam asti. tasmān nāsti gatāgatavyatirekeṇa gamyamānam. yathā caivaṁ caraṇe vicāraḥ, evaṁ paramāṇūnām api pūrva-para-digbhāga-sambandhena vicāraḥ kārya iti. MKV. p. 93.

[2] ceṣṭā yatra gatis tatra gamyamāne ca sā yataḥ;
na gate nāgate ceṣṭā gamyamāne gatis tataḥ. MK II, 2.

[3] MK. II, 3, 4, 5.

[4] dvau gantārau prasajyete prasakte gamanadvaye;
gantāraṁ hi tiraskṛtya gamanaṁ nopapadyate. MK. II, 6.

once distinguish and yet identify them. The mover is either motionless by himself apart from the motion, or he has a motion other than the motion which inheres in him. In the first case we have the anomaly of a mover without motion; in the second, there are two motions, for it is a *mover* that moves, and not a *non-mover* as in the first case.[1] With the acceptance of two motions, two movers too shall have to be accepted as disembodied motion cannot be conceived.

It might be objected that all this difficulty about a mover moving or a non-mover moving is but a verbal quibble. But the difficulty cannot be treated as a mere quibble or as an unimportant question about the suitable form to express a real situation. The difficulty is a fundamental one and concerns the substance-attribute relation. The activity (motion) can be conceived neither as identical with the mover nor as different from him.[2] If identical, the substance (mover) and the attribute (motion) cannot be distinguished; but even to assert this identity, distinction is necessary; the mover would always be moving, for he is identical with motion; and motion, for this very reason, *cannot be transferred* to any static body. But motion is not intrinsic to the body; it is its transitive property.[3] If, on the other hand, motion were different from the mover (substance), the latter can exist without activity and vice versa; motion should be possible without the moving body.[4] But disembodied motion is inconceivable. Nāgārjuna comes to the conclusion that both those things do not exist which can be conceived neither as identical with, nor as different from, each other.[5]

3. It may be thought that these difficulties are really about the locus of motion, whether it resides in a body which is itself bereft of motion or not; they have nothing to do with motion at all. There is movement, for it is begun. But where, and when does motion begin? Not at the place already traversed, nor even at that which is yet to be. And we have seen that there is no such space as the 'being

[1] gamane dve prasajyete gantā yady uta gacchati;
ganteti cocyate yena gantā san yac ca gacchati, MK. II, 11.

[2] MK. II, 18.

[3] yad eva gamanaṁ gantā sa eva hi bhaved yadi;
ekībhāvaḥ prasajyeta kartuḥ karmaṇa eva ca. MK. II, 19.

[4] anya eva punar gantā gater yadi vikalpyate;
gamanaṁ syādṛte gantur gantā syād gamanād ṛte. MK. II, 20.

[5] The dictum is expressed in the striking Kārikā:
ekībhāvena vā siddhir nānābhāvena vā yayoḥ;
na vidyate tayoḥ siddhiḥ kathaṁ nu khalu vidyate. MK. II, 21.

traversed'; for this would lead to two movements (in the space and in the moving body—kriyādvaya prasangāt) and two movers (kartṛdvaya prasangāc ca) as there cannot be motion without a substrate.[1] When does the mover begin to move? Not when he is stationary. And before he commences the motion there is no division of time into the past or the present. And motion cannot be commenced in the future.[2]

4. It might be thought that though there might be difficulty about the precise moment or place of the commencement of the motion, the distinctions of time into past, present and future, and of the space into the traversed (gatam) etc., are available. Not so; without motion, these spatial and temporal distinctions too cannot be made. For the past or the traversed space (gatam) is nothing but that time or place whence the movement has stopped, and the future is that into which movement will enter, and the present is that where the movement is progressing.[3] It is thus seen that on the basis of these distinctions alone can motion be conceived to arise, and only with its commencement are such distinctions tenable. The nerve of the entire argument is stated thus by Nāgārjuna: "Distinctions of space (and of time) into the traversed (past), to be traversed (future) and that which is being traversed (present) are dependent on the arising of motion itself;"[4] for, that alone serves as the dividing line. But the rise of motion itself is inexplicable without these very spatial and temporal distinctions which it engenders. This involves a veritable circularity.

It must be added, to make the argument complete, that space and time are inconceivable without these distinctions of the traversed, the past etc. A uniform differenceless all-pervasive space (dik) and time (kāla) like that of the Nyāya-Vaiśeṣika or of the Newtonian pattern cannot be distinguished from things which are supposed to be in them. The entire universe would be reduced to a colourless indistinguishable mass. It would not be the correct Mādhyamika view to take these distinctions themselves to be space and time. This

[1] MK. II, 12; MKV. p. 100.

[2] MK. II, 13. na pūrvaṁ gamanārambhād gamyamānaṁ na vā gatam; yatrārabhyeta gamanam agate gamanaṁ kutaḥ.

[3] sati hi gamikriyā-prārambhe, yatroparata-gamikriyā tad gatam iti parikalpyeta, yatra vartamānā tad gamyamānam, yatrājātā tad agatam iti. MKV. p. 101.

[4] gataṁ kiṁ gamyamānaṁ kim agataṁ kiṁ vikalpyate;
adṛśyamāna ārambhe gamanasyaiva sarvathā. MK. II, 14.

might be the view of the earlier Buddhism. The Ābhidharmika system might hold the view that space and time are these very distinctions, and that there is no underlying entity behind them. The essence of the Mādhyamika standpoint in this regard would be that the divisions of past, present and future etc. are of some ubiquitous substance and cannot be understood without this underlying entity. In turn, this entity too is nothing without these divisions which alone impart determinateness to it.[1]

5. Motion exists, it might be urged, for its opposite—rest—does; that exists whose opposite exists, e.g. darkness and light, or this side and the other side.[2] Logically therefore, a denial of motion involves that of rest as well. It is here precisely that Nāgārjuna proves himself a truer dialectician than Zeno.

Here too, as in the case of motion, the indispensable factors are denied. Who rests? Not the mover, nor the static—the non-mover; and there is no third who could rest. The static does not rest, for it is already stationary; there are no two rests, as this would involve two stationary bodies.[3] It is a flat contradiction to say that the mover rests, when a mover is impossible without motion; when any body rests, it is, *ipso facto*, not a mover.[4] It would be said that rest is possible, as cessation from motion is possible. The mover can stop; stopping is an opposite activity. Not so; for, whence will be the stop? Will it be from the space already traversed, yet to be traversed, or that which is being traversed?[5] Now this activity brought in to ensure rest is on a par with motion, and will be assailable on that score. There is no activity or motion in all these three spaces for the said reasons. And hence there can be no cessation of it.

Rest is possible, for it could be begun, it might be said. But is it begun when someone is at rest, or not at rest or when about to rest?—precisely the very alternatives considered in connection with the commencement of motion.

[1] Nāgārjuna refuses to attach significance to mere mental states without the underlying substratum of an ātman, nor to the ātman without these. Each is relative to the other MK. X, 16. MKV. p. 116.

[2] atrāha. vidyata eva gamanaṁ tatpratipakṣa-sadbhāvāt. yasya ca pratipakṣo'sti, tadasti; ālokāndhakāravat, pārāvāravat saṁśaya-niścayavac ca. asti ca gamanasya pratipakṣaḥ sthānam iti. MKV. p. 101.

[3] ekayā sthityā gantā, aparayā tiṣṭhatīti, sthitidvaya-prasangāt, sthātṛdvayaprasanga iti pūrvavad doṣaḥ. MKV. p. 101.

[4] MK. II, 16.

[5] MK. II, 17.

Rest being thus untenable, motion too cannot be established on the principle "that motion exists whose opposite (rest) exists." With the unavailability of motion, spatial distinctions too cannot be made; for, they are relative to the motion as seen already. The mover too cannot be conceived as either identical with or different from the motion. Being relative to each other, neither of them is real.[1] Nāgārjuna therefore reaches the conclusion: that motion, mover and space are but appearance.[2]

6. Nāgārjuna's dialectic of motion and rest suggests a comparison with Zeno's refutation of motion. For Zeno motion is appearance; but he accepted the reality of rest and the static. For Nāgārjuna neither motion nor rest is real. Being relative to each other and to the ingredients which engender them, they are appearance. Nāgārjuna is aware of the antinomical character of Reason, and refuses to accept one of the opposites as constituting the nature of the real. He is a truer dialectician.

Nāgārjuna's arguments are comprehensive and conclusive. Motion is denied because of the untenability of the ingredients that necessarily engender it. It is shown that distinctions in space depend on motion and vice versa, and that the mover cannot be understood either as identical with or different from motion. Zeno's argument, implied in the examples chosen—Achilles and the tortoise or the flying arrow etc.—is that the space between any two points consists of an infinity of discrete points and these cannot be summed up, completed, within a finite quantum of time.[3] A Bergson may answer[4] that this is an unwarranted spatialisation of time, movement. Movement cannot be cut up into a number of discrete and disjointed entities, each one of which is static and dead. Movement is one sweeping act. It cannot be *conceived*, but only 'felt' and lived through. The Mādhyamika arguments contain an implicit answer to the Bergsonian position too. If movement were one indescribable whole that is lived and felt, we are precluded, *ex hypothesi*, from comparing

[1] MK. II, 19, 20, 21 already quoted.

[2] tasmād gatiś ca gantā ca gantavyaṁ ca na vidyate, MK. II, 25.

[3] For a detailed exposition of the arguments of Zeno, see Zeller's *Pre-Socratic Philosophy*, Vol. I, pp. 619; Gomperz, *Greek Thinkers*, Vol. I, pp. 192 ff.

[4] It is also possible to point out that though a series may be infinite such as the number 1/2 . . . 1/4 . . . 1/8 . . . 1/16 . . . etc. the sum of them is a finite number (one); i.e., an infinite series is capable of summation.

any two movements, from making distinctions of past, future and present; we cannot even know whether a motion is swift or slow. Without the landmarks of the past etc. and in the absence of any rigid standard of measurement, movement will have no direction nor can the progress be measured. Distinctions of space and time are indispensable to motion, and these distinctions themselves are dependent on the commencement of motion. The Bergsonian view, consistently pressed, should lead to the real as non-conceptual, the utterly indescribable. The real is as little to be identified with time (duration or movement), which Bergson does, as with space. Without concepts, space, time and things would all collapse into an indistinguishable mass.

III EXAMINATION OF THE ĀBHIDHARMIKA CATEGORIES

The Mādhyamika dialectic as a trenchant criticism of the Modal standpoint embodied in the Ābhidharmika system devotes considerable attention to an examination of its categories—skandha, dhātu and āyatana—in their metaphysical and ethical bearings.[1] The general conception of phenomenal existence and process (saṁskṛta) is subjected to a penetrating analysis both in the *Mādhyamika Kārikās* and the *Catuḥ Śataka.*[2]

The Elements (dharmas) are ultimate existences, and they are classified variously in the Abhidharma treatises. The skandha, dhātu, āyatana classification is the one most prevalent in the schools. There is no doubt that the analysis of an individual into a number of states without the residue of any soul or substance is as old as Buddhism itself, and must be attributed to the Buddha himself. References to the five skandhas and the six āyatanas and dhātus are too persistent and universal a feature of the *Nikāyas* and other older Pāli Canons to be ignored as later accretions. Invariably this is done to show that these are not ātman, nor is there any ātman apart from these, and that the attachment to the ātman is ignorance. The classification of existences into skandha, āyatana etc. (groups or collocations) may be termed subjective, as the interest is predominantly in sentient experience, in the individual and his components. An objective classification irrespective of these moulds of thought came to be formulated in the schools. The Sthaviravādins and the Sarvāsti-

[1] MK. Chaps. II–XVII: CŚ. XIII.

[2] MK. VII (*Saṁskṛta Parīkṣā*): . XV.

vādins[1] made their own lists, and this process continued for centuries, the numbers in the total and in the sub-classes varying from time to time.[2] The *Abhidharma-kośa* of Vasubandhu represents the final form of the Sarvāstivāda doctrines, while his contemporary Buddhaghosa's *Visuddhimagga* can be taken as the final form of the Theravāda.

The details of the Ābhidharmika systems are of mere historical interest now. But it was and still remains one of the most comprehensive and systematic attempts made to explain things from the modal standpoint by a conscious rejection of an underlying substantial unity in things. Criticism of the Abhidharma system shows the untenability of every species of the modal view.

1. *The Āyatanas*

The āyatana classification is taken up in Chapter III of the *Mādhyamika Kārikās* for criticism. Āyatana is the sense-organ which functions as the door (āya, dvāra) for the ingress of sensations consequent on contact with the respective sense-data.

There are six sense-organs: five external—eye, ear, touch, taste and smell—and one internal, mind, on the one side; they are confronted on the other by the sense-data—rūpa etc.[3] The coming together of these two engenders the resultant visual and other cognitions. The general formula is that the eye (cakṣuḥ) *sees* colour (rūpa) and the ear *hears* sound etc. The function of the sense-organs can be taken as that of an active agent, that which sees (paśyatīti darśanaṁ cakṣuḥ), or as an instrument of vision—that *by* which things are seen (paśyaty aneneti karaṇasādhanam).[4] In either case the intention is to provide an account of the cognitive process without having to suppose an immutable substrate (ātman) underlying the states.

[1] 'Sarva' does not mean that they accepted the reality of everything, but only of the elements variously understood in the Buddhist scriptures; sarvaṁ sarvam iti brāhmaṇa yāvad eva pañca skandhāḥ, dvādaśāyatanāni, aṣṭādaśadhātava iti. Quoted in TSP. p. 11. BCAP. p. 375. The peculiar feature of the Sarvāstivāda was its belief in the reality (astitva) of a thing in the three times or phases of being (adhvā).

[2] For a comparative list of the number of categories admitted by Theravāda, Sarvāstivāda (Vaibhāṣika) and the Yogācāra reference may be made to McGovern's *Manual of Buddhism* Vol. I, pp. 81 ff (Cosmic analysis); Rosenberg's *Die Probleme der buddhist. Phil.* pp. 120 ff.

[3] MK. III, 1.

[4] MKV. p. 117.

The eye does not see itself, and without self-perception how can it perceive others? 'Seeing oneself' would mean the untenable bifurcation of an entity into the 'seer' and the 'seen'.[1] It may be urged that the eye need not see itself to see objects, as fire burns the wood without burning itself. But this is subject to the difficulties considered with regard to motion. What is seen cannot be that which is already seen or that which is unseen; and there is no third class of objects as the 'being seen'. Likewise, the question may be raised about the seer: Who sees? Not the seer, (for this would mean two activities etc.), nor the non-seer, (this is a flat contradiction) and there is no third alternative.[2] As there is no activity called seeing, how can there be a seer, and *a fortiori* the non-seer cannot see.[3]

The instrument-view of the eye and other sense-organs does not fare much better. An instrument implies an agent (kartā) who operates the instrument, one who *sees by* means of the eye etc. But an agent is untenable, as he cannot be conceived as *seeing himself* with the eye as his instrument, and without this self-perception how can he perceive others; nor can he be conceived as perceiving others without perceiving himself because of considerations already urged.[4] A further general difficulty is that the seer (draṣṭā) is not intelligible as identical with or different from the activity of seeing. And without the agent there can be no seeing or the object seen.[5] The considerations urged in the case of the eye apply with equal force to the other sense-organs.[6]

Advocating as he does a theory of elements (dharmamātram), discrete and momentary, emerging and subsiding without any activity or agent, the Vaibhāṣika might welcome the above Mādhyamika criticism of the agent and the activity as falling in line with his own standpoint. Perception on this view would not be the seeing of an object by the percipient, there being no activity (nirvyāpara-dharmamātram), but the momentary emergence into being of a moment called conventionally the eye simultaneous with that of another moment—the sense-datum of colour (rūpa) followed by another moment—the visual consciousness (cakṣurvijñānam). But without the activity exerted by a thing, the Mādhyamika cogently

[1] MK. III, 2.

[2] MKV. pp. 114–5.

[3] MK. III, 4–5.

[4] MKV. p. 117.

[5] tiraskṛtya draṣṭā nāsty atiraskṛtya ca darśanam; draṣṭavyaṁ darśanaṁ caiva draṣṭary asati te kutah MK. III, 6.

[6] MK. III, 9.

urges, there cannot be the emergence of the discrete moments even; they would be utterly inefficient and unreal like the sky-lotus (kriyā-rahitatvāt khapuṣpavat).

If we confine ourselves to the phenomenal point of view, if we propose merely to give a transcription of what obtains in everyday experience, we must accept, besides the states or moments, the activity and the agent. From the noumenal point of view of the Unconditioned truth, the moments too are as unreal as the activity which the earlier Buddhism rightly rejects.[1] The correct Mādhyamika standpoint is that the modes by themselves cannot offer an adequate explanation of phenomena. Substance too must be accepted. Both, however, are of empirical validity only (sāṁvṛta).

2. *Skandha classification examined*

If the āyatana classification is on the basis of sense-data and sense-organs and therefore predominantly epistemological, the skandha (group) classification is from the point of view of the derivation of things. In the former, the cognitive attitude dominates; in the latter the causal. The skandha-classification is objective and ontological. The Ābhidharmikas conceive existence as divisible into five aggregates—rūpa, vijñāna, vedanā, saṁjñā and saṁskāra—the first comprising matter and the rest mind and mental phenomena. As in the āyatana division, here too the intention is to explain all phenomena without the substance (soul)—the corner-stone of all Buddhism.

A distinction is made between primary and secondary phenomena, the original and the derivatives. Rūpa (matter) is divided into bhūta (mahābhūta) primary matter, and bhautika, empirical objects of sense. Likewise, vijñāna or citta is pure consciousness or mind *par excellence* and the others, vedanā (feelings) etc. are mentals—caitta or cetasika. A system which refused to admit any self-becoming or transformation of a substantial (potential) being into temporal modes

[1] In an illuminating passage Candrakīrti puts the issue in the proper light: ye tu manyante: nirvyāpāraṁ hīdaṁ dharmamātram utpadyamānam utpadyata iti, naiva kiṁ cit kaścid viṣayaṁ paśyati, kriyāyā abhāvāt; tasmād darśanaṁ na paśyatīti siddham etat prasādhyata iti. atrocyate. yadi kriyā vyavahārāngabhūtā na syāt, tadā dharmamātram api na syāt. kriyā virahitatvāt khapuṣpavad iti. kutaḥ kriyārahitaṁ dharmamātraṁ bhaviṣyati. *tasmād yadi vyavahārasatyaṁ dharmamātravat kriyāpy abhyupagamyatām; atha tattvacintā tadā kriyāvad dharmamātram api nāstīti bhavatābhyupagamyatām.* MKV. p. 116.

has perforce to explain the causal nexus as mere arrangement or external grouping of the discrete elements. The grouping itself is not an inherent organic feature of the elements, being a superimposition on them.

Nāgārjuna's criticism of this doctrine, which must have been inadequately developed at that time, is that the division into primary and secondary phenomena is untenable; and secondly, the causal principle which is at the basis of this classification is unintelligible.

There is no secondary matter apart from the primary causes thereof. If so, it would be adventitious (ahetukam), baseless; and there is no phenomenon that is without cause.[1] Nor is the primary matter conceivable without the secondary. For in that case there would be a cause which does not issue forth into the effect; it would be no cause at all.[2] The original and the derivative are not intelligible either as related or unrelated to each other.[3]

The effect cannot be understood as similar to (identical with) the cause.[4] For, propositions true of the one are not true of the other and vice versa. The secondary matter (or the objects of sense) are perceivable and are of a sizable magnitude; they serve various empirical uses. The primary matter is imperceptible and serves no utility. The identity of causes and effect cannot thus be countenanced.[5] We cannot, however, accept the other alternative of an ultimate difference between the two, as this would cut at the very root of the causal relation.[6]

Mutatis mutandis these considerations apply with equal force to the other groups—vijñāna, vedanā, saṁjñā and saṁskāra.[7]

3. *Examination of the Dhātus*

The Dhātus or Bases, according to the Canons, are six. These are

[1] MK. IV, 2.

[2] MK. IV, 3.

[3] rūpe satyeva rūpasya kāraṇaṁ nopapadyate;
rūpe'satyeva rūpasya kāraṇaṁ nopapadyate. MK. IV, 4.

[4] na kāraṇasya sadṛśaṁ kāryam ity upāpadyate;
na kāraṇasyāsadṛśaṁ kāryam ity upapadyate. MK. IV, 6.

[5] MKV. p. 126.

[6] For a detailed examination of the causal relation reference may be made to the previous section of this chapter.

[7] MK. IV, 7.

—earth, water, fire, air, ākāśa (ether) and consciousness.[1] The later and more well-known dhātu classification is the one into eighteen elements. This is a modification of the āyatana classification (six sense-organs and sense-data) with the respective consciousness (visual consciousness etc.) added; it does not imply any new principle of division.[2] The six-dhātu classification is an attempt exhaustively to enumerate and define the ultimate components of existence. In the well-known text of the *Pitāputra Samāgama Sūtra*,[3] it is stated that the human being (puruṣa pudgalaḥ) is composed of six basic components (ṣaḍ-dhātuḥ), implying that man (his physical and conscious part) is analysable without residue into these six elements. The differentia of each element (asādhāraṇa dharma-dhāraṇād dhātuḥ) is also given. This line of thought is interesting, as it throws light on the nature of the relation between a thing (lakṣya) and its specific property (lakṣaṇa). Nāgārjuna indeed makes it a theme for his critique of the doctrine of definition or substance-attribute relation.

Dhātus are Radical elements or Surds; they are the irreducible stuff of which phenomenal (saṁskṛta) things are composed. Two notions are involved in this conception: the fixing up of the number and nature of the components, and second the way in which these components are compounded to form things of the phenomenal sphere (samskṛta). The first is examined here and the second in the subsequent section.

A basic element, to be distinguished from another, must possess a specific character—the differentia or definition which separates it from others. The Buddhists do give us the differentia of these elements, e.g., non-obstruction of ākāśa (Space), hardness of earth, cohesion

[1] In the *Dhātuvibhanga* (p. 82 P.T.S. Edn.) it is stated that there are six dhatus viz. cha dhātuyo: paṭhavī dhātu, āpodhātu, tejodhātu, vāyodhātu, ākāsadhātu, viññāṇadhātu. See also *Majjh. N.* III, pp. 237–47.

[2] This classification is useful in dividing the universe into three planes of existence (traidhātuka) according to the types of consciousness and objects experienced in them—(Kāmadhātu, Rūpadhātu and Arūpadhātu. "All these varieties of consciousness exist only in the ordinary plane of existence (kāmadhātu). In higher worlds (rūpa-dhātu), sense-consciousness gradually disappears; in the immaterial worlds (arūpadhātu), only non-sensuous consciousness is left. A division of consciousness into various kinds is thus made necessary for the composition of formulas of elements corresponding to the denizens of various worlds." *Central Conception*, p. 10.

[3] ṣaḍ dhātur ayaṁ, mahārāja, puruṣa-pudgala iti, MKV. p. 129. The passage is cited in full in ŚS. (pp. 244 ff) and BCAP. (pp. 508 ff.).

(sneha) of water etc. Is there any distinction between the definitum (ākāśa, pṛthvī, etc.) and its differentia[1] (anāvṛtiḥ, kāṭhinyam etc.)? If there is not, we cannot define the dhātus, nor distinguish one from the other. Once a distinction is accepted, we may further ask whether the definitum (lakṣya) is prior to the defining characteristic or not. If the lakṣya, (e.g. ākāsa) could exist without its specific property, then it would be non-descript in itself; and a non-descript entity is a non-entity; such a thing is not an object of experience.[2] If there is no characteristic entity, to what will an attribute or definition apply?[3]

Moreover, the differentia (lakṣaṇa) cannot be predicated of a determinate (salakṣaṇa) or non-determinate entity (alakṣaṇa). The latter is a contradiction: how can the non-determinate be ascribed a determination? If the first, as the subject is already determinate, what further function would be served by ascribing to it this determination? Even after this determination is predicated, a second or a third may have to be applied; and this would lead to a *regress ad infinitum*; there is no third alternative of an entity which is both determinate and indeterminate or neither of them.[4]

Differentia being thus not predicable, the subject-term too is unavailable. And without the subject of predication, there can be no differentia as such. There is no positive entity which is without the subject-predicate relation.[5]

It might be urged that these objections militate against the existence of a positive entity (bhāva). But ākāśa need not be conceived as a positive existence. In fact, according to some of the Buddhist schools, it is the absence (abhāva) of obstruction. The conception of ākāśa as a negative fact is not tenable; for, a negative fact is but the negation—change, destruction or absence—of a positive entity; and if the latter is not available, the former is so too: abhāva is relative to bhāva.[6]

[1] The Buddhists may say that the differentia *is* the thing and not that the *thing has* the differentia, the use of such expressions as "The pitcher *has* colour" etc. being conventional. For a critique of this position see Candrakīrti MKV. pp. 66–9.

[2] MK. V, 1. [3] MK. V, 2.

[4] MK. V, 3 ff. MKV. p. 131.

[5] tasmān na vidyate lakṣyaṁ lakṣaṇaṁ naiva vidyate;
lakṣya-lakṣaṇa-nirmukto naiva bhāvo'pi vidyate. MK. V, 5.

[6] MKV. p. 132. yad ākāśaṁ bhāvo na bhavati, tadā bhāvasyā sattve kasyābhāvaḥ kalpyatām. vakṣyati hi: bhāvasya ced aprasiddhir abhāvo naiva siddhyati; bhāvasya hy anyathābhāvam abhāvaṁ bruvate janāḥ.

Similar considerations apply to the other dhātus, pṛthvī (earth), Consciousness etc. They do not have a svabhāva—an immutable absolute (unconditioned) nature of their own. Without svabhāva, when there is nothing as itself, how can there be an other; for an other is but the svabhāva of the different.[1] Those that have recourse to such dogmatic speculations with regard to the real, conceiving it as positive, negative, as substance or mode, as pṛthvī, vijñāna etc., miss the essence of Buddha's teaching.[2]

Nāgārjuna severely castigates them for their obtuseness: "Those that affirm the existence of things or deny their existence (the men of little wisdom), they do not perceive the ultimate truth that is the benign cessation (of the world)."[3] The Lord has clearly declared that one should not get into the muddle of the 'Is' or 'Not-is' views—that is the way of saṁsāra, and one does not thereby attain freedom from pain.[4]

4. *Criticism of the Saṁskṛta and the Pratītya-Samutpāda*

The ultimate elements of existence (the dharmas), like the letters of the alphabet, have been determined and enumerated. We have to explain the modes of their combination to make phenomena (saṁskṛta dharma), to form words and sentences to continue the analogy of the alphabet. The question is about the dynamics of the world, the way in which things arise and subside. The Lord is reported to have said: "Three are the phenomenalising characteristics (saṁskṛtalakṣaṇāni) of all phenomena (saṁskṛta): of the saṁskṛta there is the origin (utpāda), cessation (vyaya) and change of state (sthityanyathātvam)."[5]

[1] See MKV. pp. 262–6 ff.

[2] Commenting on the verse: svabhāvaṁ parabhāvaṁ ca bhāvaṁ cābhāvam eva ca;
ye paśyanti na paśyanti te tattvam buddhaśāsane. MK. XV, 6.
Candrakīrti says: ye hi tathāgata-pravacanāviparīta-vyākhyānābhimānitayā, pṛthivyāḥ kāṭhinyam svabhāvaḥ, vedanāyā viṣayānubhavaḥ, vijñānasya viṣayaprativijñaptiḥ svabhāva ity evaṁ svabhāvaṁ varṇayanti; anyad vijñānam anyad rūpam anyaiva ca vedanety evaṁ parabhāvaṁ varṇayanti, vartmānāvasthānaṁ ca vijñānādikaṁ bhāvatvena ye varṇayanti, vijñānādikam eva cātītatām āyannabhāvam iti, na te parama-gambhīrasya pratītyasamutpādasya tattvaṁ varṇayanti. MKV. p. 267.

[3] astitvaṁ ye tu paśyanti nāstitvaṁ cālpabuddhyaḥ;
bhāvānāṁ te na paśyanti draṣṭavyopaśamam śivam. MK. V, 8.

[4] MK. XV, 7 & MKV. p. 269.

[5] AKV. p. 171. *Sūtre*: trīṇimāni, bhikṣavaḥ, saṁskṛtasyasaṁskṛtalakṣaṇāni. katamāni trīṇi. saṁskṛtasya, bhikṣavaḥ, utpādo'pi prajñāyate; vyayo'pi prajñāyate; sthityanyathātvam api. *Ang. N. I*, p. 152—III. 47—Also quoted in MKV. p. 145; CŚV. p. 232.

This formula, which has all the ring of being an uncontested declaration of the Buddha, has been variously elaborated in the schools. There was unanimity of agreement that the formula denied the existence of substance—an immutable substance behind the changing states. The schools, however, differed considerably with regard to the positive interpretation, with regard to the number and nature of the elements and the manner of their interaction. It is neither possible nor even profitable to ascertain against which particular formulation of the theory of Elements is the Mādhyamika criticism directed.[1] Possibly, it is against the Vaibhāṣika; more probably, it is against the Sautrāntika. The essence of the doctrine is that there are ultimate, durationless, incomparable entities which flash into existence for a moment and as quickly subside into non-existence. The flow of these entities in a defiled way (sāsrava dharmas) is conditioned by avidyā (satkāya-dṛṣṭi) and its satellites, the saṁskāras. All things (physical and psychical) are rigidly subject to the operation of the causal law which determines their origin and subsidence. All things are anitya (impermanent, momentary) anātman (unsubstantial modes) duḥkha (restless). Impermanence is understood as the origination, continuance for a moment, and then the cessation of things.

The Mādhyamika criticism is that each one of these three characteristics is not a complete definition of the saṁskṛta. For, then we shall have the anomaly of the origination of a thing which has no duration or destruction, of something that endures but has no origination or decay, or of a thing that dies but which was not born at all.[2] To escape this predicament, it might be held that all these three together (trilakṣaṇī) characterise the phenomenal. But the three functions—origination, duration and cessation—cannot apply to a thing simultaneously (yugapad) nor successively (kramaśaḥ). It is manifestly impossible for these three functions to work on a thing at once, for they are opposed to each other in their nature.[3] Nor do they successively operate on a thing; for this would mean that at the time of origination, the thing is permanent and only later it ceases to be and vice versa.

[1] A criticism of the saṁskṛta is found in MK. Chap. VII (*Saṁskṛta Parīkṣā*); CŚ. XV.

[2] utpādādyas trayo vyastā nālaṁ lakṣaṇa-karmaṇi;
saṁskṛtasya samastāḥ syur ekatra katham ekadā.
MK. VII, 2. MKV. p. 146.

[3] utpāda-sthitibhangānāṁ yugapan nāsti sambhavaḥ;
kramaśaḥ sambhavo nāsti sambhavo vidyate kadā. CŚ. XV, 11.

As the definition of the saṁskṛta should apply universally to all compounded things, it is pertinent to ask whether it applies to each one of the three characteristics, for they are also things and must satisfy the definition of the saṁskṛta.[1] Does origination, like other entities and forces, originate, endure and cease? If it does not, there would be certain things which are unwarranted exceptions to the universal maxim, which thereby loses its compelling character as invariably true of all phenomena. If it does, this would lead to origination of origination and that to another *ad infinitum*. Some schools (as the Sāmmitīyas) did accept origination of origination too, and it is difficult to see how they escaped a regress. Possibly, they held that origination originates itself in the sense of self-origination, very much like a lamp illuminating itself and others.[2] Self-illumination is not to be taken as that of an entity being both subject and object at once.

A more serious difficulty about this notion of the saṁskṛta is: how are we to conceive origination, duration and cessation. Does the thing which is already present in its natural form come into being or that which was non-existent originate?[3] When a thing already exists and is in the form which is natural to it, why and how would it come into being again? And if it does not exist, how does *it* originate at all? When there is no entity before and after, there is no 'it' which comes into being. There is no subject of which we could predicate that 'it' has come into being; there is just origination, but it cannot be predicated of anything. The difficulty is not one concerning the correct verbal formulation. It is fundamental to any momentary or modal view of things. If whatever exists is just that moment, nothing before or after, how can 'it' be said to originate, endure or cease. We might analyse a thing away into finer, subtler moments; but each moment would be a discrete self-contained entity, and there is no

[1] It appears from the Mādhyamika criticism (MKV. pp. 545 ff) and from AKV. pp. 174 ff. that the Vaibhāṣikas held that origination, decay, duration and change—all the four forces—operate on a thing at once: yato jāti-jarā-sthity-anityatākhyāni catvāri saṁskṛtalakṣaṇāny utpadyamānasya bhāvasya bāhyādhyātmikasya vā ekasminneva kṣaṇe bhavantīti *Abhidharma-pāṭhaḥ*. The momentary cannot be accepted; because it cannot decay, being unitary; if it has an end, it must have a beginning and middle and so nothing is really momentary; and the entire structure built upon the momentary must also collapse. MKV. pp. 546–7. cf. MK. VII, 4 ff. CŚ. XV, 12.

[2] Nāgārjuna subjects the notion and the example (lamp) to a searching analysis in his *Mādhyamika Kārikās* VII, 8 ff. & VV. 34 ff.

[3] sataś ca tāvad utpattir asataś ca na yujyate;
na sataś cāsataś ceti pūrvam evopapāditam. MK. VII, 20.

movement or change *of* it into another or different state. Each distinguishable state is an entity, and nothing can be predicated of 'it'. In fact there is no 'it'—the thing—which changes or moves from one state to another; the states are all the real; they cannot even be compared with each other; they are so discrete and disconnected that no relation can obtain between them. This is the insuperable difficulty which Nāgārjuna brings home to the Vaibhāṣika in various ways by asking what originates—not that which is already present, not that which is not existent and there is no third which is neither the one nor the other;[1] what endures and what changes are also equally inexplicable.[2] Cessation cannot be understood as self-annihilation or as destruction caused by forces other to it or both or neither.[3]

Both Nāgārjuna and Āryadeva come to the conclusion, as a result of their criticism of the saṁskṛta, that origination, duration and cessation are inexplicable like māyā (illusion) the dream-object and the fairy-castle.[4] The saṁskṛta being thus untenable, the asaṁskṛta too is unavailable; for one is relative to the other.[5]

The Ābhidharmika might complain that the Mādhyamika, by his carping criticism of the origination etc. of the saṁskṛta things, has effectively reduced to nullity Buddha's key-doctrine, Pratītya Samutpāda. The Mādhyamika retorts by adverting to the obtuseness of the Vaibhāṣika who misses the real essence of the Master's teaching. "In declaring that 'this is dependent on that' the Revered Tathāgata has clearly said that there is nothing in itself—everything is relative.[6] —"whatever originates dependent (on others) is nothing by itself."

"An entity existing by itself in its own nature retains the state and form natural to itself. Being already present, it does not depend on any other. It does not come into being. Consequently, the view that things have a fixed nature of their own militates against their

[1] yadi kaścid anutpanno bhāvaḥ saṁvidyate kvacid;
utpadyeta sa kiṁ tasmin bhāva utpadyate'sati. MK. VII, 17.

yadi kaścid anutpanna utpādāt pūrvam ghaṭo nāma kvacit saṁvidyate sa utpattikriyāṁ pratītyotpadyeta; na caivam kaścid utpādāt pūrvaṁ kvacid asti. tasmin nasati ghaṭe kim utpadyate. MKV. p. 161.

[2] MK. VII, 22 ff.

[3] MK. VII 32.

[4] MK. VII, 34; CS. XIII, 25.

[5] utpāda-sthiti-bhaṅgānām asiddher nāsti saṁskṛtam;
saṁskṛtasyāprasiddhau ca kathaṁ setsyaty asaṁskṛtam. MK. VII, 33.
MKV. p. 159.

dependent origination. It is thus you, who uphold the doctrine of rigid nature of entities (sasvabhāvatā), that contradict the Pratītya Samutpāda. And in consequence thereof the entire Buddhist philosophy is vitiated. The scripture says that whosoever perceives the real nature of Pratītya Samutpāda perceives the Dharma; and whosoever perceives the Dharma perceives the Buddha."[1]

Pratītya samutpāda is not the temporal sequence of the origin and subsidence of momentary entities but their mutual dependence, their lack of thinghood or reality. It is thus equated with the unreality of things (niḥsvabhāvatva or śūnyatā). This is the revolution in Buddhist thought initiated by the Mādhyamika.

IV THE ĀTMA DOCTRINE EXAMINED

The substance-view of Reality (ātmadṛṣṭi) is equally beset with insuperable difficulties as the modal view of Buddhists. All the Brāhmanical systems, as already pointed out, conceive reality on the pattern of an inner core or soul which perdures without change and to which the changing states are attached in a more or less loose manner. A full critique of the ātmavāda will, besides laying bare the basic assumptions underlying the generic form of the doctrine, have to concern itself with some specific formulations of it. The successive application of the dialectic by the Mādhyamika teachers unmistakably shows this.[2] The ātman is part of the larger problem of the conception of the Real as static being.[3] Nāgārjuna's successors, Āryadeva and others, pay considerable attention to the Vaibhāṣika and Vaiśeṣika categaries of the asamskṛta and the nitya respectively.[4] A criticism of the ātman thus leads us, on the one hand, to the more generic question of the permanent Being (nitya) in general and to the specific formulations of the ātma-conception on the other.

The Immutables, as conceived by various philosophical systems, fall into four well-defined groups: Space (ākāśa and dik), Time (kāla),

[1] MKV. p. 160.

[2] Cf. CŚ, X for a criticism of the ātman, especially of the Sāṁkhya conception. Candrakīrti criticises the Nyāya-Vaiśeṣika conception too; Śāntideva does likewise (BCA. IX, 66 ff): The TS. examines in detail the Sāṁkhya, Nyāya, Mīmāṁsā, Jaina and Vātīsputrīyā conceptions. pp. 75–130.

[3] nitya-śabdasya svabhāva-satya-sāra-vastu-dravya-paryāyatvāt. CSV. p. 32.

[4] CŚ IV and XI.

Atom (paramāṇu) and the Soul (ātman). The first two (ākāśa and kāla) provide the two ubiquitous recepta in which finite things exist and change; themselves unchanging, they make motion and modification possible. The atom (paramāṇu) is the ultimate constituent of matter, and the ātman is the spirit which is the subject of experience.

1. The permanent is conceived as that being which has no cause; it never was not.[1] In the case of Space and Time it may further be said that they do not give rise to any effect or modification. Such things are, however, thought to exist and affect the course of things. The general criticism is that there is no entity which is by itself, uncaused. All things play a part in the engendering of entities; we cannot conceive of an entity which is not related as cause or effect to the other entities. Anything that is outside this relation altogether is non-existent. "Nowhere is there the existence of anything that is not dependent (related to other things) any time. The permanent does not thus exist anywhere."[2]

It is shown by a searching analysis of causation[3] which has become classic that the permanent cannot effect anything; it is not efficient simultaneously or successively. If the permanent precipitates all its effects in the first moment but continues to exist after that, it would give rise to the same effects in the subsequent moments *ad infinitum*. If it does not, then it really possesses two natures—efficiency (sāmarthya) in the first moment and non-efficiency (asāmarthya) in the subsequent moments of its existence with regard to the same effect. The Buddhist invokes the dictum—'that is not one which is invested with conflicting characteristics.'[4] The same result is reached on the other alternative too. If the permanent is efficient only successively, then in the moment when it is producing A, it is not efficient with regard to B (the successive effect); if it were so, why

[1] Cf. The *Vaiśeṣika Sūtras* (IV, i, 1 & 4): sad, akāraṇavan nityam. anityam iti ca viśeṣataḥ pratiṣedhābhāvaḥ.

[2] apratītyāstitā nāsti kadācit kasyacit kvacit;
na kadācit kvacit kaścid vidyate tena śāśvataḥ.
CŚ. IX, 2; MK. XXIV, 19.

[3] arthakriyākāritvaṁ hi kramākramābhyāṁ vyāptaṁ; tau hi kramākramau sthirād vyāvartamānau, arthakriyākāritvam api vyāvartayataḥ . . . etc. This sustained argument is stated in Buddhist, Jaina and Brāhmanical treatises. Cf. *Kṣaṇabhaṅgasiddhi* (*Six Buddhist Nyāya Tracts*). TS. pp. 131 ff. Dr. S. K. Mookerjee's *Buddhist Philosophy of Universal Flux* gives a brilliant exposition of momentariness (flux).

[4] yo viruddha-dharmādhyāsavān nāsāvekaḥ.

could it not produce that too then; it has no need to wait for anything else, being itself sufficient to produce the effect B then and there, (samarthasya kṣepāyogāt). Only in the succeeding moments does it produce B, C, D, etc. And as it is the same permanent entity that continues in the first and subsequent moments, it is at once efficient and non-efficient with regard to B, C, D, etc., in the first and other moments. It is a manifest contradiction to hold that one and the same entity can have two conflicting natures. The position is not much bettered by the consideration that the permanent is helped out by the presence of the auxiliaries that co-operate with it to bring about the result. The mere inoperative presence of the entities cannot mean anything to the cause; it must itself change and abandon its rigidity before it can produce anything. Āryadeva states this pointedly when he urges: "The cause must undergo modification before it can be the cause of an other; and that is not permanent which is subject to modification."[1] If it be said that which is subject to modification is impermanent and the permanent is not so subject, it might be urged that as the impermanent alone is seen actually to exist, the permanent may well be equated with the non-existent.[2]

The basic difficulty is that the permanent is so disparate in nature from the changing events that it cannot in any conceivable way be related to them. The Advaita Vedānta which takes the real to be Pure Being, immutable and uniform in nature, has perforce to deny the reality of becoming; substance appears to change but does not really do so; its position is so unique that it is unrelated to phenomena. Logically pressed, the permanent has to be taken as the absolute, and nothing can be predicated of it.

2. Space and Time are, even from the empirical point of view unsubstantial things.[3] They are admittedly not objects of perception like the everyday things such as chair, table etc. They appear to be existences owing to our inveterate tendency to objectify concepts and words. It is difficult to ascertain the nature of their existence or the mode of their influence on things.

Space is usually conceived as an all-pervasive entity—(positive or negative) which provides room for the existence of limited objects

[1] kāraṇaṁ vikṛtiṁ gacchaj jāyate'nyasya kāraṇam;
vikṛtir jāyate yasya śāśvatam iti tan na hi. CŚ. IX, 9.

[2] anityaṁ kṛtakaṁ dṛṣṭvā śāśvato'kṛtako yadi;
kṛtakasyāstitām dṛṣṭvā nāsti tenāstu śāśvataḥ. CŚ. IX, 4.

[3] CŚ. IX, 5.

that occupy space. From its all-pervasiveness (vibhutva) and lack of parts (apradeśatva) it is assumed that space is eternal and immutable.[1] But space too must have parts; for when the table exists in space, it does not cover the whole space; as in that case other things cannot exist at all anywhere; and there is no other space which is free and unoccupied. To avoid this, if it be said that the table exists not in all space but in *that part* of space where it does actually exist, leaving room for the other objects to exist elsewhere, it is clearly implied that space too has parts,[2] like objects. For, do not we speak of *this part* of space and *that part* of space, 'here', 'there', 'elsewhere' etc. Space too has distinctions and parts. That which has parts is composite; and the composite is conditioned by causes; it is impermanent as having been brought into being.

To escape this predicament, if it were held that space is an *a priori* form of our mind without any objective status, it would be accepting the Mādhyamika standpoint that things are mere subjective forms (vikalpa). A critical school of Buddhism, the Sautrāntikas—who might be considered with good reason as the precursors of the Mādhyamika—did hold that Space, Time and Nirvāṇa were mere forms of thought or words of common usage.[3]

3. [3]Time is thought to be a factor in the modification of things; it is taken as engendering the origination and cessation of the world as a whole and of the particular entities within it. It is a common expression to say that everything depends on the opportune time or moment. Time is further taken to be all-pervasive and eternal, as *all* empirical things without exception are subject to time.

There are solid reasons why Time cannot be a cause. As it is invariable and uniform, the sprout etc. which are thought to be caused by it, will always be in a state of production; a variable impermanent (kādācitkatva) factor alone can account for the production of the sprout sometimes only and not at other times. If time too is conceived to be variable, it would be non-existent at times, or be impermanent like the seed. And for this, it would have to be dependent on conditions on the occurrence of which it would happen and without which it would not.

[1] Cf. *Vaiśeṣika Sūtras* (II, 1, 29), dravyatvanityatve vāyunā vyākhyāte.

[2] pradeśini na sarvasmin pradeśo nāma vartate;
tasmāt suvyaktam anyo'pi pradeśo'sti pradeśini. CŚ. IX, 6.

[3] uktaṁ ca bhagavatā pañcemāni, bhikṣavo, nāma-mātraṁ pratijñāmātraṁ vyavahāra-mātraṁ saṁvṛtimātraṁ: tad yathātīto'dhvānāgato'dhvākāśo nirvāṇaṁ pudgalaś ceti. Quoted in CŚV. pp. 59–60; MKV. p. 389.

A cause must lead to some result (phala), for it is inconceivable that there should be a cause that does not produce anything. If time were a cause, it would itself be modified into effect. A cause further cannot produce the effect without itself being transformed and ceasing to be. The seed perishes in giving rise to the sprout. Time too would be subject to this consideration. That of which the permanent is presumed to be the cause is really uncaused or produced at random (abhūtvā jāyate); for the cause (kāla) does not do anything to it. Such an entity does not stand in need of any cause, and Time has thus no hand in its production.[1] Further, why should not an effect produced by Time, which is eternal, be itself eternal? For, disparity between cause and effect is not proper.[2]

The above arguments prove that Time as a permanent unchanging entity cannot be a cause. Its unreality even as an existent is brought home to us by the examination of this concept by Nāgārjuna. The divisions of Time into the Past, Present and Future are vital to its conception. The Present and the Future are what they are in relation to the Past; they should therefore exist in the past, for they are dependent on it.[3] If so, they too would be included in the past, or the latter would be indistinguishable from the present and the future. If, to avoid this, it were held that the present and the future do not exist in the past, *relative to what* are they the present and the future?[4] A non-relative present or future is not possible; and without distinctions, time too is unavailable.[5] The same arguments may be urged, *mutaiis mutandis*, with regard to the existence of the past or the present in the present and the future etc.[6]

The existence of time apart from things, an empty time, is not tenable; for, no such entity is apprehended apart from the momentary entities.[7] Time might be thought to exist in relation to things that

[1] CS. IX, 10.

[2] utpannaḥ śāśvatād bhāvāt katham aśāśvato bhavet;
vailakṣaṇyaṁ dvayor hetuphalayor jātu neṣyate. CŚ. IX, 11.

[3] pratyutpanno'nāgatāś ca yady atītam apekṣya hi;
pratyutpanno'nāgatāś ca kālo'tīte bhaviṣyataḥ. MK. XIXI; CŚ. XI, 1.

[4] pratyutpanno'nāgatāś ca na stas tatra punar yadi;
pratyutpanno'nāgatāś ca syātāṁ katham apekṣya tam. MK. XIIX, 2.

[5] anapekṣya punaḥ siddhir nātītaṁ vidyate tayoḥ;
pratyutpanno'nāgatāś ca tasmāt kālo na vidyate MK. XIX, 3.

[6] MK. XIX, 4.

[7] bhāvaṁ pratītya kālaś cet kālo bhāvādṛte kutaḥ;
na ca kaścana bhāvo'sti kutaḥ kālo bhaviṣyati. MK. XIX, 6.

change. But as changing things (bhāva) have been shown to be untenable, the reality of Time too is not established.

4. The atom plays an important part in the constitution of the world-picture in the Buddhist (Vaibhāṣika), Jaina and Vaiśeṣika systems. The atom is arrived at by an extension, beyond phenomenon, of the argument that production of an effect is by the mechanical combination of parts. Matter is not infinitely divisible; there is a limit to the process of partition, and the ultimate limit of it is the atom (paramāṇu). We cannot stop with a perceptible object of the least magnitude; for, that is composite, as it is related to things which are themselves composite, e.g. the sense-organs which cognise it and the gross objects which are constituted by it. Every philosophical system wants to reach the super-sensuous unconditioned ground of things. We have thus the conception of ultimate bits of matter, partless, discrete and unrelated; these somehow combine to constitute the world.

It is the Vaiśeṣika conception of the atom that has come for criticism at the hands of the Mādhyamika,[1] especially Āryadeva. His criticism brings out certain features not met with in other critics like Śaṅkara or the Vijñānavāda.

To prevent the composite entity from becoming indistinguishable from the atom, we must accept that the atomic size of the atom is not communicable to its products (the composite); i.e., the pārimāṇḍalya parimāṇa is not a cause. The atom then has two aspects; one is that aspect which is in contact with other atoms and which communicates its nature to the product, and second the incommunicable part which is thus no cause though present in the atom. The atom is thus dual in nature, i.e. is itself composite, and hence not permanent.[2]

The contact of one atom with another atom is not in its entirety (sarvātmanā) lest the resultant dual atom should be of the same size as the single atom; and we have no observed example of contact of one entity with another in entirety. If partial contact were admitted, then the atom too would have parts; and what has parts is not permanent.[3]

[1] CŚ. IX, 12 ff . . . BCA. pp. 502 ff, 516 ff; TS. pp. 185 ff.

[2] hetuḥ kaścana deśaḥ syād yasyāhetuś ca kaścana;
sa tena jāyate nānā nānā nityo na yujyate. CŚ. IX, 12.
This criticism is not generally made.

[3] CŚ. IX, 13, 14. CŚV. p. 48. This is the usual argument against atomism met with in Buddhist and other works. Cf. Vasubandhu's *Viṁśatikā*, pp. 7–8. Śaṅkara's *Bhāṣya* on the *Br. Sūtras* II, ii, 12.

Movement of the atom is also not conceivable. For, when a body moves, it moves forward to the new position by its front part, and abandons the previous position by its hind part.[1] The atom, *ex hypothesi*, has no such distinction of parts; it cannot then be a mover. If it has parts, it is not an atom; nor is it permanent.

As the atom is without extremities or middle, it cannot be perceived even by a Yogin, and its existence is a matter of conjecture.[2] A perceived object has distinguishable parts, and what has no parts cannot be perceived.

If the atom ceases when the effect emerges, as is the case with other causes, then it is not permanent. If it continues to exist unmodified, then there is no origination of a new entity.[3]

Contact, movement, perceivability and production etc. are notions exemplified and valid in the empirical sphere. To apply them in the case of atoms which are admittedly beyond the pale of experience is an illegitimate extension. Dialectical criticism lays bare the unwarranted application of the categories to the transcendent.

5. Ātman is the chief category of the permanent. In a restricted but more prevalent usage, it means the soul or spirit, the subject of experience; in a wider and more logical sense it is substance in general. There are two principal views of the Self (ātman): one is the conception, in vogue with the Brāhmanical systems, of a permanent and immutable entity identical amidst changing states and therefore different from them; the other is the Buddhistic conception of ātman as a conventional name (prajñapti-sat) for a series of discrete momentary states (skandharūpa), sensation and feeling, intellection and conation. There is nothing unitary or identical amidst the changing states, and nothing hidden beneath them as the ātman. Like all existence, the mental states too are in a state of continual flux. The Buddhists coined a very unattractive word—'pudgala'—

[1] grahaṇaṁ pūrvabhāgena paścādbhāgena varjanam;
tad dvayaṁ naiva yasyāsti sa gantāpi na jāyate. CŚ. IX, 16.
gamanābhimukha-dehyarthaṁ deśasya pūrvaḥ pradeśaḥ pīḍyate, paścād deśasya paścātpradeśaś ca tyajyate. tena gantur gantṛtvam utprekṣyate. anaṁśatvād yasya paramāṇor agrimeṇa paścimena cāvayavena grahaṇaṁ varjanaṁ ca nāsti sa na gantā. CŚV. p. 51. This acute analysis of motion and its inapplicability to the atom is not, to my knowledge, met with anywhere.

[2] ādir na vidyate yasya yasya madhyaṁ na vidyate;
vidyate na yasyāntaḥ so'vyaktaḥ kena dṛśyate. CŚ. IX, 18.

[3] naṣṭaḥ phalena yad dhetus tena hetur na śāśvataḥ;
yasmiṅś ca vidyate hetuḥ phalaṁ tasmin na vidyate. CŚ. IX, 18.

for the ātman. Besides these two principal views, there is the intermediary standpoint not only of the Jainas, but of the Vātsīputrīyas (Sāmmitīyas) within the Buddhist fold itself. They held that the ātman or pudgala was a sort of quasi-permanent entity neither different from nor identical with the states like fire and fuel.[1] The Pudgalātmavāda has been universally condemned as a heresy by the Buddhist schools, including the Mādhyamika.[2]

If the ātman were identical with the states (skandhalakṣaṇa), it would be subject to birth, decay and death. There would be as many selves (ātman) as there are states.[3] Of each self it could be urged that it was non-existent before it was born and would cease to exist later. Further, it would have been produced without causes, each self being a discrete independent entity, having no relation with the previous.[4] The full weight of this criticism is realised when we consider moral responsibility. As the former self has ceased to exist and a new one has emerged into existence, the deeds done by the previous also cease to exist; for, there is no longer that entity which performed them. If the later self were to experience the result of the acts of the previous self, it would be a clear case of gratuitous burdening of responsibility. All this is repugnant to the implications of the moral act and its consequences, as done and enjoyed by the *same* agent.[5]

This view of the states being the self really identifies the act with the agent, the feeling with the person who experiences the feeling.

[1] pudgalātmavādinas tu punarantaścara-tīrthakāḥ skandhebhyas tattvānyatvābhyām avācyaṁ pudgalanāmānam ātmānam icchanti. BCAP. p. 455. Cf. also MKV. pp. 283–4: na caivam ātmā nityā-nitya-bhūtaḥ. tasya hi skandhebhyas tattvānyatvāvaktavyavan nityatvenānityatvenāpyavaktavyatā vyavasthāpyate. AKV. (p. 700) says: yathendhanam upādāyāgniḥ prajñāpyata iti. dravyasan pudgalaḥ. *nānyo nānanya* iti. svam upādānam upādāya prajñāpyamānatvāt. yo hi bhāvo nānyo nānanya iti svam upādāya prajñāpyamānaḥ sa dravyasaṁs tad yathā'gnir iti Vātsīputrīyābhiprāyaḥ.

[2] Nāgārjuna examines the Vātsīputrīya conception of the Pudgalātman in his *Mādhyamika Kārikās* IX (*Pūrvaparīkṣā*) and the example of Fire-Fuel in the next chapter (X *Agnīndhana Parīkṣa*). BCAP.—pp. 455–6. TS. pp. 125 ff.

[3] MA. VI, 127–8 (also quoted in MKV. p. 342).

[4] nāpy abhūtvā samudbhūto doṣo hy atra prasjyate;
kṛtako vā bhaved ātmā sambhūto vāpy ahetukaḥ. MK. XXVII, 12.

[5] tasya pūrvakasyātmanas tatra naṣṭatvād iha cānyasyaiva codpādanāt pūrvakasyātmana ucchedaḥ syāt, tasmiṅś cātmany ucchinne karmaṇām adatta-phalānām evāśraya-vicchedena vicchadāt bhoktuś cābhāvān nāśa eva syāt. atha pūrvakenātmanā kṛtasya karmaṇa uttareṇātmanā phalaparibhogaḥ parikalpyeta, tathāpyanyena kṛtasya karmaṇaḥ phalasyānyena upabhogaḥ syāt. MKV. p. 580.

Such identification is unwarranted and cannot account for experience. The feeling itself is not the feeler, a content is not the *knowing* of the content. The subject of experience has to be accepted as indispensable for the occurrence of any mental state. The Buddhists, as rigorous exponents of the modal view, eschew the ātman and replace it completely by the states of feeling, sensation, conception and volition. Memory, recognition, moral responsibility and transmigration are all attempted to be explained on this hypothesis of substanceless momentary states—(upādāna-skandhas). It speaks not a little for the dialectical insight of Nāgārjuna and his followers that they are acutely alive to the halting nature of the modal view (upādānam evātmā).

"The self is not the states that originate and cease; how can the experiencing subject (upādātā) be identical with the experienced states (upādāna)?"[1] His main criticism of the modal view is that it wrongly identifies the agent with the act, the subject and the object (ekatvaṁ kartṛkarmaṇoḥ). A multitude of qualities is not substance; a bundle of states is not the self. Bereft of unity, they fall asunder and make for disorder. The substance or self is the unifying factor which integrates several acts, making mental life continuous and coherent.

The rejection of the Buddhist modal view of the ātman by the Mādhyamika does not of itself mean that he is committed to the opposite view of an identical and changeless self (substance) different from the states. As a keen dialectician, the Mādhyamika is equally aware of the pitfalls of the substance-view of the ātman. He rejects that too as a false view of the real.

The conception of the ātman is variously formulated by the different non-Buddhistic systems; but they all agree in considering it as eternal, and as existing apart from the states and as identical amidst change.[2] The main criticism of the Mādhyamika is that if the ātman were totally different from the states, it would be apprehended apart from them, as the table is perceived apart from the chair. It is not so perceived,[3] and hence it is merely thought to exist owing to transcendental thought-construction. The ātman is the egoity

[1] na copādānam evātmā vyeti tatsamudeti ca;
kathaṁ hi nāmopādānam upādātā bhaviṣyati. MK. XVII, 6.

[2] ātmā tīrthyaiḥ kalpyate nityarūpo'kartā bhoktā nirguṇo niṣkriyaś ca; kaṁcit kaṁcid bhedam āśritya tasya bhedaṁ yātā prakriyā tīrthikānām. MA. VI, 121 (as quoted in MKV. p. 344).

[3] anyaḥ punar upādānād ātmā naivopapadyate;
gṛhyeta hy anupādāno yady anyo na ca gṛhyate. MK. XXVII, 7.

(ahaṁkāra) reflected in the states, enjoying a semblance of independence, identity and permanence. It is thus a construct (vikalpa) read into the manifold of states.[1]

If the ātman were a real entity, there should be agreement about it. On the contrary one's (self) ātman is anātma (non-self) for another, and vice versa; and this should not be the case if it were an objective reality.[2]

The relation of the ātman with the states cannot be formulated in any conceivable manner: whether the states are the self or different from them; whether the states are in it, or it is in them; whether the states belong to it, or vice versa, etc. There are obvious difficulties in every formulation, and most of them have been considered already.[3]

It might be asked: if the ātman were not a real spiritual entity, then who is the mover and controller of the bodily movements? But how can an immaterial principle actuate a material thing like the body or the sense-organs and mind[4] etc. Changeless and all-pervasive (sarvagata), ātman is not active (niṣkriya); and without action, the ātman cannot be an agent (kartā). He cannot even co-ordinate and synthesise the different states into a unity.[5]

As in the modal view, here too moral and spiritual life becomes impossible, though for an opposite reason; an unchanging ātman cannot be benefited by any spiritual discipline, nor can it deteriorate if that effort were not made. In spiritual progress the ātman cannot be identical at any two stages of development. To say that the ātman is not really bound or free, but owing to avidyā he wrongly identifies himself with the body, sense-organs and mind, is to say that phenomenal life is the work of false belief and imagination (kalpanā). The saving knowledge then is not that the real is ātman or anātma, but that none of our conceptual patterns applies to it.

On the modal view, there are the different momentary states only; there is no principle of unity. Mental life is inexplicable without the

[1] See *Ratnāvalī* by Nāgārjuna as cited in MKV. p. 345. cf. the Kantian doctrine that the Transcendental Ego (I) is an empty abstraction without the categories and the manifold of sense-data.

[2] CŚ. X, 3.

[3] See MKV. pp. 432 ff. read with p. 341.

[4] bhāvasya nāsparśavataḥ preraṇā nāma jāyate;
tasmād dehasya ceṣṭāyāḥ kartā jīvo na jāyate. CŚ. X, 5.

[5] kriyāvāñ chāśvato nāsti nāsti sarvagate kriyā;
niskriyo nāstitā-tulyo nairātmyaṁ kiṁ na te priyam. CŚ. X, 17.

unity of the self. On the substance-view, there is the unitary and identical self rigid and standing aloof from the states which the ātman is presumed to shape into order. The self of the Brāhmanical systems is a bare colourless unity bereft of difference and change, which alone impart significance to it. The self has no meaning apart from the states and mental activity. The two are mutually dependent, and hence unreal.[1]

It might be thought that a view which contains the above two standpoints, the self as a unity in combination with the diversity of states, is in a position eminently to avoid the pitfalls of both the extremes. Such a view was actually advocated by the Jainas and the Sāmmitīyas (Vātsīputrīyas) in their conception of the Pudgala—the Individual as neither identical with nor different from the states. This doctrine is examined at length in two chapters of the *Mādhyamika Kārikās* (*Pūrva Parīkṣā* and *Agnīndhana Parīkṣā*).

It is difficult to formulate any conceivable relationship—identity or difference or both (ekatva, anyatva etc.) between the ātman and the states (upādāna). Does the ātman (unity) exist before, after or simultaneously with the states? If before, how is he apprehended at all without the states,[2] without the difference of mental content? If the ātman could exist without the states, the states too could exist without the ātman.[3] It may be urged that it is not prior to *all* states but only to *particular ones*. But how could it be prior to each one of the particulars in turn if it were not prior to all of them?[4] The ātman cannot be posterior to the states, as this would mean that the states could exist without the direction of the agent (self).[5] Nor are the two simultaneous; for, only those two are simultaneous which can exist apart from each other.[6]

[1] tayoś copādeyopādātroḥ parasparāpekṣayoḥ karma-kāraḳavad eva siddhir na svābhāvikī . . . "karma-kartṛbhyāṁ śeṣān bhāvān vibhāvayet." MKV. pp. 189–90.

[2] darśana-śravaṇādibhyo vedanādibhya eva ca;
yaḥ prāg vyavasthito bhāvaḥ kena prajñapyate'tha saḥ. MK. IX, 3.

[3] MK. IX, 4.

[4] sarvebhyo darśanādibhyo yadi pūrvo na vidyate;
ekaikasmāt kathaṁ pūrvo darśanādeḥ sa vidyate. MK. IX, 7.

[5] MK. IX, 10.

[6] prāk ca yo darśanādibhyaḥ sāmprataṁ cordhvam eva ca; na vidyate'sti nāstīti nivṛttās tatra kalpanāḥ. MK. IX, 12.

pṛthak pṛthag asiddhayoḥ sahabhāvādarśanāt śaśaśṛngayor iva atmopādānayoś ca paraspara-nirapekṣayoḥ pṛthak pṛthag asiddhatvāt sāmpratam api nāsti. MKV. p. 199.

In defence of the reciprocal dependence of the ātman and the states it may be pointed out that mutual dependence of two things does not necessarily mean their unreality, but that both are real. Fire does not exist apart from the fuel it burns and thrives on; on that account it does not cease to have a nature of its own as heat etc. The fuel too is the wood that is ignited by the fire, but in itself it is derived from specific sources.[1] If the two were identical, the subject and the object, consumer and consumed, would become one; this is unwarranted. If different, there should be fire without fuel, always lighted and without effort.[2] Relation is possible, it may be averred, between entities that are different from each other.[3] This is to accept their independent existence. Such a contention would be tantamount to giving up their mutual dependence. In mutual dependence, as in the example of fire and fuel, it is difficult to decide which is prior and which is posterior, and which depends on which. In fact, neither has any nature of its own; no distinction between the two is possible, as they are always together, and neither of them can be had apart from the other.[4]

The difficulties implied in mutual dependence of things, as in the adduced example of fire and fuel, infect the relation of ātman and the states and every phenomenon such as substance and attribute, whole and parts, cause and effect etc. A relational view of reality gives us only appearance.[5]

After an examination of the several views (dṛṣṭis) with regard to the ātman, Nāgārjuna concludes: "The self is not different from the states, nor identical with them; (there) is no self without the states; nor is it to be considered non-existent." [6]

The Mādhyamika position may appear to be at variance with the teaching of the Buddha; on several occasions he seems to have asserted the existence of the self. But there are texts which declare quite

[1] MKV. p. 202. sāpekṣāṇām api padārthānāṁ sasvābhāvya darśanād evam upādānasāpekṣo'pyupādātā sasvabhāvo bhaviṣyati; upādātṛsāpekṣam copādānam ity agnīndhanavad etau bhaviṣyata upādānopādātārāv iti.

[2] MK. X, 1–3.

[3] MKV. pp. 206 ff.

[4] yo'pekṣya siddhyate bhāvas tam evāpekṣya siddhyati;
yadi yo'pekṣitavyaḥ sa siddhyatāṁ kam apekṣya kaḥ. MK. X, 10.

[5] agnīndhanābhyaṁ vyākhyāta ātmopādānayoḥ kramaḥ;
sarvo niravaśeṣeṇa sārdhaṁ ghaṭa-paṭādibhiḥ.
MK. X, 15. MKV. pp. 213 ff.

[6] evam nānya upādānān na copādānam eva saḥ;
ātmā nāsty anupādāno nāpi nāsty eṣa niścayaḥ. MK. XXVII, 8.

unequivocally that he denied the self.[1] The contradiction, however, is but apparent. "The self does exist, the Buddhas have declared; they have taught the 'no-self' doctrine too; they have (finally) taught that there is neither self nor non-self."[2] Buddha's teaching is adjusted to the need of the taught as the medicine of the skilled physician is to the malady of the patient. He does not blindly, mechanically, prescribe one remedy to all and sundry, He corrects those with a nihilistic tendency by affirming the self, as there is continuity of karma and its result; to those addicted to the dogmatic belief in a changeless substantial ātman and who cling to it, he teaches the 'no-self doctrine' as an antidote; his ultimate teaching is that there is neither self nor not-self as these are subjective devices.[3] The Real as the Indeterminate (śūnya) is free from conceptual construction.[4] The indeterminacy of the Absolute allows freedom of approach; numberless are the ways by which it could be reached. The sole condition is that the method chosen should suit the disciple's disposition; this is the doctrine of upāya-kauśalya (excellence in the choice of means), and it applies to every doctrine.[5]

The seemingly divergent utterances of Buddha may also be taken as addressed not to different individuals, but to one in different stages of spiritual development. The first task is to wean one away from vice; and to achieve this end the existence of self as meaning continuity of karma and its result is taught; then to get rid of attachment the Nairātmya Doctrine is preached; finally for realising complete freedom the giving up of all views is insisted on.[6]

The application of the Dialectic to some of the important categories, Causality, Motion and Rest, Modes and Substance (ātman), shows the nature of the Mādhyamika method *in concreto*. All views on any problem can be formulated under four classes, the affirmative (sat),

[1] MKV. pp. 354 ff. e.g. ātmā hi ātmano nātha etc. and nāstīha sattva ātmā vā dharmās tu ete sahetukāḥ; anātmānaḥ sarvadharmāḥ etc.

[2] ātmetyapi prajñapitam anātmety api deśitam;
buddhair nātmā nà cānātmā kaścid ity api deśitam. MK. XVIII, 6.

[3] Cf. MKV. pp. 356–60 yataś caivam hīnamadhyotkṛṣṭa-vineya janāsaya-nānātvena ātmānātmatadubhaya-pratiṣedhena Buddhānām bhagavatām dharma-deśanā pravṛttā, tasmān nāstyāgamabādho Mādhyamikānām. MKV. p. 359.

[4] MK. XVIII, 7.

[5] sad asat sadasac ceti nobhayaṁ ceti kathyate;
nanu vyādhivaśāt sarvam auṣadhaṁ nāma jāyate. CŚ. VIII, 20.

[6] CŚ. VIII, 15.

negative (asat), conjunctive assertion of both (ubhaya) and disjunctive denial (anubhaya). Every view is rejected as it reveals, on critical analysis, inherent flaws that cannot be remedied by attention and adjustment. Rejection of one view does not mean the acceptance of the opposite or any other view. The Mādhyamika dialectic uses ***reductio ad absurdum*** arguments only (prasangāpādanam). The Dialectic is criticism only; it is not itself a view or a synthesis of view-points. Rejection of all thought-categories and views is the rejection of the competence of Reason to apprehend reality. The Real is transcendent to thought; it is non-dual (śūnya), free from the duality of 'is' and 'not-is.'

CHAPTER EIGHT

THE MĀDHYAMIKA CONCEPTION OF PHILOSOPHY AS PRAJÑĀPĀRAMITĀ

I CRITICISM OR DIALECTIC ITSELF IS PHILOSOPHY

It is usual to ask of a system of philosophy to give us its views about ultimate existences—God, soul and matter. Systems are labelled Monism, Dualism, Idealism, Realism, etc., according to the nature of the answers given. The Mādhyamika philosophy is no system in this sense. Nowhere is there any attempt to raise such problems on its own initiative. The Dialectic is not a body of doctrines, but their criticism. Philosophy, for the Mādhyamika, is not an explanation of things through conceptual patterns. That is the way of dogmatic speculation (dṛṣṭi); but this does not give us the truth. The Dialectic is intended as an effective antidote for this dogmatic procedure of reason; it is the criticism of theories (śūnyatā sarva-dṛṣṭīnām). The Dialectic itself is philosophy.

Criticism of theories is not another theory; śūnyatā of dṛṣṭis is not one more dṛṣṭi, but is prajñā—their reflective awareness. It has been shown that to be aware of a dṛṣṭi (view), we must be aware of its falsity. Reflective consciousness is necessarily the consciousness of the false.[1] As the Mādhyamika dialectic relentlessly exposes the falsity of every philosophical view, each of which pretends to give a complete and only picture of all things, it curbs the speculative disposition of dogmatic Reason. It is a reversal of the natural process of looking at things through set ideas, the disabusing of the mind of *a priori* notions which are the mainsprings of our empirical ways of life.

The essence of the Mādhyamika attitude, his philosophy (the madhyamā pratipad), consists in not allowing oneself to be entangled in views and theories, but just to observe the nature of things without standpoints (bhūta-pratyavekṣā). The *Ratnakūṭa Sūtra* (*Kāśyapa-parivarta*) states the middle position thus:

"The Bodhisattva desiring to adopt the spiritual discipline must cultivate

[1] Supra Chap. VI, Section entitled: "Is Śūnyatā a Theory."

the attitude of unceasing, critical alertness with regard to things (yoniśo dharmaprayuktena bhavitavyam). And what is this alertness? It is the perception of all things in their true form (sarvadharmāṇām bhūta-pratyavekṣā). And again, what is the nature of this true perception? Where, Kāśyapa, there is not the viewing of things as atman (substance) etc., that which does not take rūpa, (matter), vedanā, saṁjñā, saṁskāra, vijñāna as eternal (nitya), or changing (anitya). That things are unchanging (nitya), this, Kāśyapa, is one end (antaḥ); that they are changing is another . . . that reality is substance (ātmeti) is one end; that it is only modal (nairātmyam iti) is another end; the middle between these two extremes of ātman and nairātmya is the intangible, the incomparable, non-appearing, not comprehensible, without any position . . . that verily is the Middle Path—the vision of the Real in its true form.[1]

The *Prajñā-Pāramitā* texts contain innumerable passages of the same import.[2] Nāgārjuna and his school, in rejecting all views and systems and refusing to advance a view of their own, have been most consistent in this regard. Philosophy, for the Mādhyamika, is not a Weltanschaung; it is not the *explanation* of things on a particular hypothesis or pattern, however grand this may be. That is the way of science, and is valuable there, as the hypothesis can be verified by appeal to sense-experience. The procedure, however, carries a necessary limitation with it. Systems of philosophy adopt this procedure, but discard the limitation; they seek to comprehend the entire universe in their scope and attempt to reach the unconditioned. In the absence of any objective criterion that might eliminate questionable and inadequate views, the formulation of innumerable systems of thought and their inevitable conflict are necessary consequences. Deadlock in philosophy results. This should open our eyes to the irrelevance of the scientific method (hypothesis and explanation) in philosophy. Adoption of the scientific method can only result in the identity of science and philosophy to the detriment of the latter. Philosophy becomes superfluous and pretentious. Positivism, as the restriction of significant discourse to the empirically verifiable, i.e. to science, inevitably results; and positivism is inimical to true metaphysics.

The objective of all philosophy is to attain universality—knowledge of the entire reality. Philosophical knowledge is thus distinguished from the scientific, which is incomplete and piecemeal in character.

[1] *Kāśyapaparivarta*, pp. 82–87.

[2] bodhisattvena mahāsattvena prajñāpāramitāyāṁ caratā prajñā-pāramitāyāṁ bhāvayatā na rūpe sthātavyaṁ na vedanāyām. . . . ASP. p. 8.

Again, philosophy claims to give absolutely certain knowledge free from every trace of the problematic, the doubtful and the false. It is knowledge unaffected by contingencies of time, place and circumstance. There has also been the tradition that philosophy represents the highest good, and that the philosopher realises all values. The particular sciences and even the arts (literature and fine art) cater merely to the physical and the cultural needs of man; they are thus incapable of achieving the *summum bonum.*[1]

Philosophy has, however, been pursuing a method not in consonance with its objective. Though the objective is exalted and far different from that of the sciences and arts, philosophy has in the main adopted the scientific method of hypothesis and explanation or the literary method of imagination and construction. Systems of philosophy have merely universalised the scientific method and given free scope to the flight of imagination. Little do they realise that a different ideal calls for a different method. This results in chaos and conflict; it is not calculated to give us universality and absolute certitude that is the ideal of philosophy.

The Mādhyamika system is unique in this respect that it rejects the scientific or the literary method of explanation and speculative construction as utterly unsuited to philosophy. For, to pitch upon a particular concept or even a combination of them to explain things is beset with difficulties. There is nothing to justify the initial choice of the concept or *a priori* notion; this is dependent on temperament and is a matter of happy suggestion like genius.[2] Once we accept a fundamental pattern, reasoning can get under way; we can then, and only then, reject some other notions as inconsistent with or opposed to it. This merely means that *if* you accept an idea, you are necessarily committed to its implications, and not that you are committed to the

[1] Maitreyo bodhisattvo mahāsattvo na rūpaṁ nityaṁ nānityaṁ na rūpaṁ baddhaṁ na muktam atyanta-viśuddham ity abhisambhotsyate . . . evaṁ na vedanāṁ na saṁskārān. . . . ASP. p. 200.

Āryāvalokiteśvaro bodhisattvo gambhīrāyāṁ prajñāpāramitāyāṁ caryāṁ caramāṇo vyavalokayati sma; pañcaskandhāṁs tāṅśca svabhāvaśūnyān paśyati sma. iha, Śāriputra, rūpaṁ śūnyatā, śūnyataiva rūpam . . . *Prajñāpāramitā Hṛdaya Sūtra.*

[2] Cf. What Hume says in this matter: "It is not solely in poetry and music we must follow our taste and sentiment, but likewise in philosophy. When I am convinced of any principle, it is only an idea which strikes more strongly upon me. When I give the preference to one set of arguments above another I do nothing but decide from my feeling concerning the superiority of their influence." *Treatise of Human Nature.* p. 103 (Selby-Bigge's Edn.)

idea itself.[1] Moreover, the adoption of any ideal pattern necessarily restricts our scope and narrows down our vision. The entire range of reality is not, and cannot be, covered; determination is negation. Universality eludes our grasp like the horizon. Besides, as already pointed out, we have no means of settling the disputes among systems of philosophy. With the method pursued, differences should increase with time; and there are definite indications, as exemplified by the history of philosophy both in the east and the west, that this reading is correct. Differences tend to throw doubt on the doctrines of philosophy. Absolute certainty that we seek to attain in philosophy is an ideal that cannot come about through this method.

The Mādhyamika method is to *de*conceptualise the mind and to disburden it of all notions, empirical as well as *a priori*. The dialectic is not an avenue for the acquisition of information, but a catharsis; it is primarily a path of purification of the intellect. As an ancillary, purification of moral defilement is also enjoined. The method is negative. Universality and certitude are reached not by the summation of particular points of view, but by rigidly excluding them; for, a view is always particular. It is the abolition of all restrictions which conceptual patterns necessarily impose. It is not nihilism, which is itself a standpoint asserting that nothing is. The dialectic is rejection of all views including the nihilistic.

The implication of the Mādhyamika method is that the real is overlaid with the undergrowth of our notions and views. Most of them are *a priori*; this is avidyā,[2] which, in this system is equated with ideal construction screening the real. The Real is known by uncovering it, by the removal of the opacity of ideas (śūnyatā of dṛṣṭi). Philosophy performs this uncovering function. It is both this process and its culmination. Then the Intellect becomes so pure (amala) and transparent (bhāsvara) that no distinction can possibly exist between the Real and the Intellect apprehending it. The Real (tattva) can indifferently be called dharmatā (Absolute) or prajñā-pāramitā (Intuition). The Absolute as devoid of all determinations is the inexpressible ground of all phenomena; Intellectual Intuition

[1] Systems of philosophy offer no explanation of their initial principle. Every system of philosophy can be exhibited as based on one fundamental principle. Its various doctrines can be shown to follow from that principle, provided the system is well-knit. Many systems do not possess even this internal consistency.

[2] Reference may be made to the discussion of the nature of avidyā in the next chapter.

(Prajñā-Pāramitā) is also devoid of the two extremes ('Is' and 'Is not' views). Emphasising the *faculty* of knowledge, the Mādhyamika prefers to call the Absolute Prajñā-Pāramitā. Prajñā is not a special faculty depending on causes and conditions; it is the intellect freed of conceptual restrictions by the negative function of the dialectic; it is the prius of all functions, and is the universal nature of the mind.

In most systems the negative method of criticism (parapakṣa-nirākaraṇam) is employed. The purpose is to refute other views and remove opposition, strengthening thereby the view advocated. Criticism of other views is a means, not an end itself. Even in the Vedānta and the Vijñānavāda, the dialectic is in the service of a theory of the Real which these systems uphold. Only in the Mādhyamika is the dialectic not a means but an end. Criticism itself is philosophy.

Kant comes nearest to the Mādhyamika conception of philosophy.[1] His *Critique* shows the futility of all views, of Reason itself, to reveal to us the unconditioned; like the Mādhyamika dialectic, it exposes the pretensions of dogmatic philosophy to give us pure knowledge. Like the Mādhyamika, the *Critique* does not erect any view of its own on the criticism of other views, convinced as it is that all views belong to the phenomenal realm. There is, however, an important difference, almost a vital one, between the Mādhyamika dialectic and the Kantian Critique. For Kant the critique has no value *per se*; it is intended to make the path safe for faith; and it is Practical Reason that secures for Kant his noumenal values. The Critique of Pure Reason is a brilliant luxury, and is but externally related to the practical discipline which guarantees Freedom, Immortality and God. In the Mādhyamika, the dialectic itself is true metaphysic or philosophy *par excellence*. It is at once Freedom from pain as freeing man from Ignorance, the root cause of his suffering. And is his Perfection as God (Tathāgata).

II PHILOSOPHICAL KNOWLEDGE IS PRAJÑĀ—NON-DUAL INTUITION

The Mādhyamika philosophy is a systematisation of the *Prajñā-pāramitā* treatises:[2] Diṅnāga sums up admirably the Prajñā-pāramitā

[1] Infra—Chap. XII.

[2] According to Chinese sources Nāgārjuna is the author of *Mahā Prajñā-pāramitā* (*Sūtra*) *Śāstra* (Nanjio No. 1169) a circumstance which might have given rise to the allegation that the *Prajñāpāramitā Sūtras* (Aṣṭasāhasrikā etc.) are his work. See Kimura . . . *Mahāyāna and Hīnayāna* pp. 10 ff.

teaching thus: "Prajñāpāramitā (Highest wisdom) is non-dual knowledge, and that is the Tathāgata. The treatise and the spiritual discipline, as leading to this end, receive the same appellation."[1] This is pregnant with implications.

Metaphysics or true philosophy (prajñā) is non-dual knowledge—Intuition of the Real. The possibility of intellectual intuition is not only accepted but is taken to be the very heart of reality. It is the Truth. In intuition, Knowledge and the Real coincide; essence and existence are identical. It is non-dual as being the negation of the opposites. Only when we look at a thing from a distance, through the mediation of concepts and viewpoints, is there the possibility of discrepancy between what exists and our apprehension of it. Reason works through differentia and distinction. It cannot dispense with the duality of the opposites without losing its nature as Reason. The standpoint of Reason is that of a particular special viewpoint; it is not universal or disinterested knowledge. Non-dual knowledge (jñānam advayam) is the abolition of all particular viewpoints which restrict and distort reality.

Non-duality, for the Mādhyamika, is not attained, as in Hegel, by the synthesis of particular points of view, but by their negation.[2] A view is negated only when we are conscious of its falsity. The consciousness of falsity means that what appeared as unitary and simple is not really so, but turns out to be a bundle of contradictions. And only as we analyse a content into its components and are thus aware of its falsity, do we become reflective. To say then that the Mādhyamika begins with the negation and falsity of judgment and views is to say that metaphysic begins with criticism or reflective consciousness.

It is common ground between the Mādhyamika and the absolutist systems such as Vijñānavāda and Vedānta that they all begin with negation or consciousness of illusion.[3] Absolutism is established in

[1] prajñāpāramitā jñānam advayaṁ sā tathāgataḥ; sādhyā tādarthyayogena tācchabdyaṁ granthamārgayoḥ: This is from the *Prajñāpāramitā Piṇḍārtha Nirdeśa* of Dignāga, quoted in Haribhadra's *Abhisamayālaṅkārāloka twice.* (pp. 28; 153). According to Obermiller, *Prajñāpāramitārtha Saṁgraha* is another name for this—*Doctrine of Prajñā-Pāramitā*, pp. 5; 7. See also *Buston*—Vol. I, p. 51. Tucci has published the entire work with an English translation in the JRAS. 1947, pp. 53–75.

[2] For a comparison of the Mādhyamika and the Hegelian Dialectic see Chap. XII.

[3] The *Viṁśatikā* of Vasubandhu begins with an analysis of Dream-illusion (vijñaptimātram evaitad asadarthāvabhāsanāt). The *Brahma Sūtra Bhāṣya*

all of them by the negation of duality as illusion. But the illusion with which they start and the manner of formulating negation differ in each system. The Vedānta and the Vijñānavāda start with an empirical illusion—the rope-snake or dream-object. For the Vedānta, illusion consists in mistaking the given (Being) for something else, in taking the 'this' as 'snake'. The 'this' is real; it is independent of the act of knowing. Even for being mistaken as 'snake', the rope ('this') must already be there as the substrate. The 'snake', however, is false because it has no existence apart from being known (dṛśyatvāt mithyā): it is totally exhausted within the apprehension (pratibhāsa-mātra-śarīratva). This analysis of the rope-snake illusion is applied to the cosmic illusion. Brahman as Pure Being (sanmātra) corresponds to the 'this' and is real; phenomena as superimposed on the real correspond to the 'snake'.[1]

For the Vijñānavāda, illusion consists in the wrong objectification of what is essentially a state of consciousness (vijñāna): an idea is mistaken for an external object (idam).[2] In dreams and other illusions there is wrong ascription of independent existence (objectivity) to an idea or state of consciousness. The 'snake' is real as an idea, but its supposed externality to consciousness as 'this' is unreal.[3] This analysis of illusion is applied to phenomena. The given object is parikalpita (falsely constructed), while consciousness (vijñāna) is indispensably real as the constructor of the unreal object.[3]

There is a difference in the Vedānta and Vijñānavāda analysis of illusion that amounts almost to a transposition.[4] Committed as it is to the reality of the given, the 'this' (idam) is real for the Vedānta; the 'snake' as a creature of subjective construction is false. The Vedānta analysis of illusion is realistic and is from the standpoint of knowledge, where the object known is independent of the knowing act and is the self-evident thing-in-itself (vastutantra). The Vijñānavāda analyses illusion from an opposite angle. The real in this system is the constructive activity of consciousness which alone invests things with significance. Independence of the subjective act of knowing is here the very essence of the unreal; the 'this' (idam)

of Śaṁkara likewise begins with the consideration of adhyāsa, and all Vedānta treatises commence invariably with an analysis of illusion.

[1] *Advaita Siddhi*. pp. 31 ff. (N.S. Edn.).

[2] yadantar jñeyarūpaṁ tu bahirvad avabhāsate. . . .

[3] MVBT. pp. 15 and 22.

[4] The *Bhāmatī* (p. 26, N.S. Edn.) makes this very significant analysis with regard to Vijñānakhyāti.

in the context of the illusion, 'this is a snake', is false. Both the Vedānta and the Vijñānavāda have, however, one thing in common. They start with a real that is experienced and which serves as the ground (adhiṣṭhāna) for the appearance of the false. There are two stages in their approach—first the analysis of an empirical illusion, and second its analogical application to the world-illusion. This imports an element of dogmatism; for do not the Vedānta and the Vijñānavāda extend what is true of the empirical to the unconditioned? Even granting that their analysis is correct, it is possible to show that the analysis of an *empirical* illusion may not be applied in toto to the world-illusion.

The proposition that all phenomena are illusory does not necessarily follow from the fact that empirical illusions occur. The problem must present itself in all its generality affecting all things. The cue for pronouncing the world illusory and something else real as constituting the ground underlying it must be sought in an extra-logical mode of knowledge. It was indicated in a previous section[1] that the Vedānta starts with the reality of Being as *revealed* by the Upaniṣads; and the Vijñānavāda bases itself on the deliverance of the highest trance-states, where the object drops out leaving consciousness as the sole reality.

Distinct from the above, the Mādhyamika starts with the world-illusion itself in all its directness and universality. He thus avoids the dogmatic procedure of analogical extension employed by the Vedānta and the Vijñānavāda. The world-illusion is presented to the Mādhyamika as the total and persistent conflict of Reason—the interminable opposition of philosophical viewpoints. He is solely concerned with the Transcendental illusion. As the several philosophical views are views of reality, the Mādhyamika, in being aware of the illusoriness of the views, is aware of the illusoriness of the world which is characterised by these views. For instance, in rejecting the different theories of causation (satkāryavāda, asatkāryavāda etc.) the Mādhyamika has rejected causation as a constitutive feature of the real.

It must, however, be said that the Mādhyamika dialectic, being a criticism of philosophical standpoints, can get under way only when the different systems have already been formulated. It cannot be an original system. This may make the Mādhyamika philosophy appear adventitious, as it has to depend on the chance-emergence of different

[1] Chap. VI, Section V.

systems and their opposition. It has, however, been shown that the conflict is necessary and implicit in Reason itself. The Mādhyamika system may be later in time, but its emergence is logically necessary; the inner dynamism of philosophical consciousness leads to the transcendentalism of the Mādhyamika.

III DISTINCTION BETWEEN ADVAYA AND ADVAITA

In all the three absolutisms the highest knowledge is conceived as Intuition, beyond all traces of duality. A distinction must, however, be made between the *advaya* of the Mādhyamika and the advaita of the Vedānta,[1] although in the end it may turn out to be one of emphasis of approach. Advaya is knowledge free from the duality of the extremes (antas or dṛṣṭis) of 'Is' and 'Is not', Being and Becoming etc. It is *knowledge freed* of conceptual distinctions. Advaita is knowledge *of* a differenceless entity—Brahman (Pure Being) or Vijñāna (Pure consciousness). The Vijnānavāda although it uses the term *advaya* for its absolute, is really an advaita system.

'Advaya' is purely an epistemological approach; the advaita is ontological. The sole concern of the Mādhyamika advaya-vāda is the purification of the faculty of knowing. The primordial error consists in the intellect being infected by the inveterate tendency to view Reality as identity or difference, permanent or momentary, one or many etc. These views falsify reality, and the dialectic administers a cathartic corrective. With the purification of the intellect, Intuition (prajñā) emerges; the Real is known as it is, as Tathatā or bhūtakoti. The emphasis is on the correct *attitude of our knowing* and not on the known.

On the ontological standpoint of the Advaita Vedānta, the emphasis is on the thing known. When that is universal and devoid of difference, the knowing faculty too gets concentrated and lost in it (brahma veda brahmaiva bhavati); Brahma experience is non-dual (akhaṇḍa). The primary aim of the Vedānta and the Vijñānavāda is to seek the truly real and suffuse the mind exclusively with it to the extent that the mind becomes one with the real. Dialectic is employed to

[1] Professor Bhattacharya in his *Āgama Śāstra* (p. 102) draws the distinction thus: "But there is a marked difference between the two terms *advaitavāda* and *advayavāda*, while the former literally means the theory of non-difference, i.e. the non-difference between or identity of (according to the school of Śaṅkara) jīva and brahman; the latter means the theory of non-two, i.e., neither of the two extreme views."

demonstrate the falsity of the opposed views of the Real. The Vedānta employs it to demolish difference (bheda), plurality (dvaita) and particularity (pariccheda), thereby indirectly establishing the sole reality of Pure Being as changeless, universal and self-evident. The Vijñānavāda employs the dialectic to disprove the reality of the object and plurality; it thereby indirectly establishes the sole reality of consciousness (vijñāna).

The Mādhyamika, however, has no doctrine of existence, ontology. This would be, according to him, to indulge in dogmatic speculation (dṛṣṭivāda). To the Vedānta and Vijñānavāda, the Mādhyamika, with his purely epistemological approach and lack of a doctrine of reality, cannot but appear as nihilistic (sarva-vaināśika, śūnya-vāda). The 'no-doctrine' attitude of the Mādhyamika is construed by Vedānta and Vijñānavāda as a 'no-reality' doctrine; they accuse the Mādhyamika, unjustifiably, of denying the real altogether and as admitting a theory of appearance without any reality as its ground (niradhiṣṭhāna bhrama). In fact, the Mādhyamika does not deny the real; he only denies *doctrines* about the real. For him, the real as transcendent to thought can be reached only by the denial of the determinations which systems of philosophy ascribe to it. When the entire conceptual activity of Reason is dissolved by criticism, there is Prajñā-Pāramitā. The *Aṣṭasāhasrikā* declares in the clearest terms that Prajnāpāramitā is not to be construed as a doctrine of Elements, of Groups etc. These conceptual devices do not obtain in reality. The non-apprehension of things (yo'nupalambhaḥ sarvadharmāṇām) is Prajñāpāramitā.[1]

The method of the Mādhyamika is negative, not the result. His denial of the *views* of the real is not denial of the real, and he makes the denial of views—the dialectic itself—the means for realising the real.

IV THE NATURE OF THE MĀDHYAMIKA INTUITION (PRAJÑĀ)

The intuition of the Mādhyamika (prajñā) has nothing in common with sensory intuition, which is a specific empirical act. This occurs when the sense-organs are stimulated by specific sense-data under

[1] neyaṁ, Subhūte, prajñāpāramitā skandhaśo vā dhātuśo va āyatanaśo vā śakyā nirdeṣṭuṁ vā śrotuṁ vā . . . tat kasya hetoḥ? skandha-dhātvāyatanam eva hi Subhūte śūnyaṁ viviktaṁ śāntam iti hi prajñāpāramitā ca skandhadhātvāyatanaṁ *cādvayam etad advaidhīkāraṁ*, śūnyatvād viviktatvād evaṁ śāntatvān nopalabhyate. *yo'nupalambhaḥ sarva-dharmāṇāṁ sā prajñāpāramitetyucyate.* yadā na bhavati saṁjñā, saṁajñā-prajñaptir vyavahāras tadā prajñāpāramite tyucyate. ASP. p. 177.

favourable conditions of response. It is a transitory act with a limited content. But Prajñā is not a transitory state, being the very nature of all things. Though realised in its pristine form in the highest ecstatic states, it is not a special faculty with a limited scope; it is the prius of all things—(prakṛtir dharmāṇām). Intuition must be viewed as that generic and invariable form of knowledge of which other modes of apprehension are species.[1] Anti-conceptualism notwithstanding, the intellectual intuition of the Mādhyamika must not be confounded with the Bergsonian view of Intuition. For Bergson, Reason spatialises things; it freezes reality which is movement, *elan vital*—the life-principle. The Real can be apprehended, according to him, only by sympathetically identifying oneself with it. From the examples that Berson suggests and his interpretation of the course of evolution, it is evident that intuition for him is *instinctual* in nature; its position is *infra-rational*. It would not be very wrong to say that Bergson wants us to sink down to the level of birds and insects. He does not prescribe any discipline for acquiring this faculty or for suppressing reason. The Prajñā of the Mādhyamika, on the other hand, is not instinct and cannot be identified with any biotic force. It is supra-rational.

The dialectic does not bring Intuition into existence *de novo*; it only removes the obstructions and limitations which have been obscuring it. It is not an acquisition intrinsically, although it may *appear* to be so for the individual undertaking the spiritual discipline. There is novelty epistemically, not ontologically. As the non-dual knowledge is not accretion of information, it is got not through any special faculty, but by divestifying the mind of its natural disposition to bifurcate and conceptualise.

Non-dual knowledge (prajñā) is contentless Intuition. Nothing stands out against it as an other confronting it. It is thus always described as advayā (non-dual) advaidhīkārā (non-bifurcated). It might be truer to say that the absolute or the entire reality is its content and not any particular limited object. On this account, the *Prajñā-pāramitā* texts speak of the Intuition as unfathomable (gambhīrā), immeasurable (aprameyā) and Infinite (asamkhyeyā); it is really inexpressible, too deep for words, too universal for distinctions to apply.[2]

[1] gambhīrā, Bhagavan, prakrtiṛ dharmāṇām. ASP. p. 192.

[2] na mayā Ānanda, prajñāpāramitāyāḥ pramāṇaṁ vā kṣayo vā paryanto vā ākhyātaḥ. nāmakāya-padakāya-vyañjanakāyāḥ khalu punar Ānanda pramāṇa-baddhā, neyaṁ prajñāpāramitā pramāna-baddhā. ASP. p. 467.

The mind as it is freed of impediments (āvaraṇas) is perfectly diaphanous, transparent. In that state it is non-distinct from the real, and a description of the one is thus a description of the other. Intuition is the Absolute.

In the Intuition of the Absolute there is not the consciousness of realisation; for, that would militate against the purity and fullness of the intuition. To be self-conscious of the thing known, we must stand aside and away from it, distinguish it from ourselves and even contrast our present knowledge with our previous state of non-knowing. This is possible only in a discursive form of apprehension.[1]

The Mādhyamika conception of Philosophy as Prajñāpāramitā (non-dual, contentless intuition) precludes progress and surprise. Progress implies that the goal is reached successively by a series of steps in an order, and that it could be measured in quantitative terms. Prajñā is knowledge of the entire reality once for all, and it does not depend on contingent factors as a special faculty, favourable circumstances or previous information. A progressive realisation of the absolute is thus incompatible. Science which investigates the contingent order of things is a body of information, collected and collated by a team of workers investigating the field piecemeal; there is successive growth in the volume of our knowledge. The concept of progress is applicable to science, not to philosophy. It is, however, possible to conceive of the progressive falling away of the hindrances that obstruct our vision of the real. But there is neither order nor addition in the content of our knowledge of the real. The modern conception of philosophy as a universal science, co-ordinating and weaving the findings of the various sciences into a coherent system, is at variance with the Mādhyamika conception of philosophy as Prajñāpāramitā.

V PRAJÑĀ IS FREEDOM

In common with other Indian systems, philosophy for the Mādhyamika is not a theoretic consideration of things meant to satisfy idle curiosity. Of most systems of philosophy in the West it may be said that they have no ethical bearing; they could go with any kind of ethics; and even dispense with that altogether.

For the Mādhyamika, philosophy starts with the negative judgment

[1] sa cet, Subhūte, bodhisattvo mahāsattvaḥ prajñāpāramitām atyantaviviktām iti saṁjānīte, na sā prajñāpāramitā syāt. ASP. p. 440.

or illusion. Illusion is the consciousness of the inapplicability of our subjective notions to the real. On the practical side, it is the poignant feeling of pain that provides the impetus for the search of a means to end suffering. Pain is impeded willing—the inconsonance of our desires with objective circumstances. As the secular means are incapable of giving us complete and abiding freedom from pain, recourse is to be had to philosophy. Freedom from pain is achieved by the elimination of kleśas—the unconscious primordial passions impelling man towards attachment and bondage. Prajñā is the negation of all vikalpa—conceptual constructions; it is the reaching of non-dual knowledge, a state beyond the discursive level of Reason. The end of practical discipline is the spiritual good, beyond the duality of good and evil. The spiritual must be distinguished from the moral, which is a social relationship based on justice. In the moral there is still an opposition between one's good and the good of another. Even in the individual there is the conflict between the good of the moment and his real abiding good. The dialectic resolves the antinomical conflict in reason by eliminating the root-cause of it—the duality of 'is' and 'not-is'. Likewise, the spiritual discipline of attaining the Enlightenment of Buddha-hood (bodhicittotpāda) resolves the moral conflict between private and public good. The spiritual is the consummation of all values; it is value *par excellence.* "To achieve freedom from pain and attain bliss", says Śānti Deva, "let one, with strong faith, fix one's spirit on Enlightenment (bodhi)."[1]

It must not be thought that Intellectual Intuition (prajñā) and Freedom are two parallel but independent processes. Freedom is the practical implication of prajñā. Buddhist spiritual discipline had always consisted of three parts—śīla (virtue), samādhi (contemplation) and prajñā (wisdom). Practice of virtue and contemplation are ancillaries to the attainment of prajñā.[2] A person assailed by passions and distracted by worldliness cannot perceive the truth. And only on perceiving the truth is one completely freed of passions.

Broadly, the discipline can be divided into two stages: śamatha (control of mind) and vipaśyanā (Insight).[3] In the more elaborate

[1] duḥkāntaṁ kartukāmena sukhāntaṁ gantum icchatā; śraddhāmūlaṁ dṛḍhīkṛtya bodhau kāryā matir dṛḍhā. ŚS. p. 2.
bhavaduḥkha-śatāni tartukāmair api sattva-vyasanāni hartukāmaiḥ; bahu-saukhya-śatāni bhoktukāmair na vimocyaṁ hi sadaiva *bodhicittam.* BCA. I, 8.

[2] imaṁ parikaraṁ sarvaṁ prajñārthaṁ hi munir jagau;
tasmād utpādayet prajñāṁ duḥkhanivṛttikāṅkṣayā. BCA. IX, 1.

[3] BCAP. pp. 348 ff.

doctrine of the Six Pāramitās (Excellences or Perfections), the first five (dāna, śīla, kṣānti, vīrya and dhyāna) are preparatory to the last—prajñā (Intuition) which crowns them. In a celebrated passage in the *Aṣṭasāhasrikā*,[1] it is pointed out that prajñā is the leader (nāyaka) of the pāramitās; the latter are blind and directionless without prajñā. Nor are they pāramitās (Infinite) without prajñā; that alone can complete them. Practice of separate virtues and disconnected acts of contemplation cannot impart that unity and singleness of purpose so essential for spiritual life. The entire man is to be harnessed for this effort. It is prajñā which informs and directs the whole process from the beginning.

Freedom is a negative process; it is not the accumulation of merit or accession of power, but the removal of hindrances (kleśāvaraṇa) which cover the real. Attachment and aversion (the root-kleśas) are themselves dependent on imaginative construction (kalpanā).[2] It is as we invest things with glowing or grisly attributes that we attach ourselves or evince aversion to them. It cannot be maintained that things are inherently, objectively, attractive or otherwise; for, what is liked by one is disliked by another, while a third may be indifferent to it.[3] This shows the inherently subjective character of these basic attitudes. Because the kleśas are subjective, they can be helped; we can be freed of them. Nāgārjuna analyses the nature of bondage and freedom thus: "Of constructive imagination are born attachment, aversion and infatuation, depending (respectively) on our good, evil and stupid attitudes. Entities which depend on these are not anything by themselves. The kleśas are unreal."[4] "Freedom (mokṣa) is the

[1] paramatvāt sā prajñāpāramitā nāmadheyaṁ labhate . . . tasmāt tarhy, ānanda, sarvajñatāpariṇāmita-kuśala-mūlatvāt prajñā-pāramitā pañcānāṁ pāramitānāṁ pūrvangamā nāyikā pariṇāyikā. ASP. p. 81.

evam eva, kauśika, dānaṁ śīlaṁ kṣāntir vīryaṁ dhyānaṁ ca prajñāpāramitānāmadheyaṁ labhate. jātyandhabhūtaṁ bhavati vinā prajñāpāramitayā aparināyakatvād abhavyaṁ sarvajñatāmārgāvatārāya, kutaḥ punaḥ sarvajñatām anuprāpsyati. yadā punaḥ . . .

prajñāpāramitā-parigṛhītaṁ bhavati tadā pāramitā nāmadheyam pāramitā śabdam labhate. ASP. p. 172.

[2] Cf. CŚ. VIII, 3. vinā kalpanayāstitvaṁ rāgādīnām na vidyate; bhūtārthaḥ kalpanā ceti ko grahīṣyati buddhimān.

[3] Cf. CŚ. VIII, 2. tatraiva rajyate kaścit kaścit tatraiva duṣyati; kaścin muhyati tatraiva tasmāt kāmo nirarthakaḥ.

[4] saṁkalpaprabhavo rāgo dveṣo mohaś ca kathyate;
śubhāśubha-viparyāsān sambhavanti pratītya hi.
śubhāśubha-viparyāsān sambhavanti pratītya ye;
te svabhāvān na vidyante tasmāt kleśā na tattvataḥ. MK. XXII, 1, 2.

cessation of karma and kleśa (acts and passions); these arise from vikalpa (imagination); this ceases with the knowledge of their falsity (śūnyatā)."[1]

Śūnyata is the antidote for all kleśas.[2] When the real is not (mis) apprehended as an ens nor a non-ens there is cessation of kalpanā. There can then be no gain or loss, elation or depression.[3] This doctrine is as old as Buddha himself. A verse attributed to Buddha says:[4]

> "Desire, know I thy root; from imagination (sankalpa) thou springest;
> No more shall I indulge in imagination; I will have no desire any more."

The Mādhyamika doctrine of freedom implies that complete spiritual regeneration of man is possible; the human mind can be educated and trained. The problem is essentially one of knowledge—insight into the nature of the real. The supremacy of the intellect and its absolute power to control and eradicate passions is the rock on which the Mādhyamika spiritual discipline is built. Not the will but the intellect is the supreme faculty to which others are subject. Truth is the highest value. This is at variance with the Kantian conception. For Kant, the good will is higher and more valuable than the Intellect. There is a deep conflict between the theoretical and the practical Reason, and Kant's predilections led him to ascribe superiority to the latter.

In the Vedānta and Vijñānavāda too, there is the identity of Intellectual Intuition and Freedom; they also subscribe to the supremacy of knowledge over will. A distinction can, however, be made between the Mādhyamika doctrine of Freedom and that of the Vedānta. Freedom in the Vedānta *follows* from knowledge of the identity of the self with Brahman. The abandonment of the particular standpoint of the ego and identification with the universal Being (Brahman) makes passions (attachment and aversion) impossible;[5]

[1] MK. XVIII, 5.

[2] śūnyatā duḥkhaśamanī tataḥ kiṁ jāyate bhayam. BCA. IX, 56.

[3] BCA. IX, 152: evam śūnyeṣu dharmeṣu kiṁ labdhaṁ kiṁ hṛtaṁ bhavet; satkṛtaḥ paribhūto va kena kaḥ sambhaviṣyati.

[4] kāma jānāmi te mūlaṁ saṅkalpāt kila jāyase; na tvāṁ saṅkalpayiṣyāmi tato me na bhaviṣyasi. Quoted in MKV. p. 350; 451.

Cf. also *Dhammapada* 153–154.

[5] tatra ko mohaḥ kaḥ śoka ekatvam anupaśyataḥ—*Iśā Upaniṣad.* yatra sarvam atmaivābhūt—*Bṛ. Up.*

there is no other which you can like or hate. Freedom is the consequence of the attainment of universality (sarvātmatva). In the Vijñānavāda the realisation of the sole reality of consciousness means the unreality of the other—the object. Without the reality of the object, no attachment or aversion is possible. In the Mādhyamika it is more direct. Śūnyata (Intellectual Intuition) as the dissolution of the conceptual function of mind is freedom. There is not first the suffusing of the mind with Brahman or Vijñāna which makes passion incompatible with it.[1] The difference between the two standpoints in this regard is but one more implication of the fact that Vedānta and Vijñānavāda have an ontology, a doctrine of the real, and employ the dialectic as a means. For the Mādhyamika, there is no doctrine of being; dialectic itself is philosophy.

VI PRAJÑĀ-PĀRAMITĀ IS TATHĀGATA

Prajñā-pāramitā, as non-dual knowledge, is equated with Tathāgata—the Perfect Being, God.[2] We are asked to apprehend the Buddha as dharmakāya, as one with the absolute. The conception of Buddhakāya is essentially religious. The Tathāgata is viewed not merely as the reality of all·being (Śūnyatā or Bhūtakoṭi), but as a Person endowed with all divine qualities and powers. He has ten powers (daśabala), four grounds of confidence (catvāri vaiśāradyāni) and eighteen unique attributes or perfections (aṣṭādasāvenikā dharmāḥ). The personality of the Tathāgata cannot be doubted. He is credited with a free phenomenalising activity by which he assumes at will, actuated by infinite compassion, forms to succour all beings. He is not invested with creative and other cosmic functions as in the Brāhmanical conceptions of Īśvara. Karma accounts for the existence of the universe and gradation of beings (karmajaṁ loka-vaicitryam). Out of compassion, Buddha saves all beings. His compassion is a free act of grace; it knows no distinction and suffers from no limitation of time or extent. It is this mahākaruṇā which

[1] To illustrate the distinction. Sex-love can be got over by directing the mind to the Transcendent which grips it so entirely that sex ceases to have any attraction. Or, it can be got rid of by being conscious of its inherent hollowness. The latter alternative is analogous to the Mādhyamika discipline.

[2] uktaṁ hyetad bhagavatā: dharmakāyā buddhā bhagavantaḥ. nā khalu punar imaṁ, bhikṣavaḥ, satkāyaṁ kāyaṁ manyadhvam. dharmakāya-parinispattito māṁ bhikṣavo drakṣyanty eṣa ca tathāgatakāyo bhūtakoṭi-prabhāvito draṣṭavyo yad uta Prajñāpāramitā. ASP. p. 94.

makes the Tathāgata the Deity, a personal God. He takes individual interest in beings and continuously strives for their good.

A difference is sometimes made between Prajñāpāramitā (Absolute) and the Tathāgata, the personalised aspect of the Absolute. Prajñā is taken as the matrix from which the Tathāgatas have sprung.[1] Godhead is a manifestation, a particular phenomenalisation of Dharmatā which is transcendent. There is no restriction as regards the number and form of the Tathāgatas. According to the needs and circumstances, the Buddhas arise and manifest themselves. A personal god is in some sense lower in the hierarchy of the real. The relation of the Deity (tathāgata) to the Absolute (prajñā, śūnyatā) is one-sided; the former depends on the latter, and not vice versa. It is a free identity; metaphysically, the Tathāgata is a principle of a lower order than prajñā.[2]

The acceptance of God may appear to be an after-thought and even unwarranted in the Mādhyamika system. Buddhism has always laid stress on self-effort; it has even repudiated Īśvara.[3] It has been a religion of works than of grace. Simultaneous with the revolution in Buddhism which changed it from the radical pluralism of the Hīnayāna to the absolutism of the Mahāyāna, there was felt the need for a mediating principle between the absolute and phenomenal beings. Buddha is that mediator. In Prajñā he is identical with the absolute; but as a human being subjecting himself to all the limitations, he is at once phenomenal. Buddha soon came to be deified. His enlightenment was not an accident; it was deliberately and freely chosen by the Deity. And Gautama the Buddha is just *one* of those innumerable manifestations in the past and the future. Nor is Buddha different from other beings. In essence they are identical with him; every being is Buddha in the making. "The Buddhas were subjected to a six-fold process of evolution; they were multiplied, immortalised, deified, spiritualised, universalised and unified."[4] The process, however, is not historical or accidental. The logical necessity to find a mediating principle between the Absolute and phenomena

[1] ASP. p. 254. In the invocation to Prajñāpāramitā (ASP. p. 1) it is explicitly stated that Prajñā is the matrix of all the world-teachers, the Buddhas.

yo' dhikā janayitrī ca mātā tvam asi vatsalā;
yad buddhā lokaguravaḥ putrās tava kṛpālavaḥ.

[2] The position of Īśvara in the Vedānta is analogous to this.

[3] BCA. IX, 119 ff. (BCAP. p. 544 ff.) MKV. 77. TSP. pp. 414 ff.

[4] Har Dayal—*The Bodhisattva Doctrine*, p. 28.

has given rise to the religion of the Mādhyamika and the acceptance of God.

There can be no religion without the consciousness of a being that is transcendent. A contrast must be felt between the exalted Being (God) and the finite creatures. Semitic religions—Judaism, Christianity and Mahommedanism—magnify this difference to the extent of creating an unbridgeable gulf between the two; the difference between the two is one of kind and is eternal. These religions minimise and even ignore the basic fact of the affinity of God and man as spirit. The two cannot differ in kind, as this would mean lack of relationship; man cannot worship a mere *other*, and God would not condescend to save man. Any relation, even the relationship of worshipper and worshipped, presupposes a fundamental unity which provides the platform for these differences that are relative. This aspect of religion is emphasised by the philosophical religions of India, Vedānta, Buddhism and even Jainism. God and man are not different. How can religious consciousness obtain without difference, in the absence of the contrast between the transcendent being and finite beings, it might be asked. The difference, however, need not be that of one thing and another differing eternally in kind, but one of states or stages of the same being; there is enough contrast felt between the ideal and the actual to sustain the religious consciousness.

A necessary implication of the non-difference between God and man is that both of them have to be considered as aspects of a more basic being—the Absolute; they are appearances and not ultimate. God is a personal manifestation, the individualisation, of the Absolute. As this is a free phenomenalisation, there is no conceivable limit to the number, form and occasion of these manifestations. All beings have also to be considered as God; Buddha (Gautama) is not the only instance of man attaining perfection. Absolutism translated in terms of religion can only be a Pantheism. It is necessarily committed to the unity of all beings, the identity of God and man and the transcendence of the Absolute. All this is exemplified in the Mādhyamika religion of the Triple Body of the Buddha (Trikāya).

The conception of Prajñāpāramitā is the distinctive feature of the Mādhyamika system. That dominates every part of its philosophy—its metaphysic, ethics and religion. Prajñā is the non-dual knowledge (jñānam advayam). As pointed out before, the dialectic reaches its fruition through three 'moments': the antinomical conflict of opposed views of the real advanced by speculative systems (dṛṣṭivāda); their criticism, which exposes their hollowness (śūnyatā); and intuition of the Real in which the duality of 'is' and 'not is' is totally resolved (prajñā). It is the Absolute beyond Reason. Implicit in the process, Prajñā guides the entire dialectical movement.

Prajñā as non-conceptual knowledge removes avidyā, which, in this system, is the inveterate tendency to conceptualise things. Passions (attachment and aversion), all of which have their origin in this tendency, cease on the attainment of prajñā. Prajñā is not merely Intellectual Intuition but Freedom as well.

Prajñāpāramitā—the Absolute—is also identified with Tathāgata—the Deity who is its freely phenomenalised aspect. Essentially a fact of religious consciousness, the Tathāgata serves as the principle of mediation between the Absolute (śūnyaṭā) and phenomenal beings. This is the logic implied in the admission of the Triple Buddhakāya.

Anything like an adequate treatment of the implications of the Prajñāpāramitā conception would have to consider Prajñā (Intuition) as Absolute, as Freedom and as Tathāgata.

CHAPTER NINE

ABSOLUTE AND PHENOMENA

I THE ABSOLUTE IS ŚŪNYA—TRANSCENDENT

PRAJÑĀPĀRAMITĀ as non-dual Intuition is the Absolute. This was shown in the last chapter. The converse is equally significant. The Real is non-dual—free from all empirical predicates and relation. It is Śūnya, devoid of every kind of determination. The Real (tattva) is invariably defined, in the Mādhyamika treatises, as transcendent to thought[1] as non-relative, non-determinate, quiescent, non-discursive, non-dual.[2] All possible modes of predication are classified under four heads: bhāva (existence, affirmation) and abhāva (non-existence, negation) are the primary modes which are conjointly affirmed (ubhayam) or disjunctively denied (na bhāvaḥ, naivābhāvaḥ) to make the third and the fourth class of predicates respectively. Tattva cannot be characterised by any of these predicates taken singly or in combination.[3] This point has been reiterated with regard to all categories of thought—causality, motion, substance, Relation, Self (ātman) and modes.

Different systems of philosophy which conceive the Real on any of these conceptual patterns are also criticized, and the inherent flaw in their attitude is demonstrated. The dialectic demonstrates, by a series of *reductio ad absurdum* (prasangāpādana) arguments that phenomena and the categories which define them are relative, valid only under certain conditions. A thing is significant as it is related causally or otherwise to other things. It is nothing apart from the spatio-temporal continuum on which it depends for its existence. It is a narrow, false, view that considers particular entities as independent things in themselves. "There is no entity", says Nāgārjuna, "that is not dependent. An absolute non-relational entity

[1] buddher agocaras tattvaṁ buddhiḥ saṁvṛtir ucyate. BCA. IX, 2.

[2] apara-pratyayam śāntaṁ prapañcair aprapañcitam;
nirvikalpam anānārtham etat tattvasya lakṣaṇam. MK. XVIII, 9.

[3] Cf. the celebrated verse quoted at various places. (BCAP. p. 359; *Sarva Darśana Sangraha* Chap. on *Bauddha Darśana*): na san nāsan na sadasan na cāpyanubhayātmakam; catuṣkoṭi-vinirmuktaṁ tattvam Mādhyamikā viduḥ. This is probably from Saraha. See *Subhāṣitasamgrahaḥ*.

(aśūnyo dharmaḥ) does not therefore exist."[1] Relativity or dependence is an invariable mark of the unreal. The Real (tattva) is the absolute, self-conceived and self-existent (apara-pratyayam). Conversely, the dependent is an appearance. Pratītya-samutpāda is thus equated with śūnyatā, unreality.[2] The unreal lacks a nature of its own (niḥsvabhāvatā).

Two considerations stand out prominently in the Mādhyamika notion of the Absolute: its utter indeterminateness and the consequent non-accessibility to Reason. The one emphasises the logical nature of the absolute; the other the mode of its apprehension. The Absolute is very aptly termed Śūnya, as it is devoid of all predicates. Even existence, unity, selfhood and goodness cannot be affirmed of it. One is precluded from asserting that it "is" (sat), a positive ens (bhāva). It would then be subject to origination, decay and death; there is no empirical existence which is free from these characteristics.[3] An entity has its being in an environment; it derives all its meaning as co-operating with other entities which together make the universe; it affects and is affected by other entities; technically, it is saṁskṛta; but the absolute is not such an entity.[4] Moreover, in conceiving it as a bhāva (ens), we have perforce to take it as engendered by specific causes and conditions; it is not anything by itself.[5] If the Absolute could not be conceived as bhāva, *a fortiori* the category of non-existence (abhāva) cannot apply to it. Non-existence, as cessation, comes into being on the destruction of things that had been existing.[6] The Absolute as Nirvāṇa is conceived by some as the cessation of all desires and aversions. This implies that it was not existent before the destruction. The Absolute then would be as much subject to temporal limitation as the desires and aversions on whose cessation it supervenes. Moreover, the cessation has to be brought about by the operation of certain forces and conditions. And as these may not always be

[1] MK. XXIV, 19. Cf. CŚ. IX, 2; hetupratyaya-sāmagrīm pratītya jātasya parāyattātmalābhasya pratibimbasyeva kutaḥ sasvabhāvatā. BCAP. p. 354.

[2] yaḥ pratītyasamutpādaḥ śūnyatāṁ tāṁ pracakṣmahe. MK. XXIV, 18.
yaḥ pratītya-samutpādaḥ śūnyatā saiva te matā;
bhāvaḥ svatantro nāstīti siṁhanādas tavātulaḥ. quoted in BCAP. p. 417.

[3] bhāvas tāvan na nirvāṇaṁ jarāmaraṇa-lakṣaṇam;
prasajyetāsti bhāvo hi na jarāmaraṇaṁ vinā. MK. XXV, 4.

[4] bhāvaś ca yadi nirvāṇaṁ nirvāṇaṁ saṁskṛtaṁ bhavet. MK. XXV, 5.

[5] MK. XXV, 6.

[6] yady abhāvaś ca nirvāṇam anupādāya tat katham;
nirvāṇaṁ na hy abhāvo'sti yo'nupādāya vidyate. MK. XXV, 8.

available, the Absolute has to depend on the off-chance of their occurrence.[1]

These difficulties might be avoided, it might be thought, if non-existence were taken as an other to existence or as its opposite. This would be a species of existence and is subject to the objections already urged with regard to the conception of existence. Or, if it is a non-entity, like the square-circle, hare's horn etc., then it is a mere name and less than nothing.

Attempts to combine the concepts of existence and non-existence are less plausible. Hegel has made familiar the notion of a synthesis which unifies and yet retains the differences in its grip. Neither the differents without the unity nor the bare unity without the differences are significant in his view. The real is a concrete whole, a universal which subsumes particulars without annulling them.

Without entering into the intricacies and details of the Hegelian conception of the Absolute, it may be pointed out that the Mādhyamika system has had before it such a synthetic view of the absolute in the third alternative, (bhāva and abhāva, sat and asat). It has rejected this pattern too as not applicable to the absolute. If the two ingredients, existence and non-existence or identity and difference, retain their nature in the synthesis, the combination is subject to the difficulties urged with regard to each alternative.[2] We should have added to our difficulty by creating some more problems: the manifest incompatibility in affirming two opposed characteristics at once[3] and the necessity of formulating a new relationship between the composite synthesis on the one hand and the components on the other.[4]

The considered Mādhyamika criticism is that reciprocity or mutual dependence of unity on difference and vice versa is a mark of the unreal.[5] This detracts from its nature as absolute. Bound up with the above is the contention that such an absolute is within Reason (buddhi), is Reason itself. But buddhi hides the real nature of the

[1] MKV. pp. 529–30.

[2] MK. XXV, 11–13.

[3] bhaved abhāvo bhāvaś ca nirvāṇam ubhayam katham;
na tayor ekatr āstitvam ālokatamasor yathā. MK. XXV, 14.

[4] For a fuller criticism of the Hegelian conception reference may be made to Chaps. V and XII.

[5] yo'pekṣya siddhyate bhāvas tam evāpekṣya siddhyati;
yadi yo'pekṣitavyaḥ sa siddhyatāṁ kam apekṣya kaḥ. MK. X, 10.
parasparāpekṣayoḥ karmakārakavadeva siddhir, na svābhāvikī.
MKV. p. 189.

absolute. Hegel's absolute is the saṁvṛti (Appearance) of the Mādhyamika.

The fourth alternative of the negation of both existence and non-existence does not appear to be more convincing. Granting that this is true, how is one to know that to be so? There is no ego in Nirvāṇa, as the psychic functions and states are admittedly absent there.[1]

If the category of existence or non-existence cannot be applied to the absolute, there is less justification for applying other categories—permanence, change, substance (ātmạn) modes, unity, plurality, etc. Whatever may be the empirical value of these categories as devices for interpreting phenomena, they are not assignable determinations of the absolute. The Mādhyamika dialectic relentlessly exposes their relative and empirical character. They belong to the region of the empirical truth—saṁvṛti satya.

It might be considered that we are stretching the point too far; the terms Being, Substance, Unity, Becoming, Plurality may be used in a slightly different but legitimate sense to characterise the ultimately real. Such confidence, however, is born of dogmatism. There is no term, concept or category, however exalted and general, that can apply both to the absolute and phenomena *uni voce*. The two never stand on the same plane; they cannot be related, compared or contrasted. Words do not denote the absolute in any recognisable sense. The Absolute is incommensurable and inexpressible; it is utterly transcendent to thought—Śūnya.

"Appellation ceases with the absence of the objects of thought: The absolute as the essence of all things is not born, nor does it cease to be."[2]

II CONSIDERATION OF SOME MISCONCEPTIONS ABOUT ŚŪNYATĀ (THE ABSOLUTE)

If nothing can be predicated of the Absolute and no terms can be applied to it, how then do we continue to speak of it? How can it be cognised at all as the ultimately Real?

1. The Absolute, it is true, is not known in the way that particular phenomena are known. As their reality, however, it is known as the

[1] MKV. p. 533.

[2] nivṛttam abhidhātavyaṁ nivṛtte cittagocare;
anutpannāniruddhā hi nirvāṇam iva dharmatā. MK. XVIII, 7.

implicate, the norm of all things. The Absolute does not possess any attribute of its own; but its presence can be *indicated* even by an ascribed mark (samāropāt).[1] It is asked: How can the anakṣara (literally, the inexpressible) be understood and taught (declared)? The absolute is known as the reality of the appearances, what they falsely stand for. By *dis*covering, *re*moving, the superimposed character of phenomena, the true nature of the absolute is revealed. Technically, this is called adhyāropāpavādanyāya—the method of removal of the ascription. Phenomena are utilised as devices (upāya) to reach the unconditioned (paramārtha) which is their end (upeya). There is no other means of expressing the inexpressible.[2]

Although an ascribed character may not constitute the real, yet it can indicate it as its ground. Even an ascribed mark can serve the purpose of definition. In one sense, it may be said that the cognition of everything is the cognition of the absolute; because it is that which appears under these varied and veiled forms.[3] In another sense, the absolute is not known through any of these forms; for it is not a particular entity. We really know it when nothing else is before us. The real language is silence.[4] The Absolute is totally free from conception; it is not open to thought.

The transcendence of the absolute must not be understood to mean that it is an other that lies outside the world of phenomena. There are not two sets of the real. The Absolute is *the reality* of the apparent (dharmāṇām dharmatā); it is their real nature (vāstavikam rūpam). Conversely, phenomena are the veiled form or false appearance of the Absolute (sāṁvṛtam rūpam). If this position is discountenanced and two reals are accepted, there would be no point in calling one of them the absolute and the other appearance. Both would be equally, unconditionedly, real. The absolute, as lacking determinations and without any recognisable content, would even be less real than the

[1] anakṣarasya dharmasya śrutiḥ kā deśanā ca kā; śrūyate deśyate cāpi samāropād anakṣaraḥ. Saying of Buddha quoted in MKV. p. 264, BCAP. p. 365.

[2] MK. XXV, 10. tasmān nirvāṇādhigamopāyatvād avaśyam eva yathāvasthitā saṁvṛtir ādāv abhyupeyā, bhājanam iva salilārthinā. MKV. p. 494.

[3] Brahman, in the Vedānta, is likewise taken as unknown (avedya) and at the same time as known in all cognition (sarvapratyayavedya).

[4] yo'nupalambhaḥ sarvadharmāṇāṁ sa Prajñāpāramitā. ASP. p. 177.
yadā na bhāvo nābhāvo mateḥ saṁtiṣṭhate puraḥ:
tadānyagatyabhāvena nirālambanā praśāmyati. BCA. IX, 35.
paramārtho hy āryāṇāṁ tūṣṇīmbhāva eva. MKV. p. 57.

empirical. The absolute is the only real; it is identical with phenomena. The difference between the two is epistemic—subjective and not real. In full accordance with this, Nāgārjuna declares that there is not the least difference between the Absolute and the universe:[1] "The Universe viewed as a whole is the Absolute, viewed as a process it is the phenomenal—Having regard to causes and conditions (constituting all phenomena; we call this world)—phenomenal world. This same world, when causes and conditions are disregarded, i.e. the world as whole, *sub specie aeternitatis*) is called the Absolute."[2]

2. Some absolutists have fallen into the illusion that there is a double process—the initial transformation of the Absolute into phenomena and its later reconversion to its pristine state through knowledge. The Vijñānavādins invariably speak of consciousness as undergoing the process of defilement (saṁkleśa) and purification (vyavadāna). In the pre-Śaṅkara Vedānta too we find a similar notion of retransformation of the world into Brahman (prapañca-pravilaya) implying that there had been an original degradation of Brahman.[3]

All this is wrong according to the Mādhyamika. There has been no initial fall, and there is no need for re-transformation. Nirvāṇa, says Nāgārjuna, is non-ceasing, unachieved.[4] There is only the dissolution of false views (kalpanākṣaya), but no becoming in the real. The Absolute has always been of one uniform nature (tathatā, sarvakālaṁ tathābhāvāt). In the last resort, the consciousness of achievement too is subjective.

The function of the Mādhyamika dialectic is not to bring about a change in things, but in our mentality. Therefore it is declared in the texts that through wisdom the real things are not made unreal; things themselves are unreal.[5] Śūnyatā is not an arbitrary prescription to

[1] na saṁsārasya nirvāṇāt kiṁcid asti viśeṣaṇam;
na nirvāṇasya saṁsārāt kiṁcid asti vśeṣaṇam. MK. XXV, 19.
Cf. also: tathāgato yatsvabhāvas tatsvabhāvam idaṁ jagat. MK. XXII, 16.

[2] ya ājavam-javībhāva upādāya pratītya vā;
so'pratītyānupādāya nirvāṇam upadiśyate. MK. XXV, 9.
(Stcherbatsky's Translation. *Nirvāṇa* p. 48)

[3] Cf. The prapañca-pravilaya-vāda of Bhartṛprapañca, Śaṅkara's *Bhāṣya* on *Br. Sūt.* III, ii, 21.

[4] aprahīṇam asamprāptam anucchinnam aśāśvatam;
aniruddham anutpannam etan nirvāṇam ucyate. MK. XXV, 3.

[5] yan na śūnyatayā dharmān śūnyān karoti, api tu dharmā eva śūnyāḥ, etc. *Kāśyapaparivarta* p. 94 (63). also quoted in MKV. p. 248.

view things as unreal; it is the revelation of their intrinsic nature.[1] And this frees the human mind of the cobwebs of false views and wrong perspectives.

3. Very often the Absolute of the Mādhyamika is taken by the misinformed as a non-entity, a mere nothing. The system is dubbed as rank nihilism. Ignorance in this matter is born of prejudice. The terms Śūnya and Śūnyatā which are used by the Mādhyamika in referring to his Absolute seem to have provided the cue for such criticism. There is, however, hardly any justification for characterising the Mādhyamika as a nihilist. No absolutism would, in that case, escape this charge,[2] for everyone of them has to negate all predicates of the absolute. There is no reason to single out the Mādhyamika as specially nihilistic. If anything, his is a very consistent form of absolutism.

Not only affirmative predicates (bhāva, sat) but also negative predicates (abhāva, asat) are denied of the real. The Mādhyamika does not specially favour the negative view. We are on the contrary expressly warned against taking Śūnyatā as abhāva[3] (non-existence).

The negative method implied in the rejection of all views by the Mādhyamika dialectic may also have led some critics to take the system as barren and nihilistic in outlook. The Mādhyamika rejects every view as falsification of the real. The rejection is, however, a *means*, the only means open to absolutism, to free the real of the accidental accretions with which the finite mind invests it through ignorance; it is not an end. It is a confusion to regard the "no views of the real" attitude of the Mādhyamika as a "no reality" view.[4]

Negation itself is significant because there is an underlying reality the subjacent ground. If there were no transcendent ground, how

[1] nāśūnyaṁ śūnyavad dṛṣṭaṁ nirvāṇam me bhaviṣyati;
mithyādṛṣṭer na nirvāṇaṁ varṇayanti tathāgatāḥ. CŚ. VIII, 7.

[2] Śaṅkara too complains that his Brahman is misunderstood as non-existent, as nothing (śūnyam), by men of weak intellect, simply because it is devoid of empirical determinations: digdeśaguṇa-gati-phala-bheda-śūnyaṁ hi paramārthasad advayam brahma mandabuddhīnām *asad iva pratibhāti*.
Śaṅkara's Commentary on the *Ch. Up.* VIII, I. (p. 437, Ānandāsrama Edn.)

[3] atra brūmaḥ: śūnyatāyāṁ na tvaṁ vetsi prayojanam;
śūnyatāṁ śūnyatārthaṁ ca tata evaṁ vihanyase. MK. XXIV, 7;
See also *Kārikā*, 13.
bhavāṁs tu nāstitvaṁ śūnyatārthaṁ parikalpayan, prapañca-jālam eva saṁvardhayamāno na śūnyatāyāṁ prayojanaṁ vetti, evaṁ pratītya-samutpāda-śabdasya yo'rthaḥ śūnyatā-śabdasyārthaḥ. abhāvaśabdārthaṁ ca śūnyatārtham ity adhyāropya bhavān asmān upālabhate. MKV. pp. 491; 499.

[4] The confusion lies in taking no determination as negative determination.

could any view be condemned as false. A view is false, because it *falsifies the real,* makes the thing appear other than what it is in itself. Falsity implies the real *that* is falsified. Phenomena are characterised as saṁvṛti, because they cover the real nature of things (sarvapadārtha-tattvācchādanāt saṁvṛtiḥ).

Nāgārjuna is emphatic in stating that without the acceptance of the paramārṭha (the ultimate reality) there can be no deliverance (Nirvāṇa) from Saṁsāra.[1] That the unconditioned (paramārtha satya) cannot be determined as this or that, but is the indeterminate *par excellence,* is not to be construed as denial of the ultimately real. That would be a deplorable misunderstanding of Śūnyatā.[2]

If the Paramārtha were not beyond concept and speech, it would cease to be that and would be identical with the empirical. As the ultimate Norm which serves as the absolute standard of evaluation, it is beyond the possibility of any change or limitation.[3]

The Mādhyamika is not a nihilist; only, he resists all attempts to determine what is essentially Indeterminate. The Absolute cannot even be identified with Being or Consciousness, as this would be to compromise its nature as the unconditioned ground of phenomena. The Tattva, however, is accepted by the Mādhyamika as the Reality of all things (dharmāṇām dharmatā), their essential nature (prakṛtir dharmāṇām). It is uniform and universal, neither decreasing, nor increasing, neither originating nor decaying. The Absolute alone is in itself (akṛtrima svabhāva). The Absolute is that intrinsic form in which things would appear to the clear vision of an Ārya (realised saint) free from ignorance.[4]

4. It might be urged that a thing which lacks all determinations is as good as nothing; it is an abstraction empty of all content and lacks

[1] paramārtham anāgamya nirvāṇam nādhigamyate. MK. XXIV, 10.
This contention of Nāgārjuna is clearly based on the well-known *Udāna* text—asti bhikṣavas tad ajātam abhūtam asaṁskṛtam etc. (*Udāna,* p. 80, VIII, 3).

[2] vināśayati durdṛṣṭā śūnyatā mandamedhasam; sarpo yathā durgṛhīto vidyā vā duṣprasādhitā. MK. XXIV, II.

[3] *Arya Satya-dvayavatara,* quoted in BCAP. p. 366; MKV. pp. 374–5.

[4] Candrakīrti puts the matter very explicitly thus:
yadi khalu tad adhyāropād bhavadbhir astīty ucyate kīdṛśam tat? yā sā *dharmāṇāṁ dharmatā* nāma saiva tatsvarūpam. atha keyaṁ dharmāṇāṁ dharmatā? dharmāṇāṁ svabhāvaḥ, prakṛtiḥ. kā ceyaṁ prakṛtiḥ? yeyaṁ śūnyatā. keyaṁ śūnyatā? naiḥsvābhāvyam. kim idaṁ naiḥ-svābhāvyam? *tathatā,* keyaṁ tathatā? *tathābhāvo'vikāritvaṁ sadaiva sthāyitā,* sarvadānutpāda eva paranirapekṣatvād akṛtrimatvāt svabhāva ity ucyate. MKV. pp. 264–5.

reality; the concrete alone is real The absolute, on this contention, contains within itself all determinations. On this account it cannot be foreign to thought; it may even be identical with it.

The possible Hegelian criticism of the Mādhyamika absolute is from a specific standpoint; it assumes a particular kind of metaphysics. If the fundamental assumption that the Real is Reason is conceded, the criticism becomes pertinent. But nothing could justify the initial assumption—"What is not accessible to thought is unreal." This is virtually to deny intellectual intuition and to restrict all cognition to judgment. All this directly traverses the Mādhyamika position, and has to be rejected as dogmatic speculation. Inaccessibility of the Absolute to thought does not mean that it is a non-entity. The Mādhyamika holds that the Absolute is cognised in a non-dual intuition—Prajñā. *It is that Intuition itself.*

III DIFFERENCE BETWEEN THE MĀDHYAMIKA AND VEDĀNTA ABSOLUTISM[1]

In the Mādhyamika, Vijñānavāda and Vedānta systems, the Absolute is non-conceptual and non-empirical; it is realised in a transcendent non-dual experience, variously called by them prajñā-pāramitā, lokottara-jñāna and aparokṣānubhūti respectively. All emphasise the inapplicability of empirical determinations to the Absolute, and employ the language of negation. They are agreed on the *formal* aspect of the absolute. The Vedānta and Vijñānavāda, however, identify the absolute with something that is experienced in some form even empirically—the Vedānta with Pure Being (sanmātra) which is ātman (substance) and the Vijñānavāda with Consciousness (willing). Taking these as real, they try to remove the wrong ascriptions which make the absolute appear as a limited empirical thing. When, however, the ātman or vijñāna is absolute, it is a misuse of words to continue to call it by such terms; for there is no *other* from which it could be distinguished. They are also reduced to the Mādhyamika position of the Absolute as the utterly inexpressible. Words can only be used metaphorically to characterise or rather to indicate it.

There is, however, this difference that the Vedānta and Vijñānavāda, owing to their identification of the real with Ātman or Vijñāna, are

[1] For a fuller discussion of the difference between these Absolutisms reference may be made to Chap. XIII.

seemingly more able to provide a bridge between the world of appearance and the Absolute. The transition seems easier. The Mādhyamika by his insistence on the sheer transcendence of the absolute and his refusal to identify it with anything met with in experience appears to do violence to our accustomed ways of approach. He is too abrupt and harsh. But in principle, however, there is no difference in the *form* of the Absolutes in all these systems. Śūnyatā represents the form of all absolutism.

The Vedānta and Vijñānavāda characterisation of the Mādhyamika as Śūnyavāda is worthy of consideration, as it brings out a difference. Both Vedānta and Vijñānavada analyse illusion and show that the illusory appears on a real ground (adhiṣṭhāna) but for which illusion itself would not be possible. The world-illusion too is thus a superimposition on Brahman or Vijñāna.[1] It is not true to say, as is done by Vedānta and Vijñānavāda, that the Mādhyamika conceives illusion to occur without any underlying ground (niradhiṣṭhānabhrama). Tattva as Dharmatā or Bhūtakoṭi is accepted by the Mādhyamika as the underlying ground of phenomena. But it is not shown by him to be immanent in experience, how Dharmatā activates and illumines empirical things. Not that the Mādhyamika takes the Absolute and the world of phenomena as two different sets of entities; but the Absolute is nowhere explicitly shown to be *in* things constituting their very soul. The relation between the two is not made abundantly clear. This may be said to constitute a drawback in the Mādhyamika conception of the Absolute.

The case is, however, different with the Vedānta and Vijñānavāda. Brahman is no doubt devoid of determinations; it cannot be made an object of thought as a particular thing is. But it is self-evident (svayaṁprakāśa) and because of this anything becomes evident; it implicitly, invariably and unconditionally illumines things. In a slightly different manner Vijñānavāda shows that the object is dependent on consciousness, and not vice versa. Vijñāna is self-conscious (svasaṁvedya) and is creative of the object. Factually, the Mādhyamika Absolute too is immanent, but epistemologically it is not shown to be such.

In the Vedānta and Vijñānavāda, it is possible to speak of the intuition *of* the absolute, Brahman or Vijñāna. But this can only be in a metaphoric, and not literal, sense. For in the highest experience,

[1] ātmadharmopacāro hi vividho yaḥ pravartate;
vijñānapariṇāme' sau. *Triṁśikā*. I

no conceivable difference can be made between Brahman or Vijñāna and the person knowing it. They become intrinsically one. In the Mādhyamika it is truer to speak of the Intuition (Prajñā) itself as the Absolute.

IV AVIDYĀ

The Absolute in itself is indeterminate (śūnya); no category of thought applies to it. It is avidyā (Ignorance) that invests it with all the colourful forms that we come across in ordinary experience. It is the cause of appearance. If the absolute is the realm of ultimate truth (paramārtha satya), avidyā belongs to appearance (saṁvṛti), is samvṛti itself.

Avidyā hides the real from us, and in its place puts forth the unreal appearance.[1] The *Śālistamba Sūtra* defines it as the non-apprehension of the Real (tattve apratipattiḥ) and its misapprehension as something else[2] (mithyā pratipattiḥ). There are thus two functions of avidyā: one is obscurative (āvaraṇa), covering the real nature of things; the other is constructive, as it throws up a false appearance (asatkhyāpana). These two correspond to the Vedānta notion of avidyā having two powers, āvṛti (veiling) and vikṣepa (creative). The two functions are inter-related: without the emergence of an unreal appearance there could be no obscuration of the real; the false has to take the place of the real; and without non-apprehension of the true nature of the real there could be no false notion about it. If we were in possession of true knowledge, the illusion could not even get started.

The precise nature of avidyā in the Mādhyamika system consists in the inveterate tendency to indulge in conceptual construction (saṅkalpa). The Real is Indeterminate (śūnya); the viewing of it through thought-forms is avidyā. For instance, to consider the real as substance (ātman), or as mode (dharma), as One or Many, as Unchanging (śāśvata) or Ceasing (uccheda), Existence (astitva) and Non-existence (nāstitva) etc., are some of the forms of falsification (viparyāsa).

[1] abhūtaṁ khyāpayaty arthaṁ bhutam āvṛtya vartate;
avidyā jāyamāneva kāmalatāṅkavṛttivat.—BCAP. p. 352.

[2] tattve'pratipattir mithyā pratipattir ajñānam avidyeti. From the *Śālistamba Sūtra* as quoted in BCAP. 352, ŚS. p. 222, MKV. p. 564, MA. VI, 28.
mohaḥ svabhāvāvaraṇddhi saṁvṛtiḥ, satyaṁ tayā khyāti yad eva kṛtrimam. avidyā hi padārthāsatsvarūpāropikā, svabhāvadarśanāvaraṇātmikā samvṛtiḥ. MA. p. 23.

Avidyā for the Vaibhāṣika or the Sautrāntika would consist in the imposition of unity, permanence and universality on what is really plural, transitory and uniquely particular. In this system the Real is identified with the changing modes—the dharmas. Avidyā is satkāyadṛṣṭi, the endowing of discrete momentary entities (anātma dharmas) with substantiality, identity and permanence, e.g. in the apprehension of the flame or the stream as one. In the Vedānta, avidyā is just the reverse. The Real is unchanging Pure Being (ātman); it is identical at all times, and there is no plurality or difference. Avidyā consists in the differentiation into 'I' and 'You' of what is essentially one indivisible whole devoid of every kind of difference. In the Vijñānavāda, the real is Consciousness without the trace of an other confronting it. Pure Consciousness (Vijñāptimātratā) is devoid of the duality of the knower and the known (grāhadvaya). Avidyā is the appearance of the object as an entity existing independently of consciousness with which it is really identical.

For the Mādhyamika not only difference but identity too is avidyā; the real is neither one nor many, neither permanent nor momentary; neither subject (vijñāna) nor object. These are relative to each other and are equally unreal. The Real is purely indeterminate, and all attempts to identify it with Being, Becoming, Consciousness etc., are vikalpa, subjective devices. Nāgārjuna says: "If the apprehension of the impermanent as permanent is illusion, why is the apprehension of the indeterminate as impermanent not illusion as well."[1]

In the Ābhidharmika, Vedānta and Vijñānavāda systems particular concepts or ways of viewing the real are avidyā; they of course differ, as shown above, in *what* they take to be avidyā. For the Mādhyamika, avidyā is much wider and more general in scope: conceptualisation as such (not merely particular concepts), any view without exception, is avidyā. Reason as the faculty of conceptualisation is avidyā. It is said: "Reason (buddhi) is not grounded in the real; it is a subjective play of the imagination (vikalpasvabhāva); and all vikalpa is avidyā —as it apprehends the non-entity (avastugrāhitvāt). Thus it is said: Vikalpa is, by its nature, of the stuff of avidyā."[2]

[1] anitye nityam ity evaṁ yadi grāho viparyayaḥ;
anityam ity api grāhaḥ śūnye kiṁ na viparyayaḥ. MK. XXII, 14.

[2] buddhiḥ samvṛtir ucyata iti. sarvā hi bhuddhir ālambana-nirālambanatayā vikalpasvabhāvā. *vikalpaś ca sarva evāvidyāsvabhāvaḥ*, avastugrāhitvāt. yad āha: "vikalpaḥ svayam evāyam avidyārūpatāṁ gataḥ" iti. BCAP. p. 366.

For the Ābhidharmika system satkāyadṛṣṭi (Substance-view) is Avidyā; for the Vijñānavāda, bāhya or viṣaya-dṛṣṭi (objectification) is avidyā; for the Vedānta bhedadṛṣṭi (differentiation) is avidyā. For the Mādhyamika all viewing, dṛṣṭi as such, is avidyā; dṛṣṭi is kalpanā, and kalpanā is the ascription of features which are non-existent in reality.[1]

In keeping with the equation of avidyā with Buddhi (reason) we are told that avidyā has its origin in pointless attention—distraction (ayoniśo manaskāra).[2] The distracted mind does not confine itself to a point, to the thing in hand; but flits, like a butterfly, from one thing to another. This ensues in comparing, differentiating, identifying and synthesising things; i.e. in viewing things in relation to each other. A related view of things comprehends only appearance. Prajñā, on the other hand, is the intensity of concentration of mind (nirvikalpa-jñāna); the thing is known then as it really is (prajñā yathābhūtam arthaṁ prajānāti).

Avidyā is beginningless; for there is no assignable limit, prior or posterior, to the existence of the phenomenal world (saṁsāra is anavarāgraḥ), and saṁsāra cannot be without avidyā and its satellite kleśas. Though beginningless, it has an end. It cannot be argued that what is without beginning is without end as well. The seed is produced from the tree and this from the seed, it is thus without any assignable prior limit. But it can be destroyed by fire or other causes.[3] Likewise, avidyā and other kleśas (passions) which are at the root of phenomena can be reduced to nullity on the attainment of insight (prajñā).[4]

What is the nature of avidyā—is it an ens or a non-ens? Is it Real or unreal? It is contended by the Realists that that which makes the false appear cannot itself be unreal. The dream-objects may be unreal, but the dreaming act and the disturbing conditions of the mind which cause the dream-objects are real. If avidyā itself were

[1] kalpanā hy abhūtasvabhāvam artham āropayati. CŚV. p. 294.

[2] uktaṁ hi *Pratītyasamutpāda Sūtre* bhagavatā: avidyāpi, bhikṣavaḥ, sahetukā sapratyayā sanidānā. kaś cāvidyāyā hetuḥ. ayoniśo, bhikṣavo, manaskāro avidyāyā hetuh.

āvilo mohajo manaskāro avidyāyā hetur ity ato avidyā saṁkalpaprabhāva bhavati. MKV. p. 452.

[3] yathā bījasya dṛṣṭo'nto na cādis tasya vidyate;
tathā kāraṇa-vaikalyāj janmano'pi na sambhavaḥ. CŚ. VIII, 25.

[4] CŚV. pp. 29–30.

unreal or non-existent how could it cause the appearance? Not only is avidyā real, by this argument, but there is a real causation. Even in the absolutism of Vijñānavāda, consciousness (citta) is credited with the two inherently real functions of initial defilement and later purification. The implied argument is that bondage and freedom are real; spiritual life would not be possible without these being considered real. Bondage is caused by Ignorance (avidyā) and other kleśas; this causation is a real process. The unreal cannot exert any influence.[1] The difference between the Vaibhāṣika and the Vijñānavāda in this matter is that for the latter both the process of defilement and purification are the internal functions of the mind, while the former takes them to be caused by factors external to the mind. Both, however, agree in taking the processes to be real.

The Mādhyamika view is that avidyā is itself unreal;[2] it is Māyā. If it were real, its products too would be real, and there could be no question of negating or even changing the world-process. We cannot help facts. Nāgārjuna puts the matter dialectically thus: If the passions belonged to one as an integrally real part of one's nature, how could they be abandoned; the real cannot be rejected by any one.[3] If the passions did not belong to any one how could they be abandoned; for who could abandon the unreal, the non-existent?[4] It is concluded that kleśas, karma and their result are of the stuff of fairy castles, mirage and dreams. They are not real as facts; they have only an epistemic status.

As for the contention that there is real exertion of influence by avidyā whereas the unreal cannot cause anything, the reverse is perhaps true. The unreal can and does influence, and even a false

[1] atrāha: yadi viparyāsa-nirodhād avidyā niruddhyate' sti tarhy avidyā yasya evaṁ viparyāsanirodhān nirodho bhavati. na tarhy avidyamānāyā gagana-cūtalatāyāḥ prahāṇopāyānveṣaṇam asti. tasmād vidyata evāvidyā. MKV. p. 470.

[2] evam avidyamānās tenocyante avidyeti. tān bālapṛthagjanā aśrutavanto' bhiniviṣṭāḥ. tair asamvidyamānāḥ sarvadharmāḥ kalpitāḥ. te tān kalpayitvā dvayor antayor āsaktāḥ tān dharmān na jānanti na paśyanti etc. ASP. p. 15.

yathoktaṁ bhagavatā: avidyayā naiva kadāci vidyate avidyata pratyayasambhavaś ca; avidyamāneyam avidyā loke tasmān mayā uktā avidyā esā. from *Suvaraṇaprabhāsa* (VI, 17–8; p. 53) quoted in MKV. p. 462.

[3] yadi bhūtāḥ svabhāvena kleśāḥ keciddhi kasya cit;
kathaṁ nāma prahīyeran kaḥ svabhāvaṁ prahāsyati. MK. XXIII, 24.

[4] yady abhūtāḥ svabhāvena kleśāḥ keciddhi kasyacit;
kathaṁ nāma prahīyeran ko'sadbhāvaṁ prahāsyati. ibid. 25.

apparition can appear and work.[1] Causal or other relation obtains essentially between appearances only; it is a mark of the unreal.

In all these, the Mādhyamika view approaches very close to the Vedāntic notion of avidyā as a beginningless positive entity that is totally destroyed by knowledge.[2] Its non-definability (anirvacanīyatva) as either real or unreal (sat or asat) makes it out as having an epistemic status only. Like the Mādhyamika, the Vedānta too holds that the unreal can be efficient, and causation is not a criterion of the real, but of the unreal.

The Vedānta, however, elaborates its conception of avidyā by defining its locus (āśraya) and object (viṣaya). Avidyā belongs to Pure Being, Brahman, as it cannot belong to any inert being (jaḍe āvaraṇakṛtyābhāvāt); only a conscious being capable of knowledge can be ignorant. And that can be only undifferentiated universal pure Being (nirvibhāga citi); for particular beings (the Jīva) presuppose difference which is the function of avidyā.[3] The object of ignorance is Brahman; for that is the object of ignorance which when known removes it. That ignorance is one, not many, follows from its locus (aśraya) and object (viṣaya) being not only one but identical. All ignorance is fundamentally self-ignorance, and knowledge is self-knowledge.

The Mādhyamika with his anti-speculative tendency refuses to be drawn into such questions about who is ignorant, etc. Dialectical objections are urged against any determinate view regarding the person ignorant, the object of his ignorance etc.[4] This is in keeping with his no-doctrine attitude and avoidance of all theorising.

[1] asaty api yathā māyā dṛśyā draṣṭṛ tathā manaḥ. BCA. IX, 28.

Vinaye ca: yantrakārakāritā yantrayuvatiḥ sadbhūta-yuvatiśūnyā sadbhūtayuvatirūpeṇa pratibhāste; tasya ca citrakārasya kāmarāgāspadībhūtā. tathā mṛṣāsvabhāvā api bhāvā bālānāṁ saṁkleśavyavadāna-nibandhanaṁ bhavanti. MKV. p. 46.

The Ratnakūṭa Sūtra (*Kāśyapaparivarta*) 138–149; pp. 200–16. recounts at length how a group of 500 monks were taught the highest wisdom by two apparitional monks created by the Lord. ity evaṁ mṛṣā-svabhāvābhyāṁ tathāgatanirmitābhyāṁ bhikṣubhyām pañcānāṁ bhikṣuśatānāṁ vyavadānanibandhanaṁ kṛtam iti MKV. p. 50.

[2] *Citsukhī*, p. 57.

[3] *Saṁkṣepa Śārīraka*, I, 319; see also I, 21, 11, 212 etc.

[4] yena gṛhṇāti yo grāho grahītā yac ca gṛhyate;
upaśāntāni sarvāṇi tasmād grāho na vidyate.
na cāpi viparītasya sambhavanti viparyayāḥ;
na cāpyaviparītasya sambhavanti viparyayāḥ. MK. XXIII, 15.

IV TWO TRUTHS AND THE "DEGREES OF REALITY".

Absolutism is committed to the doctrine of two truths; for, it makes the distinction between the thing as it is, unrelatedly, absolutely, and how it appears in relation to the percipients who look at it through views and standpoints. The Real as the Noumenon has to be contrasted with phenomena which are but appearance. The distinction is implicit in all philosophy. No serious and sustained consideration of things can rest satisfied with what appears to the untutored consciousness; it seeks to penetrate to the innermost core of things.

It cannot be claimed that the doctrine of two truths was initiated by the Mādhyamika or even by Buddha. The Upaniṣads clearly anticipate this when they speak of Brahman as the real of the reals (satyasya satyam[1]), and even as the sole reality.[2] In the teachings of Buddha too the distinction between Nirvāṇa as the absolutely real and phenomena as conventionally real is made.[3] The earlier Ābhidharmika system had already differentiated between the ultimate reality of the separate elements which is the object of Prajñā and the Prajñapti-sat which is of conventional signification (saṁvṛti). It is, however, the Mādhyamika who systematically worked out the doctrine of two truths and consistently applied it to synthesise Buddhist texts and doctrines.

All Mādhyamika treatises[4] take the two truths—Paramārtha Satya and Saṁvṛti Satya—as vital to the system; some even begin their philosophical disquisitions with the distinction. According to Nāgārjuna, "Those that are unaware of the distinction between these two truths are incapable of grasping the deep significance of the

[1] satyasya satyam. prāṇā vai satyam; teṣām eṣa satyam. *Bṛ. Up.* II, iii, 6.

[2] idaṁ sarvaṁ yad ayam ātmā; na tad dvitīyam asti yat tad vibhaktaṁ paśyet. neha nānāsti kiṁcana. yatra nānyat paśyati etc.

[3] uktaṁ *Sūtre*: tan mṛṣā moṣadharma yad idaṁ saṁskṛtam. etaddhi khalu, bhikṣavaḥ, paramaṁ satyaṁ yad idam amoṣadharma nirvāṇaṁ sarvasaṁskārāś ca mṛṣā moṣadharmāṇa iti. quoted in MKV. pp. 41 and 237. Parallel passages in the Pāli Canons:
Majj. N. II, p. 245 (Sutta, 140). etaṁ hi bhikkhu paramaṁ ariyasaccam yad idam amosadhammaṁ nibbānam. See also *Majj. N.* II, 261; *Sam. N.* III, 142 etc.

[4] Some chief references where this doctrine is discussed: MK. XXIV; MA. VI, 23 ff. BCA. IX, i ff—BCAP. pp. 352 ff. *Madhyamakārtha Sangraha*h of Bhāvaviveka.

teaching of Buddha."[1] The doctrine is already well-developed in the *Aṣṭasāhasrikā* and other *Prajñāpāramitā* texts besides *Saddharma Puṇḍarīka*, *Samādhirāja* and similar Mahāyāna Sūtras.

Paramārtha Satya or Absolute Truth is the knowledge of the real as it is without any distortion (akṛtrimam vastu-rūpam).[2] Categories of thought and points of view distort the real. They unconsciously coerce the mind to view things in a cramped, biassed way; and are thus inherently incapable of giving us the Truth. The paramārtha is the utter absence of the function of Reason (buddhi) which is therefore equated with saṁvṛti. The Absolute truth is beyond the scope of discursive thought, language and empirical activity; and conversely, the object of these is saṁvṛti satya.[3] It is said: "The paramārtha is in fact the unutterable (anabhilāpya), the unthinkable, unteachable etc."[4]

Devoid of empirical determinations, it is the object of the innermost experience of the wise.[5] It is so intimate and integral that we cannot be self-conscious of it.

Saṁvṛti satya is Truth so called; truth as conventionally believed in common parlance. Candrakīrti gives three definitions of saṁvṛti. As the etymology shows, saṁvṛti is that which covers up entirely the real nature of things and makes them appear otherwise. In this sense it is identical with avidyā—the categorising function of the mind—Reason. Tattva is the unconditioned (nirvikalpa and niṣprapañca). It may also mean the mutual dependence of things—their relativity. In this sense it is equated with phenomena, and is

[1] ye' nayor na vijānanti vibhāgaṁ satyayor dvayoḥ;
te tattvaṁ na vijānanti gambhīraṁ buddha-śāsane. MK. XXIV, 9.

[2] parama uttamo' rthaḥ paramārthaḥ. akṛtrimaṁ vasturūpam, sarva dharmāṇāṁ niḥsvabhāvatā. BCAP. p. 354.

[3] yadi hi paramārthataḥ paramārthasatyaṁ kāyavāṅmanasāṁ viṣayatām upagacchet, na tat paramārthasatyam iti saṁkhyāṁ gacchet. saṁvṛti satyam eva tad bhavet. api tu, devaputra, paramārthasatyaṁ sarvavyavahārasamatikrāntaṁ nirviśeṣam asamutpannam aniruddham, abhidheyābhidhānajñeyajñāna-vigatam, etc. from *Satyadvayāvatāra* as quoted in BCAP p. 366; see also MKV. pp. 374–5.

[4] yaḥ punaḥ paramārthaḥ so'nabhilāpyaḥ, anājñeyaḥ aparijñeyaḥ, avijñeyaḥ, adeśitaḥ, aprakāśitaḥ etc. from *Pitāputra Samāgama* as quoted in ŚS. p. 256; BCAP. p. 367.

[5] tad etad āryāṇām eva svasamvidita-svabhāvatayā pratyātmavedyam, atas tad evātra pramāṇam. BCAP. p. 367. kutas tatra paramārthe vācāṁ pravṛttiḥ kuto vā jñānasya. sa hi paramārtho' parapratyayaḥ śāntaḥ pratyātma-vedya āryāṇāṁ sarvaprapañcātītaḥ. MKV. p. 493.

in direct contrast with the absolute which is by itself, unrelated. The third definition of saṁvṛti is that which is of conventional nature (saṁvṛti—saṁketa), depending as it does on what is usually accepted by the common folk (loka-vyavahāraḥ).[1] It is the truth that does not do any violence to what obtains in our every-day world, being in close conformity with linguistic conventions and ideas. It is the object of the ignorant and the immature. Paramārtha satya is unsignified by language and belongs to the realm of the unutterable, and is experienced by the wise in a very intimate way.[2]

In calling it 'lokasaṁvṛti,' it is implied that there is some appearance which is 'aloka'—non-empirical, i.e. false for the empirical consciousness even. Cases of optical and other illusions, distorted perceptions caused by diseased and defective sense-organs, experiences in abnormal states of the mind and dream-objects are examples of the 'aloka or mithyā saṁvṛti'.[3] This corresponds to the prātibhāsika of the Vedānta. The spatio-temporal objects of the every-day world enjoy a relatively higher status as 'real objects' in contrast to these shadowy appearances. This alone provides the *raison d'être* for the vyāvahārika being considered as real (tathya samvṛti). But it is the experienced illusoriness of the prātibhāsika (mithyāsamvṛti of the Mādhyamika) that provides the cue for suspecting that the empirical objects may themselves be mere appearance from the ultimate point of view. The Mādhyamika, however, does not recognise the prātibhāsika as a different class of truth. He very conveniently subsumes it under saṁvṛti satya. The Mādhyamika advocates Two Truths unlike the Vedānta and Vijñānavāda doctrine of Three Truths.

Paramārtha satya, as the unutterable ultimate experience wherein

1 samantād āvaraṇaṁ hi saṁvṛtiḥ. ajñānaṁ hi samantāt sarvapadārtha-tattvācchādanāt samvṛtir ity ucyate; (ii) paraspara-sambhavanaṁ vā saṁvṛtir anyonyāśrayeṇety arthaḥ; (iii) atha vā saṁvrtiḥ saṁketo loka-vyavahāra ity arthaḥ. sa cābhidhānābhidheyādilakṣaṇaḥ—MKV. p. 492.

It is in the first sense of saṁvṛti as Avidyā that Śāntideva identifies saṁvṛti with buddhi. BCA. IX, 2; this is the same as dṛṣṭi. See also MA. VII, 28. mohaḥ svabhāvāvaraṇād dhi saṁvṛtiḥ, satyaṁ tayākhyāti yad eva kṛtrimam. avidyā hi padārtha-satsvarūpāropikā svabhāvadarśanāvaraṇātmikā samvṛtiḥ. MA. p. 23.

2 abhūtārthadarśināṁ pṛthagjanānāṁ mṛṣā-darśana-viṣayatayā samādarśitātmasattākam. BCAP. p. 360.

samyagdṛsāṁ yo viṣayaḥ sa tattvam;
mṛṣā-dṛśāṁ saṁvṛti-satyam uktam. MA. VI, 23.

3 MA. VI, 24, 25 and 26. vinopaghātena yadindriyāṇāṁ ṣaṇṇām api grāhyam avaiti lokaḥ; satyaṁ tal lokata eva śeṣaṁ vikalpitaṁ lokata eva mithyā.

the real and the intellect cognising it are non-different (advaya), does not admit of differentiation and degrees. Knowledge could be different on two grounds principally: because of the difference of objects or of the cognising agent. As both these differences are absent in the paramārtha, it is of one uniform, undifferentiated nature. It is therefore variously called 'Tathatā, Bhūta-Koṭi, Dharmatā, Dharmadhātu and Śūnyatā.[1]

Saṁvṛti, on the other hand, admits of differences and degrees. There may be a hierarchy among them. The dream-objects are experienced as illusory even by the common man. To the philosopher or the Yogi the objects of the everyday world that appear permanent and alluring may look transitory and hollow; his vision is truer than the common man's.[2] It is, however, within saṁvṛti. Even among the Yogins there may be the gradation of the lower and the higher. All are within the play of reason.[3]

The distinction between two truths enables the Mādhyamika to synthesise the different doctrines of the schools that rely on the utterances of Buddha often at variance with each other. The reality of the Elements (Skandhas, Dhātu and Āyatana) is empirical, not ultimate. The Lord has formulated them as a concession to commonsense. The Ābhidharmikas have in all simplicity conceived as absolute what is conditional and relative.[4] The Lord has taught this doctrine of elements as a step facilitating the understanding of the final teaching. In reality, things are neither plural nor are they momentary as it is made out in the Abhidharma system.[5]

The Real being truly indeterminate, it is, however, possible to utilise any means appropriate to the person in particular circumstances for leading him to the ultimate truth. There is no limit to the number and nature of the doctrinal devices that may be employed to

[1] śūnyatā, tathatā, bhūtakoṭi, dharmadhātur ityādi paryāyāḥ. *Mahā Vyut.* p. 30 (Bib. Buddhica) BCAP. p. 354.

[2] BCA. IX, 8.

[3] tatra loko dvidhā dṛṣṭo yogī prākṛtakas tathā;
tatra prākṛtako loko yogilokena bādhyate.
bādhyante dhīviśeṣeṇa yogino'pyuttarottaraiḥ. BCA. IX, 3, 4.

[4] bāla-janaprasiddhyaiva ca bhagavatā tad evaiṣāṁ sāṁvṛtaṁ rūpam *Abhidharme* vyavasthāpitam. MKV. p. 261. evam avidyātimiropaghātād atattvadṛśo bālā yad etat skandha-dhātvāyatanādi-svarūpam upalabhante tad eṣāṁ sāṁvṛtam rūpam. BCAP. p. 364.

[5] lokāvatāraṇārthaṁ ca bhāvā nāthena deśitāḥ;
tattvataḥ kṣaṇikā naite. . . . BCA. IX, 7.

realise this end. The only consideration is that the device must be suited to the spiritual temperament and needs of beings, like the medicine to the malady. This is the celebrated doctrine of Upāya-kauśalya (excellence in the choice of methods). Buddha is compared to a skilled physician who adjusts his remedies conforming to the nature and intensity of the disease of the patients; he does not, like a quack, prescribe one remedy for all. To one suffering from dogmatic belief in substance (ātman) he may prescribe the nairātmya doctrine as a corrective, and for the sceptic and the materialist he may prescribe as an antidote, the reality of the self and the continuance of Karma and its result. To the spiritually advanced man, he teaches that there is neither self nor the states. According to the nature of the malady to be cured the appropriate teaching could be used.[1]

Nāgārjuna says: Buddhas have taught, with a purpose, the reality of the 'I' and 'the mine' as indeed have they the doctrine of the groups, the elements and bases.[2] As the occasion required, the Buddha has affirmed the self or denied, both affirmed and denied, or done neither.[3]

Not only common notions of the layman, but philosophical view-points as embodied in systems of thought can be accorded some status and significance on the Mādhyamika notion of the empirical reality of the saṁvṛti and its transcendent (ultimate) ideality. But strangely enough, we often find among the Mādhyamika authors a spirit of intolerance towards the Brāhmanical systems and their tenets. Candrakīrti roundly condemns their systems as false from the empirical standpoint even; they are mithyā-saṁvṛti (empirically false) for him.[4]

The reason for this is that no Buddhist could recognise the ātman (substance) in any form. They could not conceive even empirical

[1] sad asad sadasac ceti nobhayaṁ ceti kathyate;
nanu vyādhivaśāt sarvam auṣadhaṁ nāma jāyate. CŚ. VIII, 20 quoted in MKV. p. 372.

[2] mamety aham iti proktaṁ yathā kāryavaśāj jinaiḥ;
tathā kārya-vaśāt proktāḥ skandhāyatana-dhātavaḥ. From the *Yuktiṣaṣṭikā* quoted in BCAP. p. 376.

[3] MK. XVIII, 6.

[4] saṁvṛtyāpi tadīyavyavasthānabhyupagamāt. satyadvaya-viparīta-darśana-paribhraṣṭā eva hi tīrthikāḥ—MKV. p. 27 see also p. 344. ajñānamid-dhotkṣubhitair yathāsvaṁ prakalpitaṁ *yat kila tīrthikaiś* ca. māyā marīcyādiṣu kalpitaṁ yat tat lokataś cāpi na vidyate hi. MA. VI, 26. satyadvayavirahāc ca na phalam āpnuvanti. tasmād etair yad guṇatrayādikaṁ kalpitaṁ, tal lokasaṁvṛtyaiva nāsti. MA. p. 23.

reality on the ātma-pattern, committed as they were to momentariness and a sequential view of things. The Vedānta too could not accommodate the Buddhist view even for the empirical realm, though it did accept the Sāṁkhya and even the Nyāya as approximate truths for the vyāvahārika.

The view of Bhāvaviveka, the great exponent of the Svatantra Mādhyamika school, is a notable exception to this. Though we have a very summary account of his position, it is still interesting. His *Madhyamārtha Saṅgrahaḥ*[1] begins with the two truths (paramārtha and samvṛti) and proceeds to subdivide them. Paramārtha is niṣprapañca (Non-Phenomenal) and admits of two kinds:[2] *Paryāya Paramārtha*—the absolute that is still capable of expression in words—and the other, *aparyāya Paramārtha,* that is beyond all expression (paryāyarahitaḥ) and totally free from any kind of empirical determination (sarvaprapanca-varjitaḥ).[3] The aparyāya paramārtha corresponds to the paramārtha of Nāgārjuna and Candrakīrti. The paryāya paramārtha is of two kinds: jātiparyāya vastu parmārtha (the Absolute that can be understood as a kind of universal positive being) and the other, janmarodha paramārtha (the absolute which is the complete extinction of all manifestations).[4] "As no light is thrown by the author on the former, he seems to have included in it the views of the Tīrthikas such as Sāṅkhyas etc."[5] The Hīnayāna conception of Nirvāṇa as the extinction of all forces, all saṁskāras and entities, seems to be meant by the janmarodha paramārtha.

Saṁvṛti is divided by Bhāvaviveka into *tathyā saṁvṛti,* which is the empirically efficient and the other *mithyā saṁvṛti,* that is not so efficient. The latter is of two kinds—one that involves ideation for its apprehension, like the illusion of rope-snake, and the other that is more or less mechanical like optical illusions, the double moon

[1] Restored from the Tibetan Version with an English translation by Pandit N. Ayyaswāmi Sāstri and published in the *Journal of Oriental Research,* Madras, Vol. V, Part I, (March, 1931). I am indebted to this valuable restoration and the introductory note for the information given here.

[2] paramārtho niṣprapancaḥ kartavyo dvividhaḥ sa ca; paryāya-paramārthaś cāparyaya-paramārthakaḥ. *Madhyamārtha Sam.* 2.

[3] sarvaprapañca-varjitaḥ; sa tu paryāyarahito vijñeyaḥ paramārthataḥ; satkoṭiś cāpy asatkoṭir dvaya-sarva-vivarjitaḥ etādṛk paramārtho hi. *Mad. Sam.* 5, 6.

[4] sa ca syāt prathamo dvedhā, jātiparyāya vastu ca;
paramārtho janmarodhaḥ, parārtho ruddhajanmakaḥ. ibid. 3, 4.

[5] *Journal of Oriental Research,* Vol. V, Part I, pp. 42–43.

and the bent-stick[1] in water. The noteworthy feature in Bhāvaviveka's account is his liberal accommodation of the Absolutes of the Brāhmanical and Hīnayāna systems as some kind of Paramārtha (paryāya paramārtha). Candrakīrti would not have accepted this.

It is, however, refreshing to find both Nāgārjuna and Candrakīrti rejecting, in some important respects, the modal view of the Ābhidharmika system as unsatisfactory for explaining phenomena. Nāgārjuna explicitly says that there can be no act without an agent or vice versa;[2] he calls them ignorant of the true meaning of the Buddha's teaching who take the reality of the ātman only or of the states as separate from it;[3] if there is no ātman apart from the states, there are no states too apart from the ātman.[4] If the cause and effect are not identical (satkāryavāda), they are not different from each other too. In fact the entire Mādhyamika position is developed by a trenchant criticism of the one-sided modal view of the Ābhidharmika system, by being alive to the other side of the picture equally exhibited in the empirical sphere.

In the same strain Candrakīrti complains that the Ābhidharmikas have not given an adequate picture of the empirical even. "If it is sought to depict the empirically real (vyavahāra-satyam) then besides momentary states, the activity and the agent too must be admitted."[5] "In taking that there could be an activity without an agent relying on the scriptural text: 'all entities are without self (substance)' the Ābhidharmikas have failed to understand the true import of the scriptures."[6]

Candrakīrti shows, in a sustained criticism of the Vaibhāṣika-Sautrāntika view of the mere attributes or states without any underlying substrate in which they inhere, that this does violence

[1] vastvarthakaraṇakṣamam; tathya-saṁvṛti-rūpaṁ hi dṛśyam arthakriyākṣamaṁ; mithyābhūtā saṁvṛtiḥ syād vijñeyā dvividhā ca sā; sakalpākalpayugmena sakalpāhigraho guṇe; śaśidvayagrāho'kalpā. . . . *Mad. Samg.* 7, 8 and 9.

[2] MK. VIII, 12. cf. also MKV. 64–5. yadi jñānaṁ karaṇaṁ viṣayasya paricchede kaḥ kartā. na ca kartāram antareṇāsti karaṇādīnāṁ sambhavaḥ.

[3] MK. X, 16.

[4] na copādānam evātmā vyeti tatsamudeti ca;
kathaṁ hi nāmopādānam upādātā bhaviṣyati. MK. XXVII, 6.

[5] MKV. p. 116. tasmād yadi vyavahārasatyaṁ, dharmamātravat kriyāpyupagamyatam. atha tattvacintā, tada kriyāvad dharmamātram api nāstīti bhavatābhyupagamyatām.

[6] MKV. p. 65.

to common modes of thought and language; it fails as a correct picture of the empirical; nor can it be taken as true of the unconditioned real.[1] He further shows that the Sautrāntika account of perception as cognising the unique particular (svalakṣaṇa) without any of the common and relational features is untenable logically, and must also be rejected as not being applicable to the generally accepted perception of the table, pitcher etc. If it were contended that the pitcher etc. is 'perceived' only in a metaphorical sense, there being, on the Sautrāntika view, no pitcher over and above the qualities, it is equally true to say that there is no quality apart from the substance, and hence the cognition of the quality itself has to be taken in a metaphorical sense."[2] "From the standpoint of the paramārtha neither the pitcher nor its quality 'blue etc.' is cognised; from the empirical standpoint, however, the perception of substances, e.g. pitcher etc. has to be accepted."[3] Moreover, all our empirical activity is bound up with the relational mode of perception and not with the non-relational mode of knowledge.[4] To cover all cases of knowledge and objects, the Mādhyamika accepts four sources of knowledge—perception (pratyakṣa), inference (anumāna), comparison (upamāna) and testimony (śabda) like the Nyāya as against the Buddhistic view of two pramāṇas—Perception and Inference based on two different kinds of objects—the particular and the universal (svalakṣaṇa and sāmānya-lakṣaṇa).[5]

In all these, the Mādhyamika appears as a champion of the empirical reality of substance, universal and relational mode of perception etc. as against the Ābhidharmika who had rejected the reality of these even empirically. This is the true Mādhyamika

[1] tasmād yadi laukiko vyavahāras tadāvaśyaṁ lakṣaṇaval lakṣyeṇāpi bhavitavyam . . . atha paramārthas tadā lakṣyābhāvāl lakṣaṇam api nāstīti. MKV. p. 69.

[2] lokavyavahārāṅgabhūto ghaṭo yadi nīlādi vyatirikto nāstīti kṛtvā tasy aupacārikaṁ pratyakṣatvaṁ parikalpyate; nanv evaṁ sati pṛthivyādi-vyatirekeṇa nīlādikam api nāstīti nīlāder apy aupacārikaṁ pratyakṣatvaṁ kalpyatām. MKV. p. 70.

[3] tattva-vidapekṣayā hi pratyakṣatvaṁ ghaṭādīnāṁ nīlādīnāṁ ca neṣyate. lokasaṁvṛtyā tvābhyupagantavyam eva pratyakṣatvaṁ ghaṭādīnām. MKV. p. 71.

[4] MKV. p. 74.

[5] parokṣa-viṣayaṁ tu jñānaṁ sādhyāvyabhicāri lingotpannam anumānam. sākṣād atīndriyārthavidām āptānām yad vacanaṁ sa āgamaḥ. sādṛśyād ananubhūtārthādhigama upamānaṁ gauriva gavaya iti yathā. tad evam *pramāṇa-catuṣṭayāl lokasyārthādhigamo* vyavasthāpyate. MKV. p. 75.

standpoint—acceptance of the empirical reality (saṁvṛti satya) of substance and modes etc., and rejection of them as not ultimate (paramārtha satya). Kant's position is similar: he accepts the empirical reality of the categories (space, time, substance etc.) though they are transcendentally ideal (unreal).

As in the case of the Absolute, the doctrine of two truths also is liable to misinterpretation. There are not two different spheres or sets of objects to which these apply. There would then be no point in calling one saṁvṛti and the other paramārtha; the two may be different, but one would not be less real than the other. It was pointed out that the relation between the Absolute and phenomena is not that of otherness; the absolute, looked at through the categories of Reason (thought-forms), is the world of phenomena; and phenomena, devoid of these falsifying thought-forms, are the Absolute. Absolute is the sole Reality. Likewise, all things put on two forms owing to the manner of our apprehension: one is the tattva which is the object of right knowledge and the other is the object of false knowledge.[1] One and the same thing is the object of either true or false knowledge. We have also to accept the deliverance of right knowledge as the truth. In fact, there is only one Truth—the paramārtha satya, as there is only one real—the Absolute.[2] The other is *truth so-called* in common parlance; it is totally false from the absolute standpoint. Saṁvṛti satya is what is conventionally believed to be true by the ignorant; it is true for empirical purposes. The absolute truth is not false from the saṁvṛti point of view; but in our ordinary activities we are not interested in the Absolute. The Mādhyamika or any other Absolutist such as the Vedāntin or Vijñānavādin does not establish the reality of the empirical objects, but they merely take cognisance of the commonly believed notion.

This effectively disposes of the objection raised by Kumārila in his *Ślokavārttika*. He asks: "saṁvṛti cannot be a kind of truth, for there is no generic feature between that and paramārtha by virtue of which it could be classified as a truth. If it is truth (satya), it could

[1] samyaṅ-mṛṣā-darśanalabdhabhāvaṁ rūpadvayaṁ bibhrati sarvabhāvāḥ; samyagdṛśāṁ yo viṣayaḥ sa tattvaṁ, mṛṣādṛśāṁ saṁvṛtisatyam uktam. MA. VI, 23.

[2] ekam eva, bhikṣavaḥ, paramaṁ satyaṁ, yadutāpramoṣadharmaṁ nirvāṇaṁ sarvasaṁskārāś ca mṛṣā moṣadharmāṇa iti. quoted in MKV. p. 41; BCAP. p. 363.

vastutas tu paramārtha evaikaṁ satyam. BCAP. p. 362.

not be samvṛti (apparent); if it is unreal (mṛṣā), how is it a truth."[1] There is only one truth, the paramārtha, and saṁvṛti does not share in that. Saṁvṛti is truth by courtesy; it is accepted as such only by the ignorant, not by the Mādhyamika.

The four Holy Truths (catvāri āryasatyāni) have to be understood as included in these two: nirodhasatya as Nirvāṇa is paramārtha; and the other three, including the mārga, are within saṁvṛti. Even the spiritual discipline (mārga) undertaken for attaining Nirvāṇa, exalted and purifying as it is, is within saṁvṛti. So too the four fruits of the discipline are within saṁvṛti. The *Prajñāpāramitā* goes so far as to say that even Buddhahood is illusory like a dream or māyā; if there were anything higher than that even, it has to be pronounced to bc within saṁvṛti.[2] The reason is that the scope of saṁvṛti is co-terminus with the range of concepts and words, with any kind of distinction and duality.

If saṁvṛti and paramārtha cannot be understood as two classes of truth, for paramārtha is the only truth, there is less justification to interpret the doctrine as meaning 'degrees' of truth and reality. Saṁvṛti cannot be taken as a lesser, partial or incomplete form of truth and that it needs the addition of some other features to make it the whole truth. The Absolute in the Mādhyamika system is not made up of particular things; it is not a synthesis or summation of different aspects and piecemeal views. The Absolute and phenomena differ qualitatively, not in quantity. The concept of degrees is applicable only when the thing to which it applies is capable of quantitative measurement and when it increases or decreases with the accretion or subtraction of entities. To accept the degrees of truth is really to reduce the distinction between truth and falsity to one of size—the real is the bigger, the fuller, while the 'false' is the smaller, the incomplete; the real is so much more of the false. This is to give up the qualitative distinction of the true and the false. Saṁvṛti is totally false; and nothing of it is taken up in forming the paramārtha.

[1] saṁvṛter na tu satyatvaṁ, satyabhedaḥ kuto nvayam; satyaṁ cet saṁvṛtiḥ keyaṁ, mṛṣā cet satyatā katham; satyatvaṁ na ca sāmānyaṁ mṛṣārthaparamārthayoḥ; virodhān na hi vṛkṣatvaṁ sāmānyaṁ vṛkṣasiṁhayoḥ. *Ślokavārt* (Nirālmbanavāda 6, 7.)

[2] māyopamāṣ te, devputra, sattvāh, svapnopamāḥ sarvadharmā api . . . samyaksambuddho'pi, samyaksambuddhatvam api.

yāvan nirvāṇam api māyopaṁ svapnopamam. sa cen nirvāṇād api kaścid dharmo viśiṣṭataraḥ syāt tam apy ahaṁ māyopaṁ svapnopamaṁ vadāmi. ASP. pp. 39–40; MKV. pp. 449–50; BCAP. p. 379.

It might be asked: if saṁvṛti is ultimately to be rejected and not retained in the paramārtha, why consider it at all? We should concern ourselves with the paramārtha alone. But can we do so without taking the help of the saṁvṛti (vyāvahārika)? If we had been already rooted in the Absolute (paramārtha), there should not be any occasion or use for the saṁvrti; we would not have then cared to draw the distinction between the two. The paramārtha, however, can be understood and realised only negatively, *only as we remove the saṁvṛti*, the forms which thought has already, unconsciously and beginninglessly, ascribed to the real. The Real is to be *uncovered*, *dis*covered, and realised as the reality of appearances (dharmāṇāṁ dharmatā). In the order of our discovery, the removal of saṁvṛti must precede our knowledge of the paramārtha. Paramārtha is the end or goal that we seek to attain, and samvṛti is the means; it is the ladder or the jumping board which enables us to reach that objective. It is therefore stated that saṁvṛti is the means (upāyabhūta) and Paramārtha is the end (upeyabhūta). Basing ourselves on vyavahāra do we advance to the paramārtha.[1]

It need not be doubted that saṁvṛti cannot be used as means to reach the ultimately real (paramārtha) when it is unreal in itself. The unreal, it might be thought, cannot lead us to the real. It has been already pointed out that even an assumption can work; an imputed mark can give us the correct knowledge. For though it does not constitute or characterise the real, it may *indicate* it truly, unerringly.[2] A further advantage of this conception of loose non-constitutive relationship between the Paramārtha and saṁvṛti is that we are not committed to one or a fixed number of such devices; nor is there any restriction with regard to the nature of such devices. The only criterion is that it should work.

Another indubitable advantage of this indicative, non-constitutive,

[1] vyavahāram anāśritya paramārtho na deśyate. MK. XXIV, 10.
tathya-saṁvṛti-sopānam antareṇa vipaścitaḥ;
tattva-prāsāda-śikharārohaṇaṁ na hi yujyate. quoted in AAA. p. 150.
upāya-bhūtaṁ vyavahāra-satyam, upeyabhūtam paramārtha-satyam; MA. VI, 80.

[2] MKV. p. 50; BCA. IX, 9, 10; BCAP, p. 380, 423 ff. In the Vedānta too, though śruti itself is within phenomena (avidyāvad-viṣaya) it can still indicate the paramārtha, Brahman: kathaṁ tv asatyena vedānta-vākyena satyasya brahmātmatvasya pratipattir upapadyeta . . . ity ādinā *tenāsatyenaiva svapnadarśanena* satyaṁ maraṇam sūcyata iti darśayati . . . tathākārādi-satyākṣarapratipattir dṛṣtā rekhānṛtākṣarapratipatteḥ. *Bhāṣya on Br. Sūtra*. II, i, 14 (quoted with gaps).

relation of phenomena to the Absolute is that the latter is not in any way affected by these; it does not become determined or limited in any manner. The Absolute can hold all the variety of content presented by aspects of the universe and of viewpoints in a sort of loose dynamic synthesis. The Hegelian absolute is a determinate synthesis, as it is the unification of things in *one* particular mode; it is a static synthesis, as not allowing of different modes of combination according to the changing times and shifting points of emphasis.[1]

The doctrine of two truths enables the Mādhyamika not only to accommodate all *views* as in some measure and manner leading to the ultimate, but also to synthesise and evaluate the scriptural texts and their doctrines. Texts are divided, on the basis of the paramārtha and vyāvahārika, into nītārtha and neyārtha respectively. Those texts which speak of the means, of the path and of the reality of this and that (ātman, skandhas etc.) are neyārtha; they are not to be taken as literally true; they are of secondary import (ābhiprāyika) only and must be subordinated to the texts which speak of the Absolute in negative terms. The nītārtha, on the other hand, are not concerned with the means, but with the end (phala), the ultimate goal; they are of primary import. The Advaita Vedānta makes a similar distinction of the śruti texts into parā and aparā.

The distinction of these two kinds of texts imparts a great measure of order and unity to Buddhistic doctines. In the absence of this division, there would be interminable conflict about the admissibility of certain texts and the relative importance to be assigned to them. A significant synthesis of all the texts and the doctrines expounded in them is possible only on this basis of two truths.

The entire Mādhyamika Śāstra rests on this foundation of the

[1] Reference may be made to the concluding chapter for an elaboration of this idea.

[2] uktaṁ ca *Āryākṣayamati Sūtre*: katame sutrāntā neyārthāḥ, katame nītārthāḥ. ye sūtrāntā mārgāvataraṇāya nirdiṣṭā ima ucyante neyārthāḥ; ye sūtrāntāḥ phalāvatārāya nirdiṣṭā ima ucyante nītārthāḥ. yāvad ye sūtrāntāḥ śūnyatānimittā-praṇihitā-nabhisaṁskārā-jātā-nutpādā-bhāva-nirātma-niḥsattva-nirjīva-niṣpudgalāsvāmikā vimokṣamukhā nirdiṣṭāḥ, ta ucyante nītārthāḥ. iyam ucyate, Bhadanta Śāradvātīputra, nītārthasūtrānta pratiśaraṇatā, na neyārtha sūtrānta pratiśaraṇatā iti. quoted in MKV. p. 43. See also *Samādhirāja Sūtra*, (VII, 5; p. 78) *Gilgit MSS*. nītārtha sūtrānta viśeṣa jānati; yathopadiṣṭā Sugatena śūnyatā; yasmin punaḥ pudgala-sattvapuruṣā neyārthatāṁ jānati sarvadharmān. This is also quoted in MKV. p. 44 and p. 276. The Vijñānavādins too make this distinction, but from a different point of view.

distinction between the nītārtha and neyārtha sūtras (Canons). Candrakīrti clearly states that Nāgārjuna has written his *Mādhyamika Śāstra* to expound this distinction.[1] This implies that evaluation is made from the absolute standpoint. Saṁvṛti or neyārtha can still have some significance as means to the end (paramārtha).

[1] ata evedaṁ *Madhyamakaśāstraṁ* praṇītam ācāryeṇa neyanītārtha-sūtrāntavibhāgopadarśanārtham. MKV. pp. 40–1. The colophon at the end of the MKV (p. 594) reads: samāptaṁ cedam Madhyamaka-śāstraṁ sakala-loka-lokottara-pravacana-nītaneyārtha-vyākhyāna-naipuṇya-viśāradam iti.

I THE CONCEPT OF FREEDOM

FREEDOM is freedom from pain; it is the eradication of suffering—actual and possible. Pain is frustrated will. We desire, consciously or otherwise, to acquire and enjoy things; we may have the utmost liberty in desiring things; but objective conditions are not always in consonance with our desires; often they are not. An unfavourable balance on the subjective side results; there is suffering. The root-cause of pain is desire, passion and attachment. Freedom is the achieving of a state of passionlessness. It is essentially a negative process and not the acquisition of merit or other values. Not that the practice of virtue or acquisition of merit (puṇya-sambhāra) is not needed for achieving freedom; but it is a means, not the end. According to the Mādhyamika, attachment is dependent on constructive imagination (vikalpa). We are attracted to things as we invest them, in our imagination, with this or that quality. This is a subjective affair; it is not real.[1] Freedom is the total cessation of imagination (sarva-kalpanā-kṣayo hi nirvāṇam). Summing up the essence of spiritual discipline Ārya Deva characterises it as a "Take away all." "Desisting from vice, freeing oneself from the substance-view and lastly giving up all (standpoints) are the stages of this process."[2]

Freedom being a process of negation or annulment of ignorance and passions it is possible to reach perfection; and this can be permanent, being natural to the spirit. If it were an acquisition, there could be no finality; the pile of merit can mount higher and higher; there is no conceivable limit to its size. The acquisition, conditioned as it must be by special causes, will be transitory, the length of the duration notwithstanding. The acquisition calls for special aptitudes

[1] vinā kalpanayāstitvaṁ rāgādīnāṁ na vidyate;
bhūtārthaḥ kalpanā ceti ko grahīṣyati buddhimān. CŚ. VIII, 3.

[2] vāraṇaṁ prāg apuṇyasya madhye vāraṇam ātmanaḥ;
sarvasya vāraṇaṁ paścād yo jānīte sa buddhimān. CŚ. VIII, 15; and CŚV p. 17.

and efforts; and the resultant merit will perforce vary with the individuals. Freedom or Nirvāṇa does not admit of degrees or hierarchy; it is equal and universal in all. The Mādhyamika treatises speak of this state as Samatā.[1] (equality). All beings, irrespective of their status and attainment, are equally heir to Buddhahood—the highest perfection as unconditioned Nirvāṇa. They contain within them the seed of Enlightenment and Perfection (Tathāgatagarbha). The *Uttaratantra*,[2] quoting the *Tathāgatagarbha Sūtra* says: "All living beings are endowed with the Essence of the Buddha." What is the meaning of this? The Body of the Supreme Buddha is all-pervading,

> The Absolute is (one) undifferentiated (whole). And the Germ of (Buddhahood) exists (in every living being),
>
> Therefore, for ever and anon, all that lives is endowed with the Essence of the Buddha.[3]

Again it is said:

> "Just as, being essentially free from (dialectical) thought-construction, the element of space is ubiquitous.
>
> In the same way the Immaculate Essence which is of Spiritual nature, pervades all that exists."[4]

Spiritual discipline is of the nature of purification or removal of the hindrances and defilements that cover up the real. Beings are found in various stages and degrees of purification, though they are essentially one as Buddha. It must not be thought that the process being negative, it is short or easy of accomplishment. The *Prajñāpāramitā* and other texts speak of the career of the Bodhisattva as difficult and arduous, calling for the intensest effort sustained for countless aeons (asaṁkhyeya kalpa). It does mean, however, that the ills and defilements, however long-standing and great they may be, are accidental accretions to the spirit. They are capable of complete removal by Intuitional knowledge (prajñā). The absolute power of the intellect over the will, the wrong exercise of which is the cause of suffering, is the basic implication of the Mādhyamika spiritual

[1] e.g. *The Samādhirāja Sūtra*, the full title of which is *Sarvadharma-svabhāva Samatā-vipañcita Samadhirāja Sūtra* illustrates the point.

[2] This is a work by Asanga from the Prāsangika Mādhyamika standpoint. See Obermiller's *The Sublime Science of Maitreya, Acta Orientalia*, IX, p. 95 and also his *Doctrine of Prajñāpāramitā*, p. 90 and pp. 99–100.

[3] *The Sublime Science of Maitreya* (trans. by Obermiller) pp. 156–7.

[4] Ibid . . . p. 184.

discipline for freedom. Evil or erratic willing is the consequence of ignorance of the real; the removal of ignorance effectively does away with all forms of evil—metaphysical evil (finitude), moral evil (vice) and physical evil (pain).

In all this, the closest parallel is offered by the Advaita Vedānta. Mokṣa is not acquisition (kārya) of any kind; it is the natural state of the spirit.[1] There is the annulment of ignorance, and only in this negative sense can it be said to be an achievement. Mokṣa does not admit of gradations, nor is it transitory; conversely, where there is gradation there is saṁsāra.[2] For both the Vedānta and the Mādhyamika the basic problem is one of knowledge; to know the real is at once to be free from saṁsāra.[3]

II FREEDOM IS SPIRITUAL

The freedom that the Mādhyamika or any other system of Indian Philosophy puts before us as the *summum bonum* is Spiritual Freedom; it is totally different from other kinds of freedom. The so-called four freedoms—freedom of speech, freedom of association, freedom of worship and freedom from want—are all secular. Attainment of them is only a means, not the final value. At best, they provide facilities for the group or the individual to realise his highest destiny. The freedoms represent particular and partial satisfactions; many, if not all of them, are liable to abuse. Freedom of speech as exercised by the moderns—by the press and the platform—is largely propaganda, an instrument to further partisan selfish interests. Individuals and nations, in their anxiety to be free from fear, may arm themselves to the teeth and commit aggression. This is happening in the present age and does not require any pointed example. Practically every nation is guilty of this. In striving for freedom from want, we may and do exploit weaker beings and nations. The freedoms to be exercised in the truest interests of humanity, of all beings, presuppose a passionless and disinterested outlook free from every

[1] brahmabhāvaś ca mokṣaḥ. *Bhāṣya* on *Br. Sūtras* I, i, 4.

[2] evam avidyādidoṣavatāṁ dharma-tāratamyanimittaṁ śarīropādāna-pūrvakaṁ sukha-duḥkha-tāratamyam anityaṁ saṁsāra-rūpaṁ śrutismṛti-nyāyaprasiddham. Ibid.

[3] api ca "brahma veda brahmaiva bhavati" . . . "abhayaṁ vai, Janaka, prāpto'si"; "tad ātmānam evāved ahaṁ brahmāsmīti tasmāt tat sarvam abhavat" . . . ity evamādyā śrutayo brahmavidyānantaraṁ mokṣam darśayantyo madhye kāryāntaraṁ vārayanti. Ibid.

vestige of egoism. They all imply spiritual freedom. And only the individual can be free spiritually.

The spiritual is capable of precise definition. There are certain unmistakable marks of the spiritual. The spiritual man is a one-level personality. In him there is no division of the inner and the outer, the surface motives and the deeper unconscious drives. He is not torn asunder by conflict and confusion; he is fully integrated and unified. The secular man does not react to a situation in a total way; the spiritual man does. All the hard knots of his heart are broken and fused into one whole by the fire of a master-idea. The entire personality is consumed in it; the dross is converted into gold. The Prajñā (Śūnyatā) of the Mādhyamika or the brahmasākṣātkāra of the Vedānta are the most potent catalytic agents which transform the man into a one-level personality.[1] He has no passions and prejudices which sway him from below. Buddha and other spiritual persons are invariably represented as having a transparent clear skin; this is the physical analogue of the spiritual.

As in the spiritual person there is no conflict of different ideals and cross purposes, there is also complete identity between the individual and the cosmic good. A man divided in himself must necessarily divide himself from others. In the spiritual realm, not only is there no such opposition, but the very possibility of it is ruled out. Self-seeking, egoity, is totally absent. The pain of another is one's own; his troubles are mine.[2] The good of one is the good of all beings without any reservation. All spirituality is the attainment of this universal interest and the elimination of private standpoints and values. The Bodhisattva ideal of the Mādhyamika and Vijñānavāda systems and the doctrine of Great Compassion (mahākaruṇā) are concrete expressions of this essential mark of the spiritual.

In the spiritual, the means and the end coincide. In the moral sphere, we do certain acts, e.g. charity, for some other-worldly good or social solidarity which would benefit us indirectly. Charity is not

[1] aśucipratimām imām gṛhītvā jinaratna-pratimāṁ karoty anarghām; rasajātam atīva vedhanīyaṁ sudṛḍhaṁ gṛhṇata bodhicitta-saṁjñam. BCA. I, 10.
ekaḥ sarvajñatācittotpāda-rasadhātuḥ kuśalamūla-pariṇāmanā-jñānasaṁgṛhītaḥ sarvakarmakleśāvaraṇalohāni paryādāya sarvadharmān sarvajñatāsuvarṇaṁ karoti. From *Ārya Maitreya Vimokṣa Sūtra* as quoted in BCAP. pp. 16–17 and in ŚS. pp. 177–8.

[2] yadā mama pareṣāṁ ca bhayaṁ duḥkhaṁ ca na priyam;
tadātmanaḥ ko viśeṣo yat taṁ rakṣāmi netaram. ŚS. p. 2.

for its own sake. Nor do moral acts carry with them their own sanction. Their observance is commended by external authority, fear of God or the approval of society. The spiritual person is good, he is chaste or charitable, not because he desires to gain something in this or the other world. It is his nature to be so; his goodness is motiveless. The spiritual act is not a means to an end; it is the end itself. It therefore necessarily carries within itself the criterion of its efficacy and soundness (pratyātmavedanīya).

III SPIRITUAL AWAKENING

Spiritual life is born of the sharp contrast felt between what is and what should be. It is the consciousness of suffering. Pain as an undesirable state is felt by all beings; they all try, in their own way, to get rid of it. The layman, however, is not aware of its magnitude or intensity. He entertains the fond hope that pain is a temporary phase, and that it can be remedied by the ordinary means. In pursuance of this, he adopts measures that are accessible to him in various spheres. The essential prerequisite of spiritual awakening is the awareness of the intensity and universality of suffering. A state of unpleasant feeling is but a sample of what could befall us at all times. The awareness is not complete unless it is extended infinitely before and after this life.[1] Its inexorability, given the causes and

[1] Buddha gives a graphic description of this fact of suffering: "What do you think, O monks! Which may be more, the flow of tears you have shed on this long way, running again and again to new birth and new death, united to the disliked, separated from the liked, complaining and weeping, or the water of the four great oceans? . . . But how is this possible? Without beginning or end, O monks, is this round of rebirth. There cannot be discerned the first beginning of beings, who sunk in ignorance and bound by thirst, are incessantly transmigrating and again and again run to a new birth. And thus, O monks, through a long time you have experienced suffering, pain and misery, and enlarged the burying ground; truly long enough to be disgusted with every kind of existence, long enough to turn away from every kind of existence, long enough to deliver yourself from it" *Sam. Nikāya* II, pp. 178 ff. (Translation quoted from Grimm: *The Doctrine of the Buddha*. pp. 96–98).

This is the duḥkha satya—the clear intuition of which forms the first four of the 16 moments of Enlightenment, *viz*: duḥkhe dharma-jñāna-kṣānti, duḥkhe dharma-jñānaṁ duḥkhe anvaya jñāna-kṣānti, duḥkhe anvaya-jñānam. See MKV. pp. 482–3; AAA. p. 151.

Jaigīṣavya (*Yogasūtra Bhāṣya*, III, 18) gives expression to the duḥkha satya in identical terms:

daśasu mahāsargeṣu bhavyatvād anabhibhūtena buddhisattvena mayā naraka-tiryagbhavaṁ duḥkhaṁ saṁpaśyatā devamanuṣyeṣu punaḥ punar utpadyamānena yat kiñcid anubhūtaṁ tat sarvaṁ duḥkham eva pratyavaimi.

conditions which engender it, must be realised. Even highly placed beings—kings or gods—do not escape suffering in some form or the other. What appears as pleasure is pain in the making; it necessarily leads to hankering for the repetition of the state; and if this is frustrated, there is anger against the impeding agents. Attachment and aversion result; this is saṁsāra (bondage).

Every Indian system begins with the problem of suffering. The parallel on the intellectual side is the consciousness of illusion. That makes us critical, reflective. Consciousness of suffering leads us to discard secular values and to go in search of the abiding. Buddhism has always laid great emphasis on suffering. The first two truths (ārya satya) are the consciousness of pain (duḥkha) and its cause (samudaya). It is convinced that all phenomena are pain—actual or potential.[1] The inescapability of suffering in the natural course of things is brought home to us with the utmost vigour in the Pratītya Samutpāda doctrine accepted by all Buddhist schools. The twelve-linked causal chain is an unending continuum of suffering (kevalasyaivam etasya duḥkhaskandhasya sambhavaḥ).[2]

There is suffering; but it can be helped, because it is conditioned (pratītyasamutpanna). If it were a brute fact of nature and not the result of avidyā and karma, our efforts would be unavailing, and there could be no spiritual life.[3] Acceptance of Karma as the basic factor in the constitution of the universe is indispensable. Buddha rejected at the very outset all forms of materialism and determinism (uccheda-vāda and akriyāvāda), as these militate against the efficacy of karma. Again, if there were other more easy or fruitful means of removing pain, none would take to philosophy. The conviction that the worldly means are no remedies, but make for tightening the grip of samsāra

[1] duḥkha is usually considered in the three-fold way; duḥkha-duḥkhatā—the actual pain; tāpa-duḥkhatā (longing, desire) and the saṁskāra duḥkhatā—the root-causes, kleśas or passions, e.g. attachment, aversion etc. In short, phenomenal existence or all the five upādāna skandhas are pain. (sankhittena pañc'upādāna kkandā pi dukkhā).

[2] MK. XXVI, 9. cf. also:
yathākṣepaṁ kramād vṛddhaḥ saṁtānaḥ kleśakarmabhiḥ;
paralokaṁ punar yātītyanādi bhava-cakrakam.
yaḥ pratītyasamutpādo dvādaśāngas trikāṇḍakaḥ.
From *Pratītya Samutpādahṛdaya* by Nāgārjuna quoted in BCAP. p. 389.

[3] duḥkha is not uncaused, natural (svayaṁ kṛtam), nor caused by an external factor (parakṛtam), nor both, nor neither, but pratītyajam, conditioned by avidyā—kalpanā. Hence it can be helped. MK. XII (*Duḥkha-parīkṣā*); *Sam. N.* II, 114 ff.

on us and that Prajnā alone can remove the root of suffering (ignorance) is the commencement of the spiritual discipline.[1]

Considering that opportunities for the cultivation of the spiritual life are rare and the obstacles many, the votary must make up his mind to cultivate the Bodhicitta at the earliest.[2] He should direct all his efforts towards the attainment of Bodhi and Buddhahood. It is the contention of the Mādhyamika that freedom cannot be attained without the realisation of the unreality (śūnyatā) of things.[3]

IV THE PĀRAMITĀ DISCIPLINE

The Ṣaṭ-Pāramitā-Naya,[4] the sixfold path of Highest Perfection, is the Mādhyamika spiritual discipline. The *Prajñā-pāramitā* treatises treat of these, especially the last Pāramitā, Prajñā—Wisdom. The Pāramitā way is distinguished from the older discipline of the Hīnayāna in three important respects: the replacement of the arhat by the bodhisattva ideal, the elaboration of the older śīla-samādhi-prajñā stadia of spiritual discipline into the six-fold path of the

[1] avidyāyāṁ niruddhāyāṁ saṁskārāṇām asambhavaḥ;
avidyāyā nirodhas tu jñānenāsyaiva bhāvanāt. MK. XXVI, 11.
asyaiva pratītya-samutpādasya yathāvad aviparīta-bhāvanāto' avidyā prahīyate. MKV. p. 559.

[2] ŚS. p. 2; BCA. pp. 595 ff.

[3] muktis tu śūnyatā-dṛṣṭes tadarthāśeṣabhāvanā. Nāgārjuna's dictum quoted in BCAP. p. 438, with the introductory words: idam eva Ācārya-pādair uktam; also quoted in *Subhāṣita Saṁgraha*. kleśajñeyāvṛtitamaḥpratipakṣo hi Śūnyatā; śīghraṁ sarvajñatākāmo na bhāvayati tāṁ katham. BCA. IX, 55 (p. 447).

[4] 'Pāramitā' is derived etymologically in two ways: pāram itā (gatā), that which has gone to the utmost limit, infinity; or from 'parama' excellent or superior. The first derivation is the generally accepted one. See AAA (p. 28):*pāram* prakarṣaparyantam *etīti* vigṛhya kvipi sarvāpahārilope 'nityam āgamaśāsanam ity atuki, "tatpuruṣe kṛti bahulam" ity aluki ca karma-vibhakteḥ kṛte *pāramis* tadbhavaḥ *pāramitā*. prajñāyā dharma-pravicayalakṣaṇāyāḥ pāramitā, mukhyā Buddho Bhagavān māyopaṁ jñānam advayam.
For the second derivation see *Bodhisattva Bhūmi* (passage quoted in the *Bodhisattva Doctrine* (p. 166) of Dr. Hardayal): "Pāramitā is really derived from Parama (and not from *pāra* with the root 'i'), as the *Bodhisattva Bhūmi* . . . clearly explains. The Pāramitās are so called because they are acquired during a long period of time (parameṇa kālena samudāgatāḥ) and supremely pure in their nature (paramayā svabhāva-viśuddhayā viśuddhāḥ). They also transcend the virtues or the qualities of the Śrāvakas and the Pratyekabuddhas, and lead to the highest result (paramaṁ ca phalam anuprayacchanti)." The *Aṣṭasāhasrikā* (p. 81) hints at this derivation: paramatvāt prajñāpāramitā-nāmadheyaṁ labhate.

pāramitās—dāna, śīla, kṣānti, vīrya, dhyāna and prajñā, and the minuter analysis of the highest stages of spiritual life into *bhūmis* or planes of yoga culminating in complete Buddhahood. These revolutionalise the ideal, the path and the final result of the spiritual discipline; they impart a unity and universality never known before in spiritual life.

(i) The ideal of the arhat is the highest state of the Hīnayāna systems. It is replaced here by the ideal of the bodhisattva. Arhathood is a lower ideal of perfection that is purely negative: the cessation of suffering (kleśāvaraṇa-nivṛttiḥ) and the nirvāṇa as conceived by them is almost a blank state of annihilation.[1] The Bodhisattva aims at complete Buddhahood, existence as Perfect Being (*ens perfectissimum*). All beings are identical with the Buddha; and Bodhi (Enlightenment) is implicit in them , but it has to be realised by the spiritual discipline. This is the positive ideal of the unity of all beings as the Buddha. Again, the Arhat rests satisfied with achieving his own private salvation; he is not necessarily and actively interested in the welfare of others. The ideal of the Arhat smacks of selfishness; and there is even a lurking fear that the world would take hold of him if he tarried here too long. The Bodhisattva makes the salvation of all his own good.[2] He shuns retiring into the final state of Nirvāṇa, though fully entitled to it, preferring, by his own free choice, to toil for even the lowest of beings for ages.[3] He is actuated by this motiveless altruism from the very start of his career. It is not that the Bodhisattva cannot achieve his freedom without achieving the freedom of all. This would involve a vicious circle: he cannot free others without first being free himself, and he cannot free himself without freeing others. No, his freedom is full and complete by itself; but he condescends to raise others to his level. This is a free phenomenalising act· of grace and compassion. A deeply religious element is introduced into Buddhism which would have otherwise remained an exalted moral naturalism. Buddha—which the Bodhisattva eventually becomes—is a person—the Highest Person. In

[1] See *Conception of Buddhist Nirvāṇa*, pp. 27–28.

[2] duṣkarakārakāḥ, Subhūte, bodhisattvā mahasattvā ye lokahitāya samprasthitā lokasukhāya, lokānukampāyai samprasthitāḥ, lokasya trāṇaṁ bhaviṣyāmo, śaraṇaṁ bhaviṣyāmaḥ—ity evaṁ rūpam anuttarāyāṁ samyaksambodhau vīryam ārabhante. ASP. p. 293.

[3] nāhaṁ tvaritarūpeṇa bodhiṁ prāptum ihotsahe;
parānta-koṭiṁ sthāsyāmi sattvasyaikasya kāraṇāt. ŚS. p. 14.

Buddha, we have the conception of a person without any trace of the ego. There is activity without attachment. There is nothing which the Bodhisattva cannot sacrifice for the good of others. He dedicates his present and future lives unreservedly in the service of all beings.[1]

With the Buddhas as his ideal the Bodhisattva aims at Bodhi, and undertakes the discipline for it (bodhicittotpāda). Śūnyatā and Karuṇā are the two principal features of the Bodhicitta.[2] Śūnyatā is prajñā, intellectual intuition, and is identical with the Absolute. Karuṇā is the active principle of compassion that gives concrete expression to Śūnyatā in phenomena. If the first is transcendent and looks to the Absolute, the second is fully immanent and looks down towards phenomena. The first is the abstract universal reality of which no determinations can be predicated; it is beyond the duality of good and evil, love and hatred, virtue and vice; the second is goodness, love and pure act; Śūnyatā is potential, Karuṇā is the actualised state. Buddha and the Bodhisattva, who models himself on him, are thus amphibious beings with one foot in the Absolute and the other in phenomena. They are virtuous and good and the source of all goodness in the world. The bodhicitta is a unique blend of Intellect and Will.

The Mahāyāna texts cannot praise the Bodhicitta too highly. It is the foundation of all good, the source of all endeavour, the refuge of all beings, a veritable treasure.[3] As the one secure foundation for the happiness of all beings and the one remedy for their suffering, it is

[1] api tu khalu punar avikalpa eva hīnamadhyotkṛṣṭānāṁ sattvānāṁ vyādhim apanayati. evam eva kulaputra Bodhisattvena mahāsattvena asmiṁś cāturmahābhautike ātmabhāve bhaiṣajya-sañjotpādayitavyā yeṣāṁ yeṣāṁ sattvānāṁ yena yenārthaḥ tat tad eva me harantu hastaṁ hastārthinaḥ, pādaṁ pādārthinaḥ . . . iti. From *Nārāyaṇa Paripṛcchā*. Quoted in ŚS. p. 21.
ayam eva mayā kāyaḥ sarvasattvānāṁ kiṅkaraṇiyeṣu kṣapayitavyaḥ. tad yathāpi nāmemāni bāhyāni catvāri mahābhūtāni pṛthivīdhātur abdhātus tejodhātur vāyu-dhātuś ca nānāsukhair nānopāyair nānārambaṇair nānopakaraṇair nānaparibhogaiḥ sattvānāṁ nānopabhogaṁ gacchanti, evam evāham kāyaṁ caturmahābhūta-samucchrāyam nānā sukhair . . . sarvasattvānām upabhogyaṁ kariṣyāmīti. From *Akṣayamati Sūtra* quoted in ŚS. pp. 21–22 and BCAP. p. 86.

[2] śūnyatā-karuṇāgarbhaṁ bodhicittam—AAA. p. 29.

[3] bodhicittaṁ hi, kulaputra, bījabhūtaṁ sarva buddha-dharmāṇāṁ, kṣetra-bhūtaṁ sarva-jagacchukla-dharmavirohaṇatayā, dharaṇībhūtaṁ sarvaloka-prati-śaraṇatayā, yāvat pitṛbhūtaṁ . . . vaiśravaṇabhūtaṁ sarvadāridryasamchedanatayā etc. from *Gaṇḍavyūha Sūtra* as quoted in ŚS. pp. 5–6 and BCAP. p. 23.

immeasurable in its purity and goodness.[1] It is not to be thought that the Bodhicitta is a preparation for some unworldly ideal having no relevance to the problems of the present-day world. Even in this world its influence is very great; as the basis of all altruism, it makes for social solidarity and happy human relationship.[2]

Bodhicitta is usually spoken of as in two stages of development. One is the preparatory stage wherein the devotee makes great resolves, and defines his ideal to attain complete Buddhahood. The next stage is the actual starting on the journey towards that goal—the practice of the pāramitās. The former is called *bodhi praṇidhi citta* and the latter *bodhi prasthāna citta.*[3]

At the beginning of his career the Bodhisattva makes the Great Resolves (mahā-praṇidhāna), usually before a Spiritual Guide (Kalyāṇa-mitra), about his intention and endeavour. The Mahāyāna treatises give the number as ten or twelve.[4] The chief ones are that the Bodhisattva would help all beings in their spiritual endeavour; "that his unlimited knowledge and means (prajñopāya) be of unending service to beings; that all beings should, leaving the inferior path (śrāvaka and pratyeka-buddhayāna), take to the Mahāyāna path of supreme enlightenment; that beings following my discipline be firm in their virtue and they be not born in evil state; that beings afflicted by various diseases, but helpless and poor, be cured of their diseases" etc.[5]

The importance of the Great Resolves cannot be overestimated. They set the goal of the Bodhisattva very clearly before him for all time. They give unerring and unfailing direction to him in his spiritual career. The resolve itself acts as an accelerating force in his progress and counteracts unspiritual tendencies. Man becomes what

[1] Cf. BCA. (I, 26) jagadānandabījasya jagad-duḥkhauṣadhasya ca;
cittaratnasya yat puṇyaṁ tat kathaṁ hi pramīyatām.
bodhicittād dhi yat puṇyaṁ tac ca rūpi bhaved yadi;
ākāśadhātuṁ sampūrya bhūyaś cottari tad bhavet.

Quoted in BCAP. p. 32.

[2] bodhi-praṇidhi-cittasya saṁsāre'pi phalaṁ mahat. BCA. I, 17.

[3] Cf. ŚS. p. 8; AAA. p. 29

BCA. I, 15, 16: tad bodhicittaṁ dvividhaṁ vijñātavyam samāsataḥ;
bodhipraṇidhicittaṁ ca bodhiprasthānacittam eva ca.
gantukāmasya gantuś ca yathā bhedaḥ pratīyate;
tathā bhedo'nayor jñeyo yathā-samkhyena paṇḍitaiḥ.

[4] The *Daśabhūmikā Sūtra.* pp. 14–16 gives 10 praṇidhānas; also quoted in ŚS. pp. 291 ff.

The *Bhaiṣajyaguru-Vaidūrya-Prabhā-Sūtra* (pp. 4 ff) mentions 12 praṇidhānas.

[5] Taken from the *Bhaiṣajya Guru Sūtra* pp. 4 ff.

he wills. He is not moulded by circumstances; he moulds the circumstances. Spiritual realisation is a growth from within, self-creative and self-determining. It is not too much to say that the nature of the resolve determines the nature of the final attainment, like the seed determining the plant. The seed of Buddhahood is sown in the initial vow that the Bodhisattva makes. The entire later discipline is the cultivation and preservation of this.

Salutation to and worship of the Buddhas and their sons (the Bodhisattvas) is an integral part of the bodhicaryā.[1] Offerings are made to them, and an elaborate ritual in the best Brāhmanical style is undergone. An unreserved confession of one's sins (pāpa-deśanā) is made before them, and the devotee asks for their active help in his path. It would be wrong to understand this as theistic worship of an *other*. The Buddhas are but the realised ideal of the devotee, his higher self. It is as it were the actual becomes the ideal, which it really is, by constantly having it before the mind's eye and venerating it. True worship is self-worship; the lower is completely transmuted into the higher which it is in fact; the lower surrenders itself, and the higher attracts and raises the lower. Buddhist religion can only be a species of Absolutist Pantheism.

(ii) Buddhist spiritual discipline has always been of the three-tier type—Śīla, Samādhi and Prajñā—Virtues, Concentration of mind and Wisdom.[2] The Pāramitā doctrine did not replace it exactly, but modified and elaborated it into the six-fold pāramitā discipline of dāna, śīla, kṣānti, vīrya, dhyāna and prajñā. This gives greater prominence to the preparatory stages, and emphasises certain virtues as Charity and Forbearance, and enjoins ceaseless and enthusiastic effort as essential for attaining Buddhahood. The place of Prajñā as the guiding and controlling factor to which all other Pāramitās tend is made abundantly clear. Though in the earlier systems too Prajñā was taken as the culmination of the discipline, there was a tendency

[1] Śānti Deva is the accredited teacher of the worship-cult in the Mādhyamika system. It would, however, be wrong to hold that he was the innovator of this. In Nāgārjuna's *Catuḥstava* we have the feature of worship in full measure.

[2] In the Pāli Canons the *locus classicus* of this is the latter portion of the *Sāmaññaphala Sutta* and the whole of *Subha Sutta*: tiṇṇaṁ kho, māṇava, khandhānaṁ so Bhagavā vaṇṇavādi ahosi, ettha ca imaṁ janataṁ samādapesi, nivesesi, patiṭṭhāpesi. katamesaṁ tiṇṇam? ariyassa *sīlakkhandhassa*, ariyassa *samādhikkhandhassa*, ariyassa *paññākkhandhassa*. *Subha Sutta*, 6 (*Dīgh. N.* I, p. 206). The *Visuddhimagga* of Buddhaghosa is based on these three topics: Sīla, Samādhi and Paññā.

to regard the spiritual path as the almost mechanical performance of virtues and practice of concentration. Here Prajñā informs and inspires the entire spiritual discipline; every virtue and each act of concentration is dedicated to the gaining of insight into the real. The stress has shifted from the moral to the metaphysical axis.

The conception of Pāramitā revolutionises the conception of virtue. Dāna (charity), Śīla (Moral restraints and observances) Kṣānti (Forbearance) Dhyāna (Meditation) are not disconnected and aimless acts. They are not performed just to conform to tradition or social pressure. They have only one aim—to make man fit for the highest knowledge. A mind swayed by passions and attached to the world (a sakleśa citta) cannot know the truth; the distracted mind (asamāhita citta) is incapable of perceiving the truth for lack of steadiness in attention. All the other pāramitās are meant to purify the mind and make it fit to receive the intuition of the absolute (prajñā). It is prajñā-pāramitā again that can complete them, make each of them a pāramitā—a perfection.[1] How can any one give away all, not expecting any return, without the conviction that the things are not his, and even that he must atone for happening to possess them. It is not possible to forbear from retaliating when the greatest injury is done to us, unless we are convinced of the fact that in reality there has been no loss, nor is the misdoer our enemy. Without the realisation of the ultimate, no virtue can be practised fully. It is therefore pointed out that prajñā is the leader of all the other Pāramitās.[2]

Spiritual culture is self-culture. There is no external compulsion or pressure to which the Bodhisattva accommodates himself; no outside authority can draw out the entire man as the bodhi discipline does. The essence of self-culture is the bringing about a *change in oneself*, not in the environment. Changing the external world to suit one's desires is the way of worldly men; that is like carpeting the whole earth to avoid being hurt by thorns.[3] The same end can be achieved

[1] eṣā hi prajñā-pāramitā ṣaṇṇāṁ pāramitānāṁ pūrvaṁgamā, nāyikā, pariṇāyikā, saṁdarśikā, janayitrī, dhātrī . . . tat kasya hetoḥ. prajñāpāramitā-virahitā hi pañca pāramitāḥ na prajñāyante nāpi pāramitā-nāmadheyaṁ labhante. ASP. p. 398. See also ASP. pp. 80–2, 101 and 172.

[2] This point has been treated at some length in Ch. VIII.

[3] bhūmiṁ chādayituṁ sarvāṁ kutaś carma bhaviṣyati;
upānac-carmamātreṇa cchannā bhavati medinī.
bāhyā bhāvā mayā tadvac chakyā vārayituṁ na hi;
sva-cittaṁ vārayiṣyāmi kiṁ mamānyair nirvāritaiḥ. BCA. V, 13 and 14.
cittādhīno dharmo, dharmādhīnā bodhir iti. From *Dharmasangīti Sūtra* quoted in BCAP. p. 105.

more effectively and less expensively by equipping oneself with a pair of shoes. Instead of acquiring control over things external to us, one must control one's mind and make it impervious to any external influence. Spiritual culture is the cultivation of the bodhicitta.

Spiritual culture must be further understood as an intense and sustained self-reflection, self-criticism. It is a ceaseless watchfulness of one's doings—speech, bodily and mental action. Passions overpower us because of our self-forgetfulness, we are not self-possessed. With mindfulness (smṛti or smṛtyupasthāna) regained, the passions cease to have hold on us. Just as the dialectic on the intellectual side is the reflective criticism of the inveterate tendency of the mind to speculate and spin theories, on the practical side it is the ever alert self-criticism of one's activity.[1]

The Prātimokṣa is the basis for the Buddhist discipline; the Mahāyāna has elaborated it with great care and deep insight into the different strata of spiritual consciousness. It is not meant for recluses only, as the Hīnayāna discipline was; for we hear of even householder (gṛhi) Bodhisattvas. The Bodhicaryā is at once liberally conceived and minutely drawn.[2]

(iii) Completing his training and the accumulation of merit (puṇya-sambhāra-mārga), the Bodhisattva enters, fully equipped, the path of illumination (darśana-mārga) and of concentrated contemplation (bhāvanā-mārga). The higher reaches of the spiritual path are traced, with a wealth of detail and an intimacy born of

[1] This is called samprajanya or smṛtyupasthāna in the Mahāyāna treatises. Samprajanaya is defined:
etad eva samāsena samprajanyasya lakṣaṇam;
yat kāyacittāvasthāyāḥ pratyavekṣā muhur muhuḥ. BCA. V, 108. See also ŚS. pp. 120 ff.
The Prajñāpāramitā describes this thus:
caraṁś carāmīti prajānāti, sthitaḥ sthito'smīti prajānāti etc.
Quoted in BCA. p. 108; ŚS. p. 120.
This is the Satipaṭṭhāna of the *Dīgha Nikāya*:
"And how does a monk become self-possessed He acts, mendicants, in full presence of mind. Whatever he may do, in going out or coming in, in looking forward or in looking round, in bending his arm, or stretching it forth, in wearing his robes, or in carrying his bowel, in eating or drinking . . . Thus let a monk be mindful and self-possessed; this is our instruction to you." *Mahā Pari Nibbāṇa Sutta* II, 12 and 13 Trans. by Rhys Davids. The whole of *Mahā Satipaṭṭhāna Sutta* (*D.N.* Sutta 22) is devoted to this topic.

[2] Śānti Deva's *Śikṣāsamuccaya* which is a compendium of Precepts culled from Mahāyāna texts and *Bodhicaryāvatāra* are our chief sources for the Mādhyamika spiritual discipline.

experience of those planes, in the *Daśabhūmikā, Bodhisattvabhūmi* and the *Pañcaviṁśati Sāhasrikā* and other Mahāyāna treatises. The *Abhisamayālaṅkāra* of Asanga and its commentaries deal with the stages of the spiritual path (abhisamaya) under eight heads.[1] It is interesting to note the concordance of the Abhisamaya and the Ten Planes of Mahāyānistic meditation.[2] Candrakīrti actually attempts, in his *Madhyamakāvatāra*, to fit in the Pāramitās with the ten Bhūmis—beginning from Pramuditā and culminating in the Dharma-meghā. As the disciple progresses, there is the progressive dissolution of the passions and falling away of the mental defilements. Great clarity is attained, till the mind becomes transparent, free from all impediments, obscurations, passions and sloth. The Bodhisattva approximates more and more to Buddha; he acquires great yogic powers. The tenth Bhūmi—Dharma-meghā—is taken to be the Buddhabhūmi,[3] though complete Buddhahood is still far off.

V ŚŪNYATĀ IS THE SOLE MEANS TO NIRVĀṆA

It is the contention of the Mādhyamikas that the final release is possible only through Śūnyatā—by the giving up of all views, stand-points and predicaments.[4] The paths advocated by other systems can

[1] Prajñā-pāramitā-ṣṭābhiḥ padārthaiḥ samudīritā;
sarvākārajñatā, mārgajñatā sarvajñatā tataḥ;
sarvākārābhisambodho murdhaprāpto' nupūrvakaḥ;
ekakṣaṇābhisambodho dharmakāyaś ca te'ṣṭadhā. *Abhisamayālaṅkāra kārikās* 4 and 5. Quoted in AAA. p. 19.

[2] The *Śatasāhasrikā* (X Chap. pp. 1454 ff) gives a full and clear account of the Bhūmis.
A historical and comparative study of the Mahāyāna and Hīnāyana planes of meditation as contained in the *Mahāvastu* and the *Daśabhūmikā* etc. is very interesting. Such a study is made in Dr. N. Dutt's "Aspects of Mahāyāna in relation to Hīnāyana."

[3] tatra kathaṁ bodhisattvo mahāsattvo daśamyāṁ bhūmau sthitas tathāgata eva vaktavyaḥ. yasya bodhisattvasya sarvapāramitāḥ paripūrṇā bhavanti, daśatathāgata-balāni, catvāri vaiśāradyāni, catasraḥ pratisamvidaḥ aṣṭādaśāveṇikā buddhadharmāḥ, sarvākārajñatājñānaṁ, sarva-vāsanānusam-dhikleśaprahāṇaṁ, mahākaruṇā, sarvabuddhadharmāś ca paripūrṇā bhavanti. *Śatasāhasrikā (X) p.* 1472.

[4] "muktis tu śūnyatādṛṣṭes tadarthāśeṣabhāvanā". A dictum of Nāgārjuna quoted in BCAP. p. 438 and also in *Subhāṣita Samgrha*. Also in Guṇaratna's commentary (p. 47) on *Saḍdarśana Samuccaya*.
buddhaiḥ pratyeka-buddhaiś ca śrāvakaiś ca niṣevitā; mārgas tvam ekā mokṣasya nāstyanya iti niścayaḥ. ASP. IX, 41.
na vinānena mārgeṇa bodhir ityāgamo yataḥ. BCA. IX, 41.

at best lead to partial release, or be a preliminary to this.[1] Consideration of the real in any particular mode, e.g. as Substance, Being, Becoming etc. necessarily creates an other, the opposite, from which it is distinguished. We cannot help being attached to what we take to be real—our view—and reject others. A view, because of its restriction, determination, carries with it duality, the root of saṁsāra. Nāgārjuna states this dialectical predicament thus: when the self is posited, an other (para) confronts it; with the division of the self and the not-self, attachment and aversion result. Depending on these all vices spring up. Attachment begets the thirst for pleasure, and thirst hides all flaws (of the objects). Blinded by this, the thirsty man imagines qualities in things, and seizes upon the means to achieve pleasure. Saṁsāra is thus present as long as there is the attachment to the 'I'.[2]

"A position (pakṣa) begets a counter-position (pratipakṣa), and neither of them is real."[3] In the practical sphere, the holding of views begets attachment and aversion. The kind of view does not matter; a view as such is exclusive, and by that very act an opposition is set up. We cannot avoid controversy and conflict in holding any view—affirmative or negative.[4]

[1] "ekaṁ hi yānaṁ dvitīyaṁ na vidyate". See also ASP. p. 319. ekam eva hi yānaṁ bhavati yad uta buddha-yānaṁ, bodhisattvānaṁ yathā āyuṣmataḥ subhūter nirdeśaḥ.

It is explicitly stated in the AAA. (p. 120) that it is the opinion of Nāgārjuna and his followers that the votaries of other paths do not gain final release, that they remain in a lower state, but are, at the end of the period, enlightened by the Buddha.

Ārya Nāgārjuna-pādāis tanmatanusāriṇaś caikayāna-nayavādina āhuḥ:
labdhvā bodhi-dvayaṁ hy ete bhavād uttrastamānasāḥ;
bhavanty āyuḥ-kṣayāt tuṣṭāḥ prāpta-nirvaṇa-saṁjñinaḥ.
na teṣām asti nirvāṇaṁ kiṁ tu janma-bhavatraye;
dhātau na vidyate teṣāṁ te'pi tiṣṭhanty anāsrave.
akliṣṭa-jñāna-hānāya paścād buddhaiḥ prabodhitāḥ;
sambhṛtya bodhi-sambhāraṁs te'pi syur lokanāyakāḥ. AAA. p. 120.

The *Catuḥ Stava* (I, 21, quoted by Advayavajra, p. 22) has a verse of this import;
dharmadhātor asambhedād yānabhedo'sti na prabho;
yānatritayam ākhyātaṁ tvayā sattvāvatārataḥ.

[2] *Ratnāvalī* of Nāgārjuna as quoted in BCAP. p. 492.

[3] pakṣāddhi pratipakṣaḥ syād ubhayaṁ tac ca nārthataḥ. From *Ratnāvalī* as quoted in MKV. p. 359.

[4] astīti nāstīti ca kalpanāvatām evam carantāna na duḥkha śāmyatīti. MKV. p. 523.

astīti nāstīti vivāda eṣaḥ; suddhī asuddhīti ayaṁ vivādaḥ; vivāda-prāptyā na duḥkhaṁ praśāmyate; avivādaprāptyā ca duḥkhaṁ niruddhyate. From *Samādhirāja Sūtra* as quoted in MKV. pp. 135–36.

The root-cause of duḥkha, in the Mādhyamika system, is the indulging in views (dṛṣṭi) or imagination (kalpanā). Kalpanā, (vikalpa) is avidyā *par excellence*. The real is the indeterminate (śūnya); investing it with a character, determining it as 'this' or 'not this', is making the Real one-sided, partial and unreal. This is unconsciously to negate the real; for all determination is negation. The dialectic then, as the Śūnyatā of dṛṣṭis, is the negation of standpoints, which are the initial negation of the real that is essentially indeterminate (nirvikalpa, niṣprapañca). Correctly understood, Śūnyatā is not annihilation, but the negation of negation; it is the conscious correction of an initial unconscious falsification of the real.

VI THE CONCEPTION OF NIRVĀṆA

Buddhism had always maintained that though the state of nirvāṇa cannot be expressed in words, it is real. "There is the not-born, the not-become, the not-created, the not-compounded. . . . If there were not this not-born etc. . . . there could be no escape from this world of compounded things." "There is the realm where there is neither earth nor water . . . neither the boundless realm of space nor boundless consciousness. . . . This I call neither coming nor going nor standing, neither origination nor annihilation. Without support, without beginning, without foundation is this. The same is the end of suffering."[1] It is even spoken of in positive terms as "a reality beyond all suffering and change, as unfading, still, undecaying, taintless, as peace and blissful. It is an island, the shelter, the refuge and the goal."[2] We are expressly forbidden to consider Nirvāṇa—the state of the Tathāgata after death—as annihilation. It is one of the four sets of questions declared inexpressible by the Lord. The Mādhyamika conception of Nirvāṇa can be understood as bringing out the deeper significance of the Buddhist conception by a trenchant criticism of the Vaibhāṣika and Sautrāntika views on the subject.

A distinction is usually made between upadhiśeṣa and nirupadhiśeṣa or pari-Nirvāṇa.[3] The former is the total cessation of Ignorance

[1] *Udāna* VIII, 3 and 2 cf. also *Itivuttaka*, p. 37 (43).

[2] asankhatam ca vo bhikkhave desissāmi asaṁkhatagāmiñca maggam . . . anāsavanca . . . saccam . . . param . . . nipuṇam . . . ajajjaram . . . dhuvam . . . sāntam . . . amatam . . . panītam . . . sivam . . . khemam . . . abbhūtam . . . antikadhamma . . . nibbānam . . . dīpam tāṇam . . . saraṇam . . . *Sam. N.* IV, p. 368 ff.

[3] MKV. p. 519.

and of the passions, though the body and the mind continue to function but without passions. This state corresponds to the jīvanmukti of the Vedānta and Sāṅkhya. Buddha after his enlightenment is a representative example. Nirupadhiśeṣa Nirvāṇa is the state of final release where even the skandhas, which constitute empirical existence, have totally ceased. The Mahāyānists added one more variety—the Apratiṣṭhita Nirvāṇa, the state of the Bodhisattva who shuns retiring into Final Release, although fully entitled to it, and who by his free choice devotes himself to the service of all beings.

The question is: Is nirupadhiśeṣa or (pari-) Nirvāṇa, the goal of spiritual discipline, a state of annihilation, a lifeless blank? Phenomenal existence is conceived by the Vaibhāṣika as the play of ultimate discrete elements (the dharmas) flowing under the force of the substance-view (satkāyadṛṣṭi) and its attendant passions; they thus engender the *upādāna* skandhas (conditioned existence) which are pain (duḥkha). By the operation of prajñā, assisted by the practice of virtues and mind-concentration, the elements are separated and converted into their non-co-operating state.[1] As the defiling forces (saṁskāras) have ceased, the elements stand in their pure undefiled state (anāsrava dharma). Is the state of Nirvāṇa that is engendered by prajñā any reality at all? Stcherbatsky holds very pronounced views on the subject:

> "When all manifestations are stopped, all forces extinct, remains the lifeless residue. It is impersonal eternal death, and it is a separate element, a reality, the reality of elements in their lifeless condition. This reality is very similar to the reality of the Sāṅkhya's undifferentiated matter (prakṛti); it is eternal absolute death. . . .
>
> "The moral law conduces through a very long process of evolution the living world into a state of final quiescence where there is no life, but something lifeless, inanimate. In this sense, the Vaibhāṣika outlook resembles the materialism of modern science.[2]

This is rather an overstatement.[3] The Vaibhāṣikas or any school of Buddhism never took Nirvaṇa as nothing, but as an *asaṁskṛta dharma*, some sort of noumenal unconditioned reality behind the play of phenomena. True, it does not have the colour and vivacity of

[1] pratisaṁkhyā-nirodho yo visaṁyogaḥ pṛthak. AKV. p. 16.

[2] *Buddhist Nirvāṇa*. pp. 27–9.

[3] Stcherbatsky's view has been subjected to a sustained criticism by Dr. N. Dutt in his *Aspects of Mahāyāna*. pp. 154 ff.

the empirical flux; it is however a dharma, an existent real. As being identical with the state of the Tathāgata after his death, no Buddhist school ever denied its reality. Only, it was in-expressible; it is not bhāva (being); because, being *asaṁskṛta* it is not subject to birth, decay and death like an empirical thing. It is not abhāva (non-being) either, as it is not merely the total cessation of things, the example of the blowing out of a lamp notwithstanding. The Vaibhāṣika is definite that nirvāṇa is not mere negation, it is a *Dharma in* which there is the absence of the saṁskāras; in itself it is a positive entity.[1] It is against this bhāva conception of Nirvāṇa that Nāgārjuna's criticism is directed principally. He shows that Nirvāṇa cannot be a bhāva and asamskṛta (anupādāna) at once.[2] For that very reason it cannot be taken as the destruction of kleśas and karma supervening at a particular stage in the course of things. Nirvāṇa would then become transitory and accidental (conditioned as it is by causes).[3]

Two chief features distinguish the Mādhyamika from the Vaibhāṣika conception of Nirvāṇa. For the latter the discrete existences (saṁskṛta dharmas) are really changed into another state of inoperative existence (asaṃskṛta dharma). The Mādhyamika brings out by his criticism that there is no change in things; if the kleśas were real, they could not be reduced to nothing. There is only change in our outlook, not in reality. Nirvāṇa is "what is not abandoned nor acquired; what is not annihilation nor eternality; what is not destroyed nor created."[4] The function of prajñā is not to transform the real, but only to create a change in our attitude towards it.[5] The change is

[1] "pradyotasyeva nirvāṇaṁ vimokṣas tasya cetasa" ity uktam. na ca pradyotasya nivṛttir bhāva ity upapadyate. ucyate naitad evaṁ vijñeyam: tṛṣṇāyāḥ kṣayaḥ tṛṣṇākṣaya iti. kiṁ tarhi tṛṣṇāyāḥ kṣayo' sminniti nirvāṇākhye dharme saṭi bhavati sa tṛṣṇākṣaya iti vaktavyam. pradīpaś ca dṛṣṭānta-mātram; tátrāpi yasmin sati cetaso vimokṣo bhavatīti veditavyam iti. MKV. p. 525.

[2] bhāvaś ca yadi nirvāṇaṁ nirvāṇaṁ saṁskṛtaṁ bhavet. nāsaṁskṛto hi vidyate bhāvaḥ kvacana kaścana bhāvaś ca yadi nirvāṇam anupādāya tat katham MK. XXV, 5–6.

[3] MK. XXV, 8–9; MKV. pp. 527 ff.

[4] svabhāvena hi vyavasthitānāṁ kleśānāṁ skandhānāṁ ca svabhāvasyānapāyitvāt kuto nivṛttir, yatas tannivṛttyā nirvāṇam . . . yadi khalu śūnyavadinaḥ kleśānāṁ skandhānāṁ vā nivrttilakṣaṇaṁ nirvāṇam necchanti, kiṁ lakṣaṇaṁ tarhīcchanti. ucyate;
"aprahīṇam asamprāptam anucchinnam aśāśvatam;
aniruddham anutpannam etan nirvāṇam ucyate." MKV. p. 521.

[5] na prajñā aśūnyān bhāvān śūnyān karoti; bhāvā eva śūnyāḥ.

epistemic (subjective), not ontological (objective). The real is as it has ever been. This is the Copernican revolution that the Mādhyamika dialectic ushered in Buddhism and in Indian philosophy.

This leads to the other contention of the Mādhyamika that there is no difference whatever between Nirvāṇa and Saṁsāra; Noumenon and Phenomena are not two separate sets of entities, nor are they two states of the same thing.[1] The absolute is the only real; it is the reality of saṁsāra, which is sustained by false construction (kalpanā). The absolute looked at through the thought-forms of constructive imagination is the empirical world; and conversely, the absolute is the world viewed *sub specie aeternitatis*, without these distorting media of thought.[2]

Nirvāṇa is not an ens (bhāva) or abhāva (non-ens), etc.; it is the *abandonment of such considerations of the real* (bhāvābhāva-parāmarśakṣayo nirvāṇam).[3] This is in full accord with the teaching of Buddha asking us to abandon the existential (bhava-dṛṣṭi) and non-existential (vibhava-dṛṣṭi) views.[4] This is the true significance of the avyākṛta (Inexpressibles) regarding the nature of the Tathāgata—whether he exists after death or does not or both or neither.[5] Nirvāṇa as one with the Absolute is free from thought-determinations. And only by leaving these do we attain Nirvāṇa.

The Mādhyamika conception of Nirvāṇa comes very close to the Advaita notion of mukti as brahmabhāva. In the Mādhyamika, however, Nirvāṇa is not identified with consciousness or bliss. For the Vedānta, mukti is not merely absolute existence, free from suffering, but consciousness and bliss as well—cit and ānanda. The Vedānta by a critique of experience shows Brahman as the unconditionedly self-evident being (sākṣād aparokṣād brahma) which makes knowledge possible.[6] The feeling of pleasure we experience in the objects is but the infinite bliss of Brahman in a limited impure form.[7] Mokṣa is the removal of these limitations; and ānanda, which

[1] MK. XXV, 19, 20.

[2] MK. XXV, 9.

[3] tad evaṁ na kasyacin nirvāṇe prahāṇaṁ nāpi kasyacin nirodha iti vijñeyam. tataś ca *sarvakalpanākṣayarūpam* eva nirvāṇam. tathoktam *Ārya Ratnāvalyām*: na cābhāvo'pi nirvāṇaṁ kuta evāsya bhāvatā; bhavābhāva-parāmarśa-kṣayo nirvāṇam ucyate. MKV. p. 524.

[4] MK. XXV, 10.

[5] MK. XXV, 17–8.

[6] cf. *Vedānta Paribhāṣā* Chap. I.

[7] etasyaivānandasya anyāni bhūtāni mātrām upajīvanti.
ko evānyāt kaḥ prāṇyād yad eṣa ākāśa ānando na syāt. *Taitt. Up.* III.

is the nature of Brahman, emerges in full measure. The Mādhyamika seems to stop with the *that* or the bare assertion of the Absolute as the implicate of phenomena; the Vedānta proceeds further to define the *what* or the nature (svarūpa) of Brahman as Consciousness and Bliss.

Metaphysically, the Mādhyamika Nirvāṇa is indèterminate and cannot be identified with the Good or Bliss. From the religious standpoint, however, it is identified with the Tathāgata—God. Nirvāṇa is the transcendent life of the Spirit.

CHAPTER ELEVEN

ABSOLUTE AND TATHĀGATA

I TATHĀGATA NECESSARY AS THE MEDIATOR BETWEEN ABSOLUTE AND PHENOMENA

THE Tathāgata, it was pointed out before, is the principle of mediation between the Absolute that is transcendent to thought (śūnya) and phenomenal beings. The need for a mediator is felt in all absolutism; Vedānta has recourse to Īśvara, apart from Brahman, to account for the revelation of truth; in the Mādhyamika and Vijñānavāda that function is performed by the Tathāgata.

Śūnyatā does not need to be declared as Śūnyatā; the Real or the Truth is not constituted by our knowing or not knowing it as such. If our knowing were to constitute it, the real would be relative to the person knowing it and the circumstances under which it is known. To accept this would be to accept the Protogorean maxim, "Man is the measure of all things", with all its implications. Nothing would, in that case, be false, every knowledge being true for the person in that particular context. But Truth is impersonal, true for all and for all time. Prajñā or Śūnyatā is bhūtakoṭi or dharmatā, the intrinsic nature of all things; it is Tathatā—the 'Thatness', invariable for all time (tathābhāvo'vikāritvam[1]). It does not suffer by *not* being taught (declared as the Truth); nor does it suffer by *being taught* either.[2] It is not a necessary part of Truth that it should be known and declared as truth.

A being confined to the phenomenal sphere cannot know the Absolute; all his experience is in and through the categories of thought which are saṁvṛti (avidyā). The Absolute cannot *know* the truth; it is itself the Truth. *A fortiori*, it cannot declare the truth; this requires,

[1] *tathābhāvo'vikāritvaṁ sadaiva sthāyitā.* sarvadānutpāda eva hy agnyādīnāṁ paranirapekṣatvād akṛtrimatvāt svabhāva ity ucyate. MKV. p. 265.

[2] yā dharmāṇāṁ dharmatā sā deśyamānāpi tāvaty eva, adeśyamānāpi tāvad eva. ASP. p. 196. See also p. 307.

cf. the *Śālistamba Sūtra* passage: utpādād vā tathāgatānām anutpādād va tathāgatānāṁ sthitaivaiṣā dharmāṇāṁ dharmatā. Quoted in MKV. p. 40; *Daśabhūmikā* VIII (p. 65); BCAP, p. 588; *Bhāmatī*, II, ii, 19 (p. 526). See *Sam. N.* II, p. 25 for the Pāli parallel.

besides knowledge, adequate and appropriate instruments of communication. Only a being which enjoys a sort of dual existence, having one foot in phenomena and the other in the Absolute, can possibly know the Absolute and reveal it to others. A difference is therefore made between Tathatā (the Real or Absolute Truth) and Tathā*gata*, who *knows* the truth.[1] Prajñāpāramitā is, at many places in the *Aṣṭasāhasrikā* and other texts, taken as the mother of the Buddhas.[2] From time to time the Buddhas, out of great compassion, condescend from their exalted position to reveal the truth to all beings (gods, men and lowly creatures).

The nature of the Absolute as Śūnyatā does not include the revelatory function that is invariably associated with Buddha—Tathāgata. The Absolute is the impersonal reality underlying all phenomena; Tathāgata is an Exalted Personality (bhagavān), a being freed of limitations and endowed with excellences. Though Śūnyatā does not necessarily imply the Tathāgata, it does not, however, lose its nature by freely manifesting itself as a Person, as God. It is the nature of the Good to 'overflow'. The Tathāgata is an emanation of the Absolute, to adopt a significant Neo-Platonic term.

Two possible objections may be raised against this position: one that there is no necessity for such a being; any one can come to have a knowledge of the absolute by self-effort; and second that a being intermediate between the Absolute and man is logically untenable; one may be the Absolute or a phenomenal being, and not both at once.

Can we dispense with revelation altogether, and yet acquire a knowledge of the Absolute through purely logical means? A being confined to the phenomenal has no obvious means of knowing what admittedly is beyond that sphere. His sense-organs and even intellect (buddhi) are conditioned by avidyā. All his knowledge is in and through the categories of thought, buddhi (Reason), and buddhi is saṁvṛti. But cannot the dialectical consciousness, because of its own inner dynamism, afford us a knowledge of the absolute? Will not the very conflict in Reason, the dialectical play of thesis and anti-thesis,

[1] atītā tathatā yadvat pratyutpannāpy anāgatā;
sarvadharmās *tathā-dṛṣṭās tenoktaḥ sa tathāgataḥ*. CŚV. p. 32.
sarvākārāviparīta-*dharma-daiśikatvena* parārtha-sampadā tathāgatāḥ.
AAA. p. 62.

[2] prajñāpāramitā tathāgatānāṁ janayitrī. ASP. p. 254.
ato nirjātās tathāgatāḥ. ibid.
buddhasya mātre. . . . *Abhisamayālaṅkāra Kārikā*, VI, 1.

resolve the conflict and lead us beyond Reason? The crust of buddhi (Reason) can break owing to internal pressure, as it may do because of external impact. It has been shown that the conflict is total and inevitable in philosophy, as systems of philosophy with totally divergent views arise and clamour for recognition as the true and only picture of reality. The intenser the conflict the quicker will be its denouement. Prajñā should emerge as the finale of the process.

The abstract possibility of such a contingent emergence of Prajñā may be conceded. Perhaps, the conception of the *Pratyeka Buddha* as a person having derived the knowledge all from himself, without reference to revelation or Buddhas, has this philosophical basis.[1]

There are some significant considerations why the above contention cannot be accepted in an unmodified form. The conflict in Reason does occur, and the dialectical consciousness is already at work within us. It is not, however, an automatic mechanical process.[2] If it were so, every one is bound, as a matter of course and in spite of himself even, to have Prajñā and reach the Absolute; the progress of the individual cannot be retarded or accelerated to any extent. This should obviate the necessity to learn or to teach philosophy. Such, however, is not the case.

All this is opposed to our mode of learning; we usually learn from the teacher. Even with regard to innate truths and axioms, it is the teacher who directs our attention to them. The dialectical consciousness is no doubt present, but it is the enlightened who can make us appreciate its significance. Buddha does not create the dialectical consciousness; but it is he who makes us appreciate its full significance. The case of Pratyeka Buddhas may appear to be an exception, as they effect their enlightenment without the help of a teacher. But here too it can be said that in their previous births they had already received the necessary instruction.[3]

[1] Nāgārjuna seems to concede this possibility when he says:
sambuddhānām anutpāde śrāvakāṇāṁ punaḥ kṣaye;
jñānaṁ Pratyeka-Buddhānām asaṁsargāt pravartate. MK. XVIII, 12.

[2] This would be a species of fortuitous origination like that of adhītyasamutpāda, which Buddha condemns most emphatically. The Ājīvaka-theory advocated this kind of automatic spiritual progress. See Barua: *Pre-Buddhistic Indian Philosophy*, pp. 316 ff.

[3] Candrakīrti actually says this: tathāpi pūrvajanmāntara-dharmatattva-śravaṇabalād eva . . . svāyambhuvaṁ jñānaṁ bhavati. MKV. p. 378.

Ārya Deva hints at this with regard to the future birth:
iha yady api tattvajño nirvāṇaṁ nādhigacchati;
prāpnoty ayatnato'vaśyaṁ punar-janmani karmavad. CŚ. VIII 22.

The other objection against the acceptance of Tathāgata is that an amphibious being partaking of both phenomena and the noumenon at once is logically unsound. Personality is incompatible with freedom and *vice versa*. Either a being is within phenomena as long as he has not achieved nirvāṇa, or he is the Absolute. There is no intermediary stage, and no intermediary being too can be admitted. The moment a man attains Prajñā, he is swallowed up in the absolute. There is no stage when he can declare that he is freed; he cannot leave any kind of record. Logically, he cannot even know that he is free: as long as he is in bondage, it would be false if he took himself to be free; and when he is free, he is not longer there to know that he is free, as he is immediately merged in the absolute. Freedom would in that case be an unconscious process. If this were a true state of affairs, how does the objector know that there is the absolute. For aught, he may become the absolute; but he cannot know anything about the absolute, even that it is, as long as he is in phenomena. Not only he cannot have that knowledge himself, but he is precluded from deriving it through others. For *ex hypothesi*, other freed men too share the same predicament, and an Īśvara or Tathāgata is not accepted. The objection involves a contradiction: it denies the possibility of knowledge of the absolute on the part of any phenomenal being; but the objection itself can be made only when a knowledge of the absolute is possessed by the objector.

Free, egoless, personality must be accepted. It is not that as one achieves freedom one is absorbed into the absolute wholly and at once. Though free, one has still enough of the phenomenal in one to feel kinship with fellow beings and help them out of saṁsāra. Freedom does not repel personality; nor does all personality mean bondage. There can be a Free Person, and Buddha is that.

The account that has come down to us of Gautama the Buddha's[1] attainment of Bodhi and his initial hesitation to teach and later acceptance of it out of compassion for beings[2] is proof of the existence and necessity of a Free Phenomenal Being.

[1] See the first Section of *Mahāvagga* (Vinaya Piṭaka).

[2] ataś ca pratyudāvṛttaṁ cittaṁ deśayituṁ muneḥ;
dharmaṁ matvāsya dharmasya mandair duravagāhatām.
MK. XXIV, 12 and MKV. p. 498.
. . . yaḥ saddharmam adeśayed; anukampām upādāya taṁ namasyāmi Gautamam. MK XXVII, 30.

II CONCEPTION OF GODHEAD

The Absolute (Śūnya) is the universal impersonal reality of the world. Although identical in essence with the absolute, Buddha is primarily a Person. He is the object of worship and devotion. Buddha's real nature can be realised only in the appropriate religious consciousness and accredited Buddhist tradition. We can logically demonstrate, at best, the need for a mediating principle between the absolute and phenomena. For the nature and the manner of the mediator we have to fall back upon religion.

Buddha is Bhagavān, God, endowed as he is with power and perfection. He possesses, in entirety, all power, splendour, fame, wealth, knowledge and act.[1] He has completely eliminated all passion and karma and the two obscurations (kleśāvaraṇa and jñeyāvaraṇa).[2] He is omniscient (sarvajñā and sarvākārajña), having a full knowledge of the Absolute Truth (prajña-pāramitā) and of the empirical world likewise. His wisdom is spoken of as consisting of five varieties: (1) "The perfectly pure intuition of the Absolute, there being no bifurcation into the 'is' and the 'is not' (advaya-jñānam); (2) the knowledge resembling a mirror wherein everything is reflected (ādarśa-jñāna); (3) the discriminative knowledge precisely cognising all the separate objects and elements without confounding any of them (pratyavekṣaṇājñāna); (4) the cognition of the unity, the equality of one-self and of others as possessed of the unique Essence of Buddhahood (samatājñāna); and (5) the active wisdom pursuing the welfare of all living beings (kṛtyanuṣṭhānajñāna)."[2] The first two forms of knowledge, especially the first, belong to the Dharmakāya of the Buddha; the third and the fourth (pratyavekṣaṇā and samatājñāna) to the Sambhoga Kāya (body of Bliss) and the pursuit of the welfare of beings to the Nirmāṇakāya (Apparitional Body). Besides omniscient knowledge, Buddha possesses several other perfections such as Ten Powers—(daśabala),[3] Four confidences (catvāri vaiśāradyāni), Thirty-two mercies (dvātriṁśat mahākaruṇāḥ) etc.

[1] "aiśvaryasya samagrasya rūpasya yaśasaḥ śriyaḥ;
jñānasyātha prayatnasya ṣaṇṇāṁ bhaga iti śrutiḥ."
so'syāstīti samagraiśvaryādimān Bhagavān.
"kleśa-karma tathā janma kleśajñeyāvṛtī tathā;
yena vaipakṣikā bhagnās teneha Bhagavān smṛtaḥ." AAA. p. 9.

[2] Obermiller's *The Doctrine of Prajñāpāramitā*, p. 45. *Acta Orientalia*, Vol. XI.

[3] *Mahāvyutpatti*. pp. 2–4 (B. Budd. Edn.).

Kumārila argues, with great force and no little ingenuity, that only the Impersonal and Eternal Word (Veda) can be omniscient, and not any person. A person is subject to passions and idiosyncracies[1] His powers of cognition are limited. It may well be that by practice he may come to possess knowledge of more things than others, but this can never lead to knowledge of all things.[2] Nor is it possible for any one to know all the minute and varied details of things and their parts.[3] This raises the question: what kind of knowledge is meant by omniscience: is it of the particulars or of the universals alone: does that knowledge function successively or simultaneously?[4] Buddha, Vardhamāna, Kapila and others all claim omniscience; it is difficult to decide who is really that and who is not.[5] One thing is certain that they contradict each other, and no two of them can be valid. Kumārila concludes: A seer of the super-sensuous does not therefore exist; whoever knows anything knows it through the Eternal Word (Veda).[6]

There is, however, no valid objection against the existence of an omniscient person. A fact cannot be denied because it is not cognised by all and sundry. There is positive evidence of the omniscience of the Buddha; for, following the path taught by him one is freed of saṁsāra. Most of the objections against the acceptance of omniscience are based on the assumption that it is the *acquisition* of a new faculty, or that it is a laborious process of accretion of information. It is on the other hand a case of divesting the mind of its accidental defects which have crept into it. In itself the intellect is transparent and has natural affinity with the real.[7] By the contemplation of the unreality of things (nairātmya-bhāvanā) it is possible to void the

1 *Śloka Vārttika*. p. 74 (Chou. Edn.)
Cf. doṣāḥ santi na santīti puṁvācyeṣu hi śaṁkyate;
śrutau kartur abhāvān nu doṣaśaṁkaiva nāsti naḥ. TS. p. 585.

2 TS. p. 826–27.
yatrāpy atiśayo dṛṣṭaḥ sa svārthānatilanghanāt;
dūrasūkṣmādi-dṛṣṭau syān na rūpe śrotravṛttitā.
Ślo. Vārt. 114 of the *Codanāsūtra*).

3 TS. p. 821.

4 TS. p. 844.

5 sugato yadi sarvajñaḥ kapilo neti kā pramā;
athobhāvapi sarvajñau matabhedas tayoḥ katham. TS. p. 822.

6 tasmād atīndriyārthānāṁ sākṣād draṣṭā na vidyate;
vacanena tu nityena yaḥ paśyati sa paśyati. TS. p. 828.

7 prabhāsvaram idaṁ cittaṁ tattvadarśana-sātmakam;
prakṛtyaiva sthitaṁ yasmān malās tv āgantavo matāḥ. TS p. 895.

intellect of all defects—kleśas. Owing to the removal of the obscuring factors omniscience shines out, as there is nothing to obstruct its vision.[1] Those that deny omniscience really deny the possibility of the intellect to be free from defects; they must logically deny freedom (mukti) too.

It might be said that when a person is freed of all defects (kleśa) he *ipso facto* loses all power of ideation, and communication of the truth is not possible. For, buddhi has ceased to function for the enlightened Buddha. He is absorbed in the contemplation of the Absolute; he is in self-contemplation. It is even held that the Buddha himself did not utter a word from the time that he attained Bodhi till his final release.[2] How then has his teaching been propagated?

Several answers have been given by the Mādhyamika teachers. Nāgārjuna says in the *Catuḥ Stava*: "Though, Lord, you have not uttered a single word, all the votaries have been satisfied by the teaching of the doctrine."[3] Candrakīrti suggests that the Lord uttered but once the word at the time of his Bodhi, and it has, according to the needs and spiritual attainments of the votaries, been active in dispelling their ignorance.[4] Buddha is also compared to the wish-fulfilling precious stone (cintāmaṇi) and the kalpataru tree, both of which give out the different favours sought of them by different votaries.[5] Likewise, the diversity of the Lord's teaching is dependent on the different spiritual temperament and maturity of the seekers after truth (vineyavaśāt). The initial incentive to propagate the truth, on the part of the Lord, is the result of his resolve (praṇidhāna) to strive for the good of all beings made previous to his attainment of Buddhahood. That benign intention of his contrives to influence

[1] pratyakṣīkṛta-nairātmye na doṣo labhate sthitim;
tadviruddhatayā dīpre pradīpe timiraṁ yathā.
sākṣātkṛtiviśeṣāc ca doṣo nāsti savāsanaḥ;
sarvjñatvam ataḥ siddhaṁ sarvāvaraṇa-muktitaḥ. TS. Verses 3338–9.

[2] yāṁ ca rātriṁ, śāntamate, tathāgato'nuttarāṁ samyak-sambodhim abhisambuddhaḥ, yāṁ ca rātrim anupādāya parinirvāsyati, atrāntare tathāgatenaikam apyakṣaram nodāhṛtaṁ na vyāhṛtaṁ nāpi pravyāharati nāpi pravyāhariṣyati. MKV. pp. 366 and 539.

[3] nodāhṛtaṁ tvayā kiṁcid ekam apyakṣaraṁ vibho;
kṛtsnaś ca vaineyajano dharma-varṣeṇa tarṣitaḥ.
Nāgārjuna's *Catuḥstava* quoted in BCAP. p. 420.

[4] MKV. p. 366.

[5] cintāmaṇiḥ kalpatarur yathecchāparipūraṇaḥ;
vineya-praṇidhānābhyāṁ jinabimbaṁ tathekṣyate. BCA. IX, 36.

his intellect even after the Bodhi, like the continuance of the rotation of the potter's wheel even after the pitcher is made.[1]

Besides his omniscience and other perfections, what makes Buddha a loving God is his great compassion (mahākaruṇā) and his active and abiding interest in the welfare not only of suffering humanity but of all beings. His karuṇā is great (mahā) as it knows no limitation of any kind; his mercy is for all, the deserving and the undeserving, for the lowly creatures especially; it is not for a short period of time but for aeons and aeons; the quality of his karuṇā is intense and pure. His love is more intense than that of a father for his only dear son; it does not expect any gain, recognition or respect.[2] "No activity of the Buddhas", says Ārya Deva, "is without intention; their very breath is for the good of beings."[3]

This Great Compassion is not of a sentimental kind, grand but blind. It is born of the realisation of the universality and unity of all being (samatā). Nāgārjuna says in his *Catuḥstava*: "Of the essential non-difference between the Buddhas and all beings, of oneself and others, is the Equality (samatā) taught by you."[4] As one with the Dharmadhātu all beings are equal. The Buddhas have realised this oneness, and it is their sacred function to lead all to a realisation of this basic truth. The Tathāgata-garbha (the germ of Buddhahood) present equally in all beings is to be made manifest.

Śūnyatā and karuṇā (Wisdom and Compassion) are the two essential characteristics of God in Mahāyāna Buddhism. Śūnyatā is Prajñā, non-dual intuition; and in having this, the Tathāgata is non-different from the Absolute-Tathatā, Śūnya. Karuṇā takes note of the plight of the suffering world, and is an unceasing act of grace, condescension. It is born of Buddha's sympathy, sense of equality,

[1] ye buddhasya bhagavato vineyāḥ, tadupādhiphalaviśeṣapratilambhahetu-kuśala-karma paripākāt; tadvaśāt. praṇidhānavaśāc ca, yat pūrvaṁ bodhisat-tvāvasthāyām aneka-prakāraṁ bhagavatā sattvārtha-sampādanaṁ praṇi-hitaṁ tasyākṣepavaśāt. kulālacakra-bhramaṇākṣepa-nyāyenābhogena pravar-tanāt. BCAP. p. 419.

[2] mahākaruṇām evāśritya, priyaikaputrādhikatara-premapātra-sakala-tribhuvana-jano, na lābha-satkāra-pratyupakārādi-lipsayā. MKV. pp. 592–3.

[3] "na ceṣtā kila buddhānām asti kācid akāraṇā;
niḥśvāso'pi hitāyaiva prāṇināṁ sampravartate." CŚ. (101) Fragments.
śarīra-vāca-manasāṁ pravṛttiḥ svārthā muner nāsti na cāpyanarthā;
mahā-kṛpāviṣṭa-viśuddha-buddheḥ parodayāyaiva punaḥ pravṛttiḥ.
Catuḥśatikā. p. 407, Fragments pd. by MM. H. P. *Ś*āstri.

[4] buddhānāṁ sattvadhātoś ca yenābhinnatvam arthataḥ; ātmanaś ca pareṣāṁ ca samatā tena te matā." BCAP. p. 590.

with creatures. As identical with Prajñāpāramitā, Buddha is the Absolute and belongs to the region of the paramārtha. As possessed of Karuṇā and owing to his essential equality with all beings, he is in the region of phenomena (saṁvṛti). He is thus an amphibious being, having one foot in the Absolute and the other in phenomena.[1] And it is because of this he performs the function of a mediator between the two.

In the Buddhist Pantheon, Mañjuśrī and Avalokiteśvara are the concrete expressions of these two aspects of god-head. A purer conception of God it would be difficult to find in other religions. In Tāntric Buddhism, these appear as Prajñā and Upāya respectively, and are comparable to Śiva and Śakti of the Brāhmanical Tantra. The dual aspect of Buddha's nature is reflected in the Bodhisattvas whose ideal He is. Their influence permeates the world.

III THE TRIKĀYA OF BUDDHA

The dual nature of Buddha, as one with the Absolute (Śūnya) and at once actively pursuing the welfare of beings, supplies the philosophical basis for the theological conception of the Trikāya of Buddha. The three bodies or aspects of Buddha are:[2]

(1) The Dharma Kāya—The Cosmical body is his essential nature; it is one with the Absolute;

(2) Sambhogakāya —The body of bliss; and the

(3) Nirmāṇakāya —Assumed body.

As the Dharmakāya, Buddha fully realises his identity with the Absolute (dharmatā, śūnyatā) and unity (samatā) with all beings. It is the oneness with the Absolute that enables Buddha to intuit the Truth, which it is his sacred function to reveal to phenomenal beings. This is the fountain-source of his implicit strength which he concretises in the finite sphere. The Sambhoga Kāya is the concrete manifestation to himself (svasambhoga) and to the elect (parasam-

[1] taduktam: yataḥ prajñā tattvaṁ bhajati karuṇā saṁvṛtim atah;
tavābhūn niḥsattvaṁ jagad iti yathārthaṁ vimṛśataḥ.
yadā cāviṣṭo'bhūr daśabala-jananyā karuṇayā;
tadā te' bhūd ārte suta iva pituḥ prema jagati. Quoted in BCAP. p. 488.

[2] svābhāvikaḥ sāmbhogiko nairmāṇiko' paras tathā;
dharmakāyaḥ sakāritraś caturdhā samudīritaḥ. AAA. p. 26.
See also *Mahāyāna Sūtrālaṅkāra* pp. 45 ff.

bhoga) the power and splendour of god-head. In furtherance of the great resolve to succour all beings, Buddha incarnates himself from time to time in forms best calculated to achieve this end (nirmāṇakāya).

The *Prajñā-pāramitā* texts repeatedly ask us to consider Buddha as Dharmakāya, and not in the overt form which appears to us.[1] Dharmakāya is the essence, the reality of the universe. It is completely free from every trace of duality. It is the very nature of the universe and is therefore also called the svābhāvika kāya.[2] It would be, however, not exactly correct to take the Dharmakāya to be the abstract metaphysical principle—Śūnyatā or Suchness (tathatā). The Dharmakāya[3] is still a Person, and innumerable merits and powers etc. are ascribed to him.[4]

[1] ye māṁ rūpeṇa cādrākṣur ye māṁ ghoṣeṇa anvayuḥ
mithyāprahāṇa-prasṛtā na māṁ drakṣyanti te janāḥ
dharmato Buddhā draṣṭavyā dharmakāyā hi nāyakāḥ
dharmatā cāpy avijñeyā na sā śakyā vijānitum
Vajracchedikā. p. 43, quoted in MKV. p. 448; BCAP. p. 421.

uktaṁ hy etad Bhagavatā:
dharmakāyā Buddhā Bhagavantaḥ. mā khalu punar imaṁ bhikṣavaḥ satkāyaṁ kāyaṁ manyadhvaṁ dharma-kāya pariniṣpattito mām bhikṣavo drakṣyanty eṣa ca Tathāgatakāyaḥ. ASP. p. 94. mukhyato dharmakāyas tathāgataḥ. AAA. p. 181. See also pp. 205, 521 ff.

[2] sarvākārāṁ viśuddhiṁ ye dharmāḥ prāptā nirāsravāḥ;
svābhāviko muneḥ kāyas teṣām prakṛti-lakṣaṇaḥ. AAA. p. 523.

[3] *The Avataṁska Sūtra*, copious excerpts from which are given by Suzuki, characterises the Dharmakāya thus:
"The Dharmakāya, though manifesting itself in the triple world, is free from impurities and desires. It unfolds itself here, there, and everywhere responding to the call of karuṇā. It is not an individual reality; it is not a false existence, but is universal and pure. It comes from nowhere, it goes to nowhere; it does not assert itself; nor is it subject to annihilation. It is for ever serene and eternal. It is the One; devoid of all determinations. This Body of Dharma has no boundary, no quarters, but is embodied in all bodies. Its freedom or spontaniety is incomprehensible, its spiritual presence in things corporeal is incomprehensible. . . . The universe becomes, but this Body for ever remains. It is free from all opposites and contraries, yet it is working in all things to lead them to Nirvāṇa." (*Outlines of Mahāyāna*, pp. 223–4.)

[4] See AAA. pp. 523 ff. Buston (*History of Buddhism*. Vol. I pp. 128–9) says: "The Sanskrit name for the cosmical Body is dharmakāya. The word Kāya is derived from the verb-root *ci*—to collect, accumulate. (The Cosmical Body) is thus regarded as the accumulation, the aggregate of all the elements, uninfluenced (by defiling agencies)! *The Satyadvaya-vibhanga* accordingly says: The cosmical Body is thus called, Being the aggregate of all the elements. The substratum of all the unthinkable virtues, And the essence of all things, the nature of which agrees with logic."

The Body of Bliss (Sambhoga-kāya) is so called because it represents (an existence characterised by) the full enjoyment of the Truth of the great Vehicle, as it is said: "Perfectly enjoying the Truth or since it takes delight in the Truth."[1] The body of Bliss is the reflection of the Cosmic Body in the empirical world in a corporeal form. Buddha appears here as a Supreme God, abiding in the Akaniṣṭha heaven, surrounded by a host of Bodhisattvas. He is endowed with 32 principal and 80 secondary marks of beauty and excellence.[2] This body is the result of the previous virtuous deeds. The descriptions given of Buddha in the opening sections of the Mahāyāna Sūtras are of this body. The *Śatasāhasrikā Prajñāpāramitā* may be cited as a good example of this. For pages on end there are descriptions of every part of Buddha's body, of rays proceeding from his head, hands and feet and even fingers, reaching up to the extremities of the world.[3] Only the Bodhisattvas who have reached the tenth stage can perceive the body of Bliss, and not others, is the opinion of some Mādhyamika teachers.[4] The Sambhogakāya is the vibhūti (glory) of the Lord, a fine example of which we have in the *Bhagavad Gītā* (Chapter XI).

The Nirmāṇa Kāya, usually translated as apparitional body, is really a body *assumed* by Buddha in fulfilment of his resolve to save beings from misery. The manifestation of the body of bliss in the empirical world as Gautama (Śākyamuni) or other previous and succeeding Tathāgatas is the Nirmāṇakāya of Buddha.[5] The advent of a Buddha in the world is not an accident, the lucky chance of a human being happening to attain enlightenment. It is a deliberate descent of the Divinity, incarnating Itself as human being; his

[1] Buston Vol. I, p. 129.

[2] AAA. p. 526: dvātriṁśal lakṣaṇāśītivyañjanātmā muner ayam;
sāmbhogiko mataḥ kāyo mahāyānopabhogataḥ.
A complete list of these characteristics is given in AAA. pp. 526 ff. *Buston* Vol. I. pp. 131–2.

[3] *Śata Sāhasrikā.* pp. 2 ff.

[4] This is the view of Dharmamitra the Mādhyamika, as we learn from *Buston* Vol. I (pp. 131 ff.). His work is called *Prasphuṭapāda*, and is preserved only in Tibetan.

[5] yena Śākyamuni-tathāgatādirūpeṇāsaṁsāraṁ sarvaloka-dhātuṣu sattvānāṁ saṁhitam arthaṁ samaṅkaroty asau kāyaḥ, prabandhatayānuparato nairmāṇiko buddhasya bhagavataḥ . . . tathā coktam:
karoti yena citrāṇi hitāni jagataḥ samam;
ābhavāt so'nupacchinnaḥ kāyo nairmāṇiko muneḥ. AAA. p. 532.

various (twelve principal) acts from birth to passing away into parinirvāṇa are make-believe acts, designed to create a sense of kinship with human beings.[1] Gautama is one of the Buddhas; and the Bodhisattvas are other forms chosen by divinity to help man and other beings. As Haribhadra says: "When some living being requires the explanation of the Doctrine or some other kind of help, then the Lord, by the force of his previous vows, fulfils the purpose of this living being manifesting himself in this or that form."[2] Buddha is the Providence that takes the keenest interest in beings. The particulars with regard to the Kāya conception cannot be logically demonstrated. They are to be taken as revealed to the elect and communicated by them to others.

In the Hīnayāna religion, Gautama the Buddha is an exalted human being, distinguished from the ordinary mankind by his unique and unaided attainment. He was not certainly God before he attained bodhi. The historicity of the Buddha (Śākayamuni) is indispensable for that religion. In Mahāyāna, though Gautama is a historical person, he is not the only Buddha, and his occurrence is *one* of the innumerable acts of divine dispensation. The Mahāyāna religion escapes the predicament of having to depend on any particular historical person as the founder of its religion.

IV ĪŚVARA AND BUDDHA

It should be of interest to compare the Vedānta conception of Īśvara with that of Buddha. In both the systems the highest is the Absolute—Brahman or Śūnya; it is the sole reality. As the absolute transcends thought and empirical modes of existence, it is not possible to attain the knowledge—that the Absolute is real—by beings confined to the phenomenal sphere. The Absolute cannot declare itself as such. There is thus the need, as pointed before, for a mediator who *reveals* the Absolute. Īśvara and the Tathāgata perform this necessary function. Though free, they are however, within phenomena,

[1] See *Buston*, pp. 133 ff. *Uttaratantra of Asanga*. pp. 254 ff. (Obermiller's Trans. *Acta Orientalia* Vol. IX, 1931).

[2] yasya sattvasya yasmin kāle dharma-deśanādikaṁ kriyamāṇam ayātipathyam bhavati, tadā tasyārthakaraṇāya pūrva-praṇi-dhānasamṛddhyā tatpratibhāsānurūpeṇākārenārthakriyākārī Bhagavān iti . . . tathā coktam:
paripākaṁ gate hetau yasya yasya yadā yadā
hitaṁ bhavati kartavyaṁ prathate tasya tasya saḥ. AAA. p. 525.

māyika;[1] they are the free manifestation of the absolute. Īśvara or the Tathāgata is a lower principle than the Absolute. The absolute is realised in the highest knowledge, in the context of the philosophical consciousness. Īśvara or Tathāgata is an object of devotion and worship, and is understood in the context of religious consciousness. Mokṣa or Nirvāṇa is possible only through knowledge (advaita or advaya-jñāna). As an implication of this, both the systems take devotion and other religious acts as but ancillary to knowledge. Religion is subordinate to philosophy, but there is no opposition between them.

The religion that is in consonance with the Mādhyamika or Vedānta absolutism can best be characterised as Pantheism. It is not theism in which there is an absolute difference between God and man as we have in the semitic religions. There is essential and inexpressible identity between man (all beings) and Īśvara or the Tathāgata; both are really the absolute; their difference is superficial, and belongs to the phenomenal region; it is, however, enough to sustain religious consciousness.[2] It need not be supposed that if the difference between the worshipper and the worshipped were not ultimate, religious devotion could not lead to fruitful result. Whether Buddha is ultimately real or not has no relevance with regard to religious acts being fruitful.[3]

The differences between Īśvara and Tathāgata, however, must not be overlooked. To Īśvara is assigned not merely the function of revealing the Truth (Veda); creation, sustenance, destruction and

[1] samyak sambudho'pi māyopamaḥ svapnopamaḥ; samyaksambuddhatvam api māyopamaṁ svapnopamam. ASP. p. 39.
mayopamāj jināt puṇyaṁ sadbhāvo'pi kathaṁ yathā. BCA. IX, 9.
tad evam avidyātmakopādhi-paricchedāpekṣam eveśvarasye-śvaratvaṁ sarvajñatvaṁ sarvaśaktitvaṁ ca na paramārthato vidyayāpāstasarvopādhi-svarūpa ātmanīśitrīśitavya-sarvajñatvādi-vyavahāra upapadyate. *Br. Sūtr. Bhāṣya*, II, i, 14.
syāt parameśvarasyāpīcchāvaśān māyāmayam rūpaṁ sādhakānugrahārtham. *Br. Sūtr. Bhāṣya*, I, i, 20.

[2] satyaṁ neśvarād anyaḥ saṁsārī . . . tathehāpi dehādi-samghātopādhi-sambandha-vivekakṛteśvara-saṁsāri-bheda-mithyābuddhiḥ. *Br. Sūtra Bhāṣya*, I, i, 5.
evam avidyā-kṛta-nāmarūpānurodhīśvaro bhavati . . . sa ca svātmabhūtān eva ghaṭākāśa-sthānīyān . . . jīvākhyān vijñānātmanaḥ pratīṣṭe vyavahāra-viṣaye. Ibid. II, i, 14.

[3] āgamāc ca phalaṁ tatra samvṛtyā tattvato'pi vā;
satyabuddhe kṛtā pūjā saphaleti kathaṁ yathā. BCA. IX, 40.
See BCAP. p. 380.

other cosmic functions (jagad-vyāpāra) are also performed by him.[1] In Buddhism karma takes the place of Īśvara in this regard.

Īśvara reveals the Absolute Truth to phenomenal beings through some extraordinary mechanism of communication, probably in the beginning of every creation; he does not incarnate himself as man for this purpose. He is always free and always the Lord (sadaiva muktaḥ, sadaiva Īśvaraḥ). The Tathāgata, however, descends from his divine plane and takes birth amongst men, conforms to their modes of life, gains their sympathy and reveals the truth through the ordinary methods of communication. The Tathāgata is, to all intents, man perfected, deified by the destruction of passions (kleśa-jñeyāvaraṇa-nivṛttiḥ).[2]

The most characteristic feature of God in Buddhism is the mahākaruṇā that is prepared for any sacrifice for any one and for all time. This active and unceasing interest and effort for the welfare and final release of all beings makes the Tathāgata a very loving and lovable God. It is easily one of the purest and most exalted conceptions of God-head. Not that Īśvara is not conceived as benign and loving, but that the ideal of mahākaruṇā and sarvamukti[3] is not so intensely and intimately expressed as in Buddhism.

[1] Īśvara is not only śāstrayoni, but also the creator and sustainer of the intra-subjective (vyāvahārika) world common to all; the jīvas are the makers of the pratibhāsika world which is private and subjective. He is also the sustainer of the moral order. Neither Brahman, who is beyond the duality of good and evil, nor the jīva, who is not unmixed with evil, can serve as the Norm of the good.

[2] Sarvajñatā, sarvākarajñatā and other godly perfections accrue on the destruction of kleśas. Buddha, to all ordinary intents, *was* in bondage previously (pūrva bandhakoṭi), though he has destroyed that now for ever. Īśvara of the Vedānta and the Yoga systems never had this prior bondage. In Jainism too, Mahāvīra and other Kevalins are conceived as having attained omniscience etc. as a result of the destruction of karma (kṣāyika-jñāna etc.). What distinguishes the Mahāyāna conception from this is that God (the Tathāgata) was never a mere man, but *incarnates himself as* man, and undergoes the usual practices etc. as enactment of his role as a teacher. It is the enactment of descent as man and of ascent to God-head (samyak sambuddhattva).

[3] There are feeble and indistinct references to the doctrine of sarvamukti (Universal Freedom) as the Vedāntic ideal. Freed jīvas attain to Īśvarabhāva or Sākṣibhāva before finally becoming merged into Brahman (bhūyaś cānte viśvamāyānivṛttiḥ). See *Siddhāntaleśa Saṅgraha*, IV, 5, for a discussion of the issue, ekamukti or sarva-mukti.

PART THREE

The Mādhyamika and Allied Systems

CHAPTER TWELVE

THE MĀDHYAMIKA AND SOME WESTERN DIALECTICAL SYSTEMS

HISTORIANS of Indian thought have noticed striking similarities between the absolutist systems of India and some western dialectical systems such as those of Kant, Hegel and Bradley.[1] A comparative study would not materially add to our knowledge of the systems under comparison; it is, however, valuable as establishing affinities, and as precisely differentiating them. There is gain in definition and distinction. A comparative study, to be fruitful, must be made between systems of thought which have *prima facie* generic affinity of standpoint. We should not, in our eagerness to discover affinities of thought, ignore the differences; in fact, our endeavour should be to throw into relief points of specific differences. A comparative study further presupposes an adequate knowledge of the systems compared.

In the course of our exposition of the Mādhyamika system, attention has been drawn at various places to the points of similarity and difference between the Mādhyamika system on the one hand and Kant, Hegel, Bradley, Vedānta and Vijñānavada on the other. It may be advantageous to consider them systematically.

I KANT AND THE MĀDHYAMIKA

1. As has already been pointed out, both the Mādhyamika and Kant initiated the critical phase in philosophy in their respective spheres. They engendered the "Copernican Revolution" by a sustained challenge to dogmatism and speculative metaphysics. They were successful in shifting the centre of philosophical interest from the object to the knowing mind, to Reason. Both were led to this reflective criticism by the impasse created principally by two opposed currents in philosophy: by Rationalism and Empiricism in the case of Kant and

[1] *I.P.* Vol. I, 648, 664 ff. Vol. II pp. 524 ff, (Śaṅkara with Bradley) 527 ff. (Śaṅkara with Kant) 538 ff. (with Hegel) etc. Stcherbatsky: *Buddhist Nirvāṇa* pp. 51 ff. (Mādhyamika with Hegel, Bradley and others).

by the ātma tradition (substance-view) and nairātmya tradition (modal view) in the case of the Mādhyamika. These views gave totally conflicting answers to problems of existence and knowledge. If anything, the opposition between the ātma and the nairātmya points of view was intenser and more sustained and of a longer duration than the one between Rationalism and Empiricism. Both were led, as a consequence of this, to envisage the conflict in all its universality and inevitability as a conflict in Reason.[1] Criticism, dialectic, was born. Dialectic is at once the consciousness of the total and inevitable (antinomical) conflict of Reason and the resolution of it by rising to a higher plane of consciousness.

The purpose of the dialectic is to demonstrate the subjectivity of the categories of thought, namely, that they are of empirical validity and can be significantly used within phenomena only; the Noumenon (tattva) is transcendent to thought. The function of the Dialectic is to show up the pretensions of reason exemplified in the several systems of thought. As analysis or resolution of theories, it is not itself a theory; the Dialectic is not one more speculative system of philosophy. Instead of the usual antithesis between two opposed speculative systems of metaphysics, a newer, deeper, antithesis—that between Dogmatism (dṛṣṭi) and Criticism (śūnyatā, prajñā)—emerges in Kant and the Mādhyamika. Their rejection of speculative philosophy (dṛṣṭi) is final and unqualified. For them, the Dialectic, Criticism, itself is philosophy.

The denial of the competence of Reason to have access to the real creates the duality of what appears in relation to the categories or *a priori* forms of thought (sāṁvṛta—erscheinung), and what is in itself, the unconditioned (tattva, śūnya—Noumenon). The post-Kantian philosophy refuses to accept this gulf as unbridgeable and attempts to resolve this duality. The systems of Fichte, Schelling, Hegel and Schopenhauer can be understood, against the Kantian background, as the diverse ways in which this objective could be attained. In India too, the utter transcendence of the Mādhyamika Absolute (Śūnya), as impervious not only to thought but as unidentifiable with anything in experience, led to the criticism by the Vijñānavāda of the Mādhyamika way, that it pours away the child

[1] "The battle-field of these endless controversies is called metaphysics." (p. 7) . . . "I do not mean by this a critique of books and systems, but of the faculty of *reason in general*, in respect of all knowledge after which it may strive independently of all experience." *Critique*, p. 9.

with the bath in its rejection of dogmatism; the real is no doubt inaccessible to thought, as the Mādhyamika rightly holds, but it can be utterly transcendent only at the peril of being unreal, nothing. To escape this predicament, the real is to be understood as implied in experience. The Vijñānavāda identifies it with Consciousness, the Vedānta with Pure Being. Their criticism of the Mādhyamika position that it advocates the theory of appearance without a ground (nirādhāra-bhrama) is inspired by the necessity to bring the absolute in intimate, though non-conceptual, relation with the phenomenal.

2. In their conception of the function of philosophy, Kant and the Mādhyamika agree. Both address themselves directly to the criticism of the philosophical consciousness as exemplified in the different systems of thought, and only *indirectly* to an investigation of the real. As such, both the systems may be taken as the philosophy of philosophies—the reflective awareness of the working of philosophy. Reflection is self-consciousness; it is possible only as we become conscious of the falsity of what we *were* taking as true; this again implies that closer scrutiny reveals incongruous elements in what appeared unitary and coherent.

The logical starting-point of their philosophy, therefore, is the transcendental illusion[1] which consists in the transcendent or unrestricted use of the ordinary categories of thought—substance, causality, whole and part etc., beyond their legitimate field of experience. Dogmatism, speculative philosophy, indulges in imaginatively constructing the real in terms of the empirical and deludes itself that this is knowledge.

3. How do Kant and the Mādhyamika prove that dogmatic philosophy ("metaphysics as a natural disposition") is an illusion and that it gives only semblance-knowledge? The Mādhyamika does this by showing, through *reductio ad absurdum* arguments (prasanga), that every philosophical system (dṛṣṭi) is riddled with contradiction. It is shown that a view is incompatible with its consequences. The absurdity of a view is brought home to the upholder of the view on principles and proofs acceptable to him. The Dialectic aims at self-conviction. But for the strong and unconscious attachment to his view, the dogmatist himself could have become aware of the absurdities.

[1] *Critique* pp. 298–9.

The procedure of Kant might appear to be different. He first of all analyses experience and discovers the functioning of the *a priori* in the sphere of Sensibility (*Trans. Aesthetic*) and the Understanding (*Trans. Analytic*). In a very imposing and intense critique, mainly directed against the Empiricists, Kant gives us a system of the *a priori*. Knowledge is the synthesis of two factors belonging to two different orders—the *a priori* categories which are subjective and the given manifold of sense-data which are things-in-themselves. Kant accepts unquestioningly the contention of Hume and of the Rationalists that experience cannot give us universality and necessity which we associate with propositions in mathematics and science. His innovation consists in pointing to the transcendental subjectivity as the source of the necessary and the universal. Hume was content to derive the notions of causality, substance etc. from experience itself through the operation of the empirical laws of association and habit. Kant acquaints us with a deeper and more universal subjectivity —the Transcendental. Both agree that the categories are not objective; they are not constitutive of the real.

The crux of the whole problem, as Hegel points out at many places, is why should the *a priori* be taken as merely subjective and not as forms of the real too. The usual Kantian answer is that we cannot explain the universality and necessity of the categories or forms of knowledge except by conceiving them as the innate ideas of the cognising mind. The argument which proves that the categories are universal and necessary—*a priori*—at once proves them valid only phenomenally.[1] Therefore, Kant, after proving the work of the *a priori* in experience, proceeds in the *Trans. Dialectic* to show their necessary confinement within the limits of experience.

This does not seem to be cogent. It would be cogent if universality and necessity *could not be secured in any other way*. There are at least two other modes by which the same end could be achieved. Instead of supposing, as Kant does, that knowledge is the interpretative synthesis, through the categories, of the manifold of sense given to the mind *ab extra* and thereby creating an irreconcilable opposition[2] between the two, we may take the given data of knowledge as the work of the mind, as an 'other' created by it through its own inner

[1] *Critique* pp. 23–4.

[2] The opposition appears in many forms: distinction between percept and concept; thing-in-itself (the given manifold of sense) and the *a priori* categories of thought; the unconditioned (Noumenon) and the Ideas of Reason.

laws of self-expression. Mind (Thought or Reason) is the only Real, and all activity is the activity of reason or consciousness. This is the idealistic solution. Hegel and Vijñānavāda came to formulate this, as a reaction against Kant and the Mādhyamika respectively. The realistic solution of the knowledge-problem would be to minimise, and even to deny, the interpretative (manipulative) work of thought; all distinctions and relations are *given* equally with the terms; not only matter but form too is objective, constitutive of the real. The Nyāya-Vaiśeṣika and other types of Indian Realism may be cited as consistent and successful examples of this attempt.

If explanation of experience were our aim, either of these explanations should do equally well. The Transcendental illusion could not have arisen then; for it arises only when our explanations are pushed beyond their legitimate field to the unconditioned. Moreover, it is not the real aim of Kant to offer an explanation of the knowledge process; the purpose of the *Critique* is not to justify science and set it on secure foundations but to "make room *for faith* by denying knowledge,"[1] by confining it within phenomena. He is interested in freeing the noumenal realities—God, Immortality and Freedom from the denials and doubts to which they had been subjected by philosophical systems. The essential part of the *Critique* then is the *Transcendental Dialectic*, where Kant exposes the pretensions of speculative metaphysics. The Transcendental illusion is the real starting point of his *Critique*. The consciousness of this illusion is engendered by the conflict in Reason as exemplified by totally opposed philosophies. Kant's pre-occupation with an explanation of experience only serves to confound his readers and to cloud the issues. And it is at variance with the anti-speculative tendency of the *Critique*.

As the Mādhyamika goes straight to the issue in hand, the conflict in Reason, his objective too is very clear; namely, to condemn all conceptual patterns as relative (śūnya) and confine them to the empirical realm (vyavahāra, saṁvṛti). This corresponds to the Kantian dictum about the transcendental ideality but empirical reality of the categories.

4. How is the Transcendental illusion removed? Can it be removed

[1] *Critique*: p. 30. "From what has already been said, it is evident that even the assumption—as made on behalf of the necessary practical employment of my reason—of *God, freedom*, and *immortality*, is not permissible unless at the same time speculative reason be deprived of its pretensions to transcendent insight."

at all? The Mādhyamika is definite that it is possible to eliminate all dogmatism and to reach the Absolute in Prajñā (non-dual knowledge). Kant speaks in a very hesitant and unhopeful tone. He says: "Transcendental illusion, on the other hand, does not cease even after it has been detected and its invalidity clearly revealed by transcendental criticism (e.g. the illusion: the world must have a beginning in time). . . . This is an *illusion* which can no more be prevented than we can prevent the sea appearing higher at the horizon than at the shore, since we see it through higher light rays; or to cite a still better example, than the astronomer can prevent the moon from appearing larger at its rising, although he is not deceived by this illusion. . . . The Transcendental dialectic will therefore content itself with exposing the illusion of transcendent judgments; and at the same time taking precautions that we be not deceived by it. That the illusion should, like logical illusion, actually disappear and cease to be an illusion, is something which transcendental dialectic can never be in a position to achieve. For here we have to do with a natural and inevitable *illusion* which rests on subjective principles and foists them upon us as objective."[1]

This should be disconcerting if it were logically sound. But is the consciousness of the Transcendental illusion possible without the consciousness of the Unconditioned? The consciousness of the Ideas of Reason as purely subjective (this much Kant grants) involves their contrast with the objective, the Noumenon. Only by being in possession of the unconditioned Real, the precise mode of this knowledge apart, can the falsity of the subjective forms be declared and laid bare. Kant cannot escape this argument by saying that we have only the *thought* of the unconditioned as a limiting concept and do not have direct knowledge of it. The reason is that illusion, as Kant understands it, is possible because of two factors: "the subjective grounds of the judgment enter into union with the objective grounds and make these latter deviate from their true function."[2] "Truth and error, therefore, and consequently also illusion as leading to error, are only to be found in the judgment, i.e. only in the relation of the object to our understanding. In any knowledge which completely accords with the laws of understanding there is no error. In a representation of senses, as containing no judgment whatsoever, there is also no error. Thus neither the under-

[1] *Critique*: pp. 299–300. [2] *Critique*: p. 298.

standing by itself (uninfluenced by another cause) nor the senses by themselves would fall into 'error'."[1]

The true significance of this admission is that illusion (Transcendental illusion included) cannot arise without an objective ground on which subjective (thought) forms are superimposed. The dilemma is: either we have no consciousness of the Transcendental illusion, and this is possible only if there were no conflicting philosophies; or if we are conscious of the illusion, we must perforce accept some kind of apprehension of the ground of that illusion. Kant might have feared that to claim to have knowledge of the unconditioned would be to phenomenalise it; for, knowledge is possible only in and through the categories. But this could be effectively warded off by refusing to predicate anything of the Noumenon. The Mādhyamika does not allow any predicates (affirmative, negative or their combination) to be ascribed of the Absolute. Secondly, by differentiating that apprehension of the Noumenon from any empirical mode of knowledge, including Reason. Intellectual intuition—direct knowledge of the thing without the categories—is not merely theoretically possible but is the very prius of all experience; it can be realised by divesting the mind of the adventitious thought-forms. We *know* the unconditioned then, but not through the Ideas of Reason, but without them as their implication.

5. Kant says that the dialectic can only expose the pretensions of Reason but cannot make the transcendental illusion disappear; for, the subjective principles through which we look at things are natural to the mind, as for example, the moon cannot but appear bigger at the horizon than at the zenith because we necessarily look at it through higher rays of light. This is indeed true if we take the dialectic or any philosophy as a mere theoretic consideration of things. In that case it could at best give us either information or warning; but it cannot transform, much less eradicate, the subjectivity that is the cause of illusion. The *a priori* cast of the mind would not be amenable to influence by knowledge. Kant was justified in looking to a non-intellectual agent—practical reason or faith—to do the work that could not be done by Pure Reason. In common with other Indian systems, the Mādhyamika, however, conceives our bondage as due to ignorance or wrong knowledge, which is completely removable by knowledge. The fundamental problem is knowing the real as it is.

[1] Ibid: p. 298.

The supremacy of the Intellect over other factors of the mind must be accepted.

Kant was not genuinely convinced of the possibility of Intellectual Intuition,[1] pure knowledge without the mediation of the categories. He vaguely admits this in the case of God, but does not seriously contemplate the human mind ever achieving that state. Nor could he formulate any spiritual discipline which would lead to this. The Mādhyamika conception of Prajñāpāramitā (the non-conceptual intuitional knowledge), as an effective antidote to vikalpa and as identical with the Absolute, meets the requirements. As we have seen, Prajñā is preceded by a discipline of moral culture and concentration of the mind, by the other pāramitās, such as dāna (Charity), śīla (Virtue), kṣānti (Forbearance), vīrya (Effort) and dhyāna (Contemplation), which purify the mind and enable it to have the insight. Prajñā in turn perfects these virtues and makes them pāramitās—infinite excellences.

The second reason for Kant's shortcoming is the divorce that he makes between Pure Reason and Practical Reason (Duty) and Faith (Religion). Convinced as he is of the inability of Pure Reason (philosophy) to lead us to the noumenal realities, God, Freedom and Immortality, Kant could only make a negative and insignificant use of the Critique of Pure Reason, namely, to silence Reason completely so as to give free scope to faith and the dictates of moral consciousness. The elaborate structure of his *Critique* should not be taken as proving this doctrine; it proceeds on that very assumption. Kant has already prejudged the issue and has decided in favour of the non-intellectual functions. His *Critique of Pure Reason* is an elaborate justification of this dogmatic assumption which he had culturally inherited, the conflict of Reason and Faith (Philosophy and Religion) being

[1] "We have not indeed been able to prove that sensible intuition is the only possible intuition but only that it is so for us. But neither have we been able to prove that another kind of intuition is possible. Consequently, although our thought can abstract from all sensibility, it is still an open question whether the notion of a noumenon be not a mere form of a concept, and whether, when this separation has been made, any object whatsoever is left." *Critique*: pp. 270–1.

"But in that case a noumenon is not for our understanding a special kind of object, namely an *intelligible object*; the (sort of) understanding to which it might belong is itself a problem. For we cannot in the least represent to ourselves the possibility of our understanding which should know its object, *not discursively through categories, but intuitively in a non-sensible intuition.*" *Critique*: pp. 272–3.

traditional in the West. Paradoxically, criticism in Kant is in the service of dogmatism.

In the Mādhyamika we find the closest affinity between Intellectual Intuition (Prajñā), Freedom (nirvāṇa) and Perfection. Prajñā as the dissolution of vikalpa (conceptual construction) is Freedom; for the root-cause of bondage and pain is vikalpa. And Prajñā as the Absolute is identical with the Tathāgata—*Ens realissimum*; the Tathāgata is a free phenomenal manifestation of Śūnyatā (Prajñā). Prajñāpāramitā is the unity of the Intellectual, moral and religious consciousness.[1]

II THE HEGELIAN AND THE MĀDHYAMIKA DIALECTIC

1. Dialectic is the central theme of the Hegelian and the Mādhyamika systems. It is common ground to both that Reason (buddhi) is antinomical, relative, in nature;[2] it works through the opposites, and the dialectic is the consciousness of this opposition. Both try to resolve the opposition by rising to a higher standpoint. For Hegel, the dialectic is the movement from the standpoint of the understanding, which isolates and abstracts things and attends to them piecemeal and in an artificial way, to the standpoint of Reason which at once comprehends and unifies the opposites of the understanding. For the Mādhyamika, however, the dialectic is a movement from the relativity of buddhi which is phenomenal to the non-dual Intuition of the absolute, from dṛṣṭi to prajñā.

2. The Hegelian Dialectic, as pointed out in a previous place,[3] tries to remove the opposition between the thesis and the antithesis (e.g. Being and not-being), by intimately relating and unifying them under a third concept in which, Hegel claims, their discord is removed; there they are harmonised. The synthesis of positions is not a bare affirmation of the togetherness of the two; that would be the Jaina view. Hegel takes the synthesis as a newer, richer, more

[1] See Chap. VIII.

[2] "That true and positive meaning of the antinomies in Kant is this: that every actual thing involves a co-existence of opposed elements. Consequently to know, or in other words, to comprehend an object is equivalent to being conscious of it as a concrete unity of opposed determinations." The *Logic of Hegel* (Trans. by Wallace) p. 100. Cf. this with the Mādhyamika dictum: "apratītya samutpanno dharmaḥ kaścin na vidyate; yasmāt tasmād aśūnyo hi dharmaḥ kaścin na vidyate, MK. XXIV, 19.

[3] Supra Chap. V.

comprehensive, and therefore higher idea providing the basis for the differences. "It is a new concept, but a higher, richer concept than that which preceded; for it has been enriched by the negation or opposition of that preceding concept and thus contains it but contains also more than it, and is the unity of it and its opposition."[1] Being and Non-Being are held together and unified in Becoming. The subject and the object are comprehended in the Absolute Spirit. As the Dialectical movement is a passage from a lower concept with a lesser content to a higher concept with a greater content, it is possible to determine the two limits of the dialectical process. The lower limit is the idea with the least content (Pure Being, bare existence)[2] and the culmination is the idea with the richest content (Absolute). The dialectical movement is a triadic process; the synthesis of the lower itself forms the starting point, the thesis, for a new triad. The dialectic is a spiral, each coil of which is a triad. It is better pictured as an inverted pyramid, as the Absolute is the most comprehensive unity of all.

Granting that the nature of thought is such as Hegel describes it, how does the investigation of the structure of thought help us to know the Real? The Hegelian answer, which has been arrived at after a searching criticism of the Kantian duality of thing-in-itself on the one hand and the thought forms on the other, is that they cannot be foreign to each other without losing significance altogether.[3] "For reason is unconditioned, only in so far as it is self-characterising, and thus in point of content is its own master."[4] The identity of Thought and Reality is the basic principle of Hegel. His proof for this amounts to saying that there is no other way of explanation. An imposing superstructure is taken to guarantee the soundness of the foundation. But there might be equally plausible and valid conceptions of the function of thought as distortive or purely representative.

3. The Hegelian dialectic raises important issues on which the Mādhyamika differs from Hegel fundamentally. The synthesis of the opposites is invariably called by Hegel higher, truer, more real. The

[1] *Logic* (Library of Philo. Edn.) Vol. I p. 65.

[2] The Beginning is Pure Being without any content or filling—Pure immediacy—Ibid p. 81–2; see also p. 84. "As it is simple immediacy, nothing can be intuited in it; it is "vacuity or empty thought." Pure Being is thus indistinguishable from nothing, Non-being. Being thus *passes over* to its opposite non-Being.

[3] *The Logic of Hegel*, p. 121. Ibid. pp. 109–110.

synthesis can be higher only if it is shown as the *reality* of the opposites, which would thus be false appearances of the real. The true and the false are not merely different. There is evaluation : the false is what is rejected, and the true is what is accepted. In Hegel there is some perception that the synthesis is *more real*, because it is inclusive and in that sense indispensable. But quantitative measurements cannot be ascribed to the real. Does it make any sense to say that a thing is more existent or less existent? We can say that it is big, bigger or smaller, that it has more stuff or less. Hegel reduces the qualitative distinction of the true and the false to one of degree.[1] The real cannot be understood as the more extensive. The opposites are partly real i.e. partly unreal as they stand, but if something were *added to them*, they would be fully real, more real. On the Mādhyamika contention, we cannot know anything as real except by rejecting the appearances, the several views. The real is reached through the negation of the views, and not by their addition. The real is the reality of the apparent; tattva is the śūnyatā of dṛṣṭis. The Mādhyamika dialectic is the negation of the differences, (sat, asat, both and neither); Hegel's is a summation (vargīkaraṇa) of them.

4. Hegel speaks of retaining and absorbing the opposites without annulling them, negation itself being understood as completion, not supplantation. The synthesis is the harmony of the discordant notes. This is termed by him the concrete universal with which is contrasted the bare universal got by abstracting the differences. The precise mode of the existence of the differences in the absolute has never been made clear by Hegel or by his followers who make such great use of this notion. This is a doctrine which we shall meet with in Bradley too. It is the very nature of a particular thing to stand out against its opposite. So long as it retains its individuality, there would be opposition and discord. Its claim for exclusive existence and attention has to be rejected *in toto*. What can be retained is its essence, what it really is. We have thus to make the distinction of what a thing is essentially and what it is superficially, between the paramārtha and saṁvṛti.

[1] The Doctrine of the Degrees of Truth and Reality is a necessary consequence of this conception of partial and fuller truth. Both in Hegel and Bradley this doctrine plays an important part. The Mādhyamika conception of the paramārtha and vyavahāra satya does not correspond to this, as we have seen. The paramārtha is the only real truth. The vyavahāra satya is truth so called in common parlance; it is absolutely false, notwithstanding its duration and empirical utility. It would be a mistake to identify 'the two truths' doctrine with that of the Degrees of Reality, although this is done by some exponents.

The Hegelian criticism of the abstact universal or the spurious infinite does not affect the Mādhyamika, or the Vedānta even. According to him, "The real infinite, far from being a mere transcendence of the finite, always involves the absorption of the finite into its own nature."[1] If the relation between the Real (Infinite) and the finite appearance were that of an other, this criticism is justified; for, the finite would fall outside the infinite and would be there as a standing mockery. The Infinite would be poorer for this. The Mādhyamika absolute, as we have taken care to point out, is not one reality set against another, the phenomenal world; it is the reality of phenomena (dharmāṇāṁ dharmatā, prakṛtir dharmāṇām). It is therefore declared by Nāgārjuna that there is not even the minutest difference between saṁsāra and nirvāṇa.[2] If there is rejection, it is of *our misapprehension*; but there is no abandoning or abridgement of the real. Even on Hegel's view, the *abstraction* of the understanding has necessarily to be transcended. It would not do to say that even this misunderstanding of things is retained.

5. This brings us to the function of thought (Reason) in Hegel and the Mādhyamika. Hegel takes thought as constituting the very texture of the real. For the Mādhyamika, buddhi is ignorance; it is the falsifying function (saṁvṛti) obscuring the real from us. To know the real as it is, it is necessary, according to the Mādhyamika, to free oneself from the relativity of buddhi. The Real is non-relative, absolute (aparapratyayam); and as buddhi functions with differentia and distinction, i.e. through relating one thing with another, the absolute is beyond its comprehension. The Absolute can be known only in intuition, Prajñāpāramitā (advayaṁ jñānam). Here the Real and the cognition of it coincide so intimately as to preclude the possibility of any discrepancy.

For Hegel, mutual dependence or relativity is the inherent feature of the Real; the non-relative, e.g. the abstract and the purely immediate, is insignificant. Every form of knowledge from the lowest (perception) to the highest (Absolute Idea) is interpreted by Hegel as stages of thought itself, thought as self-alienated and thought as returned to itself. The saṁvṛti of the Mādhyamika is the Absolute of Hegel.

[1] *The Logic of Hegel* p. 93. See also pp. 174 ff.

[2] MK. XXV, 19–20. saṁsāra-nirvāṇayoḥ parasparato nāsti kaścid viśeṣo, vicāryamāṇayos tulya-rūpatvāt. MKV. p. 535.

If Reason and Reality are identical and the logic of the one is the logic of the other, every thought should be true, not partially but in entirety. Discrepancy between them should not only be capable of being composed, but should not even occur at all. But the warring systems of philosophy and the manifest influence of these ideologies on practical life are evidence of the inadmissibility of thought as constituting the real. If it be said that the occurrence of discrepancy and discord is itself the self-determination of thought, the composition of the differences too would be equally inevitable, automatic. Reflection into the dialectical movement of thought can have no relevance in realising the absolute; we cannot possibly retard or hasten the movement, as it is actuated by its own inevitable dynamism. The dialectic of Hegel is a brilliant superfluity; it has no spiritual value.

6. Hegel identifies the Absolute with Thought, the Mādhyamika with Non-dual Intuition (Prajñāpāramitā). This influences the general structure of the Dialectic and every detail of its working in either system. For Hegel, the dialectic is a synthetic movement of the categories for binding them closer; it is *within phenomena*. For the Mādhyamika, the dialectic is the instrument of critical analysis intended for divesting the mind of the categories; it is a movement *away from phenomena*. The conflict of opposed theories and standpoints is resolved in the Mādhyamika by analysing each theory and exhibiting its inner flaw; the dialectic dissolves theories without residue; it does not precipitate another theory. In Hegel the resolution of the conflict is tried to be achieved by synthesising them in a unity. The synthesis of the opposites does not remove the opposition completely even according to Hegel; for, the first synthesis is a fresh *moment* in the next synthesis. There could be no logical limit to this unending spiral the coils of which will describe broader and broader circles. The dialectic can never culminate in anything that is in itself, the absolute. This is the dilemma: either the opposition is removed in the first triadic synthesis itself and there is no spiral movement, or even an infinite number of syntheses cannot remove it. For how can we admit that after a finite number of revolutions, the dialectical process suddenly abolishes the other and develops complete inwardness. It is the nature of thought, as thought, to be confronted by an *other* which can never be wholly one with it. In fact, to identify the Absolute with thought is to make it a spurious Infinite as Hegel understands it; for the 'other' necessarily falls outside and cannot be included within it.

There is a significant passage in Hegel himself that confirms our criticism. "The consummation of the infinite End, therefore, consists merely in *removing the illusion which make it seem yet unaccomplished.* The good, the absolutely Good, is eternally accomplishing itself in the world: and the result is that it needs not wait upon us, but is already by implication, as well as in full actuality accomplished. This is the illusion under which we live. It alone supplies at the same time the actualising force on which the interest in the world reposes. In the course of its process the Idea creates that illusion, by setting an antithesis to confront it, and its action consists in getting rid of the illusion which it has created. Only out of this error does the truth arise. In this fact lies the reconciliation with error and with finitude. Error or other-being, when superseded, is still a necessary dynamic element of truth; for truth can only be where it makes itself its own result."[1]

This might have been written by a Mādhyamika; but in Hegel it is glaringly out of consonance with the general tenor of his dialectic. The good is eternally realised, and the function of thought is to get rid of the illusion which it had, perhaps unwittingly, created. What then becomes of the Hegelian doctrine of thought as self-creative and as identical with the real? Thought is an accident, an illusion that has to be transcended on our way to the Absolute.

III BRADLEY AND THE MĀDHYAMIKA

The difficulties of Hegel have led some of the Neo-Hegelians, notably Bradley, to introduce modifications in the notion of the Absolute. Unlike Hegel, Bradley conceives the Absolute as "immediate experience" in which the differences of the finite are transmuted and unified. He thus hopes to have escaped the predicament of Hegel and yet to have retained the great merit of Hegel in unifying the differences. His dialectical criticism of the categories of experience comes very close to the Mādhyamika method, and deserves comparison on that score.

1. For Bradley, all things are infected with relativity and contradiction. "For thought what is not relative is nothing."[2] (p. 25). And yet a thing must obviously be something to be related even.

[1] *The Logic of Hegel*. pp. 351–2.

[2] Qotations in this section are from Bradley's *Appearance and Reality* 2nd Edn. (Oxford U. Press).

The ultimate contradiction is therefore one of the irreconcilability of terms and relations. Terms must exist first in order to be related, i.e., relation presupposes the relata; and yet the terms taken by themselves, without the relation, dwindle into nothing, i.e., the relata without the relation are insignificant abstractions. "Relation presupposes quality, and quality relation. Each can be something neither together with nor apart from the other; and the vicious circle in which they turn is not the truth about reality." (p. 21). "The conclusion to which I am brought," says Bradley, "is that a relational view of thought—any one that moves by the machinery of terms and relations—must give appearance and not truth. . . . Our intellect, then, has been condemned to confusion and bankruptcy, and the reality has been left outside uncomprehended." (pp. 28–9).

2. This is the principle of Bradley's dialectic stated in full in his own words; and this is similar to that of the Mādhyamika, for whom neither of those two things is real which cannot be conceived either as identical with or different from each other.[1] Bradley proceeds to apply this logic to some familiar modes of our understanding of the real, e.g. Substance-attribute, Space, Time, Action, Causality, Self etc. To illustrate this in the case of causality. The essence of causation is that one thing becomes or gives rise to another; but this process is ultimately unintelligible. "A becomes B, and this alteration is felt to be not compatible with A. Mere A would still be mere A, and if it turns to be something different, then something else is concerned." (p. 46). The basic dilemma may at once be stated thus: "If the sequence of the effect were different from the cause, how is the ascription of the difference to be rationally defended? If, on the other hand, it is not different, then causation does not exist, and its assertion is a farce. There is no escape from this fundamental dilemma." (p. 47). The difficulty is: "causation must be continuous" and yet "it cannot be continuous" (p. 51–2).[2]

3. Both Bradley and the Mādhyamika are agreed that no phenomenon is exempt from relativity.[3] They are but appearance, not real. There is, however, a significant difference between the Mādhyamika dialectic and Bradley's. The cue for the Mādhyamika

[1] Cf. MK. II, 21.

[2] Cf. hetoḥ phalasya caikatvaṁ na hi jātūpapadyate;
hetoḥ phalasya cānyatvaṁ na hi jātūpapadyate. MK. XX, 19.

[3] MK. XXIV, 19.

dialectic is the consciousness of the Transcendental illusion engendered by the conflict of totally opposed views of the real, e.g. the ātma and nairātmya views. In the entire procedure of the dialectic, the distinction between dṛṣṭi (dogmatism) and prajñā (criticism) is explicitly kept in view. The Mādhyamika rejects both the alternatives, every possible alternative, on any problem, and he has a schema (catuṣkoṭi) under which he brings all systems of philosophy. The Mādhyamika dialectic is a critique of the philosophical consciousness. We do not find in Bradley any such schema of alternatives; nor is there any explicit consciousness of the transcendental illusion. Categories of thought, like substance, quality, space, time etc., are taken almost at random and criticised.

We have also seen that the Mādhyamika, in criticising any view, does not advance any argument of his own; he does not commit himself to a position. He is consistent in adopting the *reductio ad absurdum* method (prasangāpādanam). Bradley, it must be admitted, has no definite procedure in criticising any view. He even advances a counter-position and adduces arguments that may not bring home the contradiction to the opponent. All this is evidence of lack of system.[1]

4. The greatest difference between the Mādhyamika and Bradley is in their notion of the Real and its relation to appearance. When we reject anything as appearance do we know something positive about reality? Bradley fills up the positive content of reality as:

(i) Reality must be self-consistent; (ii) Reality must own all the appearances; and (iii) Reality is experience.

That reality must be consistent and self-contained and that this can be the Absolute only is established by both. The Mādhyamika defines his Tattva (Real) as aparapratyayam (Non-dependent) nirvikalpam (Non-conceptual) etc. But how is this reached? Bradley's answer is this: we know anything to be appearance because it is self-contradictory, and the self-contradictory cannot be real." "To criticise anything is to use a criterion of reality." (p. 120) "Ultimate

[1] Radhakrishnan, however, makes a different estimate. Comparing the two systems, he says: "We are reminded of the attempt of Bradley, since the general principle is the same in the two cases. Of course, we have not here the luminous systematic application which constitutes the greatness of Bradley's metaphysics. Nāgārjuna's attempt is neither so full nor so methodical as Bradley's. He lacks the latter's passion for system and symmetry, but he is aware of the general principle, and his work has a unity in spite of much that is deficient as well as redundant." I.P. Vol. I p. 648. I have come to an opposite conclusion for the reasons adduced above.

Reality is such that it does not contradict itself. . . . Even in attempting to doubt it, we tacitly assume its validity." (p. 120) But this knowledge seems to be merely *formal* and cannot yield real knowledge; nor can it prevent any one starting with a different criterion. The sequence is not clear: do we have a knowledge of the real first and therefore condemn phenomena as not measuring up to our standard? If so, it is not shown how we could have come by such a knowledge so secretly and securely; and condemnation of appearance becomes quite gratuitous. It is rather the other way about. The inherent self-contradiction of appearance itself leads us to a knowledge of the real. This is the Mādhyamika way.

Are *things* self-contradictory? Do appearances quarrel and contradict each other? They do not do so, except in a metaphorical sense. There can be conflict and contradiction in our views of things, and not in things. Our thoughts can be and are at variance with things, and therefore they can be helped. The real starting-point for Bradley, then, is the consciousness of the transcendental illusion, the conflict of systems of philosophy. This failure to appreciate the true nature of the conflict constitutes a fundamental weakness in Bradley as a philosopher.

Probably, Bradley had unconsciously identified thought with Reality and therefore what is merely a conflict in thought is considered by him as a conflict in things as well. And this provides the clue for Bradley's rather inconsistent contention that the appearances too are somehow real and thus constitute the texture of reality. He says: "Whatever is rejected as appearance, is for that very reason no mere non-entity. It cannot bodily be shelved and got rid of, and therefore since it must fall somewhere, it must belong to reality. Reality must own, and cannot be less than appearance." (p. 404). How precisely the appearances are unified and the discordant note in them is attuned is nowhere made clear. What is the form in which pain, evil, ugliness and finitude can be retained? Can they be retained at all without phenomenalising the absolute, making it a mere bundle of incongruent entities?

Is the discord constituent of the nature of things or not? If it were, it can never be dissolved without dissolving things at the same time; then nothing remains to be taken up in the Absolute. If it were not constitutive of the real, then our viewing of things as contradictory and discordant is our error, a mistake that cannot find a place in the real. It has just an epistemic status, not an ontological one.

This is the real issue between Bradley and the Mādhyamika. According to Bradley even to reject a thing it must exist. The Mādhyamika of course would be compelled to admit that a blank nothing could not be negated. The vital point is as to the status of the negated content. For the Mādhyamika an ontological fact, existing by itself, can never be rejected. Hence if anything is to be negated at all, it must be epistemic.[1] Bradley might say that the appearance is retained in some form, without its abstraction and jarring features. But how can we assert the identity of the appearance as it appears to finite perception and the same in the Absolute experience? It need not be objected that if the appearances are not absorbed in the Absolute, the two would fall asunder, and there would be two realities. For the Mādhyamika, and this is true of the Vedānta and Vijñānavāda too, the Absolute is the reality of the appearances. Therefore the Absolute is at once transcendent and immanent: transcendent as free from the empiricality of the appearances; immanent as it is the essence of appearances and is therefore not different from them, This is a unique relation obtaining between the Absolute and Phenomena. Bradley's anxiety to retain the appearance *as appearance*, can only result in the Absolute being but the totality of appearances; there should not be any distinction, even epistemic, between the two; appearance itself would be absolute!

Departing from Hegel, Bradley conceives the Absolute as experience. "We perceive, on reflection, that to be real or even barely to exist, must be to fall within sentience—sentient experience, in short, is reality, and what is not this is not real." (p. 127). Though this is an advance on Hegel, Bradley does not make clear the nature and content of this experience. He is quite aware of the inadequacy of thought, and of the opposition inherent in it owing to the sundering of the 'that' (real) from the 'what' (ideal content). Yet Bradley does not explicitly reject thought as giving us appearance only; he even speaks of it as constituting the absolute. This is confusing and inconsistent. Bradley shows in this and in other doctrines, such as the Degrees of Reality and Truth and the relation of phenomena to the absolute, the influence of Hegel. Most of these doctrines have already been subjected to criticism. The Mādhyamika, however, is definite that the Absolute transcends thought, and as the unity and reality of all phenomena it is Non-dual Intuition—Prajñāpāramitā.

[1] Cf. MK. XXIII 24–5.

CHAPTER THIRTEEN

THE MĀDHYAMIKA, VIJÑĀNAVĀDA AND VEDĀNTA ABSOLUTISM

I THE PROBLEM OF THE DIFFERENT ABSOLUTES IN THE INDIAN SYSTEMS

FOR a critical student of Indian Philosophy the different Absolutisms present one of the crucial but unsolved problems. We are confronted with the Śūnya of the Mādhyamika, the Vijñaptimatratā of the Vijñānavādin, the Brahman of the Vedānta, Īśvarādvaita of the Pratyabhijñā system, Śabda Brahman of the Vaiyākaraṇas and possibly other advaitisms. It is a commonly held notion that there is no real difference between the absolutes of these systems; the differences are superficial and pertain only to terminology. Why then does the Vedānta refute the Mādhyamika, and the Mādhyamika the Vijñānavāda and vice versa, to mention only a few instances?[1] We are asked to believe that owing either to their faulty understanding of each other's philosophy or to religious fanaticism, they mistook a friend for a foe; hence the severe polemic found in each system against the others. It is even suggested that the refutations have been wilfully indulged in. Stcherbatsky says for example:

> There is but little difference between Buddhism and Vedānta . . . a circumstance which Śaṅkara *carefully conceals*. But in later works, e.g. *Vedānta Paribhāṣā* or *Nyāya Makaranda*, different pramāṇas are established as proofs for the existence of Brahman. When commenting upon *Vedānta Sūtras*, II, ii, 28, Śaṅkara, in combating Buddhist idealism, resorts to arguments *of which he himself does not believe a word*, since they are arguments which the most genuine realist would use. *He then argues not sva-matena, but paramatam āśritya*, a method very much in vogue among Indian Pandits. Deussen's interpretation of this point, (Op. cit. p. 260) as intended to vindicate vyavahāra satya, is a misunderstanding, since the Buddhists never denied the vyavahāra or saṁvṛti. Against M. Walleser's

[1] Mādhyamika criticism of Vijñānavāda, MKV. pp. 61 ff. BCAP. pp. 389 ff. MA. pp. 40 ff. Vijñānavāda criticism of the Mādhyamika: *Triṁśikā* I; MVBT. I. Śaṅkara's criticism of Vijñānavāda and Mādhyamika: *Br. Sūt.* II, ii, 28 ff. Śaṅkara's refutation of Sphoṭavāda (Śabdādvaita) in *Br. Sūtras* I, iii, 28 may also be noted.

(*Der ältere Vedānta* p. 43) opinion that the objectivity of our ideas themselves is meant, it must be pointed out that the Buddhists did not deny the jñānākāra, and Śaṅkara clearly states that external objects, not ideas, are meant—tasmād artha-jñānayor bhedaḥ.[1]

Such explanations are heroic, and tacitly assume that there is no other way of explaining the differences without imputing motives. The problem has remained unsolved because the approach has been linguistic and historical. We now know enough of the systems and their implications not to confound them. We want a schematism to bring under it the different absolutisms which, without ignoring the vital differences, will clearly indicate the precise place of each in a comprehensive scheme.

II THE STANDPOINT OF VEDĀNTA DISTINGUISHED FROM OTHERS

We should be in a better position to understand each of these three absolutisms, if we first attempted to understand the standpoint from which one system criticises the others.

The Vedānta criticism of the Mādhyamika is little better than a summary condemnation of it as nihilism that does not merit even a consideration. The one significant sentence in the condemnation is that "it is not possible to negate the empirical world without the acceptance of another reality; for, to negate an error is to accept the general truth on which it is based:"[2]

In the light of our exposition of the Mādhyamika conception of the Absolute based on explicit statements of the original works and the entire logic of the system, it is clearly impossible to agree with this interpretation of 'Śūnya'. It may be suggested that most critics of this system have not gone beyond the awe-inspiring term 'Śūnya' (Void). They have made it all too easy for their rejection of the system by foisting upon it a doctrine, rather an absurdity, which the Mādhyamikas had never accepted. If affirmative predicates (sat, bhāva) are denied of the Absolute, negative predicates (asat, abhāva etc.) are equally denied, perhaps with greater vehemence. We are expressly warned not to take Śūnyatā as abhāva-dṛṣṭi (Negation). Tattva (the Real) is accepted explicitly; but we are forbidden to

[1] *The Conception of Buddhist Nirvāṇa* pp. 38–9 (italics mine).

[2] śūnyavādipakṣas tu sarvapramāṇa-vipratiṣiddha iti tannirākaraṇāya nādaraḥ kriyate; nahy ayaṁ sarvapramāṇaprasiddho lokavyavahāro'*nyat tattvam anadhigamya śakyate' pahnotum apavādābhāva utsargaprasiddheḥ.* Śaṁkara's *Bhāṣya* on *Br. Sūtr.* II, ii, 31.

characterise and clothe it in empirical terms. Every absolutism, including the Vedānta, has to do this. The Absolute is taken as the reality of things (dharmāṇāṁ dharmatā), as their true nature (bhūta-koṭi) and as suchness (tathatā). It is identified with the Perfect Being—Tathāgata, as we have seen. We have, however, tried to show how possibly this mistake could have arisen. The "no-doctrine-about-reality" attitude of the Mādhyamika is mistaken for the "no-reality" doctrine. Accustomed as they are to deal with *doctrinal systems* and not finding any doctrine about the stock subjects, God, soul, matter etc. in the Mādhyamika, other systems have dubbed it as nihilism, giving it a short shrift. The purely epistemological standpoint of criticism has eluded their grasp.[1]

In contrast, Śaṅkara's exposition of Vijñānavāda is quite fair and full;[2] and his criticism is sound from his own standpoint. Śaṁkara points out that the sole reality of Vijñāna is tried to be proved on these grounds:

(i) The existence of the object in the form of atoms or a whole composed of them is untenable; this predicament infects every conception of the object as universal and particular, whole and parts, substance and attribute etc.

(ii) The existence of the object apart from knowledge is inconceivable; knowledge, however, is invariable and indispensable. This is the idealistic argument, *esse is percipi*, (sahopalambha-niyamād abhedo nīlataddhiyoḥ.)

(iii) Consciousness can exist without object, as in dreams etc. (svapnādivac cedaṁ draṣṭavyam); it cannot be denied, as it is self-revealed (svasaṁvedya).

(iv) We can easily account for the arising of the different states of knowledge with varied content on the simpler hypothesis of the inner dynamism of Vijñāna unfolding itself impelled by different seeds (vāsanās) latent in it. All these arguments are actually employed by Vijñānavāda, and Śaṁkara even uses the very expressions of their treatises.

His criticism of Vijñānavāda is an acute and brilliant performance; it brings out admirably the essential difference of the Vedānta from Vijñānavāda.[3]

[1] See supra. Chap. VIII.

[2] See his Bhāṣya on *Br. Sūtr.* II, ii, 28 ff.

[3] This may be taken as an answer to Stcherbatsky's remark quoted before.

(1) The given thing (bāhyo'rthaḥ) cannot be denied, as it is cognised in every act of knowledge.[1]

(2) It does not make sense to take the cognising act itself as the object cognised; for the nature of cognition is to reveal[2] what is present, given to us, and not to create the content out of itself. That could not be knowledge at all.

(3) Even the idealist's denial of the given thing-in-itself when he states that consciousness itself appears to apprehend forms of content as *if there were the given* object (yad antar jñeya-rūpaṁ *bahirvad* avabhāsate) admits, by implication, the reality of the object. If the idealist had no knowledge, as he pretends, of the given thing-in-itself, how does he speak of consciousness apprehending a content *as if* there were a given etc. No comparison can be made with an entity (given object) which is non-existent (according to the Idealist hypothesis).[3] Śaṅkara's contention is that even for the occurrence of the illusion of givenness, there must be something given.

(4) If there were no object, there can be no representation of it in knowledge. This is really a counter-argument to the Idealist's contention of the non-availability of the object apart from the knowing of it. Śaṁkara's position is identical with that of Kant and the Mādhyamika, viz., that without the given object there can be no knowledge either.

(5) The distinction between dream and waking consciousness, i.e. between false and true perception, cannot be made except on the ground that the object of the waking experience is given, independent of the knowing act, while in dream the object is not so given. Every content being the internal modification of vijñāna equally, on what ground can the Idealist account for the distinction between the true and the false?[4]

[1] upalabhyate hi pratipratyayaṁ bāhyo'rthaḥ, stambhaḥ kuḍyaṁ, ghaṭaḥ paṭa iti. *Bhāṣya* on *Br. Sūt.* II, ii, 28.

[2] upalabdhivyatireko'pi balād arthasyābhyupagantavyaḥ, upalabdher eva. nahi kaścid upalabdhim eva stambhaḥ kuḍyaṁ cety upalabhate. upalabdhiviṣaytvenaiva tu stambha-kuḍyādīn sarve laukikā upalabhante. *Bhāṣya* on *Br. Sūt.* II, ii, 28.

[3] yat pratyācakṣāṇā api bāhyārtham eva vyācakṣate yadantar jñeyarūpaṁ tad bahir*vad* avabhāsata iti. te'pi sarvaloka-prasiddhāṁ bahir avabhāsamānāṁ saṁvidaṁ pratilabhamānāḥ pratyākhyātukāmāś ca bāhyam artham *bahirvad iti vatkāraṁ* kurvanti. itarthā hi kasmād bahirvad iti brūyuḥ. Ibid.

[4] See Śaṅkara's *Bhāṣya* on *Br. Sūtr.* II, ii, 29.

These arguments of Śaṁkara do not mean, as is misunderstood by some modern exponents, that he accepts the reality of the empirical world *as it appears to us*. That would mean giving up of his absolutism; his Absolute, Brahman, cannot then be freed of empirical determinations; it could not be nirdharmaka. His position means that in every experience there is the real thing-in-itself, which is given; it serves as the passive substratum for the superimposition of thought-categories (e.g. difference, change and particularity). The empirical world of appearance is real, but *as* Brahman. For Śaṁkara, knowledge is *of* the given; it is dependent on the thing (vastutantraṁ hi jñānam). The *knowing* function does not create or even distort the object (the given); it just *re*veals,[1] *dis*covers, an existent complete in all respects (parinișṭhitavastu). The ideal of Pure knowledge is to know the thing as it is, without the least trace of the subjective forms, categories or representations. In no empirical experience, however, is this ideal requirement satisfied. Only the knowledge of Brahman is pure knowledge; for there the knowing act is totally devoid of any subjective bias; it is so pure and diaphanous that no distinction can be made between the knowing (ātman) and the known (brahman).

The position can be summed up by stating that knowing does not make the thing, the given; but the given (thing-in-itself) makes knowledge possible. The real object of knowledge does not exist in and through our knowing act, i.e. in *relation to our* knowing; but exists in itself, unrelated. That alone is sat (Real) which is in itself, which does not need anything to be what it is. On the contrary, what is *in relation* to our knowing act and nothing apart from it is the appearance (prātibhāsika); its existence is totally exhausted within that relationship.

On this criterion, only Being that is Pure (changeless), universal (undifferentiated into particulars) and self-evident (unrelated) is real; only that is the true object of knowledge. That is the Absolute, Brahman. A changing being (becoming) is conditioned; it is not in itself. The particular is as it is related to other particulars, as it is opposed to others. The self-evident (svayaṁprakāśa) does not need

[1] Cf. The famous argument formulated by the *Vivaraṇa* and accepted by the entire body of Vedānta writers regarding the nature of pramāṇajñāna as revealing an existent: pramāṇajñānaṁ, svaprāgabhāva-vyatirikta-svaviṣayāvaraṇa-svanivartya-svadeśagata-vastvantara-pūrvakam aprakāśitārthaprakāśakatvād, andhakāre prathamotpanna-pradīpa-prabhāvat. *Vivaraṇa*. p. 13. That the standpoint of knowledge is fundamental to Vedānta is proved by its analysis of illusion on this basis.

to be evidenced by another; it is immediate without being related to the knowing act (avedya, yet, aparokṣa). Considerations of space prevent us from analysing the implications of these propositions here.

The Vedānta analyses experience from the standpoint of knowledge; the thing-in-itself (sanmātra, Brahman) is all that exists; the knowing act merely reveals. Anything that is not by itself, but is only through *being known*, is appearance, e.g. the 'rope-snake' in the stock example. The Vedānta may be taken as realistic in its epistemology; for, it upholds the reality of the given (thing-in-itself). It is more correctly characterised as a species of critical realism or Transcendence; for, as opposed to naive realism, Vedānta shows that the true object of knowledge is beyond empirical experience, and what we empirically know is appearance of the real, not the real itself. The Vedānta has greater affinity with Kant and the Mādhyamika than with Idealism.

The Idealistic position of Vijñānavāda, on the other hand, takes the knowing act or consciousness to be the only real, and the object is projected, created, out of it. Although the Yogācāra uses the terms jñāna, vijñāna, vijñapti, citta, svasaṁvedana, etc. he is really meaning by these terms the *creative act, Will.* His Vijñāna is really Pure Act; *pure* as it is not conditioned by anything outside it with regard to its existence and function; it is *act*, as it is not a static passive Being like the Vedāntic Brahman, but an incessantly self-active creative entity. The object is just an other (idam) extruded and projected out of itself by the sheer self-creativity of Vijñāna. This creative projection is not of course empirical in character, but transcendental; it is the act of a deeper subjectivity. The object, as willed and projected out of consciousness, is therefore *in* and *through* the latter and nothing apart from that. This is idealism *par excellence*, and the Vijñānavāda is the only genuinely idealistic[1] school in India. Vijñāna is Cosmic, Impersonal Will, realising itself through the projection and retraction of the object. The Yogācāra chooses, for its analysis of illusion, such cases as dream-objects, where the creative act predominates; the Vedānta chooses those where the given (Being) predominates. Each tries to analyse illusion and all experience with the knowledge or Will bias, as it were. What is real for the Vedānta, the given (being), is appearance for Vijñānavāda, and vice versa.

[1] This statement requires to be modified to this extent that Īśvarādvaita is also a species of Absolute Idealism, as Īśvara is conceived more as Will (Śakti or Kriyā) than as knowledge or Being. Some idealistic trends have also entered the Vedānta, e.g. the doctrine of dṛṣṭisṛṣṭivāda, the main exponent of which is the author of *Vedānta Siddhānta Muktāvalī*.

The parallel for Vijñānavāda in the West is the system of Fichte or Hegel, both of whom conceive the Pure Ego (Fichte) or Reason (Hegel) as self-legislative, as containing and creating both the categories and the objects on which the categories function. The difference between Hegel and Vijñānavāda is that the Hegelian absolute is thought or Reason, and therefore has the duality of the opposites; the Vijñānavāda absolute is above reason and is non-dual (advaya). A further difference is that Hegel employs the logic of dialectic to draw out the categories, while the Vijñānavāda uses psychological analysis to exhibit the three strata of consciousness functioning in mutual co-operation.

III THE MĀDHYAMIKA AND VIJNĀNAVĀDA STANDPOINTS

The Mādhyamika criticism[1] of Vijñānavāda brings out the difference between them. The Vijñānavāda contends that consciousness can exist by itself without the object, as it admittedly does in dream-states and other illusions. Consciousness should be regarded as giving rise to the varied contents of its states from its own inner potentiality[2] (svaśakti); it is self-determining, and is governed by its own laws of development; it is creative of the object. Further, Consciousness is self-luminous: it is self-known (svasaṁvittiḥ) like a lamp.

In the course of a trenchant criticism of the above contentions both Candrakīrti and Śāntideva overthrow the Vijñānavāda position. The main criticism is that without the object[3] the knowing consciousness cannot function; if the object were unreal, as the Vijñānavādin holds, what is known at all?[4] Citta (mind) is empty, it cannot cognise itself. It has to work on something; a mere form cannot provide the content. "Even the sharpest sword cannot cut itself; the finger-tips

[1] See MKV. pp. 61 ff; pp. 274–5, MA. VI, 45 ff. (pp. 40–64) BCA. pp. 389 ff; 408 ff. 525 ff. Nāgārjuna and Āryadeva have not criticised Vijñānavāda, as it had not been formulated at that time. But there is no doubt about their approving the criticism of Vijñānavāda made by Candrakīrti and Śānti Deva.

[2] yathā tarangā mahato'mburāśeḥ samīraṇapreraṇay odbhavanti; tathā-layākhyād api sarvabījād vijñānamātraṁ bhavati svaśakteḥ. MA. VI, 46.

[3] saṁkṣepato jñeyam asad yathaiva, na dhīrapīty artham imaṁ hy avehi. jñeyasvabhāvo yathā nāsti tathā jñeyākārakadhīr api svātmato'nutpannā veditavyā . . . tasmād vijñānavastuvādāpasmāragṛhīto bāhyaviṣayā-pavādi ayaṁ kasmād ātmaprapāte na patiṣyati. MA. VI, pp. 58–9

[4] BCA. p. 390: yadā māyaiva te nāsti, tadā kim upalabhyate.

cannot be touched by the same finger-tips. Citta does not know itself:"[1] How can anything be the knower and the known at once, without splitting itself into two? If it is known by another act of knowledge, the later knowledge will be known by another, thus leading to a regress.

As for some texts which speak of the sole reality of consciousness, they have been taught by Buddha as a preparatory[2] step leading to the Śūnyatā doctrine, without unduly frightening the feeble-minded. They are neyārtha (secondary in import) and not nītārtha (ultimate teaching). The Vijñānavāda accepts the existence of something (vijñāna) and denies the existence of others (objects), and therefore it cannot be taken as the denial of both the 'is' and 'not is' standpoints[3] which is the real madhyamā-pratipad (middle position) of Buddha. Only the Mādhyamika system is that.

The Mādhyamika criticism of Vijñānavāda reminds one of the Refutation of Idealism by Kant in the *Critique* at several[4] places. Both very explicitly deny that we can have self-knowledge without knowledge of objects; mere categories or even the Transcendental 'I' are quite empty. With regard to empirical things, they are even prepared to accept the realistic outlook. They hold the view that idealism upsets the ordinary modes of understanding objective existence without any compensatory advantage. The Kantian or the Mādhyamika position can be characterised as Transcendental or Critical Idealism[5] which accepts the empirical reality of things (object and the knowing subject) with their transcendental or ultimate unreality. As mutually dependent, neither pure subject nor pure object (thing-in-itself, sense-datum) is real unconditionedly. This is a new species of Absolutism, which is neither the Absolutism of the Pure Cognising Act without any trace of the 'given' object (Vijñānavāda), nor the absolutism of the Pure Object (Being) free from the

[1] See MKV. pp. 61 ff. MA. pp. 59 ff. BCA. pp. 391 ff. for the Mādhyamika criticism of the svasaṁvitti doctrine.

[2] MKV. p. 276; BCAP. p. 406.

[3] MKV. p. 275.

[4] "In Kant's critical writings we find no less than seven different statements of his refutation of idealism." Kemp Smith—*A Commentary to the Critique*, p. 298.

[5] "The Transcendental Idealist is, therefore, an empirical realist and allows to matter, as appearance, a reality which does not permit of being inferred, but is immediately perceived." *Critique*, p. 347. Cf. yathādṛṣṭaṁ śrutaṁ jñātaṁ naiveha pratiṣiddhyate. BCA. p. 404.

mediation of the thought-forms (Brahman of the Vedānta). Reflective criticism or the Dialectical consciousness itself is the Absolute here.

The Vijñānavāda criticism of the Mādhyamika is that his interpretation of Śūnyatā is an unwarranted extremism. Sūnyatā is not the negation of all, but the negation of the Duality of Subject and Object *in* something. That, *where* the negation of duality (dvaya-śūnyatā) obtains, *does exist*; and it is something in itself, the Absolute. The formula is: "Constructive Ideation (abhūta-parikalpaḥ) is real. In it duality does not (absolutely) exist. Non-substantiality (Śūnyatā), however, exists in it. In this (Non-substantiality) too, that (Constructive Ideation) is found."[1] By the term 'abhūta-parikalpa' (translated as Constructive Ideation) is meant, not the wrong ideation itself which is phenomenal, but the *basis* of that false construction (abhūtasya parikalpo *yasmin*). This abhūtaparikalpa is the Transcendent dynamic stream of consciousness which creates from itself all phenomena, substance (ātmā), elements (dharma), or rather subject, object etc. All relations are *within* it, and not between it and some other beside it. Constructive Ideation constructs the phenomenal world of subject-object-relation, which cannot, for that reason, have an independent existence. The constructed subject-object world is unreal; but this does not make the abhūtaparikalpa unreal; for, it is the substratum for the unreal subject-object duality.[2] It is, however, non-conceptual. If it were the object of ideation, it would be unreal like any other superimposed (parikalpita) object. It is realised in lokottara or Non-dual knowledge. There is, in one sense, difference between the abhūtaparikalpa and the Absolute (pariniṣpanna), for the latter is totally free of the duality; while the former has that superimposed-on it. In another sense the two are identical; for, the Pariniṣpanna (Absolute) is none other than the Abhūtaparikapa[3] freed of the unreal duality infecting it. The relation of Absolute to the phenomena is thus both transcendent and immanent (anya, ananya).

[1] MVBT. p. 9.

[2] na khalv abhūtaparikalpo'pi na bhavati. yathā rajjuḥ śūnyā sarpatvabhāvena tatsvabhāvatvābhāvāt sarvakālaṁ śūnyā na tu rajjusvabhāvena, tathehāpi. . . .
yac chūnyaṁ tasya sadbhāvād, yena śūnyaṁ tasya tatrābhāvāt. MVBT. pp. 12–13.

[3] MVBT. p. 40 *Triṁśikā*—niṣpannas tasya pūrveṇa sadā rahitatā tu yā: 21–22, ata eva sa naivānyo nānanyaḥ paratantrataḥ.

The above position of the Vijñānavāda has been arrived at after a thorough criticism of the position of the Mādhyamika and the Realist. Vijñānavāda shows itself as an Absolutism of Consciousness as Pure Act, constructing absolutely the duality of subject-object. In contrast, Brahman is passive (Pure) Being devoid of difference. Brahman does not construct; but construction is possible on the passive ground of Brahman (adhiṣṭhāna), because Brahman lends itself to be superimposed upon. For the Vedānta, activity, which can only obtain through limitation (sopādhikaṁ kartṛtvam), presupposes an unlimited, undifferentiated Pure Being. The logic behind this is that all difference presupposes identity and not vice versa (abheda-pūrvako hi bhedaḥ). In the Vedantā, Pure Act as embodied in Īśvara is a category of a lower order; it is phenomenal, though not empirical. For the Vedānta then, the Pure Ideation (abhūtaparikalpa) of Vijñānavāda is through avidyā; the Absolute, as the basis of this, is beyond the Act. For the Vijñānavāda, however, the Vedānta Absolute—Brahman as the Pure Given (Thing-in-itself) cannot but appear as the primordial construct of Ideation. In the result, their Absolutes and Avidyā are transpositions of each other.

For the Mādhyamika both the given thing-in-itself (sanmātra of the Vedānta) and the constructive Ideation (abhūtaparikalpa of Vijñānavāda) are relative to each other; we cannot have the one without the other. As such both are conditioned (pratītya-samutpanna), and hence Śūnya. He does not therefore hesitate to consider both the thing-in-itself and the categories of Pure Reason as vikalpa, conceptual constructions. Vikalpa (as saṁvṛti) is the obscuration of Intuition which is the Real in the Mādhyamika system. It is thus seen that Non-Relative, unconditioned, Immediacy (Pure Intuition) is the prius of both Thought and things (Act and Being). In this sense Śūnyatā or Prajñā may be taken as a more general form of the Absolute than that of Pure Being or Pure Ideation.

IV THE COMMON FORM OF ALL ABSOLUTISMS

As absolutisms, the Mādhyamika, Vijñānavāda and Vedānta exhibit some common features as to their *form*; they differ in the mode of their approach, and possibly with regard to that entity with which they identify the absolute. In the actual state of the Absolute, they may be identical; at least we have no means of asserting their difference; silence is their most proper language. The centre of the circle may be reached from the periphery by any of the possible radii; short of reaching the very centre, persons adopting different radii may genuinely feel that they are on the right path to the centre and that the others are not. For, each votary may see the centre looming ahead of him; but he cannot, from the nature of his predicament, see that others also may be reaching the centre through their particular modes of approach.

In all these systems, the absolute is transcendent, totally devoid of empirical determinations (nirdharmaka, śūnya). The Absolute is immanent too, being the reality of appearance. The Absolute is but the phenomena in their essential form. It follows that the absolute is realised only in a non-empirical intuition called variously, prajñā-pāramitā, lokottarajñāna, and aparokṣānubhūti. The nature of this experience is that it is a non-discursive, immediate and unitary cognition; here essence and existence coincide. They further agree with regard to the nature and status of phenomena which are appearance. Engendered by a beginningless non-empirical avidyā, the appearance can be negated completely by the true knowledge of the absolute. The nature of avidyā and its orientation to the absolute differ in each system. Every absolutism is really an advaita or advayavāda, non-dualism; they do not establish the absolute, but just reject duality as illusion. And the rejection is dialectically made and not on the basis of positive arguments. Otherwise, *that* on the strength of which the absolute is established will stand out as another reality. What is rejected as illusory differs in these systems: the Mādhyamika negates the conceptualist tendency (vikalpa or dṛṣṭi); for, this is what falsifies reality which is Intuition (prajñā); the Vijñānavāda negates objectivity; for this makes Vijñāna appear infected with the duality of subject and object; the Vedānta negates difference (bheda); the real is Universal and Identical.

By implication every absolutism has to formulate the distinction of Reality and Appearance and the two truths (paramārtha and vyavahāra). Scriptures too are interpreted on this basis—nītārtha (para) and neyārtha (apara). The Vedāntic doctrine of three 'truths' and the admission of the prātibhāsika is necessitated by the fact that it first analyses an empirical illusion (an illusion which is cancelled in our ordinary experience even) and applies this analysis analogically to the world-illusion. The position of Vijñānavāda is similar. The Mādhyamika, however, addresses himself directly to the world-illusion as presented in the conflicting philosophies and points of view. He is concerned with what has been called by Kant the Transcendental illusion.

All three agree in their ideal of spiritual discipline. It is knowledge (prajñā, brahmajñāna) that frees us; other factors are auxiliary to this. The state of mukti (nirvāṇa) is a complete identity with the Absolute.

V THE DIFFERENT MODES OF THE ABSOLUTE AND THEIR IMPLICATIONS

The differences of the absolutes, at least in the manner of their approach, should not be overlooked. Every absolutism may be understood as a mode of the negative judgment, as negation of illusion. There is difference with regard to the illusion with which they start, and the standpoint from which they negate the illusory. By implication, this entails a difference in the way that the relation between the real and the appearance is conceived in each system.

1. The Vedānta and Vijñānavāda start with an *empirical illusion*, the 'rope-snake' or the dream-object, and extend this analysis analogically to the world-illusion superimposed on the real. The Vedānta analyses illusion from the knowledge-standpoint; the illusion consists in wrong characterisation, in mistaking the given as something else; the 'this' which is given is misperceived as the 'snake'. Even for being mistaken, the 'this' must be there as the substrate, independent of our knowing. The 'snake' is, however, exhausted in the knowledge-relation itself, and it is therefore prātibhāsika (appearance).

Vijñānavāda analyses illusion from an opposite angle; for it, the 'given' is appearance, and the ideating consciousness alone is real. The appearance of something, the 'this', independent of the act of cognition, is negated; and the true nature of the appearance as identical with the projecting consciousness is reinstated.

In both Vedānta and Vijñānavāda, the analysis of empirical illusion is extended analogically to the world. But what will tell us that the phenomenal world itself is illusory? For, here obviously we have no experience of an actual cancellation to justify this, as we had in the example of an empirical illusion. An empirical illusion (of the form 'this is snake') does not of itself necessitate being universalised of all phenomena. The problem must present itself in all its universality.

Both Vedānta and Vijñānavāda have therefore to take the cue from some extra-logical mode of cognition: the Vedānta gets it from revelation (śruti) which declares the ātman (Brahman) alone to be real, the Yogācāra depends on the deliverance of the trance-states where the object drops out leaving consciousness as the sole reality. This is made the norm for judging phenomena.[1]

But all this imports an element of dogmatism in their procedure as well as indirectness; there is first the analysis of empirical illusion and then its analogical extension to the world-illusion. Both Vedānta and Vijñānavāda are still given to metaphysical construction.

The Mādhyamika starts, not with an empirical illusion, but with the Transcendental illusion, as exhibited in the inevitable conflict of opposed standpoints and philosophies. He addresses himself primarily to the *views* about the real; only indirectly, he is concerned with the things or reality; for the views criticised are views of the real. The Mādhyamika approach is solely that of a critic of experience. Dialectic or criticism itself is philosophy; while for the Vedānta and Vijñānavāda dialectic is enlisted in the service of philosophy.

2. What is negated? If the form of illusion is set down as: "This is snake", the negating or concelling consciousness is of the form: "This is not snake." For the Vedānta the *not* applies to the 'snake'. This is *not snake*, i.e. *This* is real, but its ascribed snake-character is false. For the Vijñānavāda, the 'not' applies to the *this*, 'The snake is *not this*' i.e. the 'snake' is *not* out there as *this*, as an object independent of the projecting Ideation of consciousness, but is identical with the latter. The 'this' (given, Being) is real for the Vedānta, and the 'snake' as a creature of projective imagination is appearance; for the Vijñānavāda, it is just the reverse: the 'this' as an other, independent of consciousness, is appearance; and the 'snake' is real, being the mode of constructive Ideation. Both have this common feature however. From the context of illusion they reject one aspect—the appearance—(the 'snake' by the Vedāntin and the 'this' by the Vijñānavādin); it is totally false, unreal (svarūpato mithyā, parikalpita[2]). They, however, salvage and retrieve the other

[1] Refer to Chap. VI section 5.

[2] yena yena vikalpena yad yad vastu vikalpyate;
parikalpita evāsau svabhāvo na sa vidyate. *Triṁśikā* 20.
prathamo lakṣaṇenaiva niḥsvabhāvaḥ . . . Ibid. 23.
ataś ca svarūpābhāvāt khapuṣpavat svarūpeṇaiva niḥsvabhāvaḥ. Ibid. p. 41.

part, the real or the prius of illusion (the 'this' by the Vedāntin and the 'snake' by the Vijñānavādin); only its relationship with the appearance is false (saṁsargato mithyā); the paratantra (the stream of consciousness) is false to the extent of the imputation of the object (parikalpita); but in itself it is identical with the pariniṣpanna (Absolute).

Logically, the above analysis means that although the relation may be false, both the terms are not false, but only one; there is an absolute or non-relative term. The general formula is: the two terms sustaining a relation are not of the same order, one is *higher* and the other *lower*: the two terms are neither mutually dependent nor mutually independent; relation is neither 'internal' nor 'external'. If mutually dependent, we cannot distinguish between the two terms; as they so necessarily imply each other that one cannot exist without the other any time. We cannot even say that there are two terms, as the basis of distinction is lacking. If mutually independent, there is no basis of connection; each term is a self, a self-contained universe as it were. To escape this dilemma we have to conceive one term as basic, and thus capable of existing apart from its relation to the other; while the other is incapable of so doing and therefore dependent. One term, the higher, is not exhausted in the relationship; it has a transcendent or non-implicatory existence which is its intrinsic nature; the other term, however, is entirely exhausted within the relation, and it has no non-relative existence.

For the Mādhyamika negation applies to both the 'this' and the 'snake': *this* is not *snake*. The 'this' cannot be had apart from the 'snake', for we know the 'this' only as identified with the 'snake' (predicate) and not in isolation; the 'snake' too can be had only as identified with the 'this' (substrate, subject). They are relative to each other, and this constitutes their falsity. Neither the constructive Ideation of the Vijñānavāda, nor the Pure Being (of the Vedānta) which allows, as the Passive ground, for the superimposition to occur, is real for the Mādhyamika. For, what can tell us that either the one or the other is real. Not the context of illusion itself; for there each is relative to the other (the 'this' is apprehended as related with the 'snake' and vice versa). And if we bring to the analysis of illusion, an extra-philosophical knowledge of the real, that would be a dogmatic assumption. The Vedāntin and the Vijñānavādin might point out that the justification consists in the very impossibility of explaining illusion except by taking the 'this' as real and the 'snake' as false, or vice versa.[1] The Mādhyamika will, however, answer that, in that case, there should be one and only one way of explaining illusion; but obviously the Vedānta analyses illusion with a knowledge-bias and the Vijñānavāda with the will-bias. For, do they not choose, from among several possible ways of explanation, one as *the* true one? The illusion-context itself does not disclose its mind, its inner essence; but if we come to it with a made-up mind, the explanation could be justified. But nothing can justify that initial bias itself. This means that even in explaining illusion, we are still theorising, indulging in speculation. The illusion itself shows, on the contrary, that the two ('this' and 'snake') are relative to each other.

Can anything be retrieved from the relativity of the two terms? Not the two moments, certainly; they are relative and have no nature of their own (niḥsvabhāva[2]). But the *reflective consciousness to* which *they both appear* is absolute; for it is outside the conflict. Pictorially, in a duel of equals, both the combatants fall down exhausted; the spectator is the residue. Likewise, the Mādhyamā Pratipad as the Reflective awareness of the antinomical conflict of reason (dharmāṇāṁ bhūta-pratyavekṣā) is at once above the conflict and is an inner insight into it. We cannot dispense with this critical awareness *to which* the conflict appears, which appreciates and appraises the conflict. It is the philosophical consciousness come

[1] As pointed out, illusion for the Vedāntin and Vijñānavādin is the wrong identification of entities belonging to two different orders—one is real and the other unreal (satyānṛte mithunī-kṛtya). They may very well consider the Mādhyamika contention of the equal status of the 'rope' and 'snake' in the context of illusion as contrary to facts. They may further point out that the function of the Mādhyamika dialectic is in the preliminary stage; it is to bring home the nature of Transcendent illusion. How that illusion is constituted, what are the ingredients necessary for its occurrence, etc. are questions that need analysis of actual experience; and dialectical criticism is irrelevant then. This is how both Vedānta and Vijñānavāda might escape the Mādhyamika charge of dogmatism levelled against them.

[2] For the Mādhyamika, both the terms of a relational complex are false; as mutually dependent, they lack an essential nature of their own (tat tat prāpya yad utpannaṁ *notpannaṁ tat svabhāvataḥ*); the relativity of things is their unreality. The Vedāntin and the Vijñānavādin will not reject both the terms as relative; they accept one as the reality or the basis of the other. For the Mādhyamika the substance and the attributes are equally unreal, as neither of them can be had apart from the other. The Vedāntin would say that the attributes are mere ascriptions of substance, the particulars are negations of the universal and are therefore unreal by their very nature (svarūpato mithyā); but the substance or the universal is inherently real, only its seeming relationship with the attributes or particulars is false (samsargato mithyā); it has a transcendent nature without the relation.

of age. It cannot be got at as a thing; but it is there, as the deepest and innermost attitude of things. It is Prajñā.

The Mādhyamika Absolute (Śūnyatā) has to be understood as the Reflective awareness of the dialectical play of reason, of the 'is' and 'not-is'; it is none other than this critical consciousness. To deny this is to deny critical reflection. That would be to hold that we can *do* a thing, but *cannot know that we do it*: that we can theorise and speculate, but *cannot know that we theorise or speculate*. This amounts to a contradiction, for the denial itself betrays *knowledge* of the theory.

The understanding of Śūnyatā as Reflection or criticism provides the reason why nothing can be predicated of it. As the *awareness* of 'is' (bhāva) and 'not-is' (abhāva), of 'nitya' and 'anitya', it cannot be identified with either of them. The *review* of positions is no position: it is neither one of the positions reviewed, nor another position; as in that case it would lose its nature as *re*flection (self-consciousness). This is why the Mādhyamika consistently refuses to characterise it as sat, asat, both or neither (catuṣkoṭi-vinirmukta). Prajñā is transcendent to thought (Śūnya).

As reflection is not another position, but the *same* position simplified, analysed and clarified, the Mādhyamika absolute is immanent; it is essentially identical with the views (sat, 'asat' etc.) criticised. To reflect on a problem is to resolve it.

We shall miss the true nature of the Mādhyamika Śūnyatā if we failed to understand the true nature of critical reflection, which is the philosophical consciousness *par excellence*. All misrepresentations of the Mādhyamika and cheap criticism of it as Nihilism etc. spring from the failure to appreciate the nature of philosophical reflection. Let the critics pause and make clear to themselves what is the nature and status of reflction. They will have then found the key for the understanding of the Mādhyamika system.

To sum up the discussion. Brahman is the Absolute of Pure Being; and the method of approach is from the standpoint of knowledge. Vijñaptimātratā is Pure Act (Transcendental Ideation), and the approach is from the standpoint of the will consciousness. Śūnyatā is Prajñā, non-dual Intuition, and the approach is from the standpoint of philosophical reflection or criticism. It is that contentless and positionless awareness itself. Brahman and Vijñaptimātratā too are contentless; for in Pure Being there is no *other* from which it could be distinguished and related. Nothing can be predicated of it, and one cannot even speak of it literally. Can we still continue to call it

Being, Vijñāna, or by any other term? In the end every consistent absolutist is reduced to the Mādhyamika position of 'No-position'. The differences pertain to the mode of approach, to the standpoint from which these systems reach the Absolute, like the centre of a circle which is reached from the periphery by different radii.

Orientating from Kant we may understand the three absolutisms (Vedānta, Vijñānavāda and the Mādhyamika) as the three most consistent forms of what are left in Kant as indications and demands. There are two distinct trends in the *Critique*: the constructive as exemplified in the *Trans. Analytic* and the other critical or dialectical as exemplified in the *Trans. Dialectic*. In the *Analytic*, Kant attempts to give a constructive theory of experience as the composition of two factors belonging to two different spheres: on the one hand, there are the *a priori* categories that are innate to the mind; on the other, we have the thing-in-itself, the given which is interpreted in terms of the *a priori*. In spite of Hegelian or other criticism, we can dispense with neither. The demand is for a discipline to realise either of them, apart from the other, in a non-phenomenal experience. We must realise, in a non-empirical way, the pure thing-in-itself without the mediation of the categories of thought; likewise, we must realise the categories of pure thought without the spectre of *the other* (the given thing-in-itself). The logic of the demand is: if empirical experience is a composite of two factors, the constitutents must be had apart from the other; otherwise there could be no question of a composition; the two factors would be really one.

The Advaita Vedānta is that consistent discipline by which we realise the Thing-in-itself, the Pure Object (sanmātra) immediately, self-evidently, unrelatedly, without the categories. The Vijñānavāda is the attempt to reach the Transcendental categories (Pure Thought) without any trace of the given. In both ways, we reach an absolutism; for, there is no other either of thought or of the given. As pointed out already, both Vedānta and Vijñānavāda reach their characteristic position by an analysis of illusion from their respective standpoints.

The other and more dominant trend in Kant's *Critique* is the dialectical consciousness that is alive to the antinomical conflict in philosophy. Dogmatic, speculative theories try to reach the unconditioned by unduly extending empirical principles; they come into necessary clash with each other. Dialectic or criticism results. Avoiding speculation, criticism addresses itself to an analytic understanding of how philosophical construction works. Implicit in all dogmatic metaphysics, philosophy, or the dialectical consciousness, emerges through its own inner dynamism of conflict. This ever-vigilant dialectical consciousness of all philosophy is another kind of absolute, if we correctly appraise its worth. For, it rises above all positions, transcending the duality of the thesis and the antithesis which eminently contain the whole universe. It is unfortunate that Kant missed the startling discovery that he had made. Prejudiced in favour of faith, Kant makes only a negative and trivial use of criticism. He should have taken criticism itself as philosophy, the true metaphysic as a science. The Mādhyamika, however, most consistently develops this. His absolute is the critical Reflection itself.

CHAPTER FOURTEEN

THE MADHYAMIKA SYSTEM—AN ESTIMATE

A HISTORICAL, analytic and comparative survey of the Mādhyamika system has been made. It now remains to assess critically the soundness and value of the system as philosophy and religion. Is Śūnyatā a consistent absolutism? Even if consistent, is it significant? What has been its contribution to Indian philosophy, and can it prove of help in solving our present-day problems?

We have a right to expect adequate answers to these and similar questions.

I ŚŪNYATĀ IS ABSOLUTISM, NOT NIHILISM OR POSITIVISM

1. Dialectic is the pivot of the Mādhyamika system. And this could emerge as the inherent and inevitable conflict developed between the ātma and anātma traditions, one drawing its inspiration from the Upaniṣads and the other from the teachings of Buddha. Dialectic is the consciousness of the antinomical conflict of Reason in the opposition of the two 'moments'—'is' and 'not-is'; it is at once their resolution by arising to a higher plane of critical awareness. It has been shown that the Mādhyamika dialectic is but the systematic form of the suggestions already found in the teachings of Buddha as embodied in the Pāli and other Canons. The Mādhyamika develops his characteristic 'middle-position', which is really no position, by a trenchant criticism of the various systems and points of view, especially of the Ābhidharmika system. All this has been treated at sufficient length, and it is not proposed to cover the ground over again.

The Jaina system and Hegel attempt to resolve the antinomical conflict in Reason by synthesising the view-points and evolving a new system incorporating the views. For them the conflict is engendered by one-sidedness, and this, they aver, is removed in a synthesis. For the Mādhyamika, the synthesis of views is but another view, and it does not escape the predicament inherent in all views.[1] To get rid

[1] The Jaina and the Mādhyamika positions are antipodal to each other: for the Jaina, all views are true, and the real is a conspectus of view-points; for the Mādhyamika, no view is true and the Real transcends thought.

of the conflict, then, we have to transcend all views and standpoints that cramp our understanding and make reality an appearance. Every view must be given up to reach the real as it is. The rejection is done by exhibiting the inherent, but unnoticed, contradiction present in every thesis to the upholder of the thesis on principles and arguments acceptable to him; it is done by prasanga or *reductio ad absurdum* arguments. Not only affirmative views, but negative ones and even a conjunction of them, are negated by the Mādhyamika dialectic.

The one legitimate conclusion that can follow from this procedure is that the Real is transcendent to thought, and that it cannot be conceived in terms of the empirical. The dialectic should not be taken, as is done by the uninformed, as the denial of the Real—Nihilism. As we have pointed out before, the 'no-doctrine-about-the-real' attitude of the Mādhyamika is confounded with the 'no-reality' doctrine. Any consistent absolutism has necessarily to exclude empirical determinations of the real; and all determinations are empirical. This may appear to men accustomed to assess things with the norm of the empirical as non-existent; but it is not non-existent in itself. The objection assumes that the spatio-temporal world perceived by the senses is real, and that that alone is real.[1]

We are explicitly warned by the Mādhyamikas not to consider Śūnyatā as abhāva, non-existence.[2] To deny the accessibility of the real to thought is not to deny the real, unless we assumed the identity of the real with thought. A Hegel might urge that what lacks thought-determinations and is inaccessible to Reason is nothing. The objection has force only when you have accepted, assumed, that the Real is Reason and nothing else. And what will justify this assumption? It may be said that we know nothing else beside this, and that provides the justification for the criterion of the real. But thought does not exhaust the modes of our cognition; nor is it the prius. For the Mādhyamika, the total negation of thought-modes is Prajñā—Intuition. Prajñā is Absolute, as the Real and the knowledge of it are non-dual (advaya), non-different.

If Prajñā is Intuition and is, therefore, positive, why should the

[1] Śaṁkara too complains that Brahman, the Absolute, may appear to the ignorant as nothing, Śūnya: digdeśaguṇagatiphalabhedaśūnyaṁ hi paramārthasad advayaṁ Brahma mandabuddhīnām asad iva pratibhāti. *Bhāṣya on Chh. Up.* (beginning of VIII Chap.)

[2] Nāgārjuna and Candrakīrti answer these and similar objections in the MK. XXIV—(*Ārya Satya Parīkṣā*). For a discussion of these points and textual citations, reference may be made to the chapter on *Absolute & Phenomena.*

Mādhyamika identify it with Śūnyatā, and use the negative method of the Dialectic to attain this end? The objection betrays ignorance of the logic of absolutism. We cannot know the real except by negating appearance: the real is the *reality of the apparent*, and only as we tear off the superficial vestures in which it is clothed do we know the real, not otherwise. Intuition is not one other mode of knowledge beside thought; if it were so, we should have two alternative, even complementary, modes of knowing. And nothing can then decide between their rival claims. But thought is inherently incapable of revealing the real; for it looks at it through conceptual patterns, through differentia and distinction; it sunders and distorts the real. Buddhi[1] (Reason) is therefore characterised as saṁvṛti, the veil that covers the real. And the soul of buddhi is in the 'antas', in the 'is' and 'not-is' attitudes or a combination of them. To know the real, then, we have necessarily to remove the function of buddhi, i.e. negate the 'antas' or attitudes of 'is' and 'not-is' Prajñā is very rightly taken as the Śūnyatā of dṛṣṭi, the negation of concepts (antadvaya-śūnya).

This allows us to understand the nature of the absolute as at once transcendent and immanent. It is transcendent as it is beyond the categories of thought, untouched by empirical predicates (catuṣkoṭi-vinirmukta, nirvikalpa); it is immanent, as it is not another thing beside the world, but is the world itself known truly, without the distorting medium of buddhi. It is no accident then that the Mādhyamika uses the language of negation. The real is not to be brought into existence *de novo*; nor can a knowledge of it be taken as a new acquisition. Misconceptions alone require to be removed. And this function the Dialectic performs; that alone is its function.

2. *Śūnyatā is not Positivism*: it has a spiritual goal.

The critic of the Mādhyamika may not be easily satisfied. "Your logic," he might say, "is impeccable; but your logic ends in nothing." To him the dialectic may possibly appear to be an elaborate game designed to cover up the hollowness of the void (Śūnya). There is nothing to distinguish the Mādhyamika system from positivism, like that of Logical Positivism of the present age, or the forthright materialism of old.[2] All these are anti-metaphysical and anti-

[1] BCA. IX. 2; MKV. p. 492.

[2] Some of the Cārvākas, like Jayarāśi, have also adopted the negative method of the Mādhyamika. In his *Tattvopaplava Siṁha*, Jayarāśi subjects the various

religious in their objective. With his rejection of all views, of all constructive metaphysics which give us access to the ultimately real, the Mādhyamika is a species of positivism.

The objection is by no means new. It had been raised against Nāgārjuna and his successors, and has been answered by them.[1] Though the external form of denial and refutation may be common to positivism and the Mādhyamika dialectic, they have two totally different and opposite objectives. The positivist denies the significance of metaphysics, calling it sheer nonsense even, because for him all significance is confined to the propositions that are empirically verifiable, such as those of science. For him, the sense-given is, in the last resort, the only real; he has neither use for nor knowledge of the transcendent. He is a materialist at heart. The Mādhyamika rejects speculative (dogmatic) metaphysics, not because there is no real that is transcendent, but because by its defective procedure dogmatic metaphysics wrongly understands the transcendent in terms of the empirical modes; it illegitimately extends, to the unconditioned, the categories of thought that are true within phenomena alone. To safeguard the purity of his tattva (Real) it is necessary for the Mādhyamika to deny the pretensions of dogmatic metaphysics. His position is akin to that of Kant. Kant's Transcendental dialectic is directed against speculative metaphysics (against Rational Psychology, Cosmology and Theology) not because he did not believe in the reality of God, Freedom and Immortality of the Soul, but because he wanted to make them safe from the unwarranted ascriptions of pure Reason. The difference between the two, as has been pointed out previously, is that Kant seeks to realise these noumenal realities in a non-intellectual mode—Faith and practical Reason; the Mādhyamika does it in Intellectual Intuition—Prajñāpāramitā. The Mādhyamika is spiritual to the core. His absolute is not

conceptions of Pramāṇa to a searching analysis and condemns them as untenable. Without the pramāṇas there can be no determination of the real. But empirical activity is possible, because things appear as attractive and real superficially. He concludes: tad evam upapluteṣv eva tattveṣu avicāritaramaṇīyāḥ sarve vyavahārāḥ ghaṭante. *Tattvopaplava* p. 125.

[1] Cf. MKV. pp. 273 ff & 368 ff. atraike paricodayanti: nāstikā-viśiṣṭā Mādhyamikāḥ yasmāt kuśalākuśalaṁ karma kartāraṁ ca phalaṁ ca sarvaṁ ca lokaṁ bhāvasvabhāva-śūnyam iti bruvate. nāstikā api hyetan nāstīti bruvate. tasmān nāstikāviśiṣṭā Mādhyamikā iti—naivam. pratītyasamutpādavādino hi Mādhyamikāḥ etc. p. 368.

void, but *devoid* of finitude and imperfection. It is nothing but Spirit.[1]

The objective of his dialectic is spiritual; it is to free the mind of all vikalpa by resolving the antas, alternatives. By this, freedom from kleśas—passions, attachment and aversion—is achieved; for the kleśas have their root in vikalpa or false construction.[2] Prajñā is Nirvāṇa—the state of freedom. It is also the attainment of Buddhahood; Prajñā-pāramitā is Tathāgata, the *Ens realissimum.* Prajñā consummates the moral and the religious ideal; it is spiritual. The spiritual is a state of undivided personality: the person is not divided in himself; nor does he divide himself from others. The internal conflict between various levels of personality and the external conflict of one's good as antagonistic to the good of others are both resolved. This is possible in the advaita or advaya, where all our faculties and interests are unified as Brahman or Prajñāpāramitā. It is possible *only* in advaita, for that alone abolishes private standpoints and interests, which make for the ego-centric outlook. In the last analysis, the ego is the root of the unspiritual; the universal is the spiritual. Śūnyatā, as the negation of all particular views and standpoints, is the universal *par excellence.*

Not only has the Mādhyamika dialectic the spiritual for its objective, it is not also incompatible with any empirical activity. It is not opposed to commonsense or science, where our aim is to know and handle things presented to sense in the phenomenal sphere. The categories of thought, causality, substance, identity and difference, good and bad etc., are certainly not applicable to the ultimately real, being relative; but the Mādhyamika does not deny their utility as patterns of explanation in the empirical region. It is the dogmatic theorist with his insistence upon the sole truth of his particular conception of the real who makes empirical activity

[1] Hiriyanna thinks that the Mādhyamika Śūnyatā is Nothing; he relies entirely on the superficial characterisation of it by the orthodox Hindu systems (*Outlines of Ind. Phil.* p. 221). This is a bare statement without much argument or textual support. The professor, however, has the candour to say: "Our object here being chiefly to present later Buddhism as it was understood by Hindu thinkers and is found set forth in their works, it is easy to answer the question, for they all alike agree in holding that the void is the only truth according to the Mādhyamika." Professor Radhakrishnan correctly interprets "Śūnyatā as a positive principle"; "To call it being is wrong, only concrete things are. To call it non-being is equally wrong. It is best to avoid all descriptions of it." I.P. Vol. I. pp. 663–4.

[2] MK. XVIII, 5.

impossible.[1] Transcendental ideality (unreality) and empirical reality well go together.

II SOME UNIQUE FEATURES OF THE MĀDHYAMIKA SYSTEM

Very often the criticism is made that the Mādhyamika system is destructive in its function. The dialectic may be efficient as a logical weapon, but it savours of ill-will symptomatic of a disposition that sees no good in others. How does it escape being a species of philosophical sadism? Rightly understood, the Mādhyamika, however, is the one system that is completely free from every trace of dogmatism. The dialectic is not condemnation of others, but is self-criticism. It is the self-consciousness of philosophy. This self-consciousness is born of the necessary conflict in dogmatic metaphysics. The contrast implied is between the dogmatic procedure of reason that is intent on weaving theories about things and the self-conscious awareness of the weaving of theories. Through dogmatism and the necessary conflict of Reason, philosophical consciousness comes into its own.

In theorising, we make use of assumptions and pre-suppositions that are unnoticed at the time. Dialectic makes us aware of the pre-suppositions, the foundations on which our edifice rests. It may be claimed for the Mādhyamika Dialectic that it is the impartial tribunal which alone can assess the true nature of every philosophical system. We know the inside of a system only as we analyse it and subject it to a penetrating criticism. The Mādhyamika dialectic is the search-light that illumines the darkest recesses of reason. If it had been a theory, one among others, it would singularly fail in its high office as the Norm of all philosophy.

Philosophy is the quest for knowledge that is universal in scope and absolutely certain in its quality. The demand is to possess knowledge that does not leave anything out of its comprehension and which is at once free from the possibility of doubt. This demand, however, cannot be satisfied by science or speculative metaphysics. Knowledge gained by science is piecemeal in character and is progressively accumulative; there can possibly be no conceivable limit to the acquisition of information. The scientific method of

[1] Cf. svabhāvād yadi bhāvānāṁ sadbhāvam anupaśyasi;
ahetupratyayān bhāvāṁs tvam evam sati paśyasi.
sarva-saṁvyavahārāṁś ca laukikān pratibādhase;
yat pratītyasamutpāda-śūnyatāṁ pratibādhase. MK. XXIV, 16, 36.

explanation, through hypothesis and verification by appeal to sense-experience, necessarily restricts the scope of science to the empirical.

Speculative metaphysics has certainly freed itself of this limitation; as it does not depend on empirical verification, it can *claim* to give us universal (unrestricted) and final knowledge of the entire reality. But there are two fatal drawbacks which vitiate dogmatic philosophy. Each philosophical system selects a particular pattern and views reality from that standpoint; it becomes a view (a dṛṣṭi), a standpoint or position. The position selected may be attractive and advantageous; but it is *one* view, a particular standpoint, and therefore necessarily *restricts* our vision. A view is one-sided (ekāntavāda) and cannot give us the whole reality. The second drawback is that there is nothing that can *validate our* picture of reality. Among a number of possible ways of conceiving the real, we have no *a priori* or other means of deciding in favour of one. We cannot appeal to empirical experience as we do in science; for the propositions of philosophy are of the super-sensible, the unconditionedly real. Consistent and elaborate working out of a particular philosophical pattern does not mean that it conforms to the real; it just evidences our powers of imagination and logical attention. If internal consistency and elaboration were the criterion of the truth of any philosophy, this would be satisfied by many systems. We cannot admit that all or even any two of them are true as they contradict each other. For example, the systems of the ātma and the anātma tradition are internally consistent and elaborate; but they are diametrically opposed to each other in their standpoints. This throws doubt on philosophy, on every system. Certitude and finality have eluded us.

Can universality and certitude be attained by synthesising all possible views, thus obviating restriction of scope and uncertainty. The Jain system in India and Hegel in the West can be cited as examples of this attempt; the Jaina attempts a disjunctive synthesis of possible views and Hegel a conjunctive or integrating synthesis.[1] Combination of views is another view. For, we have to marshal all views according to a pre-arranged plan; there would be shifting of emphasis with regard to the constituents of the synthesis. And, owing to the emphasis placed on identity or difference, the synthesis too

[1] See Chaps. V and IX.

would become different. Syntheses become many and varied and are subject to the predicaments already adduced.

The Mādhyamika dialectic avoids all this by its negative method, as pointed out before. Universality is attained not by a combination of particular viewpoints, but by abolishing viewpoints. Certitude is gained, not by dogmatic assertion, but by critical reflection (bhūta-pratyavekṣā). We do not advance theories, but we become *aware of* theories. The Mādhyamika goes to the tendency which is the root-cause of our inability to know the real in itself—conceptual construction, dṛṣṭi; this is concretely expressed in the various ideologies and philosophical systems. It is avidyā or saṁvṛti. The antidote is to void the mind of this tendency to conceptualise the real; to resolve the dṛṣṭis, both of the affirmative and the negative kind. As special standpoints and particular positions are abolished, the knowing Intellect becomes transparent (bhāsvara, amala), free from obscuration (āvaraṇa-prahāṇa). The Real is no longer looked at through the categories of thought, mediately, wrongly; the Intellect is not different from the Real. That is Prajñāpāramitā—Intuition or Non-Dual knowledge, free from the concepts of 'is' and 'not-is'. We do not acquire the absolute or Prajñā; we only remove the impediments.

Strange as it may appear, the Mādhyamika Śūnyatā (Absolute) can serve as the basis for a synthesis of philosophical systems. Because of its rigorous eschewing of all thought-content from the Real (Śūnya), it is no doubt transcendent to thought. But on that very score, it can be 'freely' phenomenalised, and one need not restrict oneself to any *particular mode* of synthesis to serve for all time and for all people. In the Hegelian synthesis, there is emphasis on unity and the differences are subordinated to it. The opposite may well be the case: difference can be made the prius and identity subordinated to it. The order of the synthesised categories may be varied. In Hegel, the synthesis is a blocked series; it cannot be replaced without replacing his conception of the Absolute too. In the Mādhyamika, one mode of synthesis may be replaced by another without necessitating any change in the Absolute. This may be called a loose dynamic synthesis. It must, however, be borne in mind that all these modes of phenomenalisation are merely 'devices' (upāya): ultimately false, but eminently useful, both for the empirical world and as means for reaching the absolute. That they are false does not make them less useful; even the false can work. Secondly, such syntheses[1] can be formulated only

[1] This is the celebrated upāyakauśalya of the Buddhas.

by those that have spiritual realisation; it is not just a matter of logical skill and imaginative manipulation. For, each device must serve the purpose of reaching us to the Absolute by the path most suited to the person concerned. Only one who has trodden the path before can lead others to it.

In one sense, the Mādhyamika may seem one of the most intolerant of systems, as it negates all possible views without exception. In another sense, in the manner shown above, it can accommodate and give significance to all systems and shades of views. As pointed out before Śūnyatā does not militate against vyavahāra. Justly can Nāgārjuna claim:

All is concord indeed for him who to Śūnyatā conforms;[1]
All is not concordant for him who conforms not to Śūnyatā.

III THE VALUE OF THE MĀDHYAMIKA SYSTEM AS BASIS FOR WORLD CULTURE

The Mādhyamika is not an academic system. It profoundly influenced the philosophy and religion of India and a good part of Asia for several centuries. It is the first Absolutist system (advayavāda) to be formulated in India or elsewhere. To the Mādhyamika should also belong the honour of establishing advayavāda through the Dialectic. This ushered in a revolution, as we have traced, in Buddhism, in the entire range of its metaphysics, ethics and religion. Śūnyatā, mahākaruṇā and the Tathāgata's Trikāya became the fundamental ideas for all subsequent philosophy and religion. The non-Buddhist systems may not have borrowed the tenets of the Mādhyamika or Vijnānavāda; but they were conceivably profited by their technique. Advaitism came to be established as the most dominant feature of the spiritual culture of India. The essence of this consists in the inner realisation of the unity of all being and the utter negation of all egoity. The great measure of unity and stability of social structure which still persists is the reflection of the Śūnyatā (Absolutist) conception in the practical affairs of men. It permeated every walk of life—literature, fine art, social sciences, religion and philosophy. A stable and exalted civilisation was built up and sustained for centuries in the greater part of Asia, in India, China, Japan, Tibet and other countries.

[1] sarvaṁ ca yujyate tasya, śūnyatā yasya yujyate;
sarvaṁ na yujyate tasya śūnyaṁ yasya na yujyate. MK. XXIV, 14.

Its influence cannot be confined to the past. What could be done once can be done once again. And there is all the greater need to emphasise the spiritual unity of the world, torn as it is by ever so many conflicts and warring ideologies that threaten to engulf the entire world in speedy ruin. Everywhere the hold of tradition has loosened. During the Middle Ages the civilised world enjoyed, with a few exceptions, a period of peace and stability never known before. No doubt the known world was divided into three well-defined blocks, the Christian zone in the West, the Moslem in the Middle East and the Hindu (including Buddhist) in the East and Far East. Feeling of brotherhood and unity of man were vital forces. These traditional influences are no longer at work. The Christian world has been disintegrating for centuries, since the Renaissance. There is little hope that it could regain the lost ground and reassert itself. The East is hardly better, though the disintegration has not proceeded to to such an extent; but the spiritual is no longer an active force.

Owing to the phenomenal discoveries in science and their practical application, the peoples of the world have been brought together; the geographical and physical oneness of the world has been brought home to us. But our differences and divergences have increased tremendously; strife and bitterness are rampant. War has become chronic and global in its proportions. The present-day world lacks unity and goodwill; it has no soul or spirit to animate and unify it.

The causes are not hidden. Western civilisation, which has become the norm for all, has developed, since the Renaissance, along materialistic lines. "The contrast between the success of modern European minds in controlling almost any situation in which the elements are physical bodies and the forces physical forces, and their inability to control situations in which the elements are human beings and the forces mental forces" is too evident to need elaboration. Man has conquered Nature or is very near doing that; but he has not the rudimentary control over himself. The consequences are disastrous. Organised life with any pretence to stability and security has become precarious. We have gained the world, but have lost our soul.

It has been suggested that the remedy lies in increased production by the harnessing of all our ingenuity and resources, and by a more equitable distribution by concentration on the reorganisation of the social structure on a classless basis. Fascism and Communism are the concrete forms of this urge. Accepting the material as the *only* value, these try to work out a civilisation to the best advantage. The experiment needs to be tried, if only as a matter of dialectical necessity. We have to be convinced of the utter futility of the material norm before we could give it up.

It may bring about temporary and even partial relief, but it is bound to fail as a final solution. The basic principles underlying it are vicious. If material goods, earthly life, were the only good, how can one have too much of these. One would try to secure them as much as possible and by every means; fair and foul can have no moral signification, but can be judged by the measure of material success they bring about. How can the possessive instinct be conquered, or even kept under control? This is done, in a materialistic society, by checks and counter-checks and by the balancing of forces in the society. But what prevents the guardians of such a society, the ruling class, from appropriating more to themselves. Fear of public opinion may prove somewhat of a check, but a skilful determined man can easily manipulate the cards. In the last resort, there must be some considerable body of men who cannot be compelled to behave by external pressure, but who are intrinsically convinced of the worthlessness of material goods. They should have transcended the instinct of possession and must have risen above class and property, like the guardians of state in Plato's *Republic*.

Increased production and organisation cannot *per se* result in good. Goodwill must be there. And goodwill can be born of inner spiritual conviction alone; it cannot be commanded into existence by faith or secular authority. For that would fail miserably and can succeed in making us hypocritical. We have to realise that the good of all is the good of oneself, and that there can be no room for the ego. In the last analysis, the transcending of the standpoint of the ego, or more positively, the attainment of the Universal is the essence of the spiritual. And only the spiritual can provide the basis for the society and can be conducive for the realisation of other values.

In this regard, Mahāyāna absolutism and the Advaita Vedānta are valuable as providing the basis on which a world-culture can be built. It is only absolutism that can make for the fundamental unity of existence and at the same time allow for differences. Catholicity of outlook and tolerance of differences are their very soul; both insist on the universality of the Real and transcendence of the ego-centric standpoint. The Vedānta, however, is traditional in outlook and is bound to the authority of the Veda, and perhaps it presupposes a specific milieu in which alone it can thrive. The Mahāyāna is quite liberal, and it has proved its capacity to accommodate itself to various religious and social structures, to revitalise and absorb them; this is seen in Tibet, Mongolia, China and Japan. It has further the concrete expression of Śūnyatā and Mahākaruṇā in the exalted Bodhisattva ideal.

Thinkers[1] in the West and the East are becoming increasingly alive to the impending crisis in our civilisation and are suggesting the ways of saving it. The issue is not between Capitalism and Communism, although their quarrel tends to cloud the real nature of the malady. The need is for the spiritual regeneration of the world. Denominational religions with their dogmas and organisational sanctions deservedly stand discredited. There is something inherently secular and unspiritual in any organisation. It tends to create vested interests and to breed corruption. In stifling freedom of expression and setting up a norm of dogmas to which the votaries are required to conform, organised religion (the church) succeeds only in antagonising other religious groups and creating schisms and heresies within its own fold. What we need is the realisation of the spiritual which is the bed-rock of all our endeavour. Only mystical religion, which eminently combines

[1] In his numerous works, especially in *The Idealist View of Life* and *Eastern Religions and Western Thought*, the great Eastern Philosopher, Professor Radhakrishnan, advocates the necessity for the revival of the deeply spiritual mystical experience which is the basis of all religions and which is expressed in a pure form in Hinduism. He says: "In spite of all appearances to the contrary, we discern in the present unrest the gradual dawning of a great light, a converging life-endeavour, a growing realisation that there is a secret spirit in which we are all one, and of which humanity is the highest vehicle on earth, and an increasing desire to live out this knowledge and establish a kingdom of spirit on earth." (*Eastern Religions and Western Thought*, p. 33). "The different religions have now come together, and if they are not to continue in a state of conflict or competition, they must develop a spirit of comprehension which will break down prejudice and misunderstanding and bind them together as varied expressions of a single truth. Such a spirit characterised the development of Hinduism, which has not been interrupted for nearly fifty centuries." (ibid. p. 308). "We must recognise humbly the partial and defective character of our isolated traditions and seek their source in the generic tradition from which they all have sprung." (ibid. p. 347).

To take an example from the West. M. Guenon has made a commendable effort to interpret the true spirit of Hindu culture to the West in his many works, notably in *An Introduction to the Study of Hindu Doctrines*, *Man and His Becoming according to the Vedānta*, *East and West*, *The Crisis in the Modern World*, etc. The form of regeneration consists, for M. Guénon, not in a fusion or synthesis of the two cultures, but in the West regaining, as the result of a dynamic turn in its present trend, those springs of true spirituality through the help of the East. It would be hazardous to forecast the time of the change or the precise manner in which it would be brought about.

the unity of Ultimate Being with the freedom of different paths for realising it, can hope to unite the world.

The student of philosophy can only suggest that the Mādhyamika Absolutism can serve as the basis for a possible world-culture. It is not his province to show how best this could be implemented, what practical shape this would assume and at which point and time in the affairs of the world this could be introduced. These are questions which the religious reformer might answer, and even he has to depend upon the spiritual guidance and direction from above.

We must end with a note of warning. It is possible, in our enthusiasm, to over-rate the part played by scholarship and the theoretical understanding of things in the task of regeneration. It is good to remember that history does not record of a single instance of a spiritual revolution of global dimensions brought out by a band of scholars or skilful thinkers. The malady of the world is far too universal and deep-seated for remedies to be prescribed direct from books. A spiritual genius of the order of Buddha or Christ alone knows how to strike at the thing. But even a theoretic understanding of the Mādhyamika absolutism should prove of value by way of preparing the back-ground for the spiritual regeneration of the world.

GLOSSARY OF SANSKṚT TERMS

abhāva, non-being, negation, absence.

abhiniveśa, excessive attachment, dogmatic belief.

abhūta-parikalpa, literally, that where the construction of the non-existent (object) obtains; in the Yogācāra philosophy, a term for the 'paratantra' reality, the Constructive Ideation of Consciousness, the stream of ideas itself.

ācārya, teacher, master.

adhipati-pratyaya, literally, a presiding or dominant condition or cause, e.g., the organ of vision with regard to the occurrence of visual sensation; one of the four kinds of Causes. This has been differently interpreted by the Theravādins and Sarvāstivādins. According to the latter, it is the influence that any entity exerts upon all other entities excepting itself and the unconditioned noumena. See pp. 170–72.

ādi-śānta, quiescent from the very beginning.

advaita, non-dual, not two ultimate realities.

advaita-vāda, the theory of non-dualism; monism or absolutism.

advaya, *advaya-vāda*, negation of both views or extremes of the real. Though almost the same as advaita, there is still some difference between them. See pp. 217–8.

ajāti-vāda, literally, the theory of non-origination. The Mādhyamika view that there has been neither origination nor cessation of things.

ālambana, *ālambana-pratyaya*, the object viewed as a cause or condition for the occurrence of any knowledge. See p. 170.

ālaya, *ālaya-vijñāna*, in the Yogācāra philosophy, the 'store-house'. Consciousness containing potentially all the ideas and other mental states; it is also the residuam of all thoughts and deeds.

anabhilāpya, the unutterable, the inexpressible.

anāsrava, without defilement, pure.

anātma-vāda, no-self (soul) theory; the basic Buddhist doctrine that all things lack substance or permanent identical reality; same as nairātmya-vāda.

anekānta, not one-sided, manifold.

anekānta-vāda, the theory, especially of the Jainas, that reality is manifold or many-sided, not unitary.

anitya, impermanent, changing, momentary.

anta, end, one extreme or alternative; this is applied specially to views or standpoints in philosophy.

aṇu, atom; the impartite bit of matter; same as paramāṇu.

apratiṣṭhitanirvāṇa, literally, the non-fixed nirvāṇa; the non-egoistic nirvāṇa of the Mahāyāna, as contrasted with the personal salvation of the Hīnayāna. The Buddhas and the Bodhisattvas, according to the

Mahāyāna conception, disdain to pass into the state of final release, though fully entitled to it, but continue to be incessantly and actively engaged in the welfare of all beings.

ārambha-vāda, the theory that the effect is a new beginning (different from the cause), or the theory of the prior non-existence of the effect, advocated by the Nyāya-Vaiśeṣika.

arhat, the perfected Saint who has eliminated all passions and suffering. This is the highest stage of attainment according to the Hīnayāna. The Mahāyāna sharply contrasts this with the Bodhisattva ideal of attaining complete Buddhahood and of non-egoistic (altruistic) striving for the salvation of all beings.

arthakriyākāri, efficient, useful; the criterion of the real as the efficient.

ārya, a Perfected Person, Saint. When used as an adjective, it means holy, sacred, noble.

ārya-satya, The Holy Truths; the four Buddhist Truths of Suffering, its Cause, its Cessation and the Path leading to Cessation.

asaṁskṛta, *asaṁskṛta dharmas*, the Unconditioned or Noumenal entities. According to the Sarvāstivādins there are three such entities: Space (ākāśa), Nirvāṇa, and the Cessation of Elements due to the lack of favourable conditions (aprati-saṁkhyā-nirodha).

āsrava, the impure tendencies, passions (kleśas), that infect and defile the mind, causing bondage and suffering.

ātman, Self, Soul, Substance. 'ātman' is equated with dravya (substance), with the nitya (permanent, eternal), with svabhāva (nature or self-being), with sāra (essence) and vastu (real).

ātma-vāda, the theory that the real is substance, permanent and eternal, and has a nature of its own. The opposite view is the anātma-vāda or nairātmya-vāda of the Buddhists.

avayavin, one that has parts, whole.

avyākṛta (*Pāli*, *avyākata*), *avyākṛta-vastūni*, the Undeclared, the Inexpressible; the fourteen questions regarding the ultimate nature of the World, the Perfect Being (Tathāgata), and the Soul (Jīva) which Buddha declared as not capable of definition either as existent or as non-existent or as both or as neither; see pp. 36ff.

āyatana, literally, that which engenders the ingress of (sensations); sense-organs, e.g., the eye, etc., and sense-data, colour, etc.; the twelve bases of sensation and sense-data. See pp. 185–6.

bhāva, being, existence, affirmation.

bhava-diṭṭhi, affirmative or existential view.

bhūta-koṭi, the sphere of the Ultimate (Absolute).

bodhi, Enlightenment, Wisdom.

bodhi-citto-tpāda, Cultivation of the Intellect for Enlightenment; (Buddhist) Spiritual Discipline.

bodhisattva, the Aspirant for Enlightenment.

brahman, Absolute.

buddha-bhakti, devotion to Buddha.

buddhi, Intellect, Mind.

buddha-kāya, the Body of Buddha. See pp. 284–7.

citta, Mind, Pure Consciousness. In Buddhism, this is conceived as a stream or a series of momentary mental states without any abiding stratum. In the Sāṁkhya, it is the Intellect (buddhi) which is an abiding substance that is modified from time to time into the several mental states (vṛttis).

caitta, mental states.

citta-viprayukta-saṁskāras, the non-mental forces.

dāna, charity.

dāna-pāramitā, The Infinite Excellence (Perfection) of Charity.

darśana, Immediate Knowledge, Transcendental Insight, Intuition.

darśana-mārga, the Path of Insight or Illumination.

deva, *devatā*, Deity, God.

dharma, Law, especially Moral Law; Virtue or Merit; Essence or Nature of a thing; Element or Ultimate Constituent of Existence. (The last meaning obtains only in Buddhism).

dharma-dhātu, *dharmatā*, The Reality or Essence of Dharmas (Elements of Existence); the Noumenal Ground of Phenomena; synonymous with Dharma-Kāya, Śūnyatā and Tathatā.

dharma-kāya, The Cosmical Body of the Buddha: the essence of all beings.

dharma-nairātmya, the unreality of elements as separate ultimate existences; this contention of the Mādhyamika is directed against the dogmatic acceptance of the reality of elements by the Hīnayāna Schools (Ābhidharmika and Sautrāntika).

dhrama-saṁketa, the formula or law regarding the sequence of existences.

dharma-vāda, the theory of elements: the Ābhidharmika theory.

dhātu, the literal meaning is 'root' or ultimate element. In Buddhist thought, this term is used in three senses: (i) the three planes of existence (trai-dhātukạ), viz., the Kāmadhātu (Sphere of Gross Desires or Bodies), Rūpadhātu (the Sphere of Subtle Bodies), and Arūpadhātu (the Sphere of Immaterial Bodies); (ii) for the Six Ultimate Elements of Existence (the four general elements of matter, viz., Air, Fire, Water and Earth), Ākaśa (Space) and Vijñāna (pure awareness); (iii) for the eighteen elements of existence (aṣṭādaśa-dhātavaḥ), viz., the six sense-data, the six sense-organs of cognition and the six resultant cognitions or sensations (visual consciousness, etc.)

dhyāna, concentrated contemplation, same as Yoga or Samādhi.

dhyāna-pāramitā, the Infinite Excellence (Perfection) of Concentration of Mind, one of the Six Pāramitās.

dravya, substance, reality.

dravyārthika-naya, the substance-view of reality, as opposed to the modal view which takes the real as particulars or modes.

dṛṣṭi (*Pāli*, *diṭṭhi*), view, philosophical standpoint, speculative theory.

dṛṣṭi-vāda, dogmatism, speculative philosophy as contrasted with Prajñā, which is the rejection of all dogmatic views.

duḥkha, suffering, pain.

eka-naya-vāda, literally 'the sole way theory'; Nāgārjuna and his followers hold that Śūnyatā is the sole means to Nirvāṇa.

ghaṭākāśa, the space enclosed or limited by the pitcher. This is a stock-example in the Advaita Vedānta to explain the relation between the Absolute (Brahman) and the Individual Souls (Jīvas).

gotra, gens, spiritual lineage.

hetu, Cause or Condition; also used more specifically to mean the 'producing cause' (nirvarttako hetuḥ). See p. 170.

indriya, organs of sense-cognition and action.

Īśvara, Lord, God.

jaḍa, inert, matter or material.

jīva, the empirical self, individual soul.

jñāna, knowledge, cognition.

jñeyāvaraṇa, the veil or obscuration of ignorance with regard to the true nature of the real. In the Yogācāra system, this stands for the obscuration engendered by the wrong belief in the reality of the object.

kalpanā, conceptualisation; the application of thought-categories and names (forms in general) to the real.

kalpanāpodham, free from any trace of thought-activity (name and concept).

kalpita, imputed, false.

karma, free or purposeful act, volition; past deeds and their traces or results.

karuṇā, compassion, pity, especially the unmotived infinite Grace of the Buddhas and Bodhisattvas for beings; see also under Mahā-karuṇā.

kleśa, defiling forces, passions.

kleśāvaraṇa, the veiling or obscuration caused by passions; moral defilement.

kṣaṇa, *kṣaṇika*, moment, momentary being.

kṣānti, forbearance, forgiveness, patience.

kṣānti-pāramitā, the Infinite Excellence (Perfection) of Forbearance or Forgiveness.

kūṭastha-nitya, literally, unchanging as the anvil, e.g., the Self (puruṣa) according to the Sāṁkhya and the Vedānta; the unchangingly real, contrasted with the changing real (prakṛti).

lokottara, super-mundane, transcendent, non-empirical.

Madhyamaka, *Mādhyamika*, the Middle Position or Philosophy (of Nāgārjuna).

madhyamā pratipad, the Middle Path; the avoidance of extremes.

mahākaruṇā, the Great Compassion of Buddhas and Bodhisattvas towards all beings; the Condescending Grace or the Free Phenomenalising activity of the Absolute (Śunya); see pp. 259, 280-3, 337, 340.

mīmāṁsā, synthetic consideration, especially exegetical; a school of Brāhmanical philosophy.

nairātmya, soullessness, substancelessness, unreality.

nairātmya-vāda, the theory that there is no substance or soul.

neyārtha, teaching of the indirect or circumstantial import, having phenomenal validity only. See pp. 53, 122, 254–5.

niḥsvabhāvatā, devoid of real essence or reality; having no reality or independent existence; a synonym for the śūnya.

niḥsvabhāva-vāda, the theory embodying the above contention.

nirmāṇa-kāya, An Assumed Body of the Buddha acting in the world of phenomena for the good of beings.

nirupadhiśeṣa-nirvāṇa, the nirvāna without any trace of body-constituents; final release or parinirvāṇa; this corresponds to the Videhamukti of the Vedānta.

nirvikalpa, free from conceptual construction; indeterminate.

niṣprapañca, transcending speech or verbal elaboration; the absolute.

nītārtha, teaching of the direct or ultimate import. See pp. 53, 122, 254–55.

pakṣa, tenet, thesis.

paramāṇu, atom.

paramārtha, *paramārtha-sat*, the Ultimate or Noumenal Reality; Absolute.

paratantra, the relative reality. In the Yogācāra system, it stands for the mind and the mental states on which there occurs the imputation of subject-object distinction; same as abhūta-parikalpa.

pāramitā, literally, that which has gone beyond all limits; Infinite Excellence, Perfection.

parikalpita, the imputed or illusory aspect of appearance; in the Yogācāra, the entire world of objects is imputed on consciousness, and is therefore essentially unreal.

pārimāṇḍalya, the atomic size.

pariṇāma, modification, change.

pariṇāmi-nitya, real as changing: the prakṛti (primordial matter) of the Sāṁkhya.

pariniṣpanna, absolute reality; the specific term for the Yogācāra absolute.

prajñā, wisdom, non-dual knowledge, intuition.

prajñā-pāramitā, Perfection of Wisdom; the Highest Reality identified with the Buddha.

prajñapti-sat, literally, real in thought (only); subjective; unreal.

pramāṇas, sources of valid knowledge.

prapañca, verbal elaboration; the phenomenal world.

prapañcopaśama, the cessation of the world.

prasanga, *prasanga-vākya*, reductio ad absurdum.

prāsangika, one who resorts to *reductio ad absurdum* arguments; one school of the Mādhyamika; dialectician.

prātibhāsika, apparent, illusory like the 'rope-snake' in the stock example of the Vedānta.

pratipakṣa, counter-thesis.

pratītya-samutpāda, dependent origination; this is equated, in the Mādhyamika, with Śūnyatā, the Relativity of things.

pudgala, (*Pāli*, *puggala*), the empirical individual, ego.

pudgalātma-vāda, the theory, held by the Vātsīputrīyas or Sāmmitīyas, of a quasi-permanent entity (pudgala), neither completely identical with the mental states, nor totally different from them. See pp. 26, 81, 202, 205–6.

rūpa, matter, material forms or elements.

sahopalambha-niyama, the principle of the apprehension of knowledge and object together; this is the main Yogācāra argument to establish his idealism, and it corresponds to the principle: esse est percipi.

Śakti, Power; the Phenomenalising Aspect of the Absolute, Siva.

samanantara-pratyaya, the immediately preceding cessation of an entity conceived as a condition in the occurrence of an effect, especially of a mental state. See pp. 170–2, 176n.

samavāya, inherence relation in the Nyāya-Vaiśeṣika. See p. 65.

śamatha, quiescence of the mind by the elimination of passions.

sambhoga-kāya, the Buddha's Body of Enjoyment or Bliss.

saṁjñā, ideation; apprehension of determining marks, i.e., judgement; one of the Five Groups (Skandhas).

saṁsāra, literally, incessantly in motion, flux; the world of phenomena.

saṁskāra, the forces, mental and material, that condition existential (phenomenal) entities.

saṁskṛta, conditioned existence, phenomenon.

saṁvṛti, literally, the covered or the covering activity; superficial reality, appearance. See pp. 86, 122, 243ff.

saṁvṛti-satya, superficial or apparent truth, phenomenal reality. See pp. 243ff.

śānta, quiescent, tranquil.

santāna, series, continuum.

Sarvāsti-vāda, the Buddhist School which holds that all the elements (dharmas) exist in all the three times (sarvadā asti); another name for the Vaibhāṣika.

śāśvata-vāda, eternalism, the theory that the real is changeless and permanent.

satkāya-dṛṣṭi (*Pāli*, *sakkāya-diṭṭhi*), the dogmatic view which clings to the reality of ātman or substance; same as ātma-dṛṣṭi.

satkārya-vada, the (Sāṁkhya) theory that the effect is pre-existent in or identical with the cause.

Sautrāntika, the adherents of the Sūtras of Buddha who deny the canonical character of the Abhidharma treatises; the Buddhist School of Critical Realism. See pp. 81–2, 95, 192.

śīla, practice of moral virtues.

śīla-pāramitā, the Perfection of Moral Virtues.

śīla-vrata, *sīla-vrata-parāmarśa*, the mechanical performance of moral rules, rites and rituals.

Śiva, the Personal Absolute of the Tantra philosophy; as an adjective, it means 'benign', 'blessed'.

skandha (*Pāli*, *khandha*), the (Five) Groups of Elements (dharmas) into which all existences are classified in Early Buddhism. The Five are: Rūpa (matter), Vedanā (feeling), Saṁjñā (ideation), Saṁskāra (forces or drives), Vijñāna (pure consciousness or sensation). See under each head.

sopadhiśeṣa-nirvāṇa, the nirvāṇa with residue of mental and body constituents, not final release; corresponds to the Jīvanmukti of the Vedānta.

sthāpanīya, one of the four kinds of questions, one which has to be put aside as not to be answered.

Sthavira-vāda, The Doctrine of the Elders; an early school of Buddhism belonging to the Hīnayāna; same as Theravāda.

śūnya, *śūnyatā*, the terms are used in two allied meanings: (i) the phenomena are śūnya, as they are relative and lack substantiality or independent reality; they are conditioned (pratītya-samutpanna), and hence are unreal; (ii) the Absolute is śūnya or śūnyatā itself, as it is devoid of empirical forms; no thought-category or predicate ('is', 'not-is', 'is and not-is', 'neither is nor not-is') can legitimately be applied to it; it is Transcendent to thought (śūnya).

svalakṣaṇa, the unique momentary particular; the thing-in-itself; the only real according to early Buddhism; it is cognised in pure sensation.

svatantra, svātantrika, the Mādhyamika school of Bhāvaviveka and others which adduced arguments and examples of their own in refuting their opponents; this is opposed to the other Mādhyamika school (the Prāsangika) of Buddhapālita, Candrakīrti, etc., which strictly adhered to the method of reductio ad absurdum. See pp. 95ff., 132.

svābhāvika-kāya, the Essential or Natural Body of the Buddha; same as the Dharma-kāya.

Tathāgata, appellation of Buddha; one who has realised and known things as they are in reality; Perfect Being.

tathatā, Suchness, Thatness; the Real that stays unmodified; Absolute.

tattva, Essence, Ultimate Reality.

uccheda-vāda, nihilism, materialism; the theory that denies freedom (free will and its responsibility, karma and karma-phala).

upāya, means; the free phenomenal activity of the Absolute manifesting itself as karuṇā.

upāya-kauśalya, excellence in the choice of methods; the skill of Buddha in adopting appropriate and varied means in preaching the truth.

vastu-sat, objectively real; opposite of prajñapti-sat.

vedanā, feeling; the second of the Five Groups (Pañca Skandhas).

vibhava-dṛṣṭi (*Pāli, vibhava-diṭṭhi*), negative or non-existential view.

vijñāna, consciousness or pure awareness without content; the last of the Five Groups (Skandhas).

vijñaptimātratā, the sole reality of Consciousness; the Yogācāra doctrine of the Absolute.

vikalpa, conceptual construction; the subjective activity of thought interpreting the object.

vipaśyanā, analytic insight, intuition.

vīrya, effort, enthusiasm.

vīrya-pāramitā, the Perfection of Effort.

viveka, discrimination, analytic insight; wisdom.

vyakta, manifest, determinate.

vyāvahārika, phenomenal reality; relative truth or appearance.

APPENDIX

A NOTE ON THE TWENTY MODES OF ŚŪNYATĀ

SOME of the later *Prajñāpāramitās*, such as the *Pañcaviṁśatisāhasrikā*, speak of the twenty modes of Śūnyatā.[1] There is no explicit discussion of this topic in the writings of noted Mādhyamika philosophers. Probably, this is a later innovation. This does not however mean that Nāgārjuna or his successors had not considered all the implications of Śūnyatā and of the possible modes of its application.

The Twenty Modes of Śūnyatā, as enumerated in the *Pañcaviṁśati*, are as follows.

I. The Unreality of Internal Elements of Existence (adhyātmaśūnyatā);

[1] It must be noted that the present *Pañcaviṁśati* available in Sanskrit is one that had been redacted in the light of the *Abhisamayālaṁkāra*. No definite opinion can therefore be expressed whether the doctrine of the Twenty Modes of Śūnyatā is original to the *Prajñāpāramitās* or is a later addition. The *Abhisamayālaṁkārāloka* of Haribhadra treats of the modes of śūnyatā in terms identical with the *Pañcaviṁśati*. Haribhadra, in his *Āloka*, assigns each mode of Śūnyatā to one of the Ten Planes of Concentration (daśa-bhūmi) or to the preparatory or posterior stages. For instance, the first three modes of śūnyatā are said to belong to the Preparatory Stage, literally the Stage of Action in Faith (adhimukticaryābhūmi) and the fourth śūnyatā belongs to the Stage of Training (prayoga-mārga); the fifth is assigned to the First Plane of Concentration (prathamā bhūmi, pramuditā) and the sixth śūnyatā to the Second Stage, and so on. The last three modes of śūnyatā belong to the Plane of Buddahood (buddha-bhūmi), above the Tenth Plane of Concentration. This alignment of the modes of śūnyatā with the Stages of Concentration is not dealt with here.

The Madhyāntavibhāgaṭīkā (pp. 43ff.; pp. 51ff. Japanese Edn.) mentions only 16 modes of śūnyatā as the doctrine of the *Prajñāpāramitās*; the last four modes seem to be later additions. The *Madhyāntavibhāga* interpretation is largely coloured by the Yogācāra standpoint. References: *Pañcaviṁśatisāhasrikā*, pp. 24, 195-8; *Abhisamayālaṁkārāloka* of Haribhadra, pp. 89ff. *Madhyāntavibhāgaṭīkā*, pp. 43ff.; pp. 51ff. (Japanese Edn.).

Dharmasaṁgraha, pp. 8-9; *Mahāvyutpatti*, section XXXVII, lists only 18 modes of śūnyatā, omitting Nos. 17 and 20 of the list given above.

Obermiller: *A Study of the Twenty Aspects of Śūnyatā, Indian Historical Quarterly*, Vol. IX (1933), pp. 170-187;

Obermiller: *The Term Śūnyatā and its Different Interpretations*, in the *Journal of the Greater India Society*, vol. I, pp. 105-117.

II. The Unreality of the External Objects (bahirdhāśūnyatā);
III. The Unreality of Both together as in the sense organs or the body (adhyātmabahirdhāśūnyatā);
IV. The Unreality of (the Knowledge of) Unreality (śūnyata-sūnyatā);
V. The Unreality of the Great (Infinite Space), (mahāśūnyatā);
VI. The Unreality of the Ultimate Reality, Nirvāna (paramārthaśūnyatā);
VII. The Unreality of the Conditioned (saṁskṛtasūnyatā);
VIII. The Unreality of the Unconditioned (asaṁskṛtaśūnyatā);
IX. The Unreality of the Limitless (atyantaśūnyatā);
X. The Unreality of that which is Beginningless and Endless (anavarāgraśūnyatā);
XI. The Unreality of the 'Undeniable' (anavakāraśūnyatā);
XII. The Unreality of the Ultimate Essences (prakṛtiśūnyatā);
XIII. The Unreality of All Elements of Existence (sarvadharmaśūnyatā);
XIV. The Unreality of all Determination (Definition), (lakṣaṇaśūnyatā);
XV. The Unreality of the Past, the Present and the Future (anupalambhaśūnyatā);
XVI. The Unreality of Relation or Combination conceived as a Non-ens (abhāvaśvabhāvaśūnyatā);
XVII. The Unreality of the Positive Constituents of Empirical Existence (bhāvaśūnyatā);
XVIII. The Unreality of Non-Ens (of the Non-empirical), (abhāvaśūnyatā);
XIX. The Unreality of Self-Being (svabhāvaśūnyatā);
XX. The Unreality of Dependent Being (parabhāvaśūnyatā).

Although an *a priori* deduction or a logical classification of these modes of śūnyatā may not be possible, a kind of dialectical movement is perceptible if we take them in combination. The first three modes clearly go together. The first applies to psychical facts, mental states such as feelings, volitions, etc. Their nature is not discribable either as unchangingly real (akūṭastha), or as totally non-emergent (avināśi); that is, they are neither real (sat) nor unreal (asat). And this constitutes their śūnyatā, relativity or unreality. This is the stock argument that is applied to other modes also.[1] The unreality of external objects follows as a matter of dialectical necessity. The hope may be entertained that the above two are unreal as they are abstractions, and one that combines both the aspects together in itself may possibly escape being unreal. The third mode of śūnyatā repels any such contention.

The subsequent modes refer to thought-categories and doctrines of early Buddhism. Importance attaches to the fourth mode, śūnyatā of śūnyatā. The criticism that everything is relative, unreal (śūnya) may be thought to stand out as a reality; when all things are rejected, the rejection itself could not be rejected. This would, however, be a misconception. The rejection itself is as much relative, unreal, as the rejected; because, it is unintelligible without the latter. The fire of criticism which consumes all dogmatic views itself dies down, as there is nothing on which it could thrive; the medicine after curing the disease dissolves itself, and does not itself constitute a fresh disorder. If it were itself a view, a negative view, it would be as absurd as, if not worse than, other theories.[2] But the rejection of the dialectical criticism (śūnyatā) does not mean the reinstatement of the reality of the phenomenal world; it merely means that in rejecting the unreal we have to resort to means that are themselves of the same order, like the extracting of a thorn by another thorn. This śūnyatā should have been logically stated as the last.

Space is notional; our conception of it is relative to the distinctions of directions, east, west, etc. and also to things resident in them. In the absence of these, space itself crumbles away. The Śūnyatā of Space is termed Great, as space has infinite expanse.

By the Unreality of the Ultimate Reality (No. VI) is meant the unreality of Nirvāṇa as a separate reality. The Ābhidharmikas did conceive nirvāṇa as a separate entity (dharma) engendered by the cessation of all defiling forces. But the Mādhyamika view is that nirvāṇa is identical with the world of phenomena as its transcendent ground; the difference between them exists merely in thought. This

[1] tatra katmā adhyātmaśūnyatā? ādhyātmikā dharmā ucyante cakṣuḥ śrotram ghrāṇam jihvā kāyo manaḥ. tatra cakṣuś cakṣuṣā śūnyaṁ, akūtasthāvināśitām upādāya. tat kasya hetoḥ? prakṛtir asyaiṣā.

Pañcaviṁśatisāhasrikā p. 195.

[2] This point has been discussed before, see pp. 160ff. The Vedānta conception of the Illusoriness of the Illusory (mithyātva-mithyātva) may be compared to the Mādhaymika śūnyatā of śūnyatā. See pp. 161.

Śūnyatā guards against the error of regarding nirvāṇa as a separate reality.[1]

The next two modes (Nos. VII and VIII) make a natural pair. The conditioned (samskṛta) is unreal, as it is nothing in itself; it is neither permanent nor non-emergent. The Unconditioned (asamskṛta) can only be conceived in contradistinction to the conditioned; it is neither brought into being, nor destroyed by any activity of ours.

The ninth mode is with reference to our consciousness of the Limit and the Limitless. It might be thought that, in steering clear of the two extremes or ends of Eternalism and Nihilism, we are relying on a middle line of demarcation and that thereby the Middle or the Limitless might become invested with a nature of its own. Dialectic or Śūnyatā applies to this also. The Limitless is nothing in itself; the Middle position is no position at all, but a review of positions.[2]

The following mode is similar in character. It applies to distinctions in time, such as the beginning, the middle and the end. These distinctions are subjective.[3] In reality nothing stands out rigidly as the beginning, the middle and the end; the times flow into each other. Consequent on the rejection of the beginning, etc., the beginningless too turns out to be notional; and it should be recognised as relative or unreal on that score.

When we reject anything as untenable, something else is kept aside as the unrejectable, the undeniable, it might be thought. Our dialectical insight will not be complete without realising that the so-called unrejectable is itself relative to the rejected, and is hence nothing in itself. The eleventh mode of śūnyatā brings out this aspect. It seems to be identical with the fourth (sūnyatā of śūnyatā).

The dialectic or any activity on the part of Buddhas and others does not either make or mar things; for, they exist in their own right (prakṛtyā). The dialectic does not deprive them of their reality; things themselves are void, lack essential reality of their own. There is change in our notions, not in the real.[4] This is brought out by the twelfth mode of śūnyatā.

There is nothing new regarding the thirteenth mode of śūnyatā. It only reiterates that all modes of being, phenomenal and noumenal, lack essential reality, and so are unreal (sarvadharmaśūnyatā).

[1] For a discussion of this point, see pp. 274ff.

[2] This point has been discussed before; see pp. 129, 160ff.

[3] See pp. 181ff.

[4] See pp. 162, 233-34.

Early Buddhist thought, though it rejected the soul or substance (permanent and identical existence), had erected a system of discrete, unique entities (dharmas) and gave cut and precise definitions of them, e.g. impenetrability of matter (rūpa), apprehension of object of consciousness (vijñāna) etc. The dialectic brings home to us that matter and other entities lack the essence attributed to them. All definition is of the nature of a distinction within a general class (sāmānya-viśeṣa-prajñaptimātratvāt), and is therefore nominal in character. This is the Unreality of all Determination, definition (lakṣaṇaśūnyatā or svalakṣaṇaśūnyatā).

The unreality or the purely nominal character of the Past, the Present and the Future is demonstrable by the consideration that in the past itself there is no present and future, and vice versa; and yet without such relating, the consciousness of the past, etc., does not arise.[1] This constitutes their unreality (anupalambhaśūnyatā).

The dependent elements of phenomenal existence are what they are in their functional dependence on each other. And so dependent (pratītyasamutpannatvāt), they have no nature of their own in themselves. This mode of śūnyatā (abhāvasvabhāvaśūnyatā) is the basic principle of the Mādhyamika dialectic.

The Five Groups of Individuality and Existence (upādānaskandhas) do not stand for any objective reality; the collection is a non-entity, as it is a grouping subjectively imposed upon things. The dialectic shows that corresponding to words and concepts there is no entity. This is the meaning of the seventeenth mode of śūnyatā (bhāvaśūnyatā).

Likewise, the unconditioned, conceived as the absense of the Five Groups, is also unreal. For example, Space, one of the unconditioned, is defined as non-obstruction (anāvṛti). It is determined solely by the absence of positive characteristics. This is also the case with nirvāṇa, another unconditioned. Hence they are merely nominal entities. This is the nature of the eighteenth mode of śūnyatā (abhāvaśūnyata).

The last two modes of śūnyatā serve to emphasize the nature of reality as something existing in itself (svabhāva), and is not therefore constituted by wisdom and intuition on our part. For this very reason, no external factor, like the agent or his instruments, plays any part (parabhāvaśūnyatā) in making up its reality. It is pointed out that whether the Buddhas are born or they are not, the nature of

[1] See pp. 199-200.

the Ultimate Reality remains utterly unaffected.[1] This constitutes its complete freedom from others.

It may be noted that some of the enumerations are redundant (e.g. the last five); most if not all of them refer, directly or indirectly, to categories of Buddhist thought. Though it may be difficult to follow in detail the scholastic intricacies and the implied criticism in pronouncing each category unreal (śūnyā), the principle is clear. Dialectical criticism (śūnyatā) cannot spare anything; it has to include within its scope, not only all modes of being, but also modes of value and of speculative thought; it has to include itself too, to be consistent and complete. The pronouncement that everything is śūnya (relative, unreal) is itself unreal; it is not to be taken for one more entity. Otherwise, it would lead to a *regress ad infinitum* and prove a standing contradiction to the principle of Śūnyatā.

[1] See pp. 276-77.

INDEX